IF FOUND, please notify and arrange return to owner. This written test book is important for the owner's preparation for the Federal Aviation Administration Pilot Knowledge Test for the Commercial Pilot Certificate. Thank you.

Pilot's Name _____

Address _____

City	State	Zip Code

Telephone (_____) _____

Additional copies of *Commercial Pilot FAA Written Exam* are available from

Gleim Publications, Inc.
P.O. Box 12848
University Station
Gainesville, Florida 32604
(352) 375-0772
(800) 87-GLEIM or (800) 874-5346
FAX: (352) 375-6940
Internet: www.gleim.com
E-mail: admin@gleim.com

The price is $14.95 (subject to change without notice). Orders must be prepaid. Use the order form on page 284. Shipping and handling charges will be added to telephone orders. Add applicable sales tax to shipments within Florida.

Gleim Publications, Inc. guarantees the immediate refund of all resalable books returned within 30 days. Shipping and handling charges are nonrefundable.

ALSO AVAILABLE FROM GLEIM PUBLICATIONS, INC.

ORDER FORM ON PAGE 284

Private Pilot and Recreational Pilot FAA Written Exam
Private Pilot Flight Maneuvers and Practical Test Prep
Pilot Handbook
FAR/AIM
Aviation Weather and Weather Services
Private Pilot Syllabus and Logbook
Instrument Pilot Syllabus
Commercial Pilot Syllabus
Flight Computer
Navigational Plotter
Private Pilot Kit
Flight Bag

*Chapter II
IAB*

Advanced Pilot Training Books

Instrument Pilot FAA Written Exam
Instrument Pilot Flight Maneuvers and Practical Test Prep
Commercial Pilot Flight Maneuvers and Practical Test Prep
Flight/Ground Instructor FAA Written Exam
Fundamentals of Instructing FAA Written Exam
Flight Instructor Flight Maneuvers and Practical Test Prep
Airline Transport Pilot FAA Written Exam
Flight Engineer FAA Written Exam

* See page 17 for information about Instrument and Commercial Pilot Kits.

REVIEWERS AND CONTRIBUTORS

Karen A. Hom, B.A., University of Florida, is our book production coordinator. Ms. Hom coordinated the production staff and reviewed the final manuscript.

Barry A. Jones, ATP, CFII, MEI, B.S. in Air Commerce/Flight Technology, Florida Institute of Technology, drafted material in previous editions and for this edition, and provided technical assistance throughout the project.

Joshua B. Moore, CFI, B.A., University of Florida, is our aviation technical research assistant and a flight instructor with Gulf Atlantic Airways in Gainesville, FL. Mr. Moore researched questions, edited answer explanations, and incorporated revisions into the text.

John F. Rebstock, B.S., School of Accounting, University of Florida, reviewed portions of the edition.

Jan M. Strickland is our production assistant. Ms. Strickland reviewed the final manuscript and prepared the page layout.

The CFIs who have worked with me throughout the years to develop and improve my pilot training materials.

The many FAA employees who helped, in person or by telephone, primarily in Gainesville, FL, Orlando, FL, Oklahoma City, OK, and Washington, DC.

The many pilots and student pilots who have provided comments and suggestions about *Commercial Pilot Flight Maneuvers and Practical Test Prep* and *Commercial Pilot FAA Written Exam* during the past 10 years.

A PERSONAL THANKS

This manual would not have been possible without the extraordinary efforts and dedication of Jim Collis and Terry Hall, who typed the entire manuscript and all revisions, as well as prepared the camera-ready pages.

The author also appreciates the production and proofreading assistance of Melissa Gruebel, Kevin Jordan, Jessica Medina, and Shane Rapp.

Finally, I appreciate the encouragement, support, and tolerance of my family throughout this project.

Groundwood Paper and Highlighters -- This book is printed on high quality groundwood paper. It is lightweight and easy-to-recycle. We recommend that you purchase a highlighter specifically designed to be non-bleed-through (e.g., Avery *Glidestick*™) at your local office supply store.

SEVENTH EDITION

COMMERCIAL PILOT

FAA WRITTEN EXAM

for the FAA Computer-Based Pilot Knowledge Tests:

Commercial Pilot - Airplane   *Military Competency - Airplane*

by Irvin N. Gleim, Ph.D., CFII

ABOUT THE AUTHOR

Irvin N. Gleim earned his private pilot certificate in 1965 from the Institute of Aviation at the University of Illinois, where he subsequently received his Ph.D. He is a commercial pilot and flight instructor (instrument) with multiengine and seaplane ratings, and is a member of the Aircraft Owners and Pilots Association, American Bonanza Society, Civil Air Patrol, Experimental Aircraft Association, and Seaplane Pilots Association. He is also author of flight maneuvers and practical test prep books for the private, instrument, commercial, and flight instructor certificates/ratings, and study guides for the private/recreational, instrument, commercial, flight/ground instructor, fundamentals of instructing, and airline transport pilot FAA pilot knowledge tests. Three additional pilot training books are *Pilot Handbook*, *Aviation Weather and Weather Services*, and *FAR/AIM*.

Dr. Gleim has also written articles for professional accounting and business law journals, and is the author of the most widely used review manuals for the CIA exam (Certified Internal Auditor), the CMA exam (Certified Management Accountant), CFM exam (Certified in Financial Management), and the CPA exam (Certified Public Accountant). He is Professor Emeritus, Fisher School of Accounting, University of Florida, and is a CFM, CIA, CMA, and CPA.

Gleim Publications, Inc.

P. O. Box 12848
University Station
Gainesville, Florida 32604

(352) 375-0772
(800) 87-GLEIM or (800) 874-5346
FAX: (352) 375-6940

Internet: www.gleim.com
E-mail: admin@gleim.com

ISSN 1056-0599
ISBN 1-58194-012-2
Sixth Printing: November 2001

This is the sixth printing of the seventh edition of *Commercial Pilot FAA Written Exam*. Please e-mail update@gleim.com with CPWE 7-6 in the subject or text. You will receive our current update as a reply.

EXAMPLE:

To: update@gleim.com
From: your e-mail address
Subject: CPWE 7-6

SOURCES USED IN COMMERCIAL PILOT FAA WRITTEN EXAM

The first lines of the answer explanations contain citations to authoritative sources of the answers. These publications are obtainable from the FAA. These citations are abbreviated as noted below:

AC	Advisory Circular	Fl Comp	Flight Computer
ACL	Aeronautical Chart Legend	FTH	Flight Training Handbook
AFNA	Aerodynamics for Naval Aviators	IFH	Instrument Flying Handbook
AFH	Airplane Flying Handbook	NTSB	National Transportation Safety Board Regulations
AIM	Aeronautical Information Manual		
A&PM PH	Airframe & Powerplant Mechanics Powerplant Handbook	PHAK	Pilot's Handbook of Aeronautical Knowledge
AvW	Aviation Weather	PWBH	Pilot's Weight and Balance Handbook
AWS	Aviation Weather Services		
FAR	Federal Aviation Regulations		

HELP !!

This is the Seventh Edition, designed specifically for pilots who aspire to the Commercial Certificate. Please send any corrections and suggestions for subsequent editions to the author, c/o Gleim Publications, Inc. The last page in this book has been reserved for you to make comments and suggestions. It can be torn out and mailed to us.

Our *Commercial Pilot Flight Maneuvers and Practical Test Prep* book and *Commercial Pilot FAA Test Prep* software are also available. See the order form on page 284. Please bring these books and software to the attention of flight instructors, fixed-base operators, and others with a potential interest in acquiring their commercial pilot certificates. Wide distribution of these books and increased interest in flying depend on your assistance, good word, etc. Thank you.

NOTE: ANSWER DISCREPANCIES and UPDATES

Our answers have been carefully researched and reviewed. Inevitably, there will be differences with competitors' books and even the FAA. Send e-mail to update@gleim.com as described at the top right of this page, and visit our Internet site for the latest updates and information on all of our products. To continue providing our customers with first-rate service, we request that questions about our books and software be sent to us via mail, e-mail, or fax. The appropriate staff member will give each question thorough consideration and a prompt response. Questions concerning orders, prices, shipments, or payments will be handled via telephone by our competent and courteous customer service staff.

TABLE OF CONTENTS

Preface vi

Introduction: The FAA Pilot Knowledge Test 1

Chapter 1: Airplanes and Aerodynamics 19

Chapter 2: Airplane Instruments, Engines, and Systems 39

Chapter 3: Airports, Air Traffic Control, and Airspace 55

Chapter 4: Federal Aviation Regulations 69

Chapter 5: Airplane Performance and Weight and Balance 109

Chapter 6: Aeromedical Factors and Aeronautical Decision Making (ADM) 155

Chapter 7: Aviation Weather 167

Chapter 8: Aviation Weather Services 191

Chapter 9: Navigation: Charts, Publications, Flight Computers 207

Chapter 10: Navigation Systems 231

Chapter 11: Flight Operations 247

Appendix A: Commercial Pilot Practice Test 255

FAA Listing of Subject Matter Knowledge Codes 267

Cross-References to the FAA Pilot Knowledge Test Question Numbers 273

Author's Recommendation 282

Gleim Software and Book Order Form 284
    [Call (800) 87-GLEIM to purchase your FAA Test Prep software]

Index 289

Abbreviations and Acronyms 296

SIXTH PRINTING (11/01) CHANGES

1. Page 12. Explanation of the FAA's new question-numbering system.

2. Pages 13-17. Updated description of *FAA Test Prep* software.

3. The FAA made revisions to or added the following questions:

    Chapter 3:   Q. 25a (new)
    Chapter 4:   Q. 6, 6a (new), 7c (new), 9, 23a (new), 77a (new), 103a (new), 103b (new),
                 103c (new)
    Chapter 10: Q. 22a (new)
    Chapter 11: Q. 18a (new)

4. Page 204. The definition of squalls was changed in question 35.

5. Pages 273-281. Numerous updates to the Subject Matter Knowledge Codes.

PREFACE

The primary purpose of this book is to provide you with the easiest, fastest, and least expensive means of passing the commercial pilot (airplane) pilot knowledge test. We have

1.   Reproduced all of the FAA test questions (airplane) that can possibly appear on your FAA pilot knowledge test.

2.   Reordered the questions into 81 logical topics.

3.   Organized the 81 topics into 11 chapters.

4.   Explained the answer immediately to the right of each question.

5.   Provided an easy-to-study outline of exactly what you need to know (and no more) at the beginning of each chapter.

Accordingly, you can thoroughly prepare for the FAA pilot knowledge test by

1.   Studying the brief outlines at the beginning of each chapter.

2.   Answering the question on the left side of each page while covering up the answer explanations on the right side of each page.

3.   Reading the answer explanation for each question that you answer incorrectly or have difficulty with.

4.   Using Gleim's *FAA Test Prep* software which facilitates this process (see pages 13-17).

The secondary purpose of this study aid is to introduce *Commercial Pilot Flight Maneuvers and Practical Test Prep* and *Pilot Handbook*.

Commercial Pilot Flight Maneuvers and Practical Test Prep is designed to help prepare pilots for their flight training and the FAA commercial pilot practical test. Each task, objective, concept, and requirement is explained, analyzed, illustrated, and interpreted so pilots will be totally conversant with all aspects of the commercial pilot practical test.

Pilot Handbook is a textbook of aeronautical knowledge presented in easy-to-use outline format. While this book contains only the material needed to pass the FAA pilot knowledge test, *Pilot Handbook* contains the textbook knowledge required to be a safe and proficient pilot.

Most books create additional work for the user. In contrast, my books facilitate your effort. They are easy to use. The outline format, type styles, and spacing are designed to improve readability. Concepts are often presented as phrases rather than as complete sentences.

Read Chapter 1, The FAA Pilot Knowledge Test, carefully. Also, recognize that this study manual is concerned with **airplane** flight training, rather than balloon, glider, or helicopter training. I am confident this manual will facilitate speedy completion of your test. I also wish you the very best as you complete your commercial pilot certificate, in subsequent flying, and in obtaining additional ratings and certificates.

Enjoy Flying -- Safely!

Irvin N. Gleim

November 2001

INTRODUCTION
THE FAA PILOT KNOWLEDGE TEST

This introduction explains how to obtain a commercial pilot certificate, and explains the content and procedure of the Federal Aviation Administration (FAA) knowledge test, including how to take the test at a computer testing center. The remainder of this chapter discusses and illustrates Gleim's **FAA Test Prep** software. Achieving a commercial pilot certificate is fun. Begin today!

Commercial Pilot FAA Written Exam is one of three books contained in Gleim's Commercial Pilot Kit. The other two books are

1. *Commercial Pilot Flight Maneuvers and Practical Test Prep*
2. *Commercial Pilot Syllabus*

Commercial Pilot Flight Maneuvers and Practical Test Prep presents each flight maneuver you will perform in outline/illustration format so you will know what to expect and what to do before each flight lesson. This book will thoroughly prepare you to complete your FAA practical (flight) test confidently and successfully.

Commercial Pilot Syllabus is a step-by-step syllabus of ground and flight training lesson plans for your commercial pilot training.

While the following books are not included in the Commercial Pilot Kit, you may want to purchase them if you do not already have them:

Gleim's *Aviation Weather and Weather Services* combines all of the information from the FAA's *Aviation Weather* (AC 00-6A), *Aviation Weather Services* (AC 00-45E), and numerous FAA publications into one easy-to-understand book. It will help you study all aspects of aviation weather and provide you with a single reference book.

Pilot Handbook is a complete pilot reference book, which combines over 100 FAA books and documents including *AIM*, FARs, ACs, and much more.

Gleim's *FAR/AIM* is an easy-to-read reference book containing all of the Federal Aviation Regulations (FARs) applicable to general aviation flying, plus the full text of the FAA's *Aeronautical Information Manual* (*AIM*).

WHAT IS A COMMERCIAL PILOT CERTIFICATE?

A commercial pilot certificate is identical to your private pilot certificate except it allows you to fly an airplane and carry passengers and/or property for compensation or hire. The certificate is sent to you by the FAA upon satisfactory completion of your training program, the pilot knowledge test, and a practical test. A sample commercial pilot certificate is reproduced below.

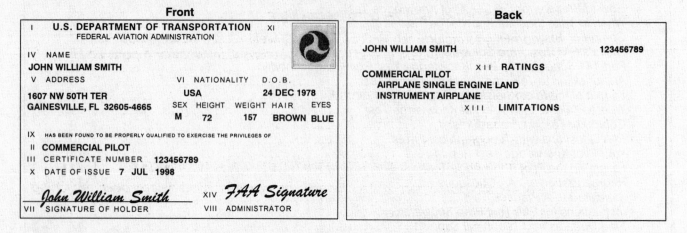

REQUIREMENTS TO OBTAIN A COMMERCIAL PILOT CERTIFICATE

1. Be at least 18 years of age and hold at least a private pilot certificate.

2. Be able to read, speak, write, and understand the English language. (Certificates with operating limitations may be available for medically related deficiencies.)

3. Hold at least a current third-class FAA medical certificate. Later, if your flying requires a commercial pilot certificate, you must hold a second-class medical certificate.

    a. You must undergo a routine medical examination which may only be administered by FAA-designated doctors called aviation medical examiners (AME).

        1) For operations requiring a commercial pilot certificate, a second-class medical certificate expires at the end of the last day of the month, 1 year after the date of examination shown on the certificate.

        2) For operations requiring a private or recreational pilot certificate, any class of medical certificate expires at the end of the last day of the month either

            a) 3 years after the date of examination shown on the certificate, if you have not reached your 40th birthday on or before the date of examination or

            b) 2 years after the date of examination shown on the certificate, if you have reached your 40th birthday on or before the date of examination

    b. Even if you have a physical handicap, medical certificates can be issued in many cases. Operating limitations may be imposed depending upon the nature of the disability.

    c. Your certificated flight instructor (CFI) or fixed-base operator (FBO) will be able to recommend an AME.

        1) Also, the FAA publishes a directory that lists all authorized AMEs by name and address. Copies of this directory are kept at all FAA offices, ATC facilities, and Flight Service Stations (FSS).

4. Receive and log ground training from an instructor or complete a home-study course (such as studying this book, *Commercial Pilot Flight Maneuvers and Practical Test Prep*, and *Pilot Handbook*) to learn

   a. Applicable Federal Aviation Regulations...that relate to commercial pilot privileges, limitations, and flight operations

   b. Accident reporting requirements of the National Transportation Safety Board

   c. Basic aerodynamics and the principles of flight

   d. Meteorology to include recognition of critical weather situations, windshear recognition and avoidance, and the use of aeronautical weather reports and forecasts

   e. Safe and efficient operation of aircraft

   f. Weight and balance computations

   g. Use of performance charts

   h. Significance and effects of exceeding aircraft performance limitations

   i. Use of aeronautical charts and a magnetic compass for pilotage and dead reckoning

   j. Use of air navigation facilities

   k. Aeronautical decision making and judgment

   l. Principles and functions of aircraft systems

   m. Maneuvers, procedures, and emergency operations appropriate to the aircraft

   n. Night and high-altitude operations

   o. Procedures for operating within the National Airspace System

5. Pass a pilot knowledge test with a score of 70% or better. All FAA pilot knowledge tests are administered at FAA-designated computer testing centers. The commercial pilot test consists of 100 multiple-choice questions selected from the airplane-related questions among the questions in the FAA's commercial pilot knowledge test bank; the balance of questions are for balloons, helicopters, etc. Each of the FAA's airplane questions is reproduced in this book with complete explanations to the right of each question.

6. Accumulate flight experience (FAR 61.129). You must log at least 250 hr. of flight time as a pilot that consists of at least

   a. 100 hr. in powered aircraft, of which 50 hr. must be in airplanes

   b. 100 hr. as pilot in command flight time, which includes at least

      1) 50 hr. in airplanes
      2) 50 hr. in cross-country flight of which at least 10 hr. must be in airplanes

   c. 20 hr. of training in the areas of operation required for a single-engine or multiengine rating that includes at least

      1) 10 hr. of instrument training of which at least 5 hr. must be in a single-engine or multiengine airplane, as appropriate

      2) 10 hr. of training in an airplane that has a retractable landing gear, flaps, and controllable pitch propeller, or is turbine-powered

         a) For a multiengine rating, the airplane must be a multiengine airplane and meet the other requirements.

      3) One cross-country flight of at least 2 hr. in a single-engine or multiengine airplane (as appropriate) in day-VFR conditions, consisting of a total straight-line distance of more than 100 NM from the original point of departure

    4)   One cross-country flight of at least 2 hr. in a single-engine or multiengine airplane (as appropriate) in night-VFR conditions, consisting of a straight-line distance of more than 100 NM from the original point of departure

    5)   3 hr. in a single-engine or multiengine airplane (as appropriate) in preparation for the practical test within the 60 days preceding the test

  d. 10 hr. of solo flight (sole occupant of the airplane) in a single-engine airplane, or 10 hr. of flight time performing the duties of pilot in command in a multiengine airplane with an authorized instructor, training in the areas of operations required for a single-engine or multiengine rating (as appropriate), which includes at least

    1)   One cross-country flight of not less than 300 NM total distance, with landings at a minimum of three points, one of which is a straight-line distance of at least 250 NM from the original departure point

        a)   In Hawaii, the longest segment need have only a straight-line distance of at least 150 NM.

    2)   5 hr. in night-VFR conditions with 10 takeoffs and 10 landings (with each landing involving a flight in the traffic pattern) at an airport with an operating control tower

  e. The 250 hr. of flight time as a pilot may include 50 hr. in an approved flight simulator or training device that is representative of a single-engine or multiengine airplane (as appropriate).

7.   Hold an instrument rating. As a commercial pilot you are presumed to have an instrument rating. If not, your commercial certificate will be endorsed with a prohibition against carrying passengers for hire on flights beyond 50 NM, or at night.

8.   Demonstrate flight proficiency (FAR 61.127). You must receive and log ground and flight training from an authorized instructor in the following areas of operations for an airplane category rating with a single-engine or multiengine class rating.

  a. *Preflight preparation*
  b. *Preflight procedures*
  c. *Airport and seaplane base operations*
  d. *Takeoffs, landings, and go-arounds*
  e. *Performance maneuvers*
  f. *Ground reference maneuvers (single-engine only)*

    1)   *Multiengine operations (multiengine only)*

  g. *Navigation*
  h. *Slow flight and stalls*
  i. *Emergency operations*
  j. *High-altitude operations*
  k. *Postflight procedures*

9.   Alternatively, enroll in an FAA-certificated pilot school or training center that has an approved commercial pilot certification or test course (airplane).

  a. These are known as Part 141 schools or Part 142 training centers because they are authorized by Part 141 or Part 142 of the FARs.

    1)   All other regulations concerning the certification of pilots are found in Part 61 of the FARs.

10. Successfully complete a practical (flight) test which will be given as a final exam by an FAA inspector or designated pilot examiner. The flight test will be conducted as specified in the FAA's Commercial Pilot Practical Test Standards (FAA-S-8081-12A), dated May 1997, with Change 1 (May 1997, Change 2 (August 1997), and Change 3 (December 1997).

a.   FAA inspectors are FAA employees and do not charge for their services.

b.   FAA-designated pilot examiners are proficient, experienced flight instructors and pilots who are authorized by the FAA to conduct practical tests. They do charge a fee.

c.   The FAA's Commercial Pilot Practical Test Standards are outlined and reprinted in Gleim's *Commercial Pilot Flight Maneuvers and Practical Test Prep*.

FAA PILOT KNOWLEDGE TEST

1.   This book can be used in your preparation for the following FAA pilot knowledge tests:

a.   Commercial Pilot-Airplane (CAX), which consists of 100 questions and a 3-hour time limit

b.   Military Competency-Airplane (MCA), which consists of 50 questions covering the FARs, which are covered in Chapter 4 and the airspace questions in Chapter 3.

1)   The MCA knowledge test time allowed is 2 hr.

NON-AIRPLANE TESTS

If you are using this book to study for a non-airplane pilot knowledge test, you should skip all of the obviously airplane-related questions. Then, go to www.gleim.com/Aviation/nonairplane/ for the appropriate non-airplane questions.

2.   In an effort to develop better test questions, the **FAA frequently pretests questions** on pilot knowledge tests by adding up to 5 "pretest" questions. Thus, rather than the number of questions listed above, you may be required to answer up to 5 extra pretest questions. The pretest questions will not be graded. You will NOT know which questions are "real" and which are "pretest." Accordingly, you must attempt to answer all questions correctly.

3.   All of the questions in the FAA's commercial pilot knowledge test bank that are applicable to airplanes have been grouped into the following 11 categories, which are the titles of Chapters 1 through 11:

Chapter 1 -- Airplanes and Aerodynamics
Chapter 2 -- Airplane Instruments, Engines, and Systems
Chapter 3 -- Airports, Air Traffic Control, and Airspace
Chapter 4 -- Federal Aviation Regulations
Chapter 5 -- Airplane Performance and Weight and Balance
Chapter 6 -- Aeromedical Factors and Aeronautical Decision Making (ADM)
Chapter 7 -- Aviation Weather
Chapter 8 -- Aviation Weather Services
Chapter 9 -- Navigation: Charts, Publications, Flight Computers
Chapter 10 -- Navigation Systems
Chapter 11 -- Flight Operations

Note that, in the official FAA commercial pilot knowledge test, the FAA's questions are **not** grouped together by topic. We have unscrambled them for you in this book.

4.   Within each of the chapters listed, questions relating to the same subtopic (e.g., duration of medical certificates, stalls, carburetor heat, etc.) are grouped together to facilitate your study program. Each subtopic is called a module.

5.   To the right of each question are

a.   The correct answer,

b.   The FAA question number, and

    c.   A reference for the answer explanation.

        1)   See page iv for a listing of abbreviations used for authoritative sources.

        2)   EXAMPLE: *FTH Chap 1* means *Flight Training Handbook*, Chapter 1.

6.   Each chapter begins with an outline of the material tested on the FAA pilot knowledge test. The outlines in this part of the book are very brief and have only one purpose: to help you pass the FAA pilot knowledge test for the commercial pilot certificate.

    a.   **CAUTION:** The **sole purpose** of this book is to expedite your passing the FAA pilot knowledge test for the commercial pilot certificate. Accordingly, all extraneous material (i.e., not directly tested on the FAA pilot knowledge test) is omitted even though much more information and knowledge are necessary to fly safely. This additional material is presented in two related books: Gleim's *Commercial Pilot Flight Maneuvers and Practical Test Prep* and *Pilot Handbook*.

Follow the suggestions given throughout this chapter and you will have no trouble passing the test the first time you take it.

HOW TO PREPARE FOR THE FAA PILOT KNOWLEDGE TEST

1.   Begin by carefully reading the rest of this chapter. You need to have a complete understanding of the examination process prior to beginning to study for it. This knowledge will make your studying more efficient.

2.   After you have spent an hour studying this chapter, set up a study schedule, including a target date for taking your pilot knowledge test.

    a.   Do not let the study process drag on because it will be discouraging, i.e., the quicker the better.

    b.   Consider enrolling in an organized ground school course at your local FBO, community college, etc.

    c.   Determine where and when you are going to take your pilot knowledge test.

3.   Work through each of Chapters 1 through 11.

    a.   Each chapter begins with a list of its module titles. The number in parentheses after each title is the number of FAA questions that cover the information in that module. The two numbers following the parentheses are the page numbers on which the outline and the questions for that particular module begin, respectively.

    b.   Begin by studying the outlines slowly and carefully.

    c.   Cover the answer explanations on the right side of each page with your hand or a piece of paper while you answer the multiple-choice questions.

        1)   Remember, it is very important to the learning (and understanding) process that you honestly commit yourself to an answer. If you are wrong, your memory will be reinforced by having discovered your error. Therefore, it is crucial to cover up the answer and make an honest attempt to answer the question before reading the answer.

        2)   Study the answer explanation for each question that you answer incorrectly, do not understand, or have difficulty with.

4.   Note that this test book (in contrast to most other question and answer books) contains the FAA questions grouped by topic. Thus, some questions may appear repetitive, while others may be duplicates or near-duplicates. Accordingly, do not work question after question (i.e., waste time and effort) if you are already conversant with a topic and the type of questions asked.

5. As you move from module to module and chapter to chapter, you may need further explanation or clarification of certain topics. You may wish to obtain and use the following Gleim books described on page 1.

    a. *Commercial Pilot Flight Maneuvers and Practical Test Prep*
    b. *Pilot Handbook*

6. Keep track of your work!!! As you complete a module in Chapters 1 through 11, grade yourself with an A, B, C, or ? (use a ? if you need help on the subject) next to the module title at the front of the respective chapter.

    a. The A, B, C, or ? is your self-evaluation of your comprehension of the material in that module and your ability to answer the questions.

        A   means a good understanding.
        B   means a fair understanding.
        C   means a shaky understanding.
        ?   means to ask your CFI or others about the material and/or questions and read the pertinent sections in *Commercial Pilot Flight Maneuvers and Practical Test Prep* and/or *Pilot Handbook*.

    b. This procedure will provide you with the ability to see quickly (by looking at the first page of Chapters 1 through 11) how much studying you have done (and how much remains) and how well you have done.

    c. This procedure will also facilitate review. You can spend more time on the modules with which you had difficulty.

WHEN TO TAKE THE PILOT KNOWLEDGE TEST

1. You must be at least 16 years of age to take the commercial pilot knowledge test.

2. You must prepare for the test by successfully completing a ground instruction course, or you may use this book as your self-developed home study course.

    a. See Authorization to Take the Pilot Knowledge Test, on page 8.

3. Take the pilot knowledge test within the next 30 days.

    a. Get the test behind you.

4. Your practical test must follow within 24 months

    a. Or you will have to retake your pilot knowledge test.

COMPUTER TESTING CENTERS

The FAA has contracted with several computer testing services to administer FAA pilot knowledge tests. Each of these computer testing services has testing centers throughout the country. You register by calling an 800 number. Call the following testing services for information regarding the location of testing centers most convenient to you and the time allowed and cost to take the commercial pilot (airplane) or military competency (airplane) pilot knowledge test.

        CATS   (800) 947-4228
        LaserGrade   (800) 211-2754

Also, about twenty Part 141 schools use the AvTEST computer testing system, which is very similar to the computer testing services described above.

GLEIM'S *FAA TEST PREP* SOFTWARE

Computer testing is consistent with modern aviation's use of computers (e.g., DUATS, flight simulators, computerized cockpits, etc.). All FAA pilot knowledge tests are administered by computer.

Computer testing is natural after computer study. Computer assisted instruction is a very efficient and effective method of study. Gleim's *FAA Test Prep* software is designed to prepare you for computer testing. *FAA Test Prep* software contains all of the questions in this book (but not the outlines and figures). You choose either STUDY MODE or TEST MODE.

In STUDY MODE, the software provides you with an explanation of each answer you choose (correct or incorrect). You design each study session:

> Topic(s) you wish to cover
> Number of questions
> Order of questions -- FAA, Gleim, or random
> Order of answers to each question -- FAA or random
> Questions missed from last session -- test, study, or both
> Questions missed from all sessions -- test, study, or both
> Questions never answered correctly

In TEST MODE, you decide the format -- CATS, LaserGrade, AvTEST, or Gleim. When you finish your test, you can study the questions missed and access answer explanations. The software imitates the operation of the FAA-approved computer testing companies above. Thus, you have a complete understanding of exactly how to take an FAA pilot knowledge test before you go to a computer testing center.

For more information on Gleim's *FAA Test Prep* software, see page 13.

PART 141 SCHOOLS WITH PILOT KNOWLEDGE TEST EXAMINING AUTHORITY

The FAA permits some FAR Part 141 schools to develop, administer, and grade their own pilot knowledge tests as long as they use the FAA pilot knowledge test questions, i.e., the same questions as in this book. The FAA does not provide the correct answers to the Part 141 schools, and the FAA only reviews the Part 141 school test question selection sheets. Thus, some of the answers used by Part 141 test examiners may not agree with the FAA or those in this book. The latter is not a problem but may explain why you may miss a question on a Part 141 pilot knowledge test using an answer presented in this book.

AUTHORIZATION TO TAKE THE PILOT KNOWLEDGE TEST

Before taking the pilot knowledge test, you must receive an endorsement from an authorized instructor who conducted the ground training or reviewed your home study in the required aeronautical knowledge areas. The 15 required aeronautical knowledge areas are listed under item 4., Requirements to Obtain a Commercial Pilot Certificate, beginning on page 2.

For your convenience, a standard authorization form for the commercial pilot knowledge test is reproduced on page 285. It can be easily completed, signed by a flight or ground instructor, torn out, and taken to the computer testing site.

FORMAT OF THE PILOT KNOWLEDGE TEST

The FAA's commercial pilot knowledge test for airplanes consists of 100 multiple-choice questions selected from the questions that appear in the next 11 chapters.

Note that the FAA test will be taken from exactly the same questions that are reproduced in this book. If you study the next 11 chapters, including all the questions and answers, **you should be assured of passing your FAA pilot knowledge test.**

Additionally, all of the FAA figures are contained in a book titled *Computer Testing Supplement for Commercial Pilot*, which you will be given for your use at the time of your test. All of the airplane-related FAA figures for the commercial pilot knowledge test are reproduced in this book.

We need your help identifying which questions the FAA is pretesting (but not grading - see page 5). After you take your exam, please e-mail, fax, or mail us a description of these questions so we can anticipate their future use by the FAA.

WHAT TO TAKE TO THE FAA PILOT KNOWLEDGE TEST

1. The same flight computer that you have used to solve the test questions in this book, i.e., one you are familiar with and have used before
2. Navigational plotter
3. A pocket calculator you are familiar with and have used before (no instructional material for the calculator allowed)
4. Authorization to take the examination (see page 285)
5. Picture identification of yourself

NOTE: Paper and pencils are supplied at the examination site.

COMPUTER TESTING PROCEDURES

To register for the pilot knowledge test, you should call one of the computer testing services listed in Computer Testing Centers, on page 7, or you may call one of their testing centers. These testing centers and telephone numbers are listed in Gleim's *FAA Test Prep* software under Vendors in the main menu. When you register, you will pay the fee with a credit card.

When you arrive at the computer testing center, you will be required to provide positive proof of identification and documentary evidence of your age. The identification presented must include your photograph, signature, and actual residential address, if different from the mailing address. This information may be presented in more than one form of identification. Next, you will sign in on the testing center's daily log. Your signature on the logsheet certifies that, if this is a retest, you meet the applicable requirements (see Failure on the Pilot Knowledge Test, on page 11) and that you have not passed this test in the past 2 years. Finally, you will present your logbook endorsement or authorization form from your instructor, which authorizes you to take the test. A standard authorization form is provided on page 285 for your use.

Next, you will be taken into the testing room and seated at a computer terminal. A person from the testing center will assist you in logging on the system, and you will be asked to confirm your personal data (e.g., name, Social Security number, etc.). Then you will be prompted and given an online introduction to the computer testing system and you will take a sample test. If you have used our *FAA Test Prep* software, you will be conversant with the computer testing methodology and environment, and you will probably want to skip the sample test and begin the actual test immediately. You will be allowed 3 hr. to complete the actual test. This is 1.8 minutes per question. Confirm the time permitted when you call the testing center to register to take the test by computer. When you have completed your test, an Airman Computer Test Report will be printed out, validated (usually with an embossed seal), and given to you by a person from the testing center. Before you leave, you will be required to sign out on the testing center's daily log.

Each computer testing center has certain idiosyncrasies in its paperwork, scheduling, telephone procedures, as well as in its software. It is for this reason that our *FAA Test Prep* software emulates each of these FAA-approved computer testing companies.

FAA QUESTIONS WITH TYPOGRAPHICAL ERRORS

Occasionally, FAA test questions contain typographical errors such that there is no correct answer. The FAA test development process involves many steps and people, and as you would expect, glitches occur in the system that are beyond the control of any one person. We indicate "best" rather than correct answers for some questions. Use these best answers for the indicated questions.

Note that the FAA corrects (rewrites) defective questions on the computer tests, which it cannot currently do with respect to faulty figures printed in FAA Computer Testing Supplements. Thus, it is important to carefully study questions that are noted to have a best answer in this book.

YOUR PILOT KNOWLEDGE TEST REPORT

1. You will receive your Airman Computer Test Report upon completion of the test. An example computer test report is reproduced on the next page.

    a. Note that you will receive only one grade as illustrated.

    b. The expiration date is the date by which you must take your FAA practical test.

c.   The report lists the FAA subject matter knowledge codes of the questions you missed, so you can review the topics you missed prior to your practical test.

```
┌─────────────────────────────────────────────────────────────┐
│                Federal Aviation Administration                │
│                  Airman Computer Test Report                  │
│                                                               │
│   EXAM TITLE:  Commercial Pilot Airplane                      │
│   NAME:  Jones David John                                     │
│   ID NUMBER:  123456789           TAKE:  1                    │
│   DATE:  08/14/01          SCORE:  82         GRADE:  Pass    │
│   ---------------------------------------------------------   │
│   Knowledge area codes in which questions were answered       │
│   incorrectly.  See appropriate FAA knowledge test study      │
│   guide.  A code may represent more than one incorrect        │
│   response.                                                   │
│   A24 B08 B09 B12 D38 E04                                     │
│                                                               │
│   EXPIRATION DATE:  08/31/03                                  │
│                                                               │
│                  DO NOT LOSE THIS REPORT                      │
│   ---------------------------------------------------------   │
│   Authorized instructor's statement.  (If Applicable)         │
│                                                               │
│   I have given Mr./Ms. _____ additional           │
│   instruction in each subject area shown to be deficient and  │
│   consider the applicant competent to pass the test.          │
│                                                               │
│   Last _____ Initial ____ Cert. No. _____ Type ____   │
│   (Print Clearly)                                             │
│                                                               │
│   Signature _____                                  │
│                                      CTD's Embossed Seal      │
└─────────────────────────────────────────────────────────────┘
```

2.   Use the FAA List of Subject Matter Knowledge Codes on pages 267 to 270 to determine the topics with which you had difficulty.

  a.   Look them over and review them with your CFI so (s)he can certify that (s)he reviewed the deficient areas and found you competent in them when you take your practical test.

3.   Keep your Airman Computer Test Report in a safe place, as you must submit it to the FAA examiner when you take your practical test.

FAILURE ON THE PILOT KNOWLEDGE TEST

1.   If you fail (less than 70%) the pilot knowledge test (virtually impossible if you follow the previous instructions), you may retake it after your CFI endorses the bottom of your Airman Computer Test Report certifying that you have received the necessary ground training to retake the test.

2.   Upon your retaking the test, everything is the same except you must also submit your Airman Computer Test Report indicating the previous failure to the examiner.

3. Note that the pass rate on the commercial pilot knowledge test is about 80%; i.e., 2 out of 10 fail the test initially. Reasons for failure include

   a. Failure to study the material tested (contained in the outlines at the beginning of Chapters 1 through 11 of this book)

   b. Failure to practice working the FAA exam questions under test conditions. All of the FAA questions on airplanes appear in Chapters 1 through 11 of this book.

   c. Poor examination technique, such as misreading questions and not understanding the requirements

REORGANIZATION OF FAA QUESTIONS

1. The questions in the FAA's Commercial Pilot Knowledge Test Bank are numbered 5001 to 5963. The FAA questions appear to be presented randomly.

   a. We have reorganized and renumbered the FAA questions into chapters and modules.

   b. The FAA question number is presented in the middle of the first line of the explanation of each answer.

2. Pages 273 through 281 contain a list of the FAA questions numbers 5001 to 5963 with cross-references to the FAA's subject matter knowledge codes and the chapters and question numbers in this book.

   a. For example, we have coded question 5001 as G10 and 8-112, which means it is covered in NTSB Part 830, General, and is found in Chapter 8 as question 112.

   b. Note that, although 5001 to 5963 implies more questions than those in this book, numerous FAA questions have two or more questions using the same question number and 22 question numbers without a question.

      1) The remaining 381 questions relate to helicopters, gliders, balloons, etc., and have been omitted from this book.

         a) These questions are indicated as NA in our cross-reference table beginning on page 273.

   c. In June 2001, the FAA test bank was released without the familiar four-digit FAA questions numbers. We identified all of the new questions and added them to the end of our cross-reference chart using our own question numbering system.

      1) The first four digits of this code refer to the month and year the question first appeared. The remaining digits identify the question number used in that particular FAA test bank release.

         a) For example, 0601-35 refers to the 35th question in the FAA's June 2001 test bank. It is found in Gleim Chapter 4 as question 23a.

With this overview of exam requirements, you are ready to begin the easy-to-study outlines and rearranged questions with answers to build your knowledge and confidence and PASS THE FAA's COMMERCIAL PILOT KNOWLEDGE TEST.

The feedback that we receive indicates that our books and software reduce anxiety, improve FAA test scores, and build knowledge. Studying for each test becomes a useful step toward advanced certificates and ratings.

SIMULATED FAA PRACTICE TEST

Appendix A, Commercial Pilot Practice Test, beginning on page 255, allows you to practice taking the FAA pilot knowledge test without the answers next to the questions. This test has 100 questions that have been randomly selected from the airplane-related questions in the FAA's Commercial Pilot Knowledge Test Bank. Topical coverage in this practice test is similar to that of the FAA commercial pilot test.

It is very important that you answer all 100 questions at one sitting. You should not consult the answers, especially when being referred to figures (charts, tables, etc.) throughout this book where the questions are answered and explained. Analyze your performance based on the answer key which follows the practice test.

Also rely on Gleim's *FAA Test Prep* software to simulate actual computer testing conditions including the screen layouts, instructions, etc., for CATS, LaserGrade, and AvTEST.

INSTRUCTIONS FOR THE *FAA TEST PREP* SOFTWARE

To install *FAA Test Prep*, put your CD-ROM in your CD-ROM drive. If an autoplay window appears after you insert the CD, follow the Setup wizard. If no screen appears after you have inserted the CD, click on the Windows Start button, and select "Run" from a list of options. Type x:\setup.exe (if x is the drive letter of your CD-ROM), and click "OK." Follow the on-screen instructions to finalize the installation.

Gleim Publications requires all *FAA Test Prep* users to register their software for unlimited use, free updates, and technical support. To register, simply use the Personal Registration Number and Library Passkey(s) that were shipped with your CD-ROM, call (800) 87-GLEIM, or register online at (http://www.gleim.com/license.html).

Once you have installed *FAA Test Prep* onto your system, you can begin studying at any time by clicking on the icon placed on your desktop or the Windows Start Menu. Use the Tutorial in the HELP menu to go step by step through the study process, or start studying right away by clicking on Create Session. *FAA Test Prep* allows you to customize your study process using several different options.

Study Session

Study Sessions give you immediate feedback on why your answer selection for a particular FAA question is correct or incorrect and allows you to access the context-sensitive outline material that helps to explain concepts related to the question. Choose from several different question sources: all questions available for that library, questions from a certain topic (chapters and modules from Gleim books), questions that you missed or marked in the last session you created, questions that you have never answered correctly, questions from certain FAA subject codes, etc. You can mix up the questions by selecting to randomize the question and/or answer order so that you do not memorize answer letters.

You may then grade your study sessions and track your study progress using the performance analysis charts and graphs. The Performance Analysis information helps you to focus on areas where you need the most improvement, saving you time in the overall study process. You may then want to go back and study questions that you missed in a previous session, or you may want to create a study session of questions that you marked in the previous session, and all of these options are made easy with *FAA Test Prep*'s Study Sessions.

After studying the outlines and questions in a Study, you can switch to a Test Session. In a Test Session, you will not know which questions you have answered correctly until the session is graded. You can further test your skills with a Standard Test Session, which gives you the option of taking your pilot knowledge test under actual testing conditions using one of the emulations of the major testing centers.

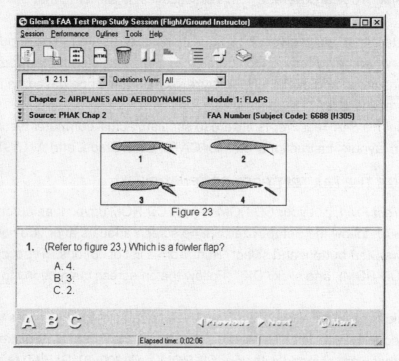

Standard Test Session

Take an exam in the actual testing environment of any of the major testing centers: CATS, AvTest, or Lasergrade. *FAA Test Prep* emulates the testing formats of these testing centers making it easy for you to study FAA questions under actual exam conditions. After studying with *FAA Test Prep*, you will know exactly what to expect when you go in to take your pilot knowledge test.

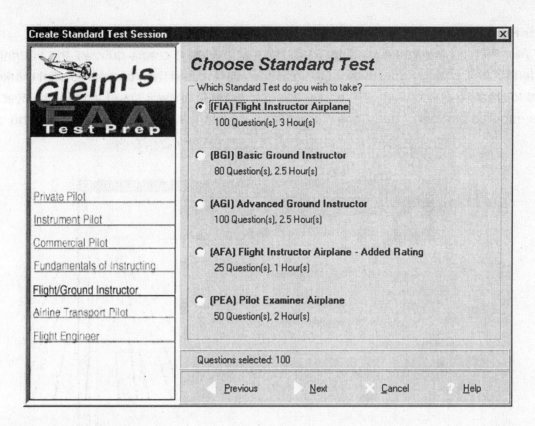

On-Screen Charts and Figures

One of the most convenient features of *FAA Test Prep* is the easily accessible on-screen charts and figures. Several of the FAA questions refer to drawings, maps, charts, and other pictures that provide information to help answer the question. In *FAA Test Prep*, you can pull up any of these figures with the click of a button. You can increase or decrease the size of the images, and you may also use our drawing feature to calculate the true course between two given points (required only on the private pilot knowledge test).

Instructor Print Options

FAA Test Prep is also a useful tool for instructors who want to create quizzes and assignments for their students. An instructor may mark questions in a session and then choose to print marked questions to create a quiz or test. (S)he may select to print an answer sheet, a blank answer sheet, and a renumbered printout of questions marked and any instructions that go along with the quiz or test.

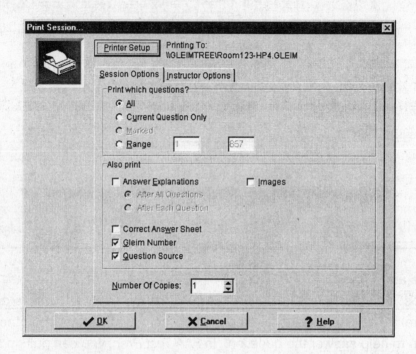

INSTRUCTOR SIGN-OFF SHEETS

FAA Test Prep is capable of generating an instructor sign-off for FAA knowledge tests which require one. This sign-off has been approved by the FAA and can be presented at the computer testing center as authorization to take your test—you do NOT need an additional endorsement from your instructor.

In order to obtain the instructor sign-off sheet for your test, you must first answer all questions in *FAA Test Prep* correctly. Then, select "Instructor Sign-Off Sheets" under the PERFORMANCE menu and select the appropriate test acronym using the index tabs (test acronyms are explained on page 5). If you have answered all of the required questions, the instructor sign-off sheet will appear for you to print. If you have not yet answered all required questions, a list of the unanswered questions, along with their location, will appear.

FAA Test Prep also contains a listing by state of all major testing center locations for CATS, AvTest, and LaserGrade. Gleim's *FAA Test Prep* is an all-in-one program designed to help anyone with a computer, Internet access, and an interest in flying to pass the pilot knowledge tests.

FREE Updates and Technical Support

Gleim offers FREE technical support to all registered users. Call (800) 87-GLEIM, send e-mail to support@gleim.com, or fill out the technical support request form online (www.gleim.com/techform.html). Gleim's new Online Updates feature makes updating your software and libraries even easier than before. Simply connect to the Internet, start the Gleim software, select Online Updates from the Test Prep Tools screen, and follow the on-screen instructions. Downloadable library updates will also be available online (www.gleim.com/updates.html) free to registered users of our CD-ROM software. For more information on our update service by e-mail, turn to page 367.

Obtain your copy of *FAA Test Prep* today. Order online at http://www.gleim.com/Aviation/IndivOrderForm.html or call 800 87-GLEIM.

If this Gleim test book saves you time and frustration in preparing for the FAA commercial pilot knowledge test, you should use Gleim's *Commercial Pilot Flight Maneuvers and Practical Test Prep* to prepare for the FAA practical test. *Commercial Pilot Flight Maneuvers and Practical Test Prep* will assist you in developing the competence and confidence to pass your FAA practical test, just as this book organizes and explains the knowledge needed to pass your FAA pilot knowledge test.

Also, flight maneuvers are quickly perfected when you understand exactly what to expect before you get into an airplane to practice the flight maneuvers. You must be ahead of (not behind) your CFI and your airplane. Gleim's flight maneuvers books explain and illustrate all flight maneuvers so the maneuvers and their execution are intuitively appealing to you.

INSTRUMENT AND COMMERCIAL PILOT KITS

Due to customer feedback and requests, we have created kits for pilots with an interest in the instrument rating and commercial certificate. Gleim kits contain everything necessary to prepare for their FAA knowledge test, each flight lesson, and their FAA practical test (assuming previous purchase of *FAR/AIM* and *Pilot Handbook*). Our state-of-the-art *FAA Test Prep* software on CD-ROM is standard with each kit. Gleim kits are available at leading FBOs, flight schools, and aviation retailers or directly from Gleim.

Instrument Pilot Kit -- $114.95 (save $50.75)

Includes:
Instrument Pilot Syllabus
*Instrument Pilot Flight Maneuvers and
 Practical Test Prep*
Instrument Pilot FAA Written Exam
Aviation Weather and Weather Services
FAA Test Prep CD-ROM for Instrument Pilot
Gleim Flight Bag

Commercial Pilot Kit -- $97.95 (save $36.80)

Includes:
Commercial Pilot Syllabus
*Commercial Pilot Flight Maneuvers and
 Practical Test Prep*
Commercial Pilot FAA Written Exam
FAA Test Prep CD-ROM for Commercial Pilot
Gleim Flight Bag

END OF INTRODUCTION

18

CHAPTER ONE
AIRPLANES AND AERODYNAMICS

This chapter contains outlines of major concepts tested, all FAA test questions and answers regarding aerodynamics, and an explanation of each answer. Each module, or subtopic, within this chapter is listed above with the number of questions from the FAA pilot knowledge test pertaining to that particular module. For each module, the first number following the parentheses is the page number on which the outline begins, and the next number is the page number on which the questions begin.

CAUTION: Recall that the **sole purpose** of this book is to expedite your passing the FAA pilot knowledge test for the commercial pilot certificate. Accordingly, all extraneous material (i.e., topics or regulations not directly tested on the FAA pilot knowledge test) is omitted, even though much more information and knowledge are necessary to become a proficient commercial pilot. This additional material is presented in *Commercial Pilot Flight Maneuvers and Practical Test Prep* and *Pilot Handbook*, available from Gleim Publications, Inc. See the order form on page 284.

1.1 FLAPS (Questions 1-2)

1. One of the main functions of flaps during the approach and landing is to increase angle of attack, which causes the wing to produce the same amount of lift at a slower airspeed.

2. The raising of flaps increases the stall speed.

1.2 AIRPLANE WINGS (Questions 3-6)

1. Rectangular wings generally are designed so that the wing root stalls first, with the stall progression toward the wingtip.

2. A change in the angle of attack of the wing changes the lift, drag, and airspeed.

3. The angle of attack of a wing directly controls the distribution of positive and negative pressure acting on the wing.

4. Frost on the upper surface of airplane wings disrupts the smooth flow of air over the top of the wing (which increases drag) and causes the airplane to stall at higher airspeeds and lower angles of attack than normal.

1.3 STALLS (Questions 7-15)

1. The angle of attack at which a wing stalls (critical angle of attack) remains constant regardless of

   a. Weight

   b. Dynamic pressure (a component of the Bernoulli equation which explains lift in pressure differentials)

   c. Bank angle

   d. Pitch attitude

2. Stall speed is affected by the airplane's

   a. Weight
   b. Load factor
   c. Power setting

3. The stalling speed is most affected by variations in airplane loading, i.e., weight and CG.

4. Turbulence can increase stall speed due to increased load factors.

   a. Slowing to V_A protects the airplane from excessive load stresses while providing a safe margin above stall speed.

5. Stall recovery becomes progressively more difficult when the CG moves aft.

6. Stall speed tables for various configurations at different angles of bank are provided for some airplanes, such as illustrated in Fig. 2 on page 27.

   a. Note that the table portrays situations for a given weight at four angles of bank in two configurations (gear and flaps up or down) and with power on or off.

   b. Generally, note that stall speeds are lower with gear and flaps down.

   c. Also, stall speeds are higher as bank increases.

1.4 SPINS (Question 16)

1. Recovery from spins as well as stalls may become difficult when the CG is too far rearward.

   a. The rotation of a spin is always around the CG.

1.5 LIFT AND DRAG (Questions 17-36)

1. An airplane wing produces lift resulting from relatively higher air pressure below the wing surface and lower air pressure above the wing surface.

   a. Lift is defined as the force acting perpendicular to the relative wind.
   b. An increase in the angle of attack will increase drag.

      1) Drag acts parallel to the flight path.

2. In all steady-state flight, including descent, the sum of all forward forces equals the sum of all rearward forces, and the sum of all upward forces equals the sum of all downward forces.

   a. During the transition from straight-and-level flight to a climb, the angle of attack must be increased and lift is momentarily increased.

3. Any given angle of attack has a corresponding airspeed to provide sufficient lift to maintain a given altitude.

   a. As airspeed decreases, the airfoils generate less lift. Accordingly, to maintain altitude, the angle of attack must be increased to compensate for the decrease in lift.

   b. To generate the same amount of lift as altitude increases, the airplane must be flown at a higher true airspeed for any given angle of attack.

4.   As the angle of bank increases, the vertical component of lift decreases and the horizontal component of lift increases.

5.   As airspeed increases, lift and parasite drag increase as the square of the increase in airspeed; e.g., doubling airspeed quadruples lift and parasite drag.

   a.   Induced drag is a by-product of lift and is also greatly affected by changes in airspeed.

6.   Graphs including curves of the component of lift, the component of drag, and the lift/drag (L/D) ratio are frequently prepared to study the effect of the angle of attack on drag, lift, and the lift/drag ratio.

   a.   An example appears in Fig. 3 on page 30.

   b.   For any given angle of attack, the L/D ratio can be converted into altitude loss (in feet) per forward distance traveled.

   c.   Of interest is that the L/D ratio can be the same for two different angles of attack.

      1)   EXAMPLE: At 3° angle of attack and at slightly over 12° angle of attack, the L/D ratio is approximately 10.

7.   In the diagram below, as airspeed increases above the maximum lift/drag (L/D$_{MAX}$) speed, total drag on the airplane increases due to the increased parasite drag. Note that Fig. 1 on page 32 is basically the same graph.

   a.   As airspeed decreases below the L/D$_{MAX}$ speed, total drag increases due to increased induced drag.

8.   By definition, the L/D$_{MAX}$ ratio is at the minimum (lowest) point of the total drag curve.

   a.   The minimum point in the total drag curve is the point where the parasite drag and induced drag curves intersect.

9.   In a propeller-driven airplane, the airspeed resulting in L/D$_{MAX}$ will provide the maximum range and maximum glide distance.

1.6 GROUND EFFECT (Questions 37-39)

1.   Ground effect is due to the interference of the ground (or water) surface with the airflow patterns about the airplane in flight.

    a.   When an airplane is within a distance of its wingspan to the surface, a change occurs in the three-dimensional flow pattern around the airplane because the vertical component of the airflow around the wing is restricted by the Earth's surface.

        1)   This change alters the wing's upwash, downwash, and wingtip vortices.

            a)   The reduction of the wingtip vortices alters the spanwise lift distribution and reduces the induced angle of attack and induced drag.

2.   An airplane leaving ground effect experiences an increase in induced drag and requires more thrust.

3.   While in ground effect, an airplane needs a lower angle of attack to produce the same lift as when out of ground effect.

    a.   If the same angle of attack is maintained in ground effect as when out of ground effect, lift will increase and induced drag will decrease.

1.7 AIRPLANE STABILITY (Questions 40-44)

1.   Stability is the inherent ability of an object (e.g., airplane), after its equilibrium is disturbed, to return to its original position. In other words, a stable airplane will tend to return to the original condition of flight if disturbed by a force such as turbulent air.

2.   Static stability is the initial tendency that the airplane displays after its equilibrium is disturbed.

    a.   Positive static stability can be illustrated by a ball inside a round bowl. If the ball is displaced from its normal resting place, it will eventually return to its original position at the bottom of the bowl.

    b.   Neutral static stability can be illustrated by a ball on a flat plane. If the ball is displaced, it will come to rest at some new, neutral position and show no tendency to return to its original position.

    c.   Negative static stability is actually instability. It can be illustrated by a ball on the top of an inverted round bowl. Even the slightest displacement of the ball will activate greater forces, which will cause the ball to continue to move in the direction of the applied force (e.g., gravity).

3.   Dynamic stability is the overall tendency that the airplane displays after its equilibrium is disturbed.

    a.   Positive dynamic stability is a property which dampens the oscillations set up by a statically stable airplane, enabling the oscillations to become smaller and smaller in magnitude until the airplane eventually settles down to its original condition of flight.

    b.   Neutral dynamic stability means the oscillations remain unchanged.

    c.   Negative dynamic stability is actually dynamic instability. It means the oscillations tend to increase.

4.   An airplane is said to have

    a.   Longitudinal stability about the lateral axis

    b.   Lateral stability about the longitudinal axis

    c.   Directional stability about the vertical axis

5.   If an airplane is loaded to the rear of its CG range, it will tend to be unstable about its lateral axis.

1.8 TURNS (Questions 45-52)

1. At a constant altitude in a coordinated turn, for each angle of bank each airspeed has a specific rate and radius of turn, and they do not vary.

   a. An increase in airspeed in a level coordinated turn with a constant bank results in

      1) An increase in the radius of turn and
      2) A decrease in the rate of turn.

   b. Steepening the bank and decreasing the airspeed result in an increase in the rate of turn and a decrease in the radius.

2. With a constant bank angle, the load factor will be constant regardless of

   a. The rate of turn
   b. Airspeed
   c. Weight

3. As bank is increased, additional vertical lift converts into horizontal lift, decreasing available vertical lift.

   a. Thus, an increased angle of attack (back elevator pressure) is required in order to maintain a constant altitude during the turn.

4. When airspeed is increased during a level turn, the angle of attack must be decreased or the angle of bank increased to maintain level altitude.

5. A standard rate turn is, by definition, 2 min. for 360°, or 3°/sec.

1.9 LOAD FACTOR (Questions 53-61)

1. Load factor is the ratio between the total airload imposed on the wing in flight and the gross weight of the airplane.

   a. The amount of excess load that can be imposed on an airplane's wings varies directly with the airplane's speed and the excess lift available.

      1) At low speeds, very little excess lift is available, so very little excess load can be imposed.

      2) At high speeds, the wings' lifting capacity is so great that the load factor can quickly exceed safety limits.

   b. An increased load factor will cause an airplane to stall at a higher airspeed.

   c. As bank angle increases, the load factor increases. The wings not only must carry the airplane's weight but also must bear the centrifugal force.

      1) The only determinant of load factor in level coordinated turns is the amount of bank.

      2) A change of airspeed does not affect load factor given a constant angle of bank, although it does directly affect the rate and radius of turn.

2. Load factor (or G units) is a multiple of the regular weight or, alternatively, a multiple of the force of gravity.

   a. Unaccelerated straight flight has a load factor of 1.0 (by definition).

   b. A 60° level bank has a load factor of 2.0. Thus, a 3,000-lb. airplane in a 60° bank would require the wings to provide lift for 6,000 lb.

3.   Maximum safe load factors (limit load factors):

   a.   Normal category airplanes are limited to +3.8 and −1.52 G's.
   b.   Utility aircraft are limited to +4.4 and −1.76 G's.
   c.   Aerobatic aircraft are limited to +6.0 and −3.0 G's.

4.   When baggage or other areas of the plane are placarded for weight, they are placarded for gross weight. The airplane is designed to accommodate the specified G's (3.8, 4.4, 6.0) given the weight placarded.

5.   A "stall speed/load factor" graph relates these variables to the degree of bank angle for a particular airplane, as illustrated in Fig. 4 on page 38.

   a.   Determine the load factor (or G units) for any bank angle by finding the bank angle on the horizontal axis, moving vertically up to the intersection with the load factor curve, and then proceeding horizontally to the left of the graph to find the number of G units on the vertical load factor scale.

   b.   To determine the increase in stall speed for any load factor, begin with the load factor on the far left vertical scale and move horizontally to the graph on the right to intersect the load factor curve. From that point of intersection, move up vertically to the intersection with the stall speed curve. From that point, move horizontally to the left to the vertical axis to determine the percentage increase in stall speed.

QUESTIONS AND ANSWER EXPLANATIONS

   All the FAA questions from the pilot knowledge test for the commercial pilot certificate relating to aerodynamics and the material outlined on the previous pages are reproduced on the following pages in the same modules as the outlines. To the immediate right of each question are the correct answer and answer explanation. You should cover these answers and answer explanations while responding to the questions. (A bookmark for this purpose has ben provided in the back of the book.) Refer to the general discussion in the Introduction on how to take the FAA pilot knowledge test.

   Remember that the questions from the FAA pilot knowledge test bank have been reordered by topic, and the topics have been organized into a meaningful sequence. Accordingly, the first line of the answer explanation gives the FAA question number and the citation of the authoritative source for the answer.

1.1 Flaps

1.
5182. One of the main functions of flaps during the approach and landing is to

A— decrease the angle of descent without increasing the airspeed.
B— provide the same amount of lift at a slower airspeed.
C— decrease lift, thus enabling a steeper-than-normal approach to be made.

Answer (B) is correct (5182). *(PHAK Chap 2)*
   Extending the flaps increases the wing camber, the wing area (some types), and the angle of attack of the wing. This allows the wing to provide the same amount of lift at a slower airspeed.
   Answer (A) is incorrect because flaps increase, not decrease, the angle of descent without increasing the airspeed. Answer (C) is incorrect because flaps increase, not decrease, lift. They also increase induced drag.

2.
5181. Which is true regarding the use of flaps during level turns?

A— The lowering of flaps increases the stall speed.
B— The raising of flaps increases the stall speed.
C— Raising flaps will require added forward pressure on the yoke or stick.

Answer (B) is correct (5181). *(PHAK Chap 2)*
   Raising the flaps decreases the wing camber and the angle of attack of the wing. This decreases wing lift and results in a higher stall speed.
   Answer (A) is incorrect because flaps decrease, not increase, the stall speed. Answer (C) is incorrect because raising the flaps will decrease the lift provided by the wings. Thus, back, not forward, pressure on the yoke or stick is required to maintain altitude.

1.2 Airplane Wings

3.
5197. A rectangular wing, as compared to other wing planforms, has a tendency to stall first at the

A— wingtip, with the stall progression toward the wing root.
B— wing root, with the stall progression toward the wingtip.
C— center trailing edge, with the stall progression outward toward the wing root and tip.

Answer (B) is correct (5197). *(FTH Chap 17)*
A rectangular wing, as compared to other wing planforms, has a tendency to stall first at the wing root, with the stall progression toward the wingtip. Because the wingtips and the ailerons stall later, the pilot can use aileron control in avoiding and recovering from the stall.
Answer (A) is incorrect because the wing root, not wingtip, will stall first. Answer (C) is incorrect because the wing root, not center trailing edges, will stall first.

4.
5198. By changing the angle of attack of a wing, the pilot can control the airplane's

A— lift, airspeed, and drag.
B— lift, airspeed, and CG.
C— lift and airspeed, but not drag.

Answer (A) is correct (5198). *(FTH Chap 17)*
The pilot can control the airplane's lift, airspeed, and drag by changing the angle of attack of the wing. As the angle of attack is increased, the lift increases to the critical angle of attack, airspeed decreases, and induced drag increases with the increase in lift.
Answer (B) is incorrect because the angle of attack has no effect on the CG of an airplane. Answer (C) is incorrect because drag as well as lift and airspeed is determined by the angle of attack.

5.
5199. The angle of attack of a wing directly controls the

A— angle of incidence of the wing.
B— amount of airflow above and below the wing.
C— distribution of pressures acting on the wing.

Answer (C) is correct (5199). *(FTH Chap 17)*
The angle of attack of an airfoil directly controls the distribution of pressure below and above it. When a wing is at a low but positive angle of attack, most of the lift is due to the wing's negative pressure (upper surface) and downwash. Note: Negative pressure is any pressure less than atmospheric, and positive pressure is pressure greater than atmospheric.
Answer (A) is incorrect because the angle of incidence is a fixed relationship between the wing chord line and the longitudinal axis of the airplane and is thus unrelated to the angle of attack. Answer (B) is incorrect because the same amount of air must flow above and below (over and under) the wing.

6.
5739. Frost covering the upper surface of an airplane wing usually will cause

A— the airplane to stall at an angle of attack that is higher than normal.
B— the airplane to stall at an angle of attack that is lower than normal.
C— drag factors so large that sufficient speed cannot be obtained for takeoff.

Answer (B) is correct (5739). *(PHAK Chap 5)*
Frost on the surface of a wing interferes with the smooth flow of air over the wing surface; i.e., parasite drag is increased. The air flowing over the wing is thus disrupted and stalls at a lower angle of attack (a higher speed) when there is frost on the wing surface.
Answer (A) is incorrect because frost on the wing surface will usually cause the airplane to stall at a lower, not higher, angle of attack. Answer (C) is incorrect because the drag created by frost usually will not be so disruptive as to prevent the aircraft from obtaining takeoff speed.

1.3 Stalls

7.
5204. The angle of attack at which a wing stalls remains constant regardless of

A— weight, dynamic pressure, bank angle, or pitch attitude.
B— dynamic pressure, but varies with weight, bank angle, and pitch attitude.
C— weight and pitch attitude, but varies with dynamic pressure and bank angle.

Answer (A) is correct (5204). *(FTH Chap 17)*
The angle of attack at which a wing stalls is constant regardless of weight, bank, pitch, etc.
Answer (B) is incorrect because the stall speed, not angle of attack, varies with weight and bank angle. Answer (C) is incorrect because the stall speed, not angle of attack, varies with bank angle.

8.
5160. The need to slow an aircraft below V$_A$ is brought about by the following weather phenomenon:

A— High density altitude which increases the indicated stall speed.
B— Turbulence which causes an increase in stall speed.
C— Turbulence which causes a decrease in stall speed.

Answer (B) is correct (5160). *(PHAK Chap 1)*
Turbulence, in the form of vertical air currents, can cause severe load stress on a wing. It is wise, in extremely rough air, to reduce the speed to V$_A$ (design maneuvering speed). Yet, V$_A$ allows a sufficient margin of safety above stall speed, which may be increased in turbulent air due to increased load factors.
Answer (A) is incorrect because changes in density altitude do not affect indicated stall speed. Answer (C) is incorrect because turbulence increases the load factors imposed on the aircraft, which increases, not decreases, stall speed.

9.
5196. Stall speed is affected by

A— weight, load factor, and power.
B— load factor, angle of attack, and power.
C— angle of attack, weight, and air density.

Answer (A) is correct (5196). *(FTH Chap 17)*
Stall speed may vary under different circumstances. Factors such as weight, load factor, power, center of gravity, altitude, temperature, and the presence of snow, ice, or frost on the wings will affect an aircraft's stall speed.
Answer (B) is incorrect because stall speed is not affected by the angle of attack. Answer (C) is incorrect because stall speed is not affected by the angle of attack.

10.
5211. The stalling speed of an airplane is most affected by

A— changes in air density.
B— variations in flight altitude.
C— variations in airplane loading.

Answer (C) is correct (5211). *(FTH Chap 17)*
Indicated stall speed is most affected by the gross weight and how it is distributed within the airplane.
Answer (A) is incorrect because air density does not affect indicated stall speed. Answer (B) is incorrect because flight altitude does not affect indicated stall speed.

11.
5212. An airplane will stall at the same

A— angle of attack regardless of the attitude with relation to the horizon.
B— airspeed regardless of the attitude with relation to the horizon.
C— angle of attack and attitude with relation to the horizon.

Answer (A) is correct (5212). *(FTH Chap 17)*
An airplane will always stall at the same angle of attack. The airplane's attitude with relation to the horizon has no significance to the stall.
Answer (B) is incorrect because the stall speed will vary with changing load factors, weight, and power. Answer (C) is incorrect because an airplane can stall in any attitude with relation to the horizon.

12.
5155. In a rapid recovery from a dive, the effects of load factor would cause the stall speed to

A— increase.
B— decrease.
C— not vary.

Answer (A) is correct (5155). *(FTH Chap 17)*
In a rapid recovery from a dive, the load factor would be increased because of the rapid change in the angle of attack, since gravity and centrifugal force would prevent the airplane from immediately altering its flight path. Because the relative wind is opposite the flight path, the critical angle of attack will be reached at a higher airspeed.
Answer (B) is incorrect because, as load factor increases, so does stall speed. Answer (C) is incorrect because, as load factor increases, so does stall speed.

13.
5206. Recovery from a stall in any airplane becomes more difficult when its

A—center of gravity moves aft.
B—center of gravity moves forward.
C—elevator trim is adjusted nosedown.

Answer (A) is correct (5206). *(FTH Chap 17)*
The recovery from a stall in any airplane becomes progressively more difficult as the airplane's center of gravity moves aft. This difficulty is due to the decreasing stability in pitch, which results in the decrease of elevator effectiveness in lowering the nose.
Answer (B) is incorrect because recovery from a stall becomes easier, not more difficult, as the center of gravity moves forward. Answer (C) is incorrect because the center of gravity, not the elevator trim adjustment, has an effect on the stall recovery characteristics of an airplane.

14.
5179. (Refer to figure 2 below.) Select the correct statement regarding stall speeds.

A— Power-off stalls occur at higher airspeeds with the gear and flaps down.
B— In a 60° bank the airplane stalls at a lower airspeed with the gear up.
C— Power-on stalls occur at lower airspeeds in shallower banks.

Answer (C) is correct (5179). *(PHAK Chap 4)*
Using Fig. 2, work through each of the answers to determine which is true. Power-on stalls occur at lower airspeeds in shallower banks.
Answer (A) is incorrect because, with power off, stall speed is lower, not higher, with gear and flaps down. Answer (B) is incorrect because, in a 60° bank, the gear position alone will not affect stall speed.

GROSS WEIGHT 2750 LBS		ANGLE OF BANK			
		LEVEL	30°	45°	60°
POWER		GEAR AND FLAPS UP			
ON	MPH	62	67	74	88
	KTS	54	58	64	76
OFF	MPH	75	81	89	106
	KTS	65	70	77	92
		GEAR AND FLAPS DOWN			
ON	MPH	54	58	64	76
	KTS	47	50	56	66
OFF	MPH	66	71	78	93
	KTS	57	62	68	81

FIGURE 2.—Stall Speeds.

15.
5180. (Refer to figure 2 above.) Select the correct statement regarding stall speeds. The airplane will stall

A— 10 knots higher in a power-on, 60° bank, with gear and flaps up, than with gear and flaps down.
B— 25 knots lower in a power-off, flaps-up, 60° bank, than in a power-off, flaps-down, wings-level configuration.
C— 10 knots higher in a 45° bank, power-on stall, than in a wings-level stall.

Answer (A) is correct (5180). *(PHAK Chap 4)*
The airplane stalls at 76 kt. with power on, gear and flaps up at 60° bank but stalls at 66 kt. with gear and flaps down (i.e., a difference of 10 kt.).
Answer (B) is incorrect because the airplane stalls 35 kt. higher, not 25 kt. lower, with power off, flaps up, and a 60° bank than with power off, flaps down, and wings level. Answer (C) is incorrect because gear and flap position are not specified, so there is not enough information to make a proper determination.

1.4 Spins

16.
5205. In small airplanes, normal recovery from spins may become difficult if the

A— CG is too far rearward, and rotation is around the longitudinal axis.
B— CG is too far rearward, and rotation is around the CG.
C— spin is entered before the stall is fully developed.

Answer (B) is correct (5205). *(AC 61-67B)*
Because rotation is around the CG in a spin, with a rearward CG, the control arm at the rudder is sufficiently shortened that it may make spin recovery difficult, if not impossible. Intuitively, if there is too much weight near the tail, it is also hard to get the nose down to produce an angle of attack below the critical angle.
Answer (A) is incorrect because rotation is around the CG, not the longitudinal axis, in a spin. Answer (C) is incorrect because in order for an airplane to spin it must first stall.

1.5 Lift and Drag

17.
5167. Which statement is true relative to changing angle of attack?

A— A decrease in angle of attack will increase pressure below the wing, and decrease drag.
B— An increase in angle of attack will increase drag.
C— An increase in angle of attack will decrease pressure below the wing, and increase drag.

Answer (B) is correct (5167). *(PHAK Chap 1)*
As the angle of attack is increased, up to the critical angle of attack, the greater the amount of lift is developed, and the greater the induced drag.
Answer (A) is incorrect because a decrease in the angle of attack will decrease, not increase, the pressure below the wing. Answer (C) is incorrect because an increase in angle of attack will increase, not decrease, the pressure below the wing.

18.
5223. To generate the same amount of lift as altitude is increased, an airplane must be flown at

A— the same true airspeed regardless of angle of attack.
B— a lower true airspeed and a greater angle of attack.
C— a higher true airspeed for any given angle of attack.

Answer (C) is correct (5223). *(FTH Chap 17)*
At an altitude of 18,000 ft. MSL, the air has one-half the density of air at sea level. Thus, in order to maintain the same amount of lift as altitude increases, an airplane must be flown at a higher true airspeed for any given angle of attack.
Answer (A) is incorrect because true airspeed must be increased, not remain the same, as altitude increases to generate the same amount of lift. Answer (B) is incorrect because true airspeed must be increased, not decreased, as altitude increases to generate the same amount of lift.

19.
5225. As the angle of bank is increased, the vertical component of lift

A— decreases and the horizontal component of lift increases.
B— increases and the horizontal component of lift decreases.
C— decreases and the horizontal component of lift remains constant.

Answer (A) is correct (5225). *(FTH Chap 17)*
In level flight, all lift is vertical (upwards). As bank is increased, however, a portion of the airplane's lift is transferred from a vertical component to a horizontal component. Thus, the vertical component of lift decreases and the horizontal component of lift increases as the angle of bank is increased.
Answer (B) is incorrect because the vertical component of lift decreases and the horizontal component of lift increases. Answer (C) is incorrect because the horizontal component of lift increases.

20.
5218. Which is true regarding the forces acting on an aircraft in a steady-state descent? The sum of all

A— upward forces is less than the sum of all downward forces.
B— rearward forces is greater than the sum of all forward forces.
C— forward forces is equal to the sum of all rearward forces.

Answer (C) is correct (5218). *(FTH Chap 17)*
In any steady-state flight, whether level flight, climbs, or descents, the sum of all forward forces is equal to the sum of all rearward forces, and the upward forces equal the downward forces.
Answer (A) is incorrect because upward forces are equal to, not less than, downward forces in steady-state flight. Answer (B) is incorrect because rearward forces are equal to, not greater than, forward forces in steady-state flight.

21.
5220. During the transition from straight-and-level flight to a climb, the angle of attack is increased and lift

A— is momentarily decreased.
B— remains the same.
C— is momentarily increased.

Answer (C) is correct (5220). *(FTH Chap 17)*
During the transition from straight-and-level flight to a climb, a change in lift occurs as back elevator pressure is first applied, causing an increase in the angle of attack. Lift at this moment is now greater than weight and starts the airplane's climb.
Answer (A) is incorrect because, during the transition from straight-and-level flight to a climb, lift is momentarily increased, not decreased, as the angle of attack is increased. Answer (B) is incorrect because, during the transition from straight-and-level flight to a climb, lift is momentarily increased, rather than remaining the same, as the angle of attack is increased.

22.
5229. What changes in airplane longitudinal control must be made to maintain altitude while the airspeed is being decreased?

A— Increase the angle of attack to produce more lift than drag.
B— Increase the angle of attack to compensate for the decreasing lift.
C— Decrease the angle of attack to compensate for the increasing drag.

23.
5219. Which is true regarding the force of lift in steady, unaccelerated flight?

A— At lower airspeeds the angle of attack must be less to generate sufficient lift to maintain altitude.
B— There is a corresponding indicated airspeed required for every angle of attack to generate sufficient lift to maintain altitude.
C— An airfoil will always stall at the same indicated airspeed; therefore, an increase in weight will require an increase in speed to generate sufficient lift to maintain altitude.

24.
5161. In theory, if the airspeed of an airplane is doubled while in level flight, parasite drag will become

A— twice as great.
B— half as great.
C— four times greater.

25.
5162. As airspeed decreases in level flight below that speed for maximum lift/drag ratio, total drag of an airplane

A— decreases because of lower parasite drag.
B— increases because of increased induced drag.
C— increases because of increased parasite drag.

26.
5217. What performance is characteristic of flight at maximum lift/drag ratio in a propeller-driven airplane? Maximum

A— gain in altitude over a given distance.
B— range and maximum distance glide.
C— coefficient of lift and minimum coefficient of drag.

Answer (B) is correct (5229). *(FTH Chap 6)*
As airspeed decreases, the airfoils generate less lift. Accordingly, to maintain altitude, the angle of attack must be adjusted to compensate for the decrease in lift.
Answer (A) is incorrect because, if the angle of attack is increased to produce more lift than weight, not drag, the airplane will begin to climb. Answer (C) is incorrect because the angle of attack must be increased, not decreased, and the objective is to compensate for the decreased lift, not increased drag.

Answer (B) is correct (5219). *(FTH Chap 17)*
Different angles of attack provide different lift coefficients (amounts of lift). Accordingly, any given angle of attack has a corresponding airspeed to provide sufficient lift to maintain altitude.
Answer (A) is incorrect because, as airspeed is reduced, the angle of attack must be increased, not decreased, to provide sufficient lift. Answer (C) is incorrect because an airfoil will always stall at the same angle of attack, not the same indicated airspeed.

Answer (C) is correct (5161). *(PHAK Chap 1)*
Tests show that lift and drag vary as the square of the velocity. The velocity of the air passing over the wing in flight is determined by the airspeed of the airplane. Thus, if an airplane doubles its airspeed, lift and drag will be four times greater (assuming that the angle of attack remains the same).
Answer (A) is incorrect because the relationship between parasite drag and airspeed is not linear. Answer (B) is incorrect because parasite drag will increase, not decrease, with an increase in airspeed.

Answer (B) is correct (5162). *(FTH Chap 17)*
Total drag is at a minimum for the maximum lift/drag (L/D_{MAX}) ratio at one specific angle of attack and lift coefficient. As airspeed decreases, the induced drag will increase because a greater angle of attack is required to maintain level flight. The amount of induced drag varies inversely as the square of the airspeed.
Answer (A) is incorrect because total drag increases, not decreases, with decreases in airspeed below L/D_{MAX} because of increased induced drag. Answer (C) is incorrect because parasite drag changes directly, not inversely, with airspeed. Thus, below L/D_{MAX}, parasite drag decreases, not increases.

Answer (B) is correct (5217). *(FTH Chap 17)*
If the airplane is operated in steady flight at L/D_{MAX}, the total drag is at a minimum. Many important items of airplane performance are obtained in flight at L/D_{MAX}. For a propeller-driven airplane, these items include maximum range and maximum power-off glide range.
Answer (A) is incorrect because the best angle of climb (e.g., to clear an obstacle) is at a high angle of attack with both high lift and high drag coefficients, which would not result in an L/D_{MAX} ratio. Answer (C) is incorrect because L/D_{MAX} is neither at the maximum coefficient of lift nor at the minimum coefficient of drag, but at a point somewhere in between.

27.
5200. In theory, if the angle of attack and other factors remain constant and the airspeed is doubled, the lift produced at the higher speed will be

A— the same as at the lower speed.
B— two times greater than at the lower speed.
C— four times greater than at the lower speed.

Answer (C) is correct (5200). *(FTH Chap 17)*
    If the angle of attack and other factors remain constant, lift is proportional to the square of the airplane's velocity. For example, an airplane traveling at 200 kt. has four times the lift as the same airplane traveling at 100 kt.
    Answer (A) is incorrect because, as airspeed is doubled, lift produced will be four times greater than, not the same as, at the lower speed. Answer (B) is incorrect because, as airspeed is doubled, lift produced will be four, not two, times greater than at the lower speed.

28.
5201. An aircraft wing is designed to produce lift resulting from a difference in the

A— negative air pressure below and a vacuum above the wing's surface.
B— vacuum below the wing's surface and greater air pressure above the wing's surface.
C— higher air pressure below the wing's surface and lower air pressure above the wing's surface.

Answer (C) is correct (5201). *(FTH Chap 17)*
    An airplane's lift is produced by a pressure differential resulting from relatively lower (i.e., less than atmospheric) pressure above the wing and higher (i.e., greater than atmospheric) pressure below the wing's surface.
    Answer (A) is incorrect because the air pressure below the wing is relatively higher, not negative, and the pressure above the wing is lower, not a vacuum. Answer (B) is incorrect because the air pressure below the wing is relatively higher, not a vacuum, and the pressure above the wing is lower, not higher.

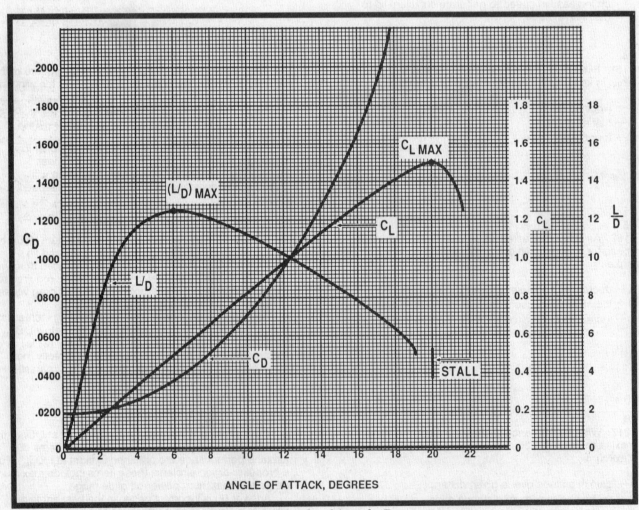

FIGURE 3.—Angle of Attack, Degrees.

29.
5213. (Refer to figure 3 on page 30.) If an airplane glides at an angle of attack of 10°, how much altitude will it lose in 1 mile?

A— 240 feet.
B— 480 feet.
C— 960 feet.

Answer (B) is correct (5213). *(FTH Chap 17)*
Use Fig. 3 to determine the L/D ratio for a given angle of attack. At the bottom of the chart, locate 10 (i.e., 10° angle of attack) and move vertically up to the L/D curve (the third curve as you move up). Then move right to the margin to determine the L/D ratio of 11:1 (i.e., 1-ft. loss of altitude for every 11 ft. of horizontal distance traveled). Thus, at a distance of 5,280 ft. (1 SM), the airplane will lose 480 ft. (5,280 ÷ 11) of altitude.
Answer (A) is incorrect because the airplane would lose 240 ft. in ½, not 1, SM at an angle of attack of 10°. Answer (C) is incorrect because the airplane would lose 960 ft. of altitude in 1 SM at an angle of attack of 1.5° or 19°, not 10°.

30.
5214. (Refer to figure 3 on page 30.) How much altitude will this airplane lose in 3 statute miles of gliding at an angle of attack of 8°?

A— 440 feet.
B— 880 feet.
C— 1,320 feet.

Answer (C) is correct (5214). *(FTH Chap 17)*
Use Fig. 3 to determine the L/D ratio for a given angle of attack. At the bottom of the chart, locate 8 (i.e., 8° angle of attack) and move vertically up to the L/D curve (the third curve as you move up). Then move right to the margin to determine the L/D ratio of 12:1 (i.e., 1-ft. loss of altitude for every 12 ft. horizontal distance traveled). Thus, at a distance of 15,840 ft. (5,280 ft./SM x 3 SM), the airplane will lose 1,320 ft. (15,840 ÷ 12) of altitude.
Answer (A) is incorrect because the airplane would lose 440 ft. in 1 mi. Answer (B) is incorrect because the airplane would lose 880 ft. in 2 mi.

31.
5215. (Refer to figure 3 on page 30.) The L/D ratio at a 2° angle of attack is approximately the same as the L/D ratio for a

A— 9.75° angle of attack.
B— 10.5° angle of attack.
C— 16.5° angle of attack.

Answer (C) is correct (5215). *(PHAK Chap 4)*
Enter the bottom of the chart in Fig. 3 at 2° angle of attack and move vertically up to the L/D curve. From this point move right horizontally to the point where the L/D curve intersects. Then move vertically down to the bottom of the chart to determine a 16.5° angle of attack. Thus, the L/D ratio is approximately the same at both 2° and 16.5° angle of attack.
Answer (A) is incorrect because an angle of attack of 9.75° would have the same L/D ratio as a 3.75°, not 2.0°, angle of attack. Answer (B) is incorrect because an angle of attack of 10.5° would have the same L/D ratio as a 3.5°, not 2.0°, angle of attack.

32.
5165. (Refer to figure 1 below.) At the airspeed represented by point A, in steady flight, the airplane will

A— have its maximum L/D ratio.
B— have its minimum L/D ratio.
C— be developing its maximum coefficient of lift.

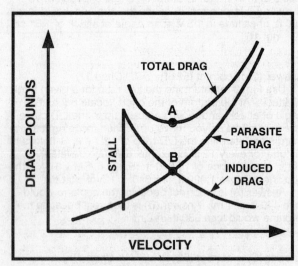

FIGURE 1—Drag Chart

33.
5166. (Refer to figure 1 above.) At an airspeed represented by point B, in steady flight, the pilot can expect to obtain the airplane's maximum

A— endurance.
B— glide range.
C— coefficient of lift.

34.
5158. Lift on a wing is most properly defined as the

A— force acting perpendicular to the relative wind.
B— differential pressure acting perpendicular to the chord of the wing.
C— reduced pressure resulting from a laminar flow over the upper camber of an airfoil, which acts perpendicular to the mean camber.

35.
5202. On a wing, the force of lift acts perpendicular to and the force of drag acts parallel to the

A— chord line.
B— flightpath.
C— longitudinal axis.

Answer (A) is correct (5165). *(FTH Chap 17)*
Point A (Fig. 1) is at the minimum point on the total drag curve. By definition, this is the point of maximum L/D ratio. Note that airspeed is on the horizontal axis and drag is on the vertical axis.
Answer (B) is incorrect because the minimum, not maximum, L/D ratio occurs at high airspeeds at which parasite drag is very high. Answer (C) is incorrect because the maximum coefficient of lift is produced at lower airspeeds, which have high induced drag and resulting lower L/D ratio.

Answer (B) is correct (5166). *(FTH Chap 17)*
Point B (Fig. 1) is the intersection of the parasite and induced drag curves, which is the point where the total drag is at its minimum (also known as the point of maximum L/D ratio). L/D_{MAX} is the airspeed at which the pilot of either a jet or a propeller-driven airplane can expect to obtain that airplane's maximum glide range.
Answer (A) is incorrect because only a jet-powered aircraft will obtain its maximum endurance at L/D_{MAX}. Answer (C) is incorrect because the maximum coefficient of lift is at the critical angle of attack, where total drag is also high because of an increase in induced drag.

Answer (A) is correct (5158). *(FTH Chap 17)*
Lift opposes the downward force of weight, is produced by the dynamic effect of the air acting on the wing, and acts perpendicular to the relative wind through the wing's center of lift.
Answer (B) is incorrect because lift acts perpendicular to the relative wind, not the chord line. Answer (C) is incorrect because lift is produced by pressure resulting from flow under as well as over the wing, and it acts perpendicular to relative wind, not the mean camber of the wing.

Answer (B) is correct (5202). *(FTH Chap 17)*
Lift acts perpendicular to the relative wind, which is opposite the flight path. Drag acts parallel to the flight path.
Answer (A) is incorrect because there is no fixed relationship between lift and drag with respect to the chord line. Answer (C) is incorrect because there is no fixed relationship between lift and drag and the longitudinal axis.

36.

5203. Which statement is true, regarding the opposing forces acting on an airplane in steady-state level flight?

A— These forces are equal.
B— Thrust is greater than drag and weight and lift are equal.
C— Thrust is greater than drag and lift is greater than weight.

Answer (A) is correct (5203). *(FTH Chap 17)*
In steady-state level flight, the sum of the opposing forces is equal to zero.
Answer (B) is incorrect because thrust is equal to, not greater than, drag in steady-state level flight. If thrust is greater than drag, airspeed will increase. Answer (C) is incorrect because thrust is equal to, not greater than, drag and lift is equal to, not greater than, weight in steady-state level flight. If lift is greater than weight, the airplane will enter a climb.

1.6 Ground Effect

37.

5209. An airplane leaving ground effect will

A— experience a reduction in ground friction and require a slight power reduction.
B— experience an increase in induced drag and require more thrust.
C— require a lower angle of attack to maintain the same lift coefficient.

Answer (B) is correct (5209). *(FTH Chap 17)*
An airplane leaving ground effect (a height greater than the wingspan) will

1. Require an increase in angle of attack to maintain the same lift coefficient,
2. Experience an increase in induced drag and thrust required,
3. Experience a decrease in stability and a nose-up change in moment, and
4. Produce a reduction in static source pressure and increase in indicated airspeed.

Answer (A) is incorrect because ground friction is reduced when breaking ground, not leaving ground effect, and an increase, not decrease, in power may be required. Answer (C) is incorrect because a higher, not lower, angle of attack is required to maintain the same lift coefficient when leaving ground effect.

38.

5224. To produce the same lift while in ground effect as when out of ground effect, the airplane requires

A— a lower angle of attack.
B— the same angle of attack.
C— a greater angle of attack.

Answer (A) is correct (5224). *(FTH Chap 17)*
In ground effect, induced drag decreases due to a reduction in wingtip vortices (caused by a reduction in the wing's downwash), which alters the spanwise lift distribution and reduces the induced angle of attack. Thus, the wing will require a lower angle of attack in ground effect to produce the same lift as when out of ground effect.
Answer (B) is incorrect because a lower, not the same, angle of attack is required to maintain the same lift while in ground effect as when out of ground effect. Answer (C) is incorrect because a lower, not greater, angle of attack is required to maintain the same lift while in ground effect as when out of ground effect.

39.

5216. If the same angle of attack is maintained in ground effect as when out of ground effect, lift will

A— increase, and induced drag will decrease.
B— decrease, and parasite drag will increase.
C— increase, and induced drag will increase.

Answer (A) is correct (5216). *(FTH Chap 17)*
In ground effect, induced drag decreases due to a reduction in wingtip vortices (caused by a reduction in the wing's downwash), which alters the spanwise lift distribution and reduces the induced angle of attack. Thus, if an airplane is brought into ground effect with a constant angle of attack, an increase in lift will result.
Answer (B) is incorrect because, at the same angle of attack in ground effect as when out of ground effect, lift will increase, not decrease, and parasite drag does not significantly change in ground effect. Answer (C) is incorrect because induced drag decreases, not increases, in ground effect.

1.7 Airplane Stability

40.
5226. If the airplane attitude remains in a new position after the elevator control is pressed forward and released, the airplane displays

A— neutral longitudinal static stability.
B— positive longitudinal static stability.
C— neutral longitudinal dynamic stability.

Answer (A) is correct (5226). *(FTH Chap 17)*
When an airplane's attitude is momentarily displaced and it remains at its new attitude, it is said to have neutral longitudinal static stability. Longitudinal stability is the quality which makes an airplane stable about its lateral axis (pitch).
Answer (B) is incorrect because positive longitudinal static stability is the initial tendency of the airplane to return to its original attitude after the elevator control is pressed forward and released. Answer (C) is incorrect because the longitudinal dynamic stability is the overall, not initial, tendency that the airplane displays after the elevator control is pressed forward and released. Neutral dynamic stability is indicated if the airplane attempts to return to its original state of equilibrium, but the pitch oscillations neither increase nor decrease in magnitude in time.

41.
5228. Longitudinal stability involves the motion of the airplane controlled by its

A— rudder.
B— elevator.
C— ailerons.

Answer (B) is correct (5228). *(FTH Chap 17)*
Longitudinal stability is the quality which makes an airplane stable about its lateral (i.e., pitch) axis. This motion is controlled by the elevators.
Answer (A) is incorrect because the rudder affects the directional, not longitudinal, stability of the airplane. Answer (C) is incorrect because the ailerons affect the lateral, not longitudinal, stability of the airplane.

42.
5227. Longitudinal dynamic instability in an airplane can be identified by

A— bank oscillations becoming progressively steeper.
B— pitch oscillations becoming progressively steeper.
C— Trilatitudinal roll oscillations becoming progressively steeper.

Answer (B) is correct (5227). *(FTH Chap 17)*
Dynamic stability is the overall tendency that the airplane displays after its equilibrium is disturbed. Negative dynamic stability (dynamic instability) is a property which causes oscillations set up by a statically stable airplane to become progressively greater. Longitudinal instability refers to pitch oscillations.
Answer (A) is incorrect because roll (bank) oscillations refer to lateral, not longitudinal, stability. Answer (C) is incorrect because roll (bank) oscillations refer to lateral, not longitudinal, stability.

43.
5230. If the airplane attitude initially tends to return to its original position after the elevator control is pressed forward and released, the airplane displays

A— positive dynamic stability.
B— positive static stability.
C— neutral dynamic stability.

Answer (B) is correct (5230). *(FTH Chap 17)*
When an airplane's elevator control is pressed forward and released and its attitude initially tends to return to its original position, the airplane displays positive static stability.
Answer (A) is incorrect because dynamic stability is the overall, not initial, tendency the airplane displays after its equilibrium is disturbed. Positive dynamic stability means the airplane will return to its original position directly, or through a series of decreasing pitch oscillations in time. Answer (C) is incorrect because dynamic stability is the overall, not initial, tendency the airplane displays after its equilibrium is disturbed. Neutral dynamic stability means the airplane attempts to return to its original position, but the pitch oscillations neither increase nor decrease in magnitude in time.

44.
5207. If an airplane is loaded to the rear of its CG range, it will tend to be unstable about its

A— vertical axis.
B— lateral axis.
C— longitudinal axis.

Answer (B) is correct (5207). *(FTH Chap 17)*
As the CG is moved rearward, it may move behind the center of lift, in which case the airplane is said to have negative stability about its lateral axis. Recall that the CG should be forward of the center of lift and that the tail surface is designed to have negative lift.
Answer (A) is incorrect because the CG position has relatively little to do with the stability about the vertical axis. Answer (C) is incorrect because stability about the longitudinal axis is not greatly affected by CG location. Remember that the airplane rolls about the longitudinal axis.

1.8 Turns

45.
5210. If airspeed is increased during a level turn, what action would be necessary to maintain altitude? The angle of attack

A— and angle of bank must be decreased.
B— must be increased or angle of bank decreased.
C— must be decreased or angle of bank increased.

Answer (C) is correct (5210). *(FTH Chap 17)*
To compensate for the added lift that would result if the airspeed were increased during a turn, the angle of attack must be decreased, or the angle of bank increased, to maintain a constant altitude.
Answer (A) is incorrect because either the angle of attack can be decreased or the angle of bank increased, not decreased, to maintain altitude as airspeed is increased in a turn. Answer (B) is incorrect because, to maintain a constant altitude in a turn as the airspeed is decreased, not increased, the angle of attack must be increased or angle of bank decreased.

46.
5159. While holding the angle of bank constant in a level turn, if the rate of turn is varied the load factor would

A— remain constant regardless of air density and the resultant lift vector.
B— vary depending upon speed and air density provided the resultant lift vector varies proportionately.
C— vary depending upon the resultant lift vector.

Answer (A) is correct (5159). *(PHAK Chap 1)*
For any given angle of bank, the rate of turn varies with the airspeed. For example, if the angle of bank is held constant and the airspeed is increased, the rate of turn will decrease and vice versa. Because of this, there is no change in centrifugal force while holding a constant angle of bank; thus, the load factor remains constant.
Answer (B) is incorrect because the rate of turn, not load factor, will vary depending on airspeed while holding a constant angle of bank. Answer (C) is incorrect because load factor will vary depending on the resultant load, not lift, vector.

47.
5192. To increase the rate of turn and at the same time decrease the radius, a pilot should

A— maintain the bank and decrease airspeed.
B— increase the bank and increase airspeed.
C— increase the bank and decrease airspeed.

Answer (C) is the best answer (5192). *(FTH Chap 17)*
At slower airspeeds, an airplane can make a turn in less distance (smaller radius) and at a faster rate. Thus, to decrease the radius and increase the rate, one steepens the bank and decreases airspeed.
Answer (A) is also correct in that, at a given angle of bank, a decrease in airspeed will increase the rate of turn and decrease the radius. However, the effect achieved will not be the same as achieved by steepening the bank and decreasing airspeed; thus, this is not the best answer. Answer (B) is incorrect because you decrease, not increase, airspeed to decrease the turn radius.

48.
5193. Which is correct with respect to rate and radius of turn for an airplane flown in a coordinated turn at a constant altitude?

A— For a specific angle of bank and airspeed, the rate and radius of turn will not vary.
B— To maintain a steady rate of turn, the angle of bank must be increased as the airspeed is decreased.
C— The faster the true airspeed, the faster the rate and larger the radius of turn regardless of the angle of bank.

Answer (A) is correct (5193). *(FTH Chap 17)*
At a constant altitude in a coordinated turn, for each angle of bank each airspeed has a specific rate and radius of turn, and they do not vary.
Answer (B) is incorrect because you must decrease, not increase, the angle of bank when the airspeed is decreased if you are to maintain a steady rate of turn. Answer (C) is incorrect because the faster the airspeed, the slower, not faster, the rate of turn at a constant angle of bank.

49.
5157. While maintaining a constant angle of bank and altitude in a coordinated turn, an increase in airspeed will

A— decrease the rate of turn resulting in a decreased load factor.
B— decrease the rate of turn resulting in no change in load factor.
C— increase the rate of turn resulting in no change in load factor.

Answer (B) is correct (5157). *(FTH Chap 17)*
When in a constant bank in a coordinated turn, an increase in airspeed will decrease the rate of turn. Because the bank is held constant, there will be no change in load factor.
Answer (A) is incorrect because there is no change in load factor in a coordinated turn if the angle of bank is held constant. Answer (C) is incorrect because the rate of turn decreases, not increases, with an increase in airspeed, and since the angle of bank is held constant, the load factor remains constant, not decreases.

50.
5194. Why is it necessary to increase back elevator pressure to maintain altitude during a turn? To compensate for the

A— loss of the vertical component of lift.
B— loss of the horizontal component of lift and the increase in centrifugal force.
C— rudder deflection and slight opposite aileron throughout the turn.

Answer (A) is correct (5194). *(FTH Chap 11)*
    As you enter a turn, lift is divided into horizontal and vertical components. This division reduces the amount of lift which is opposing weight, and thus the airplane loses altitude unless additional lift is created. This is done by increasing back elevator pressure to increase the angle of attack until the vertical component of lift is equal to the weight to maintain altitude without a change in thrust.
    Answer (B) is incorrect because, when the horizontal component of lift is less than centrifugal force, the airplane is in a skidding turn, which is corrected by increasing bank or decreasing the rate of turn (or a combination of both). Answer (C) is incorrect because slight opposite aileron pressure may be needed in a steep bank to overcome the airplane's overbanking tendency.

51.
5195. To maintain altitude during a turn, the angle of attack must be increased to compensate for the decrease in the

A— forces opposing the resultant component of drag.
B— vertical component of lift.
C— horizontal component of lift.

Answer (B) is correct (5195). *(FTH Chap 11)*
    As you enter a turn, lift is divided into horizontal and vertical components. This division reduces the amount of lift which is opposing weight, and thus the airplane loses altitude unless additional lift is created. This is done by increasing back elevator pressure to increase the angle of attack until the vertical component of lift is equal to the weight to maintain altitude without a change in thrust.
    Answer (A) is incorrect because the resultant component of drag is a nonsense term. Answer (C) is incorrect because, as the horizontal component of lift decreases, the vertical component increases; thus, the angle of attack will need to be decreased, not increased.

52.
5270. If a standard rate turn is maintained, how long would it take to turn 360°?

A— 1 minute.
B— 2 minutes.
C— 3 minutes.

Answer (B) is correct (5270). *(FTH Chap 13)*
    A standard rate turn is one during which the heading changes at a rate of 3°/sec. Thus, a 360° turn would take 2 min. (360° ÷ 3°/sec. = 120 sec., or 2 min.).
    Answer (A) is incorrect because at standard rate a 180°, not 360°, turn would take 1 min. Answer (C) is incorrect because at standard rate a 540°, not 360°, turn would take 3 min.

1.9 Load Factor

53.
5151. The ratio between the total airload imposed on the wing and the gross weight of an aircraft in flight is known as

A— load factor and directly affects stall speed.
B— aspect load and directly affects stall speed.
C— load factor and has no relation with stall speed.

Answer (A) is correct (5151). *(PHAK Chap 1)*
    A load factor is the ratio of the total airload acting on the airplane to the gross weight of the airplane. For example, if the airload imposed on the wing is twice the actual weight of the airplane, the load factor is said to be 2 G's, and the stall speed increases.
    Answer (B) is incorrect because the ratio between the total airload imposed on the wing and the gross weight of an airplane is known as a load, not aspect, factor. Answer (C) is incorrect because the airplane's stalling speed increases in proportion to the square root of the load factor. Thus, a load factor of 4 will double the normal unaccelerated stalling speed of an airplane.

54.
5152. Load factor is the lift generated by the wings of an aircraft at any given time

A— divided by the total weight of the aircraft.
B— multiplied by the total weight of the aircraft.
C— divided by the basic empty weight of the aircraft.

Answer (A) is correct (5152). *(PHAK Chap 1)*
    Since the load factor is the ratio between the total airload imposed on the wing and the gross weight of the airplane, the load factor is the lift generated by the wings divided by the total weight of the airplane. For example, an airplane weighing 2,000 lb. and having a load factor of 2.0 would require 4,000 lb. of lift by the wings. Thus, the load factor of 2.0 is equal to the 4,000 lb. of wing lift divided by the gross weight of 2,000 lb.
    Answer (B) is incorrect because load factor times airplane weight equals required lift. Answer (C) is incorrect because the total weight of the airplane, not the basic empty weight, is relevant.

55.

5153. For a given angle of bank, in any airplane, the load factor imposed in a coordinated constant-altitude turn

A— is constant and the stall speed increases.
B— varies with the rate of turn.
C— is constant and the stall speed decreases.

Answer (A) is correct (5153). *(PHAK Chap 1)*
In any airplane at any airspeed, if a constant altitude is maintained during the turn, the load factor for a given degree of bank is the same, which is the resultant of weight and centrifugal force. Because of the increased load factor in a turn, the stall speed is also increased in proportion to the square root of the load factor.
Answer (B) is incorrect because the load factor is not affected by changes in the rate of turn (which is determined by airspeed when at a constant bank). Answer (C) is incorrect because, when the load factor is increased as a turn is entered, the stall speed is also increased in proportion to the square root of the load factor.

56.

5154. Airplane wing loading during a level coordinated turn in smooth air depends upon the

A— rate of turn.
B— angle of bank.
C— true airspeed.

Answer (B) is correct (5154). *(PHAK Chap 1)*
The load factor for a given airplane during a level coordinated turn is determined solely by the angle of bank.
Answer (A) is incorrect because, in a coordinated turn, rate of turn has no impact on load factor. Answer (C) is incorrect because, in a coordinated turn, true airspeed has no impact on wing loading.

57.

5156. If an aircraft with a gross weight of 2,000 pounds was subjected to a 60° constant-altitude bank, the total load would be

A— 3,000 pounds.
B— 4,000 pounds.
C— 12,000 pounds.

Answer (B) is correct (5156). *(PHAK Chap 1)*
In a constant-altitude, 60° bank turn, the wings are loaded at 2 G's. Therefore, the total load of a 2,000-lb. airplane is 4,000 lb. (2,000 x 2).
Answer (A) is incorrect because 3,000 lb. would be the total load of a 1,500-lb. airplane in a 60° bank. Answer (C) is incorrect because 12,000 lb. would be the total load of a 6,000-lb. airplane in a 60° bank.

58.

5163. If the airspeed is increased from 90 knots to 135 knots during a level 60° banked turn, the load factor will

A— increase as well as the stall speed.
B— decrease and the stall speed will increase.
C— remain the same but the radius of turn will increase.

Answer (C) is correct (5163). *(FTH Chap 17)*
Since the only determinant of load factor in level coordinated turns is the amount of bank, a change in airspeed does not change the load factor. When airspeed is increased, however, the rate of turn decreases and the radius of turn increases.
Answer (A) is incorrect because the load factor and stall speed will remain the same for a constant-altitude, constant-banked turn. Answer (B) is incorrect because the load factor and stall speed will remain the same for a constant-altitude, constant-banked turn.

59.

5164. Baggage weighing 90 pounds is placed in a normal category airplane's baggage compartment which is placarded at 100 pounds. If this airplane is subjected to a positive load factor of 3.5 G's, the total load of the baggage would be

A— 315 pounds and would be excessive.
B— 315 pounds and would not be excessive.
C— 350 pounds and would not be excessive.

Answer (B) is correct (5164). *(FTH Chap 17)*
Since 90 lb. is less than the amount of placarded weight (100 lb.), there is no problem with the weight. The positive load factor of 3.5 G's is within the normal operational limit of 3.8 G's of normal category airplanes. The placarded weight does not have to be divided by the design load factor of the airplane. When 100 lb. was set as a baggage limit in this particular case, the designers recognized that, since this is a normal category airplane, it may be subjected to 3.8 G's, i.e., 380 lb. The baggage weight of 90 lb. is multiplied by 3.5 G's to get a load of 315 lb.
Answer (A) is incorrect because the baggage weight is not excessive. Load factor does not need to be figured in to determine maximum weight for any compartment. Answer (C) is incorrect because 350 lb. would be the total load of 100 lb. of baggage at 3.5 G's.

60.
5222. (Refer to figure 4 below.) What increase in load factor would take place if the angle of bank were increased from 60° to 80°?

A— 3 G's.
B— 3.5 G's.
C— 4 G's.

Answer (C) is correct (5222). *(FTH Chap 17)*
In Fig. 4, the relationship between bank angle degrees on the horizontal axis is related to both load factor or "G" units on the vertical scale and percent increase in stall speed on the vertical axis. There are two curves on the graph. Each curve relates to the vertical scale or the vertical axis. At a 60° bank, find 60° on the horizontal axis, go up to the load factor curve, and then horizontally left to the far left vertical scale to determine approximately 2 G's. At 80° there are approximately 6 G's. Thus, the increase in load factor is 4 G's (6 – 2) when the angle of bank is increased from 60° to 80°.
Answer (A) is incorrect because an additional 3 G's would result from an increase of bank from 60° to 77°. Answer (B) is incorrect because an additional 3.5 G's would result from an increase of bank from 60° to 78°.

61.
5221. (Refer to figure 4 below.) What is the stall speed of an airplane under a load factor of 2 G's if the unaccelerated stall speed is 60 knots?

A— 66 knots.
B— 74 knots.
C— 84 knots.

Answer (C) is correct (5221). *(FTH Chap 17)*
Use Fig. 4 to determine the percentage increase in stall speed under a load factor of 2 G's. First, find 2 G's on the far left vertical scale and move horizontally to the right to the load factor curve, which intersects at about a 60° bank. Then move vertically up from that point to the intersection of the stall speed increase curve. Next move left horizontally to the vertical axis to determine a 40% increase in stall speed. If the unaccelerated stall speed is 60 kt., the accelerated stall speed is 84 kt. (60 kt. x 140%).
Answer (A) is incorrect because 66 kt. is a 10%, not 40%, increase in stall speed. Answer (B) is incorrect because 74 kt. is a 23%, not 40%, increase in stall speed.

FIGURE 4.—Stall Speed/Load Factor.

END OF CHAPTER

CHAPTER TWO
AIRPLANE INSTRUMENTS, ENGINES, AND SYSTEMS

This chapter contains outlines of major concepts tested; all FAA test questions and answers regarding airplane instruments, engines, and systems; and an explanation of each answer. Each module, or subtopic, within this chapter is listed above with the number of questions from the FAA pilot knowledge test pertaining to that particular module. For each module, the first number following the parentheses is the page number on which the outline begins, and the next number is the page number on which the questions begin.

CAUTION: Recall that the **sole purpose** of this book is to expedite your passing the FAA pilot knowledge test for the commercial pilot certificate. Accordingly, all extraneous material (i.e., topics or regulations not directly tested on the FAA pilot knowledge test) is omitted, even though much more information and knowledge are necessary to become a proficient commercial pilot. This additional material is presented in *Commercial Pilot Flight Maneuvers and Practical Test Prep* and *Pilot Handbook*, available from Gleim Publications, Inc. See the order form on page 284.

2.1 MAGNETIC COMPASS (Question 1)

1. The difference between direction indicated by a magnetic compass not installed in an airplane and one installed in an airplane is called compass deviation.

   a. Magnetic fields produced by metals and electrical accessories in an airplane disturb the compass needle.

   b. The compass deviation usually varies for different headings of the same aircraft.

2.2 AIRSPEED INDICATOR (Questions 2-9)

1. Airspeed indicators have several color-coded markings.

   a. The white arc is the flap operating range.

      1) The lower limit is the power-off stalling speed or the minimum steady flight speed with wing flaps and landing gear in the landing position (V_{S0}).

      2) The upper limit is the maximum flap extended speed (V_{FE}).

b.   The green arc is the normal operating range.

1)   The lower limit is the power-off stalling speed with the wing flaps up and landing gear retracted (V_{S1}).

2)   The upper limit is the maximum structural cruising speed for normal operation (V_{NO}).

c.   The yellow arc is the range of airspeed that is safe in smooth air only.

1)   It is known as the caution range.

d.   The red line is the speed that should never be exceeded (V_{NE}).

1)   Design limit load factors could be exceeded with airspeeds in excess of V_{NE} from a variety of phenomena.

2.   The most important airspeed limitation which is **not** color-coded is the maneuvering speed (V_A).

a.   The maneuvering speed is the maximum speed at which abrupt full deflection of aircraft controls can be made without causing structural damage.

b.   It is the maximum speed for flight in turbulent air.

3.   The maximum landing gear extended speed (V_{LE}) is not color coded.

a.   It is usually placarded and is included in the airplane's flight manual.

4.   Types of airspeed

a.   Indicated airspeed (IAS) is read directly off the airspeed indicator.

b.   Calibrated airspeed (CAS) is IAS corrected for installation and instrument error.

c.   True airspeed (TAS) is CAS corrected for pressure altitude and nonstandard temperature.

5.   The V-G diagram (velocity versus "G" loads) shows the flight operating strength of an airplane.

a.   In the diagram on page 41, load factor is on the vertical axis with airspeed on the horizontal axis.

b.   The lines of maximum lift capability (dashed lines) are the first items of importance on the V-G diagram.

1)   The subject airplane in the diagram on the opposite page is capable of developing no more than one positive "G" at 64 mph, which is the wings-level stall speed of the airplane.

2)   The maximum load factor increases dramatically with airspeed. The maximum positive lift capability of this airplane is 2 "G" at 96 mph, 3 "G" at 116 mph, 3.8 "G" at 126 mph, etc.

a)   These are the "coordinates" of points on the curved line up to point C.

3)   Any load factor above this dashed line is unavailable aerodynamically. That is, the subject airplane cannot fly above the line of maximum lift capability (it will stall).

c.   Point C is the intersection of the positive limit load factor (line CDE) and the line of maximum positive lift capability (dashed line up to point C).

1)   The airspeed at this point is the minimum airspeed at which the limit load can be developed aerodynamically.

2) Any airspeed greater than point C provides a positive lift capability sufficient to damage the airplane.

   a) Any airspeed less than point C does **not** provide positive lift capability sufficient to cause damage from excessive flight loads.

3) The usual term given to the speed at point C is the design maneuvering speed (V_A).

d. The limit airspeed V_{NE} is a design reference point for the airplane. The subject airplane is limited to 196 mph (line EF).

   1) If flight is attempted beyond the limit airspeed, structural damage or structural failure may result from a variety of phenomena.

e. Thus, the airplane in flight is limited to a regime of airspeeds and G's which do not exceed

   1) The limit (or red-line) speed (line EF)
   2) Normal stall speed (line AJ)
   3) The positive and negative limit load factors (lines CDE and IHG)
   4) The maximum lift capability (dashed lines up to C, down to I)

f. A caution range is indicated between points D, E, F, and G. Within this range, certain factors must be considered to maintain flight in the envelope.

   1) Line DG represents the maximum structural cruising speed (V_{NO}).

2.3 TURN COORDINATOR/TURN-AND-SLIP INDICATOR (Questions 10-11)

1.   The turn coordinator and the turn-and-slip indicator are usually electric-driven instruments. Each instrument has an inclinometer (i.e., ball).

     a.   The turn coordinator indicates roll rate, rate of turn, and coordination.
     b.   The turn-and-slip indicator indicates rate of turn and coordination.

2.   The advantage of having an electric turn coordinator (or turn-and-slip indicator) is to provide bank information in case the vacuum-driven attitude indicator and heading indicator fail.

2.4 FUEL/AIR MIXTURE (Questions 12-21)

1.   As altitude increases, the density (weight) of air entering the carburetor decreases.

     a.   If no adjustment is made, the amount of fuel remains constant and the fuel/air ratio (mixture) becomes excessively rich.

     b.   Thus, the pilot adjusts the fuel flow with the mixture control to maintain the proper fuel/air ratio at all altitudes.

2.   The fuel/air ratio, by definition, is the ratio between the weight of fuel and the weight of air entering the cylinder.

     a.   The best power mixture refers to the fuel/air ratio that will provide the most power at any given power setting.

3.   Spark plug fouling results from operating at high altitudes with an excessively rich mixture due to the below-normal temperatures in the combustion chambers.

4.   In gas turbine (as well as reciprocating) engines, as temperature increases and air density decreases, thrust decreases.

2.5 CARBURETOR HEAT (Questions 22-24)

1.   Carburetor heat enriches the fuel/air mixture because warm air is less dense than cold air.

2.   Applying carburetor heat decreases engine output and increases operating temperature due to the warmer, less dense air entering the carburetor.

     a.   Leaving the carburetor heat on during takeoff will increase the ground roll.

2.6 DETONATION AND PREIGNITION (Questions 25-28)

1.   Detonation occurs in a reciprocating aircraft engine when the unburned fuel/air charge in the cylinders is subjected to instantaneous combustion.

2.   Detonation is usually caused by using a lower-than-specified grade of aviation fuel and too lean a mixture or by excessive engine temperature caused by high-power settings.

3.   Preignition is the uncontrolled firing of the fuel/air charge in advance of the normal spark ignition.

2.7 AIRPLANE IGNITION SYSTEMS (Questions 29-33)

1. Dual ignition systems provide improved combustion of the fuel/air mixture.

2. Aircraft magnetos generate their own electricity by self-contained magnets.

3. An engine that continues to run after the ignition switch has been turned off probably has a broken or disconnected ground wire between the magneto and the ignition switch.

    a. Thus, a potentially dangerous situation exists because the engine could accidentally start if the propeller is moved with fuel in the cylinder.

4. A good practice before shutdown is to idle the engine and momentarily turn the ignition off.

5. Rapid opening and closing of the throttle may cause detuning of engine crankshaft counterweights (throwing the crankshaft out of balance).

2.8 ENGINE COOLING (Questions 34-36)

1. Aircraft engines are largely cooled by the flow of oil through the lubrication system.

2. An excessively low oil level will prevent the oil from cooling adequately and result in an abnormally high engine oil temperature.

3. You should inspect aircraft exhaust manifold-type heating systems on a regular basis to minimize the possibility of cracks or other problems which would permit exhaust gases to leak into the cockpit.

2.9 AIRPLANE PROPELLERS (Questions 37-45)

1. Propeller efficiency is the ratio of thrust horsepower to brake horsepower.

2. A fixed-pitch propeller can be most efficient only at a specified combination of airspeed and RPM.

3. The propeller's geometric pitch varies along the propeller blade because the propeller tip goes through the air faster than the section of propeller near the hub.

    a. This pitch variation permits a relatively constant angle of attack along the blade's length when in cruising flight.

4. A constant-speed (controllable-pitch) propeller adjusts the pitch angle of the propeller blade so that the engine is maintained at a selected RPM.

5. For takeoff, to develop maximum power and thrust, you should use a small angle of attack and high RPM on a controllable-pitch (constant-speed) propeller.

6. To establish climb power after takeoff in an airplane equipped with a constant-speed propeller, you should first decrease manifold pressure and then decrease RPM. When the propeller control is moved to reduce the RPM, the propeller blade angle increases.

    a. When increasing power, increase RPM first; then increase manifold pressure to avoid placing undue stress on the engine.

7. Spiraling slipstream describes the propeller blade forcing air rearward in a spiraling clockwise direction around the fuselage when the propeller rotates through the air in a clockwise direction as viewed from the rear.

    a. As a result, the airplane yaws left around the vertical axis.
    b. Also, the airplane rolls right around the longitudinal axis.

QUESTIONS AND ANSWER EXPLANATIONS

All the FAA questions from the pilot knowledge test for the commercial pilot certificate relating to airplane instruments, engines, and systems, and the material outlined previously are reproduced on the following pages in the same modules as the outlines. To the immediate right of each question are the correct answer and answer explanation. You should cover these answers and answer explanations while responding to the questions. (A bookmark for this purpose has been provided in the back of the book.) Refer to the general discussion in the Introduction on how to take the FAA pilot knowledge test.

Remember that the questions from the FAA pilot knowledge test bank have been reordered by topic, and the topics have been organized into a meaningful sequence. Accordingly, the first line of the answer explanation gives the FAA question number and the citation of the authoritative source for the answer.

2.1 Magnetic Compass

1.
5178. Which statement is true about magnetic deviation of a compass? Deviation

A— varies over time as the agonic line shifts.
B— varies for different headings of the same aircraft.
C— is the same for all aircraft in the same locality.

Answer (B) is correct (5178). *(PHAK Chap 3)*
The difference between the direction indicated by a compass not installed in an airplane and one installed in an airplane is called compass deviation. Magnetic fields produced by the metal and electrical accessories in the airplane disturb the compass needle and produce errors. The amount of deviation varies with different headings.
Answer (A) is incorrect because the position of the agonic line determines magnetic variation, not compass deviation. Answer (C) is incorrect because compass deviation varies from aircraft to aircraft.

2.2 Airspeed Indicator

2.
5605. Maximum structural cruising speed is the maximum speed at which an airplane can be operated during

A— abrupt maneuvers.
B— normal operations.
C— flight in smooth air.

Answer (B) is correct (5605). *(PHAK Chap 3)*
The maximum structural cruising speed (V_{NO}) is the upper limit of the green arc on the airspeed indicator. It is the maximum speed for normal operations.
Answer (A) is incorrect because V_A is the design maneuvering speed, which is the rough air penetration speed and maximum speed for abrupt maneuvers. Answer (C) is incorrect because the yellow arc (V_{NO} to V_{NE}) is the caution range where flight is allowed only in smooth air.

3.
5604. Why should flight speeds above V_{NE} be avoided?

A— Excessive induced drag will result in structural failure.
B— Design limit load factors may be exceeded, if gusts are encountered.
C— Control effectiveness is so impaired that the aircraft becomes uncontrollable.

Answer (B) is correct (5604). *(PHAK Chap 3)*
At speeds above V_{NE}, the design limit load factors for the airplane may be exceeded if gusts are encountered. Thus, this airspeed should never be exceeded, even in smooth air.
Answer (A) is incorrect because induced drag decreases, not increases, as airspeed increases. Answer (C) is incorrect because control effectiveness increases, not decreases, as airspeed increases.

4.
5231. (Refer to figure 5 on page 45.) The horizontal dashed line from point C to point E represents the

A— ultimate load factor.
B— positive limit load factor.
C— airspeed range for normal operations.

Answer (B) is correct (5231). *(FTH Chap 17)*
In Fig. 5, the line from point C to point E represents the positive limit load factor, i.e., the greatest positive load that may be placed on the aircraft without risk of structural damage.
Answer (A) is incorrect because ultimate load factor is the limit load factor multiplied by 1.5 as a safety measure. While structural damage may occur at the limit load factor, structural failure may occur at the ultimate load factor. Answer (C) is incorrect because the airspeed range for normal operations, the green arc on the airspeed indicator, is the horizontal distance from the vertical line from point A to point J to the vertical line from point D to point G.

Figure 5.—Velocity vs. G-Loads.

5.
5232. (Refer to figure 5 above.) The vertical line from point E to point F is represented on the airspeed indicator by the

A— upper limit of the yellow arc.
B— upper limit of the green arc.
C— blue radial line.

Answer (A) is correct (5232). *(FTH Chap 17)*
In Fig. 5, the line from point E to point F is labeled as the never-exceed speed (V_{NE}). This speed is represented on the airspeed indicator by the upper limit of the yellow arc (the red radial line).
Answer (B) is incorrect because the upper limit of the green arc represents the maximum structural cruising speed (V_{NO}), which is the line from point D to point G, not E to F. Answer (C) is incorrect because the blue radial line represents the single-engine best rate-of-climb speed (V_{YSE}) in a multiengine airplane. V_{YSE} is not shown on the V-G diagram.

6.
5233. (Refer to figure 5 above.) The vertical line from point D to point G is represented on the airspeed indicator by the maximum speed limit of the

A— green arc.
B— yellow arc.
C— white arc.

Answer (A) is correct (5233). *(FTH Chap 17)*
In Fig. 5, the line from point D to point G is labeled as the maximum structural cruising speed (V_{NO}). This speed is represented on the airspeed indicator by the upper limit of the green arc.
Answer (B) is incorrect because the upper limit of the yellow arc represents the never-exceed speed (V_{NE}), which is the line from point E to point F, not D to G. Answer (C) is incorrect because the upper limit of the white arc is the maximum flap extended speed (V_{FE}), which is not shown on the V-G diagram.

7.
5177. Which airspeed would a pilot be unable to identify by the color coding of an airspeed indicator?

A— The never-exceed speed.
B— The power-off stall speed.
C— The maneuvering speed.

Answer (C) is correct (5177). *(PHAK Chap 3)*
The maneuvering speed (V_A) is not color coded on an airspeed indicator. It is usually placarded and included in the airplane's flight manual.
Answer (A) is incorrect because the never-exceed speed is identified by the red radial line at the top of the yellow arc. Answer (B) is incorrect because two power-off stall speeds are represented on the airspeed indicator; the stall speeds in the landing and clean configurations are represented by the lower limits of the white and green arcs, respectively.

8.
5601. Calibrated airspeed is best described as indicated airspeed corrected for

A—installation and instrument error.
B—instrument error.
C—non-standard temperature.

Answer (A) is correct (5601). *(PHAK Chap 3)*
Calibrated airspeed (CAS) is indicated airspeed corrected for installation and instrument error. An airspeed calibration chart is provided in the airplane's *Pilot's Operating Handbook (POH)*.
Answer (B) is incorrect because calibrated airspeed is indicated airspeed corrected for both installation and instrument error, not only for instrument error. Answer (C) is incorrect because calibrated airspeed is indicated airspeed corrected for installation and instrument error, not for nonstandard temperature.

9.
5602. True airspeed is best described as calibrated airspeed corrected for

A—installation or instrument error.
B—non-standard temperature.
C—altitude and nonstandard temperature.

Answer (C) is correct (5602). *(PHAK Chap 3)*
True airspeed (TAS) is calibrated airspeed corrected for pressure altitude and nonstandard temperature. Thus, TAS is calibrated airspeed corrected for density altitude.
Answer (A) is incorrect because calibrated airspeed, not true airspeed, is indicated airspeed corrected for installation and, not or, instrument error. Answer (B) is incorrect because true airspeed is calibrated airspeed corrected for both nonstandard temperature and pressure altitude, not only nonstandard temperature.

2.3 Turn Coordinator/Turn-and-Slip Indicator

10.
5269. What is an advantage of an electric turn coordinator if the airplane has a vacuum system for other gyroscopic instruments?

A— It is a backup in case of vacuum system failure.
B— It is more reliable than the vacuum-driven indicators.
C— It will not tumble as will vacuum-driven turn indicators.

Answer (A) is correct (5269). *(PHAK Chap 3)*
The principal uses of the turn coordinator are to indicate rate of turn and to serve as an emergency source of bank information in case the vacuum-driven attitude indicator fails.
Answer (B) is incorrect because the vacuum-driven and electric-driven indicators are equally reliable. Answer (C) is incorrect because both the vacuum-driven and the electric-driven turn indicator can tumble.

11.
5268. What is an operational difference between the turn coordinator and the turn-and-slip indicator? The turn coordinator

A— is always electric; the turn-and-slip indicator is always vacuum-driven.
B— indicates bank angle only; the turn-and-slip indicator indicates rate of turn and coordination.
C— indicates roll rate, rate of turn, and coordination; the turn-and-slip indicator indicates rate of turn and coordination.

Answer (C) is correct (5268). *(PHAK Chap 3)*
The turn-and-slip indicator indicates the rate and direction of the turn. The turn coordinator displays the movement of the aircraft along the longitudinal axis in an amount proportional to the roll rate. When the roll rate is reduced to zero (i.e., a constant bank), the instrument provides an indication of rate of turn. Both the turn coordinator and the turn indicator possess a ball which indicates rudder/aileron coordination.
Answer (A) is incorrect because the turn coordinator and the turn-and-slip indicator are usually electric-driven instruments. Answer (B) is incorrect because the turn coordinator indicates roll rate and coordination, not angle of bank.

2.4 Fuel/Air Mixture

12.
5172. Fouling of spark plugs is more apt to occur if the aircraft

A— gains altitude with no mixture adjustment.
B— descends from altitude with no mixture adjustment.
C— throttle is advanced very abruptly.

Answer (A) is correct (5172). *(PHAK Chap 2)*
As an aircraft gains altitude, the mixture must be leaned to compensate for the decrease in air density. If the mixture is not adjusted, it becomes too rich, i.e., contains too much fuel in terms of the weight of the air. Because of excessive fuel, a cooling effect takes place, which causes below-normal temperatures in the combustion chambers, resulting in spark plug fouling.
Answer (B) is incorrect because descending with no mixture adjustment, i.e., operating with an excessively lean mixture, results in overheating, rough engine operation, a loss of power, and detonation, not spark plug fouling. Answer (C) is incorrect because advancing the throttle abruptly may cause the engine to sputter or stop, not foul the spark plugs.

13.
5608. What will occur if no leaning is made with the mixture control as the flight altitude increases?

A— The volume of air entering the carburetor decreases and the amount of fuel decreases.
B— The density of air entering the carburetor decreases and the amount of fuel increases.
C— The density of air entering the carburetor decreases and the amount of fuel remains constant.

Answer (C) is correct (5608). *(PHAK Chap 2)*
As altitude increases, the density of air entering the carburetor decreases. If no leaning is done with the mixture control, the amount of fuel will remain constant, resulting in an excessively rich mixture.
Answer (A) is incorrect because the density, not volume, of air decreases, and the amount of fuel remains the same, not decreases. Answer (B) is incorrect because the amount of fuel remains the same, not decreases.

14.
5609. Unless adjusted, the fuel/air mixture becomes richer with an increase in altitude because the amount of fuel

A— decreases while the volume of air decreases.
B— remains constant while the volume of air decreases.
C— remains constant while the density of air decreases.

Answer (C) is correct (5609). *(PHAK Chap 2)*
As altitude increases, the density of air entering the carburetor decreases. If no leaning is done with the mixture control, the amount of fuel will remain constant, resulting in an excessively rich mixture.
Answer (A) is incorrect because the amount of fuel remains the same, not decreases, and the density, not volume, of air decreases. Answer (B) is incorrect because the density, not the volume of air, decreases.

15.
5610. The basic purpose of adjusting the fuel/air mixture control at altitude is to

A— decrease the fuel flow to compensate for decreased air density.
B— decrease the amount of fuel in the mixture to compensate for increased air density.
C— increase the amount of fuel in the mixture to compensate for the decrease in pressure and density of the air.

Answer (A) is correct (5610). *(PHAK Chap 2)*
The purpose of adjusting the fuel/air mixture control at altitude is to decrease the fuel flow to compensate for the decreased air density.
Answer (B) is incorrect because air density decreases, not increases, at altitude. Answer (C) is incorrect because at altitude the amount of fuel is decreased, not increased, to compensate for decreased air density.

16.
5611. At high altitudes, an excessively rich mixture will cause the

A— engine to overheat.
B— fouling of spark plugs.
C— engine to operate smoother even though fuel consumption is increased.

Answer (B) is correct (5611). *(PHAK Chap 2)*
As an aircraft gains altitude, the mixture must be leaned to compensate for the decrease in air density. If the mixture is not adjusted, it becomes too rich, i.e., contains too much fuel in terms of the weight of the air. Because of excessive fuel, a cooling effect takes place, which causes below-normal temperatures in the combustion chambers, resulting in spark plug fouling.
Answer (A) is incorrect because a lean, not rich, mixture will cause the engine to overheat. Answer (C) is incorrect because an engine runs smoothest when the mixture is appropriate, not excessively rich.

17.
5176. The pilot controls the air/fuel ratio with the

A— throttle.
B— manifold pressure.
C— mixture control.

Answer (C) is correct (5176). *(PHAK Chap 2)*
The mixture control is used to adjust the ratio of fuel-to-air mixture entering the combustion chamber.
Answer (A) is incorrect because the throttle regulates the total volume of fuel and air, not the fuel-to-air ratio, entering the combustion chamber. Answer (B) is incorrect because the manifold pressure is an indication of an engine's power output as controlled by the throttle; it is not directly related to the air/fuel mixture.

18.
5187. Fuel/air ratio is the ratio between the

A— volume of fuel and volume of air entering the cylinder.
B— weight of fuel and weight of air entering the cylinder.
C— weight of fuel and weight of air entering the carburetor.

Answer (B) is correct (5187). *(PHAK Chap 2)*
The fuel/air ratio, i.e., mixture, is the ratio between the weight of fuel and the weight of air entering the cylinder.
Answer (A) is incorrect because, as altitude increases, the amount of air in a fixed volume (i.e., air density) decreases. Thus, the ratio is between weights, not volume. Answer (C) is incorrect because the carburetor is where the fuel/air ratio is established prior to entering the cylinders.

19.
5298. The best power mixture is that fuel/air ratio at which

A— cylinder head temperatures are the coolest.
B— the most power can be obtained for any given throttle setting.
C— a given power can be obtained with the highest manifold pressure or throttle setting.

Answer (B) is correct (5298). *(FTH Chap 2)*
Engines are more efficient when they are supplied the proper mixture of fuel and air. The best power mixture refers to the fuel/air ratio that provides the most power at any given throttle setting.
Answer (A) is incorrect because the engine's cylinder heads will be coolest when the mixture is richest, not when it is at its best power setting. Answer (C) is incorrect because it describes the highest power setting, not the best power mixture.

20.
5188. The mixture control can be adjusted, which

A— prevents the fuel/air combination from becoming too rich at higher altitudes.
B— regulates the amount of airflow through the carburetor's venturi.
C— prevents the fuel/air combination from becoming lean as the airplane climbs.

Answer (A) is correct (5188). *(PHAK Chap 2)*
As an aircraft gains altitude, the mixture must be leaned to compensate for the decrease in air density. If the mixture is not adjusted, it becomes too rich, i.e., contains too much fuel in terms of the weight of the air.
Answer (B) is incorrect because the throttle, not the mixture control, regulates the airflow through the carburetor's venturi. Answer (C) is incorrect because the fuel/air ratio becomes richer, not leaner, as the airplane climbs.

21.
5300. What effect, if any, would a change in ambient temperature or air density have on gas turbine engine performance?

A— As air density decreases, thrust increases.
B— As temperature increases, thrust increases.
C— As temperature increases, thrust decreases.

Answer (C) is correct (5300). *(AFNA Chap 2)*
A high ambient air temperature at a given pressure altitude relates to a high density altitude, or a decrease in air density. Thrust is reduced because of low air density and low mass flow. Also, thrust and fuel flow are reduced further because of high compressor inlet temperature.
Answer (A) is incorrect because as air density decreases, thrust decreases, not increases. Answer (B) is incorrect because thrust decreases, not increases, with an increase in temperature.

2.5 Carburetor Heat

22.
5189. Which statement is true concerning the effect of the application of carburetor heat?

A— It enriches the fuel/air mixture.
B— It leans the fuel/air mixture.
C— It has no effect on the fuel/air mixture.

Answer (A) is correct (5189). *(PHAK Chap 2)*
The application of carburetor heat reduces the density of air entering the carburetor because the air is warmer. As a result, it enriches the fuel/air mixture because there is no change in the weight of fuel being combusted.
Answer (B) is incorrect because warmer air is less dense so the mixture is enriched, not leaned. Answer (C) is incorrect because warmer air is less dense so the mixture is enriched, not unaffected.

23.
5606. Applying carburetor heat will

A— not affect the mixture.
B— lean the fuel/air mixture.
C— enrich the fuel/air mixture.

Answer (C) is correct (5606). *(PHAK Chap 2)*
The application of carburetor heat reduces the density of air entering the carburetor because the air is warmer. As a result, it enriches the fuel/air mixture because there is no change in the weight of fuel being combusted.
Answer (A) is incorrect because warmer air is less dense so the mixture is enriched, not unaffected. Answer (B) is incorrect because warmer air is less dense so the mixture is enriched, not leaned.

24.
5170. Leaving the carburetor heat on during takeoff

A— leans the mixture for more power on takeoff.
B— will decrease the takeoff distance.
C— will increase the ground roll.

Answer (C) is correct (5170). *(PHAK Chap 2)*
Use of carburetor heat tends to reduce the output of the engine due to the warmer, less dense air entering the carburetor. Thus, the use of carburetor heat reduces performance during critical phases of flight, e.g., takeoff and climb. During the takeoff, it will increase the ground roll.
Answer (A) is incorrect because carburetor heat enriches, not leans, the mixture for less, not more, power. Answer (B) is incorrect because the use of carburetor heat will increase, not decrease, takeoff performance.

2.6 Detonation and Preignition

25.
5190. Detonation occurs in a reciprocating aircraft engine when

A— there is an explosive increase of fuel caused by too rich a fuel/air mixture.
B— the spark plugs receive an electrical jolt caused by a short in the wiring.
C— the unburned fuel/air charge in the cylinders is subjected to instantaneous combustion.

Answer (C) is correct (5190). *(PHAK Chap 2)*
Detonation (or knock) is a sudden explosion, or instantaneous combustion, of the fuel/air mixture in the cylinders, producing extreme heat and severe structural stresses on the engine. It is caused by low-grade fuel, too lean a mixture, or excessively high engine temperatures.
Answer (A) is incorrect because detonation is caused by too lean, not too rich, a mixture. Answer (B) is incorrect because detonation is caused by excessively high engine temperatures, not a short in spark plug wiring.

26.
5185b. Detonation can be caused by

A— a "rich" mixture.
B— low engine temperatures.
C— using a lower grade of fuel than recommended.

Answer (C) is correct (5185b.). *(PHAK Chap 2)*
Detonation (or knock) is a sudden explosion, or instantaneous combustion, of the fuel/air mixture in the cylinders, producing extreme heat and severe structural stresses on the engine. It is caused by low-grade fuel, too lean a mixture, or excessively high engine temperatures.
Answer (A) is incorrect because detonation is caused by the mixture being too lean, not rich. Answer (B) is incorrect because detonation is caused by excessively high, not low, engine temperatures.

27.
5186. The uncontrolled firing of the fuel/air charge in advance of normal spark ignition is known as

A— instantaneous combustion.
B— detonation.
C— pre-ignition.

Answer (C) is correct (5186). *(FTH Chap 2)*
Preignition is the ignition of the fuel prior to normal ignition or ignition before the electrical arcing occurs at the spark plug. Preignition may be caused by excessively hot exhaust valves, carbon particles, or spark plugs and electrodes heated to an incandescent, or glowing, state. These hot spots are usually caused by high temperatures encountered during detonation. A significant difference between preignition and detonation is that, if the conditions for detonation exist in one cylinder, they may exist in all cylinders, but preignition could take place in only one or two cylinders.
Answer (A) is incorrect because instantaneous combustion is detonation, which will cause extremely high engine temperatures and can result in preignition. Answer (B) is incorrect because detonation is the instantaneous combustion of the fuel/air mixture, which can be caused by using too lean a mixture, by using too low a grade of fuel, or by operating in temperatures that are too high.

28.
5185a. Detonation may occur at high-power settings when

A— the fuel mixture ignites instantaneously instead of burning progressively and evenly.
B— an excessively rich fuel mixture causes an explosive gain in power.
C— the fuel mixture is ignited too early by hot carbon deposits in the cylinder.

Answer (A) is correct (5185a.). *(PHAK Chap 2)*
Detonation (or knock) is a sudden explosion, or instantaneous combustion, of the fuel/air mixture in the cylinders, producing extreme heat and severe structural stresses on the engine. It is caused by low-grade fuel, too lean a mixture, or excessively high engine temperatures.
Answer (B) is incorrect because detonation may occur with an excessively lean, not rich, fuel mixture that causes a loss, not gain, in power. Answer (C) is incorrect because the fuel mixture being ignited too early describes preignition, not detonation.

2.7 Airplane Ignition Systems

29.
5169. Before shutdown, while at idle, the ignition key is momentarily turned OFF. The engine continues to run with no interruption; this

A— is normal because the engine is usually stopped by moving the mixture to idle cutoff.
B— should not normally happen. Indicates a magneto not grounding in OFF position.
C— is an undesirable practice, but indicates that nothing is wrong.

Answer (B) is correct (5169). *(PHAK Chap 2)*
An engine that continues to run after the ignition switch has been turned off probably has a broken magneto ground wire. The ignition switch is not able to ground the magneto to stop the generation of electrical impulses that provide electricity to the spark plug. Thus, momentarily turning off the ignition prior to shutdown is a recommended procedure to check for a faulty ground wire.
Answer (A) is incorrect because turning the ignition key to OFF should stop the engine. Answer (C) is incorrect because turning off the ignition key is a recommended procedure prior to shutdown to check for a faulty ground wire.

30.
5171. A way to detect a broken magneto primary grounding lead is to

A— idle the engine and momentarily turn the ignition off.
B— add full power, while holding the brakes, and momentarily turn off the ignition.
C— run on one magneto, lean the mixture, and look for a rise in manifold pressure.

Answer (A) is correct (5171). *(PHAK Chap 2)*
An engine that continues to run after the ignition switch has been turned off probably has a broken magneto ground wire. The ignition switch is not able to ground the magneto to stop the generation of electrical impulses that provide electricity to the spark plug. Thus, momentarily turning off the ignition prior to shutdown is a recommended procedure to check for a faulty ground wire.
Answer (B) is incorrect because it is not necessary to add full power when performing this check. Answer (C) is incorrect because this is a nonsense procedure.

31.
5173. The most probable reason an engine continues to run after the ignition switch has been turned off is

A— carbon deposits glowing on the spark plugs.
B— a magneto ground wire is in contact with the engine casing.
C— a broken magneto ground wire.

Answer (C) is correct (5173). *(PHAK Chap 2)*
An engine that continues to run after the ignition switch has been turned off probably has a broken magneto ground wire. The ignition switch is not able to ground the magneto to stop the generation of electrical impulses that provide electricity to the spark plug. Thus, momentarily turning off the ignition prior to shutdown is a recommended procedure to check for a faulty ground wire.
Answer (A) is incorrect because glowing carbon deposits result in preignition, not in the continued running of the engine. Answer (B) is incorrect because the magneto ground wire should be in contact with the engine casing to provide effective grounding.

32.
5271. A detuning of engine crankshaft counterweights is a source of overstress that may be caused by

A— rapid opening and closing of the throttle.
B— carburetor ice forming on the throttle valve.
C— operating with an excessively rich fuel/air mixture.

Answer (A) is correct (5271). *(AC 20-103)*
A detuning of counterweights on balance weight-equipped crankshafts is a source of overstress for the crankshaft. The counterweights are designed to position themselves by the inertia forces generated during crankshaft rotation and to absorb and dampen crankshaft vibration effectively. If the counterweights are detuned (allowed to slam on mounts), the vibrations are not properly dampened and crankshaft failure can occur. Counterweight detuning can occur from rapid opening and closing of the throttle, excessive speed, excessive power, and operating at high RPMs and low manifold pressure.
Answer (B) is incorrect because carburetor ice will cause the engine to stop running when the carburetor is sufficiently clogged with ice and will not affect the engine crankshaft counterweights. Answer (C) is incorrect because operating with an excessively rich fuel/air mixture fouls the spark plugs but does not affect the crankshaft.

33.
5174. If the ground wire between the magneto and the ignition switch becomes disconnected, the engine

A— will not operate on one magneto.
B— cannot be started with the switch in the BOTH position.
C— could accidently start if the propeller is moved with fuel in the cylinder.

Answer (C) is correct (5174). *(PHAK Chap 2)*
If the magneto switch ground wire is disconnected, the magneto is ON even though the ignition switch is in the OFF position. Thus, the engine could fire if the propeller is moved from outside the airplane.
Answer (A) is incorrect because disconnecting the ground wire causes both magnetos to remain on; i.e., they will operate even when the ignition switch is in the OFF position. The dual ignition system is designed so that, in case one magneto fails, the other magneto can operate alone. Answer (B) is incorrect because the engine can still be started; the magnetos cannot be turned OFF.

2.8 Engine Cooling

34.
5175. For internal cooling, reciprocating aircraft engines are especially dependent on

A— a properly functioning cowl flap augmenter.
B— the circulation of lubricating oil.
C— the proper freon/compressor output ratio.

Answer (B) is correct (5175). *(PHAK Chap 2)*
An engine accomplishes much of its cooling by the flow of oil through the lubrication system. The lubrication system aids in cooling by reducing friction as well as by absorbing heat from internal engine parts. Many airplane engines also use an oil cooler, a small radiator device that cools the oil before it is recirculated through the engine.
Answer (A) is incorrect because the cowl flaps aid in controlling engine temperatures but are not the primary cooling source. Answer (C) is incorrect because the freon/compressor output ratio determines the effectiveness of cabin, not engine, cooling.

35.
5607. An abnormally high engine oil temperature indication may be caused by

A— a defective bearing.
B— the oil level being too low.
C— operating with an excessively rich mixture.

Answer (B) is correct (5607). *(A&PM PH Chap 10)*
Operating with an excessively low oil level prevents the oil from cooling adequately; i.e., an inadequate supply of oil will not be able to transfer engine heat to the engine's oil cooler (similar to a car engine's water radiator). Insufficient oil may also damage an engine from excessive friction within the cylinders and on other metal-to-metal contact parts.
Answer (A) is incorrect because a defective bearing results in local heat and wear which will probably increase metal particles in the oil, but it should not affect oil temperature significantly. Answer (C) is incorrect because a rich fuel/air mixture results in lower engine operating temperatures and thus does not increase engine oil temperature.

36.
5653. Frequent inspections should be made of aircraft exhaust manifold-type heating systems to minimize the possibility of

A— exhaust gases leaking into the cockpit.
B— a power loss due to back pressure in the exhaust system.
C— a cold-running engine due to the heat withdrawn by the heater.

Answer (A) is correct (5653). *(PHAK Chap 2)*
You should inspect exhaust manifold-type heating systems regularly. Heating systems that rely on air being heated by the exhaust manifold could carry exhaust gases to the cockpit if a crack or leak develops in the exhaust manifold.
Answer (B) is incorrect because a leak in the exhaust system decreases, not increases, back pressure. Answer (C) is incorrect because engine temperature is not affected by withdrawing heat to a cockpit heater.

2.9 Airplane Propellers

37.
5235. Propeller efficiency is the

A— ratio of thrust horsepower to brake horsepower.
B— actual distance a propeller advances in one revolution.
C— ratio of geometric pitch to effective pitch.

Answer (A) is correct (5235). *(FTH Chap 17)*
The efficiency of any machine is the ratio of useful power output to actual power output. Thus, propeller efficiency is the ratio of thrust horsepower (amount of thrust the propeller produces) to brake horsepower (amount of torque the engine imparts on the propeller). Propeller efficiency generally varies between 50% and 85%, depending upon propeller slippage.
Answer (B) is incorrect because the distance a propeller travels in one revolution is effective pitch, not propeller efficiency. Answer (C) is incorrect because the ratio of geometric pitch to effective pitch is propeller slippage, which is related to, but is not, propeller efficiency.

38.

5237. The reason for variations in geometric pitch (twisting) along a propeller blade is that it

A— permits a relatively constant angle of incidence along its length when in cruising flight.

B— prevents the portion of the blade near the hub from stalling during cruising flight.

C— permits a relatively constant angle of attack along its length when in cruising flight.

Answer (C) is correct (5237). *(FTH Chap 17)*

Variations in the geometric pitch of the blades permit the propeller to operate with a relatively constant angle of attack along its length when in cruising flight. Propeller blades have variations to change the blade in proportion to the differences in speed of rotation along the length of the propeller and thereby keep thrust more nearly equalized along this length.

Answer (A) is incorrect because variations in geometric pitch permit a constant angle of attack, not incidence, along its length. Answer (B) is incorrect because, if there were no variation in geometric pitch, the propeller tips, not the root, would be stalled during cruising flight.

39.

5236. A fixed-pitch propeller is designed for best efficiency only at a given combination of

A— altitude and RPM.

B— airspeed and RPM.

C— airspeed and altitude.

Answer (B) is correct (5236). *(FTH Chap 17)*

A fixed-pitch propeller is most efficient only at a specified combination of airspeed and RPM. When designing a fixed-pitch propeller, the manufacturer usually selects a pitch which will operate most efficiently at the expected cruising speed of the airplane.

Answer (A) is incorrect because altitude does not affect the efficiency of a fixed-pitch propeller, *per se*. Answer (C) is incorrect because altitude does not affect the efficiency of a fixed-pitch propeller, *per se*.

40.

5183. Which statement best describes the operating principle of a constant-speed propeller?

A— As throttle setting is changed by the pilot, the prop governor causes pitch angle of the propeller blades to remain unchanged.

B— A high blade angle, or increased pitch, reduces the propeller drag and allows more engine power for takeoffs.

C— The propeller control regulates the engine RPM and in turn the propeller RPM.

Answer (C) is correct (5183). *(PHAK Chap 2)*

A constant-speed propeller, as the name implies, adjusts the pitch angle of the propeller blades so that the engine is maintained at a selected RPM. This variation permits use of a blade angle that will result in the most efficient performance for each particular flight condition.

Answer (A) is incorrect because the prop governor causes pitch angle of the propeller blades to change, not remain unchanged, to maintain a specified RPM. Answer (B) is incorrect because a high blade angle increases, not reduces, propeller drag, and allows less, not more, engine power.

41.

5667. To develop maximum power and thrust, a constant-speed propeller should be set to a blade angle that will produce a

A— large angle of attack and low RPM.

B— small angle of attack and high RPM.

C— large angle of attack and high RPM.

Answer (B) is correct (5667). *(PHAK Chap 2)*

When using a constant-speed propeller, the maximum engine power for maximum thrust can be obtained by using a small angle of attack, which results in a high RPM.

Answer (A) is incorrect because a large angle of attack and low RPM result in less, not maximum, power and thrust. Answer (C) is incorrect because maximum power is obtained by using a small, not large, propeller angle of attack.

42.

5668. For takeoff, the blade angle of a controllable-pitch propeller should be set at a

A— small angle of attack and high RPM.

B— large angle of attack and low RPM.

C— large angle of attack and high RPM.

Answer (A) is correct (5668). *(PHAK Chap 2)*

For takeoff with a controllable-pitch (i.e., constant-speed) propeller, the blade angle should be set for maximum power, which is a small angle of attack and high RPM.

Answer (B) is incorrect because a large angle of attack and low RPM result in less, not maximum, power. Answer (C) is incorrect because maximum takeoff power requires a small, not large, propeller angle of attack.

43.
5654. To establish a climb after takeoff in an aircraft equipped with a constant-speed propeller, the output of the engine is reduced to climb power by decreasing manifold pressure and

A— increasing RPM by decreasing propeller blade angle.
B— decreasing RPM by decreasing propeller blade angle.
C— decreasing RPM by increasing propeller blade angle.

44.
5184. In aircraft equipped with constant-speed propellers and normally-aspirated engines, which procedure should be used to avoid placing undue stress on the engine components? When power is being

A— decreased, reduce the RPM before reducing the manifold pressure.
B— increased, increase the RPM before increasing the manifold pressure.
C— increased or decreased, the RPM should be adjusted before the manifold pressure.

45.
5238. A propeller rotating clockwise as seen from the rear, creates a spiraling slipstream that tends to rotate the airplane to the

A— right around the vertical axis, and to the left around the longitudinal axis.
B— left around the vertical axis, and to the right around the longitudinal axis.
C— left around the vertical axis, and to the left around the longitudinal axis.

Answer (C) is correct (5654). *(FTH Chap 17)*
To establish climb power after takeoff using a constant-speed propeller, you should first decrease manifold pressure and then decrease RPM. When the propeller control is moved to reduce the RPM, the propeller blade angle increases.
Answer (A) is incorrect because, to reduce power, you should decrease, not increase, RPM by increasing, not decreasing, propeller blade angle. Answer (B) is incorrect because, to reduce power, you should decrease RPM by increasing, not decreasing, propeller blade angle.

Answer (B) is correct (5184). *(PHAK Chap 2)*
To avoid placing undue stress on an engine equipped with a constant-speed propeller, you should avoid high manifold pressure settings with low RPMs. Thus, when power is being increased, you should increase the RPM before increasing the manifold pressure.
Answer (A) is incorrect because, when power is being decreased, you should reduce the manifold pressure before reducing the RPM, not vice versa. Answer (C) is incorrect because, when power is being decreased, you should reduce the manifold pressure before reducing the RPM, not vice versa.

Answer (B) is correct (5238). *(FTH Chap 17)*
As the airplane propeller rotates through the air in a clockwise direction as viewed from the rear, the propeller blade forces the air rearward in a spiraling, clockwise direction of flow around the fuselage. A portion of this spiraling slipstream strikes the left side of the vertical stabilizer, forcing the airplane's tail to the right and the nose to the left and causing the airplane to rotate around the vertical axis. The clockwise flow of air about the fuselage attempts to rotate the airplane to the right around the longitudinal axis. Note that this is the opposite of the reactive force attempting to rotate the aircraft to the left due to the right rotation of the propeller.
Answer (A) is incorrect because the slipstream rotates the airplane to the left, not right, about the vertical axis and to the right, not left, about the longitudinal axis. Answer (C) is incorrect because the slipstream rotates the airplane to the right, not left, about the longitudinal axis.

END OF CHAPTER

CHAPTER THREE
AIRPORTS, AIR TRAFFIC CONTROL, AND AIRSPACE

This chapter contains outlines of major concepts tested; all FAA test questions and answers regarding airports, air traffic control, and airspace; and an explanation of each answer. Each module, or subtopic, within this chapter is listed above with the number of questions from the FAA pilot knowledge test pertaining to that particular module. For each module, the first number following the parentheses is the page number on which the outline begins, and the next number is the page number on which the questions begin.

CAUTION: Recall that the **sole purpose** of this book is to expedite your passing the FAA pilot knowledge test for the commercial pilot certificate. Accordingly, all extraneous material (i.e., topics or regulations not directly tested on the FAA pilot knowledge test) is omitted, even though much more information and knowledge are necessary to become a proficient commercial pilot. This additional material is presented in *Commercial Pilot Flight Maneuvers and Practical Test Prep* and *Pilot Handbook*, available from Gleim Publications, Inc. See the order form on page 284.

3.1 AIRSPACE (Questions 1-19)

1. Flight operations in Class A airspace must be conducted under instrument flight rules (IFR).

2. All aircraft operating in Class A airspace must be equipped with an ATC transponder and altitude reporting equipment.

3. You must receive an ATC clearance before operating an airplane in Class B airspace.

4. To take off or land at an airport within Class B airspace or to operate an airplane within Class B airspace, the pilot in command must hold at least a private pilot certificate.

    a. A student pilot or a recreational pilot may fly solo in Class B airspace only if the pilot has met the requirements listed in FAR 61.95.

5. To operate in Class B airspace, the airplane must be equipped with an operating ATC (4096 code or Mode S) transponder and automatic altitude reporting equipment (Mode C).

6. The maximum indicated speed authorized when operating an airplane in the airspace underlying Class B airspace is 200 kt.

7. Unless otherwise authorized or required by ATC, the maximum indicated airspeed permitted when at or below 2,500 ft. AGL within 4 NM of the primary airport of a Class C or Class D airspace is 200 kt.

8. If the minimum safe airspeed for any particular operation is greater than the maximum airspeed prescribed in FAR Part 91, the airplane may be operated at that speed.

    a. In such cases, you are expected to advise ATC of the airspeed that will be used.

9. To operate in Class C airspace, an airplane must be equipped with an ATC transponder and automatic altitude reporting capability (Mode C).

10. Prior to entering Class C airspace, you must establish and maintain communications with the ATC facility providing air traffic services.

11. The flight requirements to operate under special VFR in Class D airspace are

    a. Remain clear of clouds, and
    b. Have flight visibility of at least 1 SM, if ground visibility is not reported.

12. Flight under special VFR clearance at night is permitted only if the pilot is instrument rated and the airplane is equipped for instrument flight.

13. To take off or land under special VFR requires ground visibility of at least 1 SM.

    a. If ground visibility is not reported, flight visibility during landing or takeoff must be at least 1 SM.

14. When a part-time control tower at the primary airport in Class D airspace is not in operation, the airspace at the surface becomes either Class E, if weather reporting is available, or Class G.

15. When approaching to land at an airport in Class D airspace, you must establish communications with ATC prior to entering Class D airspace (which extends up to and includes 2,500 ft. AGL and has its lateral dimensions, such as 4 NM, set by local needs).

16. When operating in the vicinity of an airport with an operating control tower in Class E airspace, you must establish communications prior to 4 NM from the airport, up to and including 2,500 ft. AGL.

17. When approaching to land at an airport without an operating control tower in Class G airspace, you should make all turns to the left, unless otherwise indicated.

18. The Federal airways are Class E airspace areas. Unless otherwise specified, they extend upward from 1,200 ft. AGL to, but not including, 18,000 ft. MSL.

3.2 VHF/DF (Question 20)

1. VHF/DF, when seen in the *A/FD* for a particular airport, indicates a "very high frequency direction finder" facility at an FSS that can determine the direction of your airplane from the station.

2. To use VHF/DF facilities for assistance, you must have an operative VHF transmitter and receiver.

3.3 AIRPORT SIGNS (Questions 21-25a)

1.   Airport signs are used to provide information to pilots.

2.   A no entry sign (see below) is a type of mandatory instruction sign that has a red background with a white inscription.

RED

   a.   A no entry sign prohibits an aircraft from entering an area.

   b.   Typically, this sign is located on a taxiway intended to be used in only one direction or at the intersection of vehicle roadways with runways, taxiways, or aprons where the roadway may be mistaken as a taxiway or other aircraft movement surface.

3.   A runway boundary sign (see below) is a type of location sign that has a yellow background with a black inscription and graphic depicting the pavement holding position marking.

YELLOW

   a.   This sign, which faces the runway and is visible to you when you are exiting the runway, is located adjacent to the holding position marking on the pavement.

       1)   The sign is intended to provide you with another visual cue in deciding when you are clear of the runway.

   b.   You are clear of the runway when your airplane is on the solid-line side of the holding position marking.

4.   An ILS critical area boundary sign (see below) is another type of location sign that has a yellow background with a black inscription and graphic depicting the ILS pavement holding position marking.

YELLOW

    a.   This sign is located adjacent to the ILS holding position marking on the pavement. You can see it when you are leaving or approaching the critical area.

        1)   The sign is intended to provide you with another visual cue to use as a guide in deciding when you are clear of, or about to enter, the ILS critical area.

5.   A taxiway ending marker sign is a type of information sign that consists of alternating yellow and black diagonal stripes.

    a.   This sign indicates that the taxiway does not continue beyond the sign.

3.4 COLLISION AVOIDANCE (Questions 26-28)

1.   Navigation lights consist of a steady red light on the left wing, a steady green light on the right wing, and a steady white light on the tail. In night flight,

    a.   When an airplane is heading away from you, you will observe a steady white light and a rotating red light.

2.   Any aircraft which has no apparent relative motion is likely to be on a collision course.

3.   In the vicinity of VORs, you should look carefully for other aircraft converging on the VOR from all directions.

3.5 WAKE TURBULENCE (Questions 29-35)

1.   Wingtip vortices (wake turbulence) are created when airplanes develop lift.

2.   The greatest wingtip vortex strength occurs behind heavy, clean (flaps and gear up), and slow aircraft.

3.   When landing behind a large aircraft on the same runway, stay at or above the other aircraft's final approach flight path and land beyond that airplane's touchdown point.

    a.   When taking off after a large aircraft has just landed, become airborne past the large airplane's touchdown point.

4.   When taking off behind a departing jet, take off before the rotation point of the jet, and then climb above and stay upwind of the jet aircraft's flight path until you are able to turn clear of the wake.

5.   Wingtip vortex turbulence tends to sink into the flight path of airplanes operating below the airplane generating the turbulence.

    a.   Thus, you should fly above the flight path of a large jet rather than below.

6.   The primary hazard of wake turbulence is loss of control because of induced roll.

7.   In forward flight, helicopters produce a pair of high velocity trailing vortices similar to wing tip vortices of large fixed wing aircraft.

3.6 LAND AND HOLD SHORT OPERATIONS (LAHSO) (Questions 36-38)

1.   Land and hold short operations (LAHSO) take place at some airports with an operating control tower in order to increase airport capacity and improve the flow of traffic.

    a.   LAHSO requires that you land and hold short of an intersecting runway, an intersecting taxiway, or some other designated point on a runway.

2.   Before accepting a clearance to land and hold short, you must determine that you can safely land and stop in the available landing distance (ALD).

3.   The pilot in command has the final authority to accept or decline any LAHSO clearance.

    a.   You are expected to decline a LAHSO clearance if you determine it will compromise safety.

4.   You should receive a LAHSO clearance only when there is a minimum ceiling of 1,000 ft. and 3 SM visibility.

   a.   The intent of having "basic" VFR weather conditions is to allow pilots to maintain visual contact with other aircraft and ground vehicle operations.

QUESTIONS AND ANSWER EXPLANATIONS

   All the FAA questions from the pilot knowledge test for the commercial pilot certificate relating to airports and air traffic control and the material outlined previously are reproduced on the following pages in the same modules as the outlines. To the immediate right of each question are the correct answer and answer explanation. You should cover these answers and answer explanations while responding to the questions. (A bookmark for this purpose has been provided in the back of the book.) Refer to the general discussion in the Introduction on how to take the FAA pilot knowledge test.

   Remember that the questions from the FAA pilot knowledge test bank have been reordered by topic, and the topics have been organized into a meaningful sequence. Accordingly, the first line of the answer explanation gives the FAA question number and the citation of the authoritative source for the answer.

3.1 Airspace

1.
5120a. Which is true regarding flight operations in Class A airspace?

A— Aircraft must be equipped with approved distance measuring equipment (DME).
B— Must conduct operations under instrument flight rules.
C— Aircraft must be equipped with an approved ATC transponder.

Answer (B) is correct (5120a). (FAR 91.135)
   Each person operating an airplane in Class A airspace must conduct that operation under instrument flight rules (IFR).
   Answer (A) is incorrect because, if VOR navigational equipment is required, the airplane must be equipped with DME for operations at or above FL 240. Since Class A airspace begins at FL 180, DME is not required for all operations. Answer (C) is incorrect because, in Class A airspace, all airplanes must be equipped with an operable transponder and altitude reporting equipment, not only an approved ATC transponder.

2.
5120b. Which is true regarding flight operations in Class A airspace?

A— Aircraft must be equipped with approved distance measuring equipment (DME).
B— Aircraft must be equipped with an ATC transponder and altitude reporting equipment.
C— May conduct operations under visual flight rules.

Answer (B) is correct (5120b). (FAR 91.135)
   All aircraft operating in Class A airspace must be equipped with an ATC transponder and altitude reporting capability, unless otherwise authorized by ATC.
   Answer (A) is incorrect because, if VOR equipment is required, the airplane must be equipped with DME for operations at or above FL 240. Since Class A airspace begins at FL 180, DME is not required for all operations in Class A airspace. Answer (C) is incorrect because flight operations in Class A airspace are conducted under IFR, not VFR.

3.
5082a. Which is true regarding flight operations in Class B airspace?

A— Flight under VFR is not authorized unless the pilot in command is instrument rated.
B— The pilot must receive an ATC clearance before operating an aircraft in that area.
C— Solo student pilot operations are not authorized.

Answer (B) is correct (5082a). (FAR 91.131)
   The pilot must receive an ATC clearance before operating an airplane in Class B airspace.
   Answer (A) is incorrect because flight under special VFR at night, not VFR operations in Class B airspace, requires the pilot in command to be instrument rated. Answer (C) is incorrect because solo student pilot operations are authorized in Class B airspace, as long as the requirements of FAR 61.95 have been met.

4.

5082b. Which is true regarding pilot certification requirements for operations in Class B airspace?

A— The pilot in command must hold at least a private pilot certificate with an instrument rating.

B— The pilot in command must hold at least a private pilot certificate.

C— Solo student pilot operations are not authorized.

Answer (B) is correct (5082b). *(FAR 91.131)*
No person may take off or land at an airport within Class B airspace or operate an airplane within Class B airspace unless the pilot in command holds at least a private pilot certificate. However, a student pilot or a recreational pilot seeking private pilot certification may fly solo in Class B airspace if (s)he has met the requirements listed in FAR 61.95.
Answer (A) is incorrect because there is no requirement for the pilot in command to be instrument rated if (s)he is operating under VFR in Class B airspace. Answer (C) is incorrect because solo student pilot operations are authorized in Class B airspace, as long as the requirements of FAR 61.95 have been met.

5.

5072b. What transponder equipment is required for airplane operations within Class B airspace? A transponder

A— with 4096 code or Mode S, and Mode C capability.

B— with 4096 code capability is required except when operating at or below 1,000 feet AGL under the terms of a letter of agreement.

C— is required for airplane operations when visibility is less than 3 miles.

Answer (A) is correct (5072b). *(FAR 91.215)*
Unless otherwise authorized or directed by ATC, no person may operate an airplane within Class B airspace unless it is equipped with an operable transponder having either 4096 code capability or Mode S capability. Additionally, the airplane must be equipped with automatic pressure altitude reporting equipment having Mode C capability.
Answer (B) is incorrect because, in Class B airspace, the transponder must have both 4096 code capability and Mode C capability, not only 4096 code capability. Additionally, any letter of agreement with the controlling ATC facility would be geographically specific; it would not make an exception simply for any operation below 1,000 ft. AGL. Answer (C) is incorrect because an operable transponder with 4096 code, or Mode S, capability and Mode C capability is required at all times within Class B airspace, not only at times when the visibility is less than 3 SM.

6.

5082c. Which is true regarding flight operations in Class B airspace?

A— The aircraft must be equipped with an ATC transponder and altitude reporting equipment.

B— The pilot in command must hold at least a private pilot certificate with an instrument rating.

C— The pilot in command must hold at least a student pilot certificate.

Answer (A) is correct (5082c). *(FAR 91.131)*
To operate in Class B airspace, the airplane must be equipped with an operating ATC transponder and automatic altitude reporting equipment.
Answer (B) is incorrect because the pilot in command is not required to be instrument rated to operate in Class B airspace under VFR. Answer (C) is incorrect because, to operate solo in Class B airspace, a student pilot must also have met the requirements of FAR 61.65.

7.

5077. What is the maximum indicated airspeed authorized in the airspace underlying Class B airspace?

A— 156 knots.

B— 200 knots.

C— 230 knots.

Answer (B) is correct (5077). *(FAR 91.117)*
No person may operate an aircraft in the airspace underlying a Class B airspace area designated for an airport at an indicated airspeed of more than 200 kt. (230 mph).
Answer (A) is incorrect because 156 kt. is not a maximum speed associated with any type of airspace. Answer (C) is incorrect because 230 mph, not 230 kt., is the maximum indicated airspeed allowed in the airspace underlying Class B airspace.

8.
5078. Unless otherwise authorized or required by ATC, the maximum indicated airspeed permitted when at or below 2,500 feet AGL within 4 NM of the primary airport within Class C or D airspace is

A— 180 knots.
B— 200 knots.
C— 230 knots.

Answer (B) is the best answer (5078). *(FAR 91.117)*
Unless otherwise authorized or required by ATC, the maximum airspeed permitted when at or below 2,500 ft. AGL within 4 NM of the primary airport of a Class C or Class D airspace is 200 kt. (230 mph).
Answer (A) is incorrect because 180 kt. is not a maximum indicated airspeed associated with any airspace classification and/or altitude. Answer (C) is incorrect because 230 mph, not 230 kt., is the maximum indicated airspeed permitted when at or below 2,500 ft. AGL within 4 NM of the primary airport in Class C or Class D airspace.

9.
5112. If the minimum safe speed for any particular operation is greater than the maximum speed prescribed in 14 CFR Part 91, the

A— operator must have a Memorandum of Agreement (MOA) with the controlling agency.
B— aircraft may be operated at that speed.
C— operator must have a Letter of Agreement with ATC.

Answer (B) is correct (5112). *(FAR 91.117)*
If the minimum safe airspeed for any particular operation is greater than the maximum airspeed prescribed in Part 91, the aircraft may be operated at that minimum airspeed. In such cases, the pilot is expected to advise ATC of the airspeed that will be used.
Answer (A) is incorrect because, if the minimum safe airspeed for any particular operation is greater than the maximum airspeed prescribed in Part 91, the aircraft may be operated at that airspeed. The pilot is expected to advise ATC of the airspeed to be used. A memorandum of agreement is not required. Answer (C) is incorrect because, if the minimum safe airspeed for any particular operation is greater than the maximum airspeed prescribed in Part 91, the aircraft may be operated at that minimum airspeed. The pilot is expected to advise ATC of the airspeed to be used. A letter of agreement is not required.

10.
5119a. Which is true regarding flight operations to or from a satellite airport, without an operating control tower, within the Class C airspace area?

A— Prior to takeoff, a pilot must establish communication with the ATC controlling facility.
B— Aircraft must be equipped with an ATC transponder and altitude reporting equipment.
C— Prior to landing, a pilot must establish and maintain communication with an ATC facility.

Answer (B) is correct (5119a). *(FAR 91.130)*
No person may operate an airplane within Class C airspace unless the airplane is equipped with an ATC transponder and altitude reporting equipment (Mode C transponder).
Answer (A) is incorrect because, when departing a satellite airport without an operating control tower, you must establish communication with the ATC controlling facility as soon as practicable after, not prior to, takeoff. Answer (C) is incorrect because, prior to entering Class C airspace, not prior to landing at a satellite airport without an operating control tower, you must establish communication with the controlling ATC facility.

11.
5119b. Which is true regarding flight operations to or from a satellite airport, without an operating control tower, within the Class C airspace area?

A— Prior to entering that airspace, a pilot must establish and maintain communication with the ATC serving facility.
B— Aircraft must be equipped with an ATC transponder.
C— Prior to takeoff, a pilot must establish communication with the ATC controlling facility.

Answer (A) is correct (5119b). *(FAR 91.130)*
Prior to entering Class C airspace, a pilot must establish and maintain two-way radio communications with the ATC facility providing air traffic services.
Answer (B) is incorrect because, to operate in Class C airspace, an aircraft must be equipped with an ATC transponder and altitude reporting equipment (Mode C transponder), not just a transponder. Answer (C) is incorrect because, when departing from a satellite airport without an operating control tower, you must establish communication with the ATC controlling facility as soon as practicable after, not prior to, takeoff.

12.
5089. At some airports located in Class D airspace where ground visibility is not reported, takeoffs and landings under special VFR are

A— not authorized.
B— authorized by ATC if the flight visibility is at least 1 SM.
C— authorized only if the ground visibility is observed to be at least 3 SM.

13.
5088. When operating an airplane for the purpose of takeoff or landing within Class D airspace under special VFR, what minimum distance from clouds and what visibility are required?

A— Remain clear of clouds, and the ground visibility must be at least 1 SM.
B— 500 feet beneath clouds, and the ground visibility must be at least 1 SM.
C— Remain clear of clouds, and the flight visibility must be at least 1 NM.

14.
5090. To operate an airplane under SPECIAL VFR (SVFR) within Class D airspace at night, which is required?

A— The pilot must hold an instrument rating, but the airplane need not be equipped for instrument flight, as long as the weather will remain at or above SVFR minimums.
B— The Class D airspace must be specifically designated as a night SVFR area.
C— The pilot must hold an instrument rating, and the airplane must be equipped for instrument flight.

15.
5009. What designated airspace associated with an airport becomes inactive when the control tower at that airport is not in operation?

A— Class D, which then becomes Class C.
B— Class D, which then becomes Class E.
C— Class B.

Answer (B) is correct (5089). *(FAR 91.157)*
No person may take off or land an aircraft (other than a helicopter) at any airport in Class D airspace under special VFR unless ground visibility at that airport is at least 1 SM or, if ground visibility is not reported at that airport, unless flight visibility during landing or takeoff is at least 1 SM.
Answer (A) is incorrect because special VFR is still authorized if flight visibility is at least 1 SM. Answer (C) is incorrect because the visibility requirement for special VFR is 1 SM, not 3 SM.

Answer (A) is correct (5088). *(FAR 91.157)*
Under special VFR weather minimums, you may take off or land an airplane within Class D airspace if you remain clear of clouds and if the ground visibility is at least 1 SM.
Answer (B) is incorrect because you must only remain clear of clouds, not 500 ft. below the clouds, when operating an airplane under special VFR in Class D airspace. Answer (C) is incorrect because, if ground visibility is not reported, the flight visibility must be at least 1 SM, not 1 NM.

Answer (C) is correct (5090). *(FAR 91.157)*
No person may operate an airplane in Class D airspace under special VFR at night unless that person is instrument rated and the airplane is equipped for instrument flight.
Answer (A) is incorrect because the airplane must also be equipped for instrument flight to operate under SVFR at night in Class D airspace. Answer (B) is incorrect because there is no such designation as a "night special VFR area."

Answer (B) is correct (5009). *(AIM Para 3-2-5)*
Class D airspace is located at airports that have an operating control tower which is not associated with Class B or Class C airspace. Airspace at an airport with a part-time control tower is classified as Class D airspace when the control tower is in operation and as Class E airspace (beginning at the surface) when the control tower is not in operation if an approved weather reporting system is available. Without an approved weather reporting system, Class D becomes Class G.
Answer (A) is incorrect because, when a part-time control tower is not in operation, the Class D airspace becomes Class E, not Class C, airspace. Answer (C) is incorrect because the primary airport of Class B airspace will have a control tower that operates full-time, not part-time.

16.
5118. When approaching to land at an airport with an ATC facility, in Class D airspace, the pilot must establish communications prior to

A— 10 NM, up to and including 3,000 feet AGL.
B— 30 SM, and be transponder equipped.
C— 4 NM, up to and including 2,500 feet AGL.

Answer (C) is the best answer (5118). *(FAR 91.129)*
A pilot must establish communications with ATC prior to entering Class D airspace. Class D airspace extends from the surface to 2,500 ft. AGL, and the lateral dimensions are set by local needs.

Note: When approaching to land at an airport with an ATC facility in Class E or Class G airspace, the pilot must establish communications prior to 4 NM, up to and including 2,500 ft. AGL.

Answer (A) is incorrect because a pilot must establish communications with ATC prior to entering Class D airspace, not prior to 10 NM, up to and including 3,000 ft. AGL. Answer (B) is incorrect because a pilot must establish communications with ATC prior to entering Class D airspace, not prior to 30 SM, and the airplane must be transponder equipped.

17.
5117. When operating an aircraft in the vicinity of an airport with an operating control tower, in Class E airspace, a pilot must establish communications prior to

A— 8 NM, and up to and including 3,000 feet AGL.
B— 5 NM, and up to and including 3,000 feet AGL.
C— 4 NM, and up to and including 2,500 feet AGL.

Answer (C) is correct (5117). *(FAR 91.127)*
When operating an airplane to, from, through, or on an airport with an operating control tower in Class E airspace, a pilot must establish communications prior to 4 NM from the airport, up to and including 2,500 ft. AGL.

Answer (A) is incorrect because, when operating an airplane in the vicinity of an airport with an operating control tower in Class E airspace, a pilot must establish communications prior to 4 NM, not 8 NM, from the airport, and up to and including 2,500 ft. AGL, not 3,000 ft. AGL. Answer (B) is incorrect because, when operating an airplane in the vicinity of an airport with an operating control tower in Class E airspace, a pilot must establish communications prior to 4 NM, not 5 NM, from the airport, and up to and including 2,500 ft. AGL, not 3,000 ft. AGL.

18.
5116a. When approaching to land at an airport without an operating control tower, in Class G airspace, the pilot should

A— make all turns to the left, unless otherwise indicated.
B— fly a left-hand traffic pattern at 800 feet AGL.
C— enter and fly a traffic pattern at 800 feet AGL.

Answer (A) is correct (5116a). *(FAR 91.126)*
When approaching to land at an airport without an operating control tower in Class G airspace, the pilot of an airplane must make all turns to the left, unless otherwise indicated.

Answer (B) is incorrect because, when approaching to land at an airport without an operating control tower in Class G airspace, the pilot should fly a left-hand traffic pattern, unless otherwise indicated by traffic pattern indicators around the segment circle. Additionally, the recommended pattern altitude is 1,000 ft. AGL, unless otherwise published. Answer (C) is incorrect because, when approaching to land at an airport without an operating control tower in Class G airspace, the pilot should make all turns to the left (unless otherwise indicated), not fly any traffic pattern direction. Additionally, the recommended pattern altitude is 1,000 ft. AGL, unless otherwise published.

19.
5043. Excluding Hawaii, the vertical limits of the Federal Low Altitude airways extend from

A— 700 feet AGL up to, but not including, 14,500 feet MSL.
B— 1,200 feet AGL up to, but not including, 18,000 feet MSL.
C— 1,200 feet AGL up to, but not including, 14,500 feet MSL.

Answer (B) is correct (5043). *(AIM Para 3-2-6)*
Federal airways are Class E airspace, which extends upward from 1,200 ft. AGL to, but not including, 18,000 ft. MSL.

Answer (A) is incorrect because 700 ft. AGL is the floor of Class E airspace when designated in conjunction with an airport that has an IAP, not in conjunction with a Federal airway. Also, Class E airspace extends up to, but does not include, 18,000 ft. MSL, not 14,500 ft. MSL. Answer (C) is incorrect because Class E airspace that is designated as a Federal airway extends from 1,200 ft. AGL up to, but not including, 18,000 ft. MSL, not 14,500 ft. MSL.

3.2 VHF/DF

20.
5504. To use VHF/DF facilities for assistance in locating your position, you must have an operative VHF

A— transmitter and receiver.
B— transmitter and receiver, and an operative ADF receiver.
C— transmitter and receiver, and an operative VOR receiver.

Answer (A) is correct (5504). *(FTH Chap 12)*
The VHF/direction finder facility is a ground-based radio receiver that displays the magnetic direction of the airplane from the station each time the airplane transmits a signal to it. Thus, to use such facilities for assistance in locating an airplane position, the airplane must have both a VHF transmitter (to send the signal) and a receiver (to communicate with the operator, who reads out the displayed magnetic direction).
Answer (B) is incorrect because an ADF is not required to use VHF/DF facilities. Answer (C) is incorrect because a VOR is not required to use VHF/DF facilities.

3.3 Airport Signs

21.
5657. (Refer to figure 51 on page 65.) The pilot generally calls ground control after landing when the aircraft is completely clear of the runway. This is when the aircraft

A— passes the red symbol shown at the top of the figure.
B— is on the dashed-line side of the middle symbol.
C— is past the solid-line side of the middle symbol.

Answer (C) is correct (5657). *(AIM Para 2-3-9)*
The middle symbol is a runway boundary sign that has a yellow background with a black inscription and graphic depicting the pavement holding position marking. This sign, which faces the runway and is visible to the pilot exiting the runway, is located adjacent to the holding position marking on the pavement. The sign is intended to provide you with another visual cue to use as a guide to determine when you are clear of the runway. Thus, you are clear of the runway when your entire airplane is on the solid-line side of the holding marking.
Answer (A) is incorrect because, if you pass the top symbol, you will enter an area prohibited to aircraft; it does not mean that you are clear of the runway. Answer (B) is incorrect because you are considered still on, not clear of, the runway if you are on the dashed-line side of the middle symbol.

22.
5658. (Refer to figure 51 on page 65.) The red symbol at the top would most likely be found

A— upon exiting all runways prior to calling ground control.
B— at an intersection where a roadway may be mistaken as a taxiway.
C— near the approach end of ILS runways.

Answer (B) is correct (5658). *(AIM Para 2-3-8)*
The symbol at the top (red background with white inscription) is a mandatory instruction sign that prohibits an aircraft from entering an area. Typically, this sign is located on a taxiway intended to be used in only one direction or at an intersection of vehicle roadways with runways, taxiways, or aprons where the roadway may be mistaken as a taxiway or other aircraft movement surface.
Answer (A) is incorrect because the middle, not the top, symbol would most likely be found upon exiting all runways prior to calling ground control. Answer (C) is incorrect because the bottom, not the top, symbol would most likely be found near the approach end of ILS runways.

23.
5659a. (Refer to figure 51 on page 65.) While clearing an active runway you are most likely clear of the ILS critical area when you pass which symbol?

A— Top red.
B— Middle yellow.
C— Bottom yellow.

Answer (C) is correct (5659a). *(AIM Para 2-3-9)*
The bottom symbol is an ILS critical area boundary sign which has a yellow background with a black inscription and graphic depicting the ILS pavement holding position marking. The sign is located adjacent to the ILS holding position marking on the pavement and can be seen by pilots leaving the critical area. The sign is intended to provide you with another visual cue to use as a guide in deciding when you are clear of the ILS critical area.
Answer (A) is incorrect because the top symbol is a sign prohibiting aircraft entry into an area, not a sign that you have cleared the ILS critical area. Answer (B) is incorrect because, while clearing the active runway, you are most likely clear of the runway, not the ILS critical area, when you pass the middle symbol.

RED

YELLOW

YELLOW

Figure 51.--Airport Signs.*

*NOTE: Figure 51 is in color in the FAA *Computer Testing Supplement for Commercial Pilot*, which you will use during your test.

24.
5659b. (Refer to figure 51 above.) When taxiing up to an active runway, you are likely to be clear of the ILS critical area when short of which symbol?

A— Bottom yellow.
B— Top red.
C— Middle yellow.

Answer (A) is correct (5659b). *(AIM Para 2-3-9)*
The bottom symbol is an ILS critical area boundary sign which has a yellow background with a black inscription depicting the ILS pavement holding position marking. The sign is located adjacent to the ILS holding position marking on the pavement and can be seen by pilots approaching the ILS critical area. Thus, you will be clear of the ILS critical area, when taxiing to an active runway, when short of the ILS critical area boundary sign.
Answer (B) is incorrect because the top red sign prohibits an aircraft from entering an area and is not used to mark the ILS critical area. Answer (C) is incorrect because the middle yellow sign is a runway boundary sign that faces toward the runway to help pilots to decide when they are clear of the runway, not the ILS critical area.

25.
5660. (Refer to figure 51 on page 65.) Which symbol does not directly address runway incursion with other aircraft?

A— Top red.
B— Middle yellow.
C— Bottom yellow.

Answer (A) is correct (5660). *(AIM Para 2-3-8)*
The symbol at the top (red background with white inscription) is a mandatory instruction sign which prohibits an aircraft from entering an area. Typically, this sign would be located on a taxiway intended to be used in only one direction or at an intersection of vehicle roadways with runways, taxiways, or aprons where the roadway may be mistaken as a taxiway or other aircraft movement surface. Thus, it does not directly address runway incursion with other aircraft.
Answer (B) is incorrect because the middle symbol is used to help indicate when you are clear of the runway. If you are not clear of the active runway, you will interfere with runway operations. Answer (C) is incorrect because the bottom symbol is used to help indicate when you are clear of the ILS critical area. An aircraft that is not clear of the ILS critical area may cause ILS course distortion which will interfere with ILS approaches being conducted.

25a.
1001-1. The "taxiway ending" marker

A— indicates taxiway does not continue.
B— identifies area where aircraft are prohibited.
C— provides general taxiing direction to named taxiway.

Answer (A) is correct (1001-1). *(AIM Para 2-3-12)*
A taxiway ending marker sign consists of alternating yellow and black diagonal stripes. Taxiway ending marker signs indicate that the taxiway does not continue beyond the sign.
Answer (B) is incorrect because no entry signs, not taxiway ending marker signs, identify an area where aircraft are prohibited from entering. No entry signs consist of a white horizontal line surrounded by a white circle on a red background. Answer (C) is incorrect because a direction sign, not a taxiway ending marker sign, indicates the general direction to take out of an intersection in order to taxi onto the named taxiway. Direction signs consist of black lettering on a yellow background with an arrow indicating the direction of turn.

3.4 Collision Avoidance

26.
5272. How can you determine if another aircraft is on a collision course with your aircraft?

A— The nose of each aircraft is pointed at the same point in space.
B— The other aircraft will always appear to get larger and closer at a rapid rate.
C— There will be no apparent relative motion between your aircraft and the other aircraft.

Answer (C) is correct (5272). *(AIM Para 8-1-8)*
Any aircraft that appears to have no relative motion and stays in one scan quadrant is likely to be on a collision course. Also, if a target shows no lateral or vertical movements but increases in size, take evasive action.
Answer (A) is incorrect because, even if you could determine the direction of the other airplane, you may not be able to accurately project the flight paths and speeds of the two airplanes to determine if they indeed point to the same point in space and will arrive there at the same time (i.e., collide). Answer (B) is incorrect because aircraft on collision courses may not always appear to grow larger or to close at a rapid rate. Frequently, the degree of proximity cannot be detected.

27.
5666. What is the general direction of movement of the other aircraft if during a night flight you observe a steady white light and a rotating red light ahead and at your altitude? The other aircraft is

A— headed away from you.
B— crossing to your left.
C— approaching you head-on.

Answer (A) is correct (5666). *(FTH Chap 14)*
A steady white light is the tail light. The other airplane is heading away from you. The rotating red light is the beacon light. The red and green wingtip position lights cannot be seen from the rear.
Answer (B) is incorrect because you would observe a steady red light if the other airplane was crossing to your left. Answer (C) is incorrect because you would see both the red and green wingtip (not white) position lights if the other aircraft was approaching you head-on.

28.
5749. When in the vicinity of a VOR which is being used for navigation on VFR flight, it is important to

A— make 90° left and right turns to scan for other traffic.
B— exercise sustained vigilance to avoid aircraft that may be converging on the VOR from other directions.
C— pass the VOR on the right side of the radial to allow room for aircraft flying in the opposite direction on the same radial.

Answer (B) is correct (5749). *(AIM Para 4-4-14)*
When operating VFR in highly congested areas such as in the vicinity of a VOR which is being used for VFR navigation, you should exercise constant vigilance to avoid aircraft that may be converging on the VOR from other directions.
Answer (A) is incorrect because 90° turns (i.e., clearing turns) are appropriate prior to practicing stalls, etc., but not while en route. Answer (C) is incorrect because there is no convention to pass on the right side of VORs or stay on the right side of airways. The FARs require you to be on the centerline of the airway.

3.5 Wake Turbulence

29.
5751. During a takeoff made behind a departing large jet airplane, the pilot can minimize the hazard of wingtip vortices by

A— being airborne prior to reaching the jet's flightpath until able to turn clear of its wake.
B— maintaining extra speed on takeoff and climbout.
C— extending the takeoff roll and not rotating until well beyond the jet's rotation point.

Answer (A) is correct (5751). *(AIM Para 7-3-6)*
When departing behind a larger aircraft, you should rotate prior to the larger aircraft's rotation point and climb above its climb path until turning clear of its wake.
Answer (B) is incorrect because, even at maximum speed, you will probably not have enough control effectiveness to counteract the induced roll of the vortices. Answer (C) is incorrect because the vortices sink below the jet's flight path, so you want to be above them, not below them.

30.
5753. To avoid possible wake turbulence from a large jet aircraft that has just landed prior to your takeoff, at which point on the runway should you plan to become airborne?

A— Past the point where the jet touched down.
B— At the point where the jet touched down, or just prior to this point.
C— Approximately 500 feet prior to the point where the jet touched down.

Answer (A) is correct (5753). *(AIM Para 7-3-6)*
When taking off on a runway on which a large jet aircraft has just landed, plan to become airborne past the point where the jet touched down.
Answer (B) is incorrect because you should rotate past, not at or prior to, the point where the jet touched down. Answer (C) is incorrect because you should rotate past, not 500 ft. prior to, where the jet touched down.

5750. Choose the correct statement regarding wake turbulence.

A— Vortex generation begins with the initiation of the takeoff roll.
B— The primary hazard is loss of control because of induced roll.
C— The greatest vortex strength is produced when the generating airplane is heavy, clean, and fast.

Answer (B) is correct (5750). *(AIM Para 7-3-3)*
The usual hazard associated with wake turbulence is the induced rolling movements, which can exceed the rolling capability of the encountering aircraft.
Answer (A) is incorrect because vortex generation begins at the rotation point when the airplane takes off, not the initiation of the takeoff roll. Answer (C) is incorrect because the greatest vortex strength is when the generating aircraft is slow, not fast.

32.
5752. Which procedure should you follow to avoid wake turbulence if a large jet crosses your course from left to right approximately 1 mile ahead and at your altitude?

A— Make sure you are slightly above the path of the jet.
B— Slow your airspeed to V_A and maintain altitude and course.
C— Make sure you are slightly below the path of the jet and perpendicular to the course.

Answer (A) is correct (5752). *(AIM Para 7-3-6)*
To avoid the wake turbulence of a large jet at your altitude, you should increase your altitude slightly to get above the flight path of the jet.
Answer (B) is incorrect because the greatest danger is induced roll, not turbulence. Answer (C) is incorrect because flight below and behind a larger aircraft's path should be avoided.

33.
5754. When landing behind a large aircraft, which procedure should be followed for vortex avoidance?

A— Stay above its final approach flightpath all the way to touchdown.
B— Stay below and to one side of its final approach flightpath.
C— Stay well below its final approach flightpath and land at least 2,000 feet behind.

Answer (A) is correct (5754). *(AIM Para 7-3-6)*
When landing behind a large aircraft, stay above its final approach flight path all the way to touchdown; i.e., touch down beyond the touchdown point of the large aircraft.
Answer (B) is incorrect because you should stay at or above, not below, its flight path. Answer (C) is incorrect because you should stay at or above, not below, its flight path, and land beyond, not behind, its touchdown point.

34.
5755. With respect to vortex circulation, which is true?

A— Helicopters generate downwash turbulence, not vortex circulation.
B— The vortex strength is greatest when the generating aircraft is flying fast.
C— Vortex circulation generated by helicopters in forward flight trail behind in a manner similar to wingtip vortices generated by airplanes.

Answer (C) is correct (5755). *(AIM Para 7-3-7)*
In forward flight, helicopters produce a pair of high velocity trailing vortices similar to wing tip vortices of large fixed wing aircraft.
Answer (A) is incorrect because helicopters create both downwash turbulence and wingtip vortices. Answer (B) is incorrect because the vortex strength is greatest when flying slow, not fast.

35.
5756. Which is true with respect to vortex circulation?

A— Helicopters generate downwash turbulence only, not vortex circulation.
B— The vortex strength is greatest when the generating aircraft is heavy, clean, and slow.
C— When vortex circulation sinks into ground effect, it tends to dissipate rapidly and offer little danger.

Answer (B) is correct (5756). *(AIM Para 7-3-3)*
The greatest vortex strength occurs when the generating aircraft is heavy, clean, and slow.
Answer (A) is incorrect because helicopters generate both downwash turbulence and wingtip vortices. Answer (C) is incorrect because vortices remain active in ground effect for a period of time.

3.6 Land and Hold Short Operations (LAHSO)

36.
5655a. Who has the final authority to accept or decline any "land and hold short" (LAHSO) clearance?

A— ATC tower controller.
B— Airplane owner/operator.
C— Pilot-in-Command.

Answer (C) is correct (5655a). *(AIM Para 4-3-11)*
The pilot-in-command has the final authority to accept or decline any land and hold short (LAHSO) clearance. The safety and operation of the airplane remain the responsibility of the pilot. Pilots are expected to decline a LAHSO clearance if they determine it will compromise safety.
Answer (A) is incorrect because, while an ATC tower controller will issue a LAHSO clearance, the pilot in command has the final authority to accept or decline the LAHSO clearance. Answer (B) is incorrect because the pilot in command, not the airplane owner or operator, has the final authority to accept or decline any LAHSO clearance.

37.
5656a. When should pilots decline a "land and hold short" (LAHSO) clearance?

A— When it will compromise safety.
B— If runway surface is contaminated.
C— Only when the tower controller concurs.

Answer (A) is correct (5656a). *(AIM Para 4-3-11)*
The pilot in command has the final authority to accept or decline a land and hold short (LAHSO) clearance. The safety and operation of the airplane remain the responsibility of the pilot. Pilots are expected to decline a LAHSO clearance if they determine it will compromise safety.
Answer (B) is incorrect because ATC should not issue a LAHSO clearance if the runway is contaminated (e.g., snow, ice, etc.) which would affect the braking action of an airplane. Answer (C) is incorrect because the pilot in command has the final authority to accept a LAHSO clearance whether or not the tower controller concurs.

38.
5656b. What is the minimum visibility and ceiling required for a pilot to receive a "land and hold short" clearance?

A— 3 statute miles and 1,000 feet.
B— 3 nautical miles and 1,000 feet.
C— 3 statute miles and 1,500 feet.

Answer (A) is correct (5656b). *(AIM Para 4-3-11)*
You should only receive a LAHSO clearance when there is a minimum ceiling of 1,000 ft. and 3 SM visibility. The intent of having "basic" VFR weather conditions is to allow pilots to maintain visual contact with other aircraft and ground vehicle operations.
Answer (B) is incorrect because the minimum visibility and ceiling required for you to receive a LAHSO clearance is 3 SM, not 3 NM, and 1,000 ft. Answer (C) is incorrect because the minimum visibility and ceiling required for you to receive a LAHSO clearance is 3 SM and 1,000 ft., not 1,500 ft.

END OF CHAPTER

CHAPTER FOUR
FEDERAL AVIATION REGULATIONS

This chapter contains outlines of major concepts tested, all FAA test questions and answers regarding Federal Aviation Regulations, and an explanation of each answer. Each module, or subtopic, within this chapter is listed on pages 69 and 70 with the number of questions from the FAA pilot knowledge test pertaining to that particular module. For each module, the first number following the parentheses is the page number on which the outline begins, and the next number is the page number on which the questions begin.

CAUTION: The **sole purpose** of this book is to expedite your passing the FAA pilot knowledge test for the commercial pilot certificate. All extraneous material (i.e., topics or regulations not directly tested on the FAA pilot knowledge test) is omitted, even though much more information and knowledge are necessary to become a proficient commercial pilot. This additional material is presented in *Commercial Pilot Flight Maneuvers and Practical Test Prep* and *Pilot Handbook*, available from Gleim Publications.

4.1 FAR PART 1

1.1 General Definitions (Questions 1-3)

1. Commercial operators engage in carriage by aircraft in air commerce of persons or property for compensation or hire, other than as an air carrier.

2. An operator is a person who causes the aircraft to be used or authorizes its use.

3. Operational control of a flight means exercising authority over initiating, conducting, or terminating a flight.

1.2 Abbreviations and Symbols (Questions 4-7c)

1. V_{S1} means the stalling speed or minimum steady flight speed in a specified configuration.
2. V_S means the stalling speed or minimum steady flight speed at which the airplane is controllable.
3. V_F means the design flap speed.
4. V_{NO} means the maximum structural cruising speed.
5. V_{LE} means the maximum landing gear extended speed.
6. V_{NE} means the never-exceed speed.
7. V_Y means the best rate of climb speed.

4.2 FAR PART 23

23.3 Airplane Categories (Question 8)

1. The utility operational category of an airplane permits limited acrobatics, including spins (if approved for that particular type of airplane).

4.3 FAR PART 61

61.3 Requirements for Certificates, Rating, and Authorizations (Question 9)

1. A current and appropriate pilot and medical certificate is required to be in a pilot's personal possession or readily accessible in the aircraft whenever the pilot is acting as pilot in command or as a required flight crewmember.

61.5 Certificates and Ratings Issued under This Part (Question 10)

1. Aircraft class ratings (with respect to airmen) are single-engine land, multiengine land, single-engine sea, and multiengine sea.

61.15 Offenses Involving Alcohol or Drugs (Questions 10a. - 10d.)

1. A pilot convicted of operating a motor vehicle while either intoxicated by, impaired by, or under the influence of alcohol or a drug is required to provide a written report to the FAA Civil Aviation Security Division (AMC-700) not later than 60 days after the conviction.
2. A pilot convicted for the violation of any Federal or State statute relating to the process, manufacture, transportation, distribution, or sale of narcotic drugs is grounds for suspension or revocation of any certificate, rating, or authorization issued under Part 61.
3. A pilot convicted of operating an aircraft as a crewmember under the influence of alcohol, or using drugs that affect the person's faculties (acts which are prohibited by Sec. 91.17), is grounds for denial of an application for a certificate, rating, or authorization issued under Part 61 for a period of one year after the date of that act.

61.19 Duration of Pilot and Instructor Certificates (Question 11)

1. Commercial pilot certificates are issued without a specific expiration date.

61.23 Medical Certificates: Requirement and Duration (Question 12)

1. A second-class medical certificate expires for commercial pilot purposes at the end of the last day of the 12th month after the month of the date of examination shown on the certificate.

61.31 Type Rating Requirements, Additional Training, and Authorization Requirements (Questions 13-17)

1. For flights carrying passengers, the pilot must hold a category and class rating appropriate to the aircraft being flown.

2. A type rating is required when operating any turbojet-powered airplane or an airplane having a gross weight of more than 12,500 lb.

3. To act as pilot in command of a complex airplane (an airplane that has retractable landing gear, flaps, and a controllable pitch propeller), the pilot must receive and log ground and flight training in such an airplane and obtain a logbook endorsement of competence.

4. To act as pilot in command of a high-performance airplane (an airplane with an engine of more than 200 horsepower), the pilot must receive and log ground and flight training from an authorized instructor in such an airplane.

5. To act as a pilot in command of a tailwheel airplane, without prior experience, a pilot must receive and log flight training from an authorized instructor in a tailwheel airplane and receive a one-time logbook endorsement.

61.51 Pilot Logbooks (Questions 18-19)

1. Pilots may log as second-in-command time all flight time when qualified and occupying a crewmember station in an aircraft that requires more than one pilot.

2. The aeronautical training and experience used to meet the requirements for a certificate, rating, or flight review and recent flight experience must be documented and recorded in a manner acceptable to the FAA, e.g., a logbook.

61.55 Second-in-Command Qualifications (Question 20)

1. To serve as second in command of an airplane type certificated for more than one pilot crewmember and operated under Part 91, (in part) a person, within the last 12 months, must have become familiar with the required information (systems operations, performance, limitations, etc.) and must have logged pilot time in the type of airplane for which privileges are requested.

61.56 Flight Review (Question 21)

1. To act as pilot in command of an aircraft, a commercial pilot must have satisfactorily completed a flight review or proficiency check within the preceding 24 months.

61.57 Recent Flight Experience: Pilot in Command (Questions 22-23a)

1. If a pilot does not meet the recent night experience requirements, (s)he may not carry passengers during the period 1 hr. after sunset to 1 hr. before sunrise.

2. Prior to carrying passengers, the pilot in command must accomplish required takeoffs and landings in the same category, class, and type of aircraft (if a type rating is required).

3. To act as pilot in command under IFR or in weather conditions that are less than the minimums prescribed for VFR, a pilot must have, within the preceding 6 months, performed and logged (under actual or simulated instrument conditions) at least 6 instrument approaches, holding procedures, and intercepting and tracking courses through the use of navigation systems.

    a. Alternatively, the pilot may have passed an instrument proficiency check in the appropriate category of aircraft within the preceding 6 months.

61.58 Pilot-in-Command Proficiency Check: Operation of Aircraft Requiring More than One Pilot Flight Crewmember (Question 24)

1. To serve as pilot in command of an airplane that is certificated for more than one pilot crewmember and operated under Part 91, a person must have completed a pilot-in-command proficiency check within the preceding 12 calendar months in an airplane that is type certificated for more than one pilot.

61.60 Change of Address (Question 25)

1. You must notify the FAA Airman Certification Branch in writing of any change in your permanent mailing address.

2. You may not exercise the privileges of your pilot certificate (act as pilot in command) after 30 days from moving unless you make this notification.

61.69 Glider Towing: Experience and Training Requirements (Questions 26-27)

1. To act as pilot in command of an airplane towing a glider, the tow pilot is required to hold at least a current private pilot certificate with a category rating for powered aircraft, have a logbook endorsement from an authorized glider instructor certifying receipt of ground and flight training in gliders, and be proficient with techniques and procedures for the safe towing of gliders.

2. To act as pilot in command of an airplane towing a glider, a pilot must have accomplished, within the preceding 12 months, at least three actual or simulated glider tows while accompanied by a qualified tow pilot.

61.133 Commercial Pilot Privileges and Limitations (Questions 28-30)

1. Commercial pilots without an instrument rating cannot carry passengers for hire on cross-country flights during the day beyond a radius of 50 NM.

   a. Carrying passengers for hire at night is prohibited without an instrument rating.

2. A person who holds a commercial pilot certificate may act as pilot in command of an airplane that

   a. Carries persons or property for compensation or hire, provided the person is qualified in accordance with Part 61 and any other FAR Parts that apply to the operation

   b. Operates for compensation or hire, provided the person is qualified in accordance with Part 61 and any other FAR Parts that apply to the operation

4.4 FAR PART 91

91.3 Responsibility and Authority of the Pilot in Command (Questions 31-32)

1. If you, as pilot in command, deviate from any rule in FAR Part 91 (due to an in-flight emergency requiring immediate action), you must submit a written report to the FAA, if requested.

2. The pilot in command is directly responsible for, and is the final authority as to, the operation of the airplane.

91.7 Civil Aircraft Airworthiness (Question 33)

1. You, as pilot in command, are responsible for determining whether your aircraft is in condition for safe flight.

91.9 Civil Aircraft Flight Manual, Marking, and Placard Requirements (Question 34)

1. You may not operate a U.S.-registered civil aircraft unless there is a current, approved Airplane Flight Manual available in the aircraft.

91.15 Dropping Objects (Question 35)

1.   As pilot in command of a civil aircraft, you may not allow any object to be dropped from that aircraft in flight if it creates a hazard to persons or property.

91.21 Portable Electronic Devices (Question 36-37)

1.   Portable electronic devices which may cause interference with the navigation or communication system may not be operated on any of the following U.S.-registered civil aircraft operations.

     a.   Air carrier
     b.   Any other aircraft under IFR

91.23 Truth in Leasing Clause Requirement in Leases and Conditional Sales Contracts (Question 38)

1.   In order to operate a large civil aircraft of U.S. registry which is subject to a lease, the lessee must have mailed a copy of the lease to the FAA in Oklahoma City within 24 hr. of its execution.

91.103 Preflight Action (Questions 39-42)

1.   Pilots are required to familiarize themselves with all available information concerning the flight prior to every flight, and specifically to determine

     a.   For any flight, runway lengths at airports of intended use and the airplane's takeoff and landing requirements

     b.   For IFR flights or those not in the vicinity of an airport

          1)   Weather reports and forecasts
          2)   Fuel requirements
          3)   Alternatives available if the planned flight cannot be completed
          4)   Any known traffic delays

91.105 Flight Crewmembers at Stations (Questions 43-44)

1.   Required flight crewmembers' seatbelts must be fastened while the crewmembers are at their stations.

2.   Each required flight crewmember is required to keep his/her shoulder harness fastened during takeoff and landing unless

     a.   The crewmember would be unable to perform required duties with the shoulder harness fastened.

     b.   The seat at the crewmember's station is not equipped with a shoulder harness.

91.107 Use of Safety Belts, Shoulder Harnesses, and Child Restraint Systems (Questions 45-46)

1.   All occupants of airplanes must wear a safety belt and shoulder harness (if installed) during taxiing, takeoffs, and landings.

91.109 Flight Instruction; Simulated Instrument Flight and Certain Flight Tests (Question 47)

1.   No person may operate an airplane in simulated instrument flight conditions unless the other control seat is occupied by a safety pilot who possesses at least a private pilot certificate with category and class ratings appropriate to the airplane being flown.

91.111 Operating near Other Aircraft (Question 48-50)

1. No person may operate an aircraft so close to another aircraft as to create a collision hazard.
2. Formation flights are not authorized, except by arrangement with the pilot in command of each aircraft.
3. Formation flights are not authorized when carrying passengers for hire.

91.113 Right-of-way Rules: Except Water Operations (Questions 51-56)

1. When an airplane is overtaking another, the airplane being passed has the right-of-way.
   a. The passing (overtaking) airplane shall alter course to the right to pass well clear.
2. When aircraft of the same category are converging at approximately the same altitude (except head on, or nearly so), the aircraft to the other's right has the right-of-way.
   a. Thus, on a night flight, if the pilot of aircraft #1 sees only the green navigation light of aircraft #2, and the aircraft are converging, aircraft #1 has the right-of-way because it is to the right of aircraft #2.
   b. Airplanes and helicopters are equally maneuverable and have equal rights-of-way.
3. When two or more aircraft are approaching an airport for the purpose of landing, the aircraft at the lower altitude has the right-of-way.
   a. This rule shall not be abused by cutting in front of or overtaking another aircraft.

91.121 Altimeter Settings (Question 57)

1. When a pilot is operating an airplane at or above 18,000 ft. MSL, the altimeter should be set to 29.92 in. Hg.

91.123 Compliance with ATC Clearances and Instructions (Question 58)

1. After obtaining an ATC clearance, a pilot may not deviate from that clearance unless an amended clearance is obtained, an emergency exists, or the deviation is in response to a traffic alert and collision avoidance system (TCAS) resolution advisory.

91.144 Temporary Restriction on Flight Operations during Abnormally High Barometric Pressure Conditions (Question 59)

1. When any information indicates that barometric pressure on the route of flight currently exceeds or will exceed 31.00 in. of mercury, no person may operate an aircraft or initiate a flight contrary to the requirements established by the FAA and published in NOTAMs.

91.155 Basic VFR Weather Minimums (Questions 60-61)

1. The minimum flight visibility and cloud clearance requirements in Class C, D, or E airspace at 6,500 ft. MSL are
   a. 3-SM visibility
   b. 1,000 ft. above or 500 ft. below
2. The minimum flight visibility for VFR flight increases to 5 SM at an altitude of
   a. 10,000 ft. MSL and above 1,200 ft. AGL in Class G airspace, or
   b. 10,000 ft. MSL regardless of height above ground in Class E airspace.

91.159 VFR Cruising Altitude or Flight Level (Question 62)

1. Specified altitudes are required for VFR cruising flight at more than 3,000 ft. AGL and below 18,000 ft. MSL.

    a.   The altitude prescribed is based upon the magnetic course.

91.167 Fuel Requirements for Flight in IFR Conditions (Question 63)

1. When an alternate airport is required on an IFR flight plan, you must have sufficient fuel to complete the flight to the first airport of intended landing, fly to the alternate, and thereafter fly for 45 min. at normal cruising speed.

91.169 IFR Flight Plan: Information Required (Questions 64-65)

1. For an airport with an approved instrument approach procedure to be listed as an alternate airport on an IFR flight plan, the forecasted weather conditions at the time of arrival must be at or above the following alternate airport weather minimums:

    a.   Nonprecision approach -- ceiling 800 ft. and visibility 2 SM
    b.   Precision approach -- ceiling 600 ft. and visibility 2 SM

2. For an airport with no instrument approach procedure to be listed as an alternate airport, the forecasted weather conditions at the time of arrival must have a ceiling and visibility that allow descent from the MEA, approach, and landing under basic VFR.

91.171 VOR Equipment Check for IFR Operations (Questions 66-68)

1. To operate an airplane under IFR using the VOR, you must ensure that the VOR equipment has been operationally checked within the preceding 30 days and found to be within prescribed limits.

2. The maximum bearing error allowed for an operational VOR equipment check when using an FAA-approved ground test signal (such as a VOT) is ±4°.

3. Each person making the VOR operational check must enter the date, place, and bearing error and sign the aircraft log or other record.

91.175 Takeoff and Landing under IFR (Questions 69-71)

1. One requirement for a pilot on an instrument approach to operate below the MDA or DH, or to continue the approach, is that the airplane continuously be in a position from which a descent to landing on the intended runway can be made at a normal rate using normal maneuvers.

2. A pilot is not authorized to land an airplane from an instrument approach unless the flight visibility is at, or exceeds, the visibility prescribed in the approach procedure being used.

3. In the case of a radar vector to a final approach course or fix, a timed approach from a holding fix, or an approach for which the procedure specifies "No PT," a pilot may not make a procedure turn unless cleared to do so by ATC.

91.177 Minimum Altitudes for IFR Operations (Question 72)

1. Except during takeoff or landing, the minimum altitude for IFR flight, within a horizontal distance of 4 NM from the course to be flown, is 2,000 ft. above the highest obstacle over designated mountainous terrain or 1,000 ft. above the highest obstacle over terrain elsewhere.

91.183 IFR Radio Communications (Question 73)

1. The pilot in command of an airplane operated under IFR in controlled airspace, and not in radar contact, shall report by radio as soon as possible the time and altitude of passing each designated reporting point.

91.187 Operation under IFR in Controlled Airspace: Malfunction Reports (Question 74)

1. The pilot in command of an airplane operated under IFR in controlled airspace shall report to ATC, as soon as practicable, any malfunctions of navigational, approach, or communication equipment occurring in flight.

91.205 Powered Civil Aircraft with Standard Category U.S. Airworthiness Certificates: Instrument and Equipment Requirements (Questions 75-77a)

1. For a flight for hire over water beyond power-off gliding distance from shore, approved flotation gear must be readily available to each occupant.

2. An anticollision light system is required for powered aircraft during VFR night flights.

3. An electric landing light is required for VFR night flights when operated for hire.

91.207 Emergency Locator Transmitters (Question 78)

1. ELT batteries must be replaced (or recharged, if rechargeable batteries) after 1 cumulative hr. of use or after 50% of their useful life expires.

91.209 Aircraft Lights (Questions 79-80)

1. Airplanes operating between sunset and sunrise must display lighted position (navigation) lights.

2. If an airplane is not equipped with an anticollision light system, no one may operate that airplane after sunset.

91.211 Supplemental Oxygen (Questions 81-82)

1. At cabin pressure altitudes above 15,000 ft. MSL, each passenger of the aircraft **must be provided** with supplemental oxygen.

    a. At cabin pressure altitudes above 14,000 ft. MSL, each required crewmember **must be provided and must use** supplemental oxygen.

2. If a flight is conducted at cabin pressure altitudes above 12,500 ft. MSL to and including 14,000 ft. MSL, oxygen must be used by required crewmembers for the time in excess of 30 min. at that altitude.

91.215 ATC Transponder and Altitude Reporting Equipment and Use (Questions 83-84)

1. A transponder with altitude encoding (Mode C) equipment is required in all airspace above 10,000 ft. MSL, excluding airspace at or below 2,500 ft. AGL.

2. A transponder with altitude encoding equipment is also required in Class A, Class B, and Class C airspace.

91.303 Aerobatic Flight (Question 85)

1. Aerobatic flight is prohibited

    a. With visibility of less than 3 SM
    b. Below 1,500 ft. AGL

91.311 Towing: Other Than under Sec. 91.309 (Question 86)

1.   In order to operate an aircraft towing an advertising banner, the pilot must obtain a certificate of waiver from the administrator of the FAA.

91.313 Restricted Category Civil Aircraft: Operating Limitations (Question 87)

1.   Persons or property cannot be transported for compensation or hire in a restricted category airplane.

91.315 Limited Category Civil Aircraft: Operating Limitations (Question 88)

1.   Persons or property cannot be transported for compensation or hire in a limited category aircraft.

91.319 Aircraft Having Experimental Certificates: Operating Limitations (Question 89)

1.   Persons or property cannot be transported for compensation or hire in an airplane that has an experimental certificate.

91.325 Primary Category Aircraft: Operating Limitations (Question 90)

1.   Persons or property cannot be transported for compensation or hire in a primary category aircraft.

91.403 General (Questions 91-92)

1.   The owner or operator of an aircraft is primarily responsible for

  a.   Maintaining that aircraft in an airworthy condition
  b.   Assuring compliance with all Airworthiness Directives

2.   An operator is a person who uses, causes to use, or authorizes to use an aircraft for the purpose of air navigation, including the piloting of an aircraft, with or without the right of legal control (i.e., owner, lessee, or otherwise).

  a.   Thus, the pilot in command is also responsible for maintaining the aircraft in an airworthy condition and for complying with all Airworthiness Directives.

91.405 Maintenance Required (Questions 93-94)

1.   After an annual inspection has been completed and the aircraft has been returned to service, an appropriate notation must be made in the aircraft maintenance records.

2.   A standard airworthiness certificate remains in effect as long as the airplane receives required maintenance and inspections.

91.407 Operation after Maintenance, Preventive Maintenance, Rebuilding, or Alteration (Question 95)

1.   When aircraft alterations or repairs substantially change the flight characteristics, the aircraft documents must show that it was test flown and approved for return to service prior to carrying passengers.

  a.   The pilot test flying the aircraft must be at least a private pilot and rated for the type of aircraft being tested.

91.409 Inspections (Questions 96-97)

1. For commercial operations, an inspection is required every 100 hr.

    a. The 100 hr. may be exceeded by no more than 10 hr. if necessary to reach a place at which an inspection can be performed.

    b. An annual inspection may be substituted for a 100-hr. inspection but not vice versa.

91.413 ATC Transponder Tests and Inspections (Questions 98-99)

1. An ATC transponder may not be used unless, within the preceding 24 calendar months, that transponder has been tested, inspected, and found to comply with appropriate regulations.

91.417 Maintenance Records (Questions 100-102)

1. Each owner or operator must keep maintenance records for each airplane. The records must include

    a. Current status of life-limited parts of the airframe and each engine, propeller, rotor, and appliance

    b. Current status of each Airworthiness Directive (AD)

    c. Preventive maintenance accomplished by a pilot

91.421 Rebuilt Engine Maintenance Records (Question 103)

1. A new maintenance record may be used for a rebuilt (zero-time) engine, but the new records must include the status of previous Airworthiness Directives.

4.5 FAR PART 119

119.1 Applicability (Questions 103a-103b)

1. A commercial pilot may act as pilot in command of the following operations, which are not regulated by 14 CFR Part 119 (FAR Part 119):

    a. Nonstop flights within a 25 SM radius of an airport for the purpose of carrying persons for intentional parachute jumps.

    b. Crop dusting, spraying, and bird chasing.

4.6 NTSB PART 830

830.2 Definitions (Question 103c)

1. For an injury to be defined as a "serious injury" on the basis of hospitalization, the injury must require hospitalization for more than 48 hours, commencing within 7 days from the date the injury was received.

830.5 Immediate Notification (Questions 104-111)

1. Even when no injuries occur to occupants, an airplane accident resulting in substantial damage must be reported to the nearest National Transportation Safety Board (NTSB) field office immediately.

    a. Damage to the landing gear, wheels, and tires are not considered "substantial damage," and thus no notification or report is required.

2. The following incidents must also be reported immediately to the NTSB:

    a. Inability of any required crewmember to perform normal flight duties because of in-flight injury or illness

    b. In-flight fire (but not a ground fire)

    c. Flight control system malfunction or failure

830.15 Reports and Statements to Be Filed (Questions 112-113)

1. A written accident report is required to be filed with the nearest NTSB field office within 10 days of an accident.

2. A written incident report is required only upon request.

4.1 FAR PART 1
1.1 General Definitions

1.
5010. Regulations which refer to "commercial operators" relate to that person who

A— is the owner of a small scheduled airline.
B— for compensation or hire, engages in the carriage by aircraft in air commerce of persons or property, as an air carrier.
C— for compensation or hire, engages in the carriage by aircraft in air commerce of persons or property, other than as an air carrier.

Answer (C) is correct (5010). *(FAR 1.1)*
A commercial operator is a person who, for compensation or hire, engages in the carriage by aircraft in air commerce of persons or property, other than as an air carrier or foreign air carrier or under the authority of Part 375.
Answer (A) is incorrect because commercial operations do not apply to airlines. Answer (B) is incorrect because commercial operations do not apply to airlines.

2.
5012. Regulations which refer to the "operational control" of a flight are in relation to

A— the specific duties of any required crewmember.
B— acting as the sole manipulator of the aircraft controls.
C— exercising authority over initiating, conducting, or terminating a flight.

Answer (C) is correct (5012). *(FAR 1.1)*
Operational control of a flight means the exercise of authority over initiating, conducting, or terminating a flight.
Answer (A) is incorrect because assigning specific duties to a crewmember is only a small portion of exercising operational control. Answer (B) is incorrect because acting as sole manipulator of an aircraft is a flight crew, not an operator, responsibility.

3.
5011. Regulations which refer to "operate" relate to that person who

A— acts as pilot in command of the aircraft.
B— is the sole manipulator of the aircraft controls.
C— causes the aircraft to be used or authorizes its use.

Answer (C) is correct (5011). *(FAR 1.1)*
To operate an aircraft means to use, cause to use, or authorize to use aircraft for the purpose of air navigation, including the piloting of aircraft, with or without the right of legal control (as owner, lessee, or otherwise).
Answer (A) is incorrect because the pilot in command may not necessarily be the operator of the aircraft. Answer (B) is incorrect because the sole manipulator may not necessarily be the operator of the aircraft.

1.2 Abbreviations and Symbols

4.
5013. Which is the correct symbol for the stalling speed or the minimum steady flight speed in a specified configuration?

A— V_S.
B— V_{S1}.
C— V_{S0}.

Answer (B) is correct (5013). *(FAR 1.2)*
V_{S1} means the stalling speed or the minimum steady flight speed obtained in a specified configuration. This configuration is generally specified as gear and flaps retracted.
Answer (A) is incorrect because V_S means the stalling speed or the minimum steady flight speed at which the airplane is controllable with no particular configuration specified. Answer (C) is incorrect because V_{S0} means the stalling speed or the minimum steady flight speed in the landing configuration.

5.
5014. Which is the correct symbol for the stalling speed or the minimum steady flight speed at which the airplane is controllable?

A— V_S.
B— V_{S1}.
C— V_{S0}.

Answer (A) is correct (5014). *(FAR 1.2)*
V_S means the stalling speed or the minimum steady flight speed at which the airplane is controllable. No configuration is specified.
Answer (B) is incorrect because V_{S1} means the stalling speed or the minimum steady flight speed obtained in a specified configuration. Answer (C) is incorrect because V_{S0} means the stalling speed or the minimum steady flight speed in the landing configuration.

6.
5015a. 14 CFR Part 1 defines V_F as

A— design flap speed.
B— flap operating speed.
C— maximum flap extended speed.

Answer (A) is correct (5015a). *(FAR 1.2)*
V_F means design flap speed.
Answer (B) is incorrect because the flap operating range, not speed, is indicated by the white arc on the airspeed indicator. Answer (C) is incorrect because V_{FE} means maximum flap extended speed.

6a.
5015b. 14 CFR Part 1 defines V_{NO} as

A— maximum structural cruising speed.
B— normal operating speed.
C— maximum operating speed.

Answer (A) is correct (5015b). *(FAR 1.2)*
V_{NO} means maximum structural cruising speed.
Answer (B) is incorrect because the normal operating range, not speed, is indicated by the green arc on the airspeed indicator. Answer (C) is incorrect because V_{MO}, not V_{NO}, means maximum operating limit speed.

7.
5016a. 14 CFR Part 1 defines V_{LE} as

A— maximum landing gear extended speed.
B— maximum landing gear operating speed.
C— maximum leading edge flaps extended speed.

Answer (A) is correct (5016a.). *(FAR 1.2)*
V_{LE} means maximum landing gear extended speed.
Answer (B) is incorrect because V_{LO} means maximum landing gear operating speed. Answer (C) is incorrect because maximum leading edge flaps extended speed is not defined in FAR Part 1.

7a.
5016b. 14 CFR Part 1 defines V_{NE} as

A—maximum nose wheel extend speed.
B—never-exceed speed.
C—maximum landing gear extended speed.

Answer (B) is correct (5016b.). *(FAR 1.2)*
V_{NE} is defined as the never-exceed speed.
Answer (A) is incorrect because V_{NE} means the never-exceed speed, not the maximum nosewheel extend speed. Answer (C) is incorrect because V_{LE}, not V_{NE}, means the maximum landing gear extended speed.

7b.
5016c. 14 CFR Part 1 defines V_Y as

A—speed for best rate of descent.
B—speed for best angle of climb.
C—speed for best rate of climb.

Answer (C) is correct (5016c.). *(FAR 1.2)*
V_Y means the speed for the best rate of climb.
Answer (A) is incorrect because V_Y means the speed for the best rate of climb, not descent. Answer (B) is incorrect because V_X, not V_Y, means the speed for the best angle of climb.

7c.
1001-22. 14 CFR part 1 defines V_{NO} as

A— maximum structural cruising speed.
B— maximum operating limit speed.
C— never-exceed speed.

Answer (A) is correct (1001-22). *(FAR 1.2)*
V_{NO} means maximum structural cruising speed.
Answer (B) is incorrect because V_{MO}, not V_{NO}, means maximum operating limit speed. Answer (C) is incorrect because V_{NE}, not V_{NO}, means never-exceed speed.

4.2 FAR PART 23
23.3 Airplane Categories

8.
5017. If an airplane category is listed as utility, it would mean that this airplane could be operated in which of the following maneuvers?

A— Limited acrobatics, excluding spins.
B— Any maneuver except acrobatics or spins.
C— Limited acrobatics, including spins (if approved).

Answer (C) is correct (5017). *(FAR 23.3)*
The utility operational category of airplanes is designed to accommodate 4.4 positive G's, which permits limited aerobatics, including spins (if approved for that particular type of airplane).
Answer (A) is incorrect because the utility category includes spins, if approved. Answer (B) is incorrect because the normal, not utility, category prohibits aerobatics and spins.

4.3 FAR PART 61
61.3 Requirements for Certificates, Rating, and Authorizations

9.
5018. Commercial pilots are required to have a valid and appropriate pilot certificate in their physical possession or readily accessible in the aircraft when

A— piloting for hire only.
B— acting as pilot in command.
C— carrying passengers only.

Answer (B) is correct (5018). *(FAR 61.3)*
No person may act as pilot in command or in any other capacity as a required pilot of a civil aircraft of U.S. registry unless that person has a valid and appropriate pilot certificate in that person's physical possession or readily accessible in the aircraft when exercising the privileges of that pilot certificate.
Answer (A) is incorrect because a valid and appropriate pilot certificate is required when acting as pilot in command, regardless if the flight was for hire or not. Answer (C) is incorrect because a valid and appropriate pilot certificate is required to be in your personal possession when acting as pilot in command, regardless of whether or not you are carrying passengers.

61.5 Certificates and Ratings Issued under This Part

10.
5019. Which of the following are considered aircraft class ratings?

A— Transport, normal, utility, and acrobatic.
B— Airplane, rotorcraft, glider, and lighter-than-air.
C— Single-engine land, multiengine land, single-engine sea, and multiengine sea.

Answer (C) is correct (5019). *(FAR 61.5)*
Aircraft class ratings (with respect to airmen) are single-engine land, multiengine land, single-engine sea, and multiengine sea.
Answer (A) is incorrect because transport, normal, utility, and acrobatic are aircraft categories with respect to the certification of aircraft, not airmen. Answer (B) is incorrect because airplane, rotorcraft, glider, and lighter-than-air are categories, not classes, of aircraft with respect to airmen.

61.15 Offenses Involving Alcohol or Drugs

10a.
5141. A pilot convicted of operating a motor vehicle while either intoxicated by, impaired by, or under the influence of alcohol or a drug is required to provide a

A— written report to the FAA Civil Aeromedical Institute (CAMI) within 60 days after the motor vehicle action.
B— written report to the FAA Civil Aviation Security Division (AMC-700) not later than 60 days after the conviction.
C— the notification of the conviction to an FAA Aviation Medical Examiner (AME) not later than 60 days after the motor vehicle action.

10b.
5142. A pilot convicted of a motor vehicle offense involving alcohol or drugs is required to provide a written report to the

A— nearest FAA Flight Standards District Office (FSDO) within 60 days after such action.
B— FAA Civil Aeromedical Institute (CAMI) within 60 days after the conviction.
C— FAA Civil Aviation Security Division (AMC-700) within 60 days after such action.

10c.
5143. A pilot convicted for the violation of any Federal or State statute relating to the process, manufacture, transportation, distribution, or sale of narcotic drugs is grounds for

A— a written report to be filed with the FAA Civil Aviation Security Division (AMC-700) not later than 60 days after the conviction.
B— notification of this conviction to the FAA Civil Aeromedical Institute (CAMI) within 60 days after the conviction.
C— suspension or revocation of any certificate, rating, or authorization issued under 14 CFR part 61.

10d.
5144. A pilot convicted of operating an aircraft as a crewmember under the influence of alcohol, or using drugs that affect the person's faculties, is grounds for a

A— written report to be filed with the FAA Civil Aviation Security Division (AMC-700) not later than 60 days after the conviction.
B— written notification to the FAA Civil Aeromedical Institute (CAMI) within 60 days after the conviction.
C— denial of an application for an FAA certificate, rating, or authorization issued under 14 CFR part 61.

Answer (B) is correct (5141). *(FAR 61.15)*
A pilot convicted of operating a motor vehicle while either intoxicated by, impaired by, or under the influence of alcohol or a drug is required to provide a written report to the FAA Civil Aviation Security Division (AMC-700) not later than 60 days after the conviction.
Answer (A) is incorrect because a pilot convicted of operating a motor vehicle while either intoxicated by, impaired by, or under the influence of alcohol or a drug is required to provide a written report to the FAA Civil Aviation Security Division, not the FAA Civil Aeromedical Institute (CAMI), within 60 days after the motor vehicle action. Answer (C) is incorrect because a pilot convicted of operating a motor vehicle while either intoxicated by, impaired by, or under the influence of alcohol or a drug is required to provide a written report to the FAA Civil Aviation Security Division, not notify an AME, not later than 60 days after the motor vehicle action.

Answer (C) is correct (5142). *(FAR 61.15)*
A pilot convicted of a motor vehicle offense involving alcohol or drugs is required to provide a written report to the FAA Civil Aviation Security Division (AMC-700) within 60 days after such action.
Answer (A) is incorrect because a pilot convicted of a motor vehicle offense involving alcohol or drugs is required to provide a written report to the FAA Civil Aviation Security Division, not the nearest FSDO, within 60 days after such action. Answer (B) is incorrect because a pilot convicted of a motor vehicle offense involving alcohol or drugs is required to provide a written report to the FAA Civil Aviation Security Division, not the FAA Civil Aeromedical Institute (CAMI), within 60 days after the conviction.

Answer (C) is correct (5143). *(FAR 61.15)*
A pilot convicted for the violation of any Federal or State statute relating to the process, manufacture, transportation, distribution, or sale of narcotic drugs is grounds for suspension or revocation of any certificate, rating, or authorization issued under 14 CFR Part 61.
Answer (A) is incorrect because a written report must be filed with the FAA Civil Aviation Security Division not later than 60 days after a pilot is convicted of a motor vehicle offense involving alcohol or drugs, not for a conviction for the violation of any Federal or State statute relating to the process, manufacture, transportation, or sale of narcotic drugs. Answer (B) is incorrect because a pilot convicted for the violation of any Federal or State statute relating to the process, manufacture, transportation, distribution, or sale of narcotic drugs is grounds for suspension or revocation of any certificate, rating, or authorization issued under 14 CFR part 61. The pilot is not required to notify CAMI of the conviction.

Answer (C) is correct (5144). *(FAR 61.15)*
A pilot convicted of operating an aircraft as a crewmember under the influence of alcohol, or using drugs that affect the person's faculties (acts prohibited by Sec. 91.17), is grounds for denial of an application for a certificate or rating, or authorization issued under 14 CFR part 61 for a period of one year after the date of that act.
Answer (A) is incorrect because a written report must be filed with the FAA Civil Aviation Security Division not later than 60 days after a pilot is convicted of a motor vehicle offense involving alcohol or drugs, not for being convicted of operating an aircraft as a crewmember under the influence of alcohol, or using drugs that affect the person's faculties. Answer (B) is incorrect because a pilot convicted of operating an aircraft as a crewmember under the influence of alcohol, or using drugs that affect a person's faculties, is grounds for denial of an application for an FAA certificate or rating. The pilot is not required to notify CAMI of the conviction.

61.19 Duration of Pilot and Instructor Certificates

11.
5020. Does a commercial pilot certificate have a specific expiration date?

A— No, it is issued without an expiration date.
B— Yes, it expires at the end of the 24th month after the month in which it was issued.
C— No, but commercial privileges expire if a flight review is not satisfactorily completed each 12 months.

Answer (A) is correct (5020). *(FAR 61.19)*
Any pilot certificate (other than a student pilot or flight instructor certificate) issued under Part 61 is issued without a specific expiration date.
Answer (B) is incorrect because a flight instructor certificate, not a commercial pilot certificate, expires at the end of the 24th month after the month in which it was issued. Answer (C) is incorrect because a flight review is required at the end of the 24th month, not 12th month.

61.23 Medical Certificates: Requirement and Duration

12.
5021. A second-class medical certificate issued to a commercial pilot on April 10, this year, permits the pilot to exercise which of the following privileges?

A— Commercial pilot privileges through April 30, next year.
B— Commercial pilot privileges through April 10, 2 years later.
C— Private pilot privileges through, but not after, March 31, next year.

Answer (A) is correct (5021). *(FAR 61.23)*
A second-class medical certificate expires at the end of the last day of the 12th month after the examination for operations requiring a commercial pilot certificate (e.g., April 30, next year).
Answer (B) is incorrect because a second-class medical is valid for commercial operations for 12 months, not 24 months, and expires on the last day of the month. Answer (C) is incorrect because a second-class medical is valid for private or recreational pilot operations, not commercial pilot operations, for 24 months.

61.31 Type Rating Requirements, Additional Training, and Authorization Requirements

13.
5022. When is the pilot in command required to hold a category and class rating appropriate to the aircraft being flown?

A— On flights when carrying another person.
B— All solo flights.
C— On practical tests given by an examiner or FAA inspector.

Answer (A) is correct (5022). *(FAR 61.31)*
To serve as pilot in command of an aircraft carrying passengers, a person must hold the appropriate category, class, and type rating (if a class rating and a type rating are required) for the aircraft to be flown.
Answer (B) is incorrect because the pilot in command must hold a category and class rating on flights when carrying passengers. Answer (C) is incorrect because the pilot in command is not required to hold a category and class rating to the aircraft being flown on a practical test.

14.
5023. Unless otherwise authorized, the pilot in command is required to hold a type rating when operating any

A— aircraft that is certificated for more than one pilot.
B— aircraft of more than 12,500 pounds maximum certificated takeoff weight.
C— multiengine airplane having a gross weight of more than 12,000 pounds.

Answer (B) is correct (5023). *(FAR 61.31)*
A person may not act as pilot in command of any aircraft of more than 12,500 lb. maximum takeoff weight unless (s)he holds a type rating for that aircraft.
Answer (A) is incorrect because an aircraft that is certificated for more than one pilot does not necessarily require a type rating. Answer (C) is incorrect because a type rating is required for any, not only multiengine, aircraft having a maximum gross weight of more than 12,500 lb., not 12,000 lb.

15.
5024. To act as pilot in command of an airplane that is equipped with retractable landing gear, flaps, and controllable pitch propeller, a person is required to

A— hold a multiengine airplane class rating.
B— make at least six takeoffs and landings in such an airplane within the preceding 6 months.
C— receive and log ground and flight training in such an airplane, and obtain a logbook endorsement certifying proficiency.

Answer (C) is correct (5024). *(FAR 61.31)*
No person may act as pilot in command of a complex airplane (an airplane that has retractable landing gear, flaps, and a controllable pitch propeller), unless the person has received and logged ground and flight training from an authorized instructor in a complex airplane and obtained a logbook endorsement certifying proficiency.
Answer (A) is incorrect because it is not necessary to hold a multiengine rating to pilot a single-engine complex airplane. Answer (B) is incorrect because, to act as pilot in command of a complex airplane, a person is required to receive and log ground and flight training in a complex airplane and obtain a logbook endorsement certifying proficiency, not just make at least six takeoffs and landings in a complex airplane within the preceding 6 months.

16.
5106. To act as pilot-in-command of an airplane with more than 200 horsepower, a person is required to

A— receive and log ground and flight training from a qualified pilot in such an airplane.
B— obtain an endorsement from a qualified pilot stating that the person is proficient to operate such an airplane.
C— receive and log ground and flight training from an authorized instructor in such an airplane.

Answer (C) is correct (5106). *(FAR 61.31)*
To act as pilot in command of an airplane with an engine of more than 200 hp. (high-performance), a person is required to receive and log ground and flight training from an authorized instructor in a high-performance airplane, simulator, or flight training device and receive a one-time logbook endorsement from an authorized instructor who certifies the person is proficient to operate a high-performance airplane.
Answer (A) is incorrect because the ground and flight training must be given by an authorized instructor, not a qualified pilot. Additionally, a one-time logbook endorsement, stating that the person is proficient to operate a high-performance airplane, is required. Answer (B) is incorrect because the endorsement must be given by an authorized instructor, not any qualified pilot, and the endorsement will certify, not state, that the person is proficient to operate such an airplane.

17.
5128. To act as pilot in command of a tailwheel airplane, without prior experience, a pilot must

A— log ground and flight training from an authorized instructor.
B— pass a competency check and receive an endorsement from an authorized instructor.
C— receive and log flight training from an authorized instructor.

Answer (C) is correct (5128). *(FAR 61.31)*
To act as pilot in command of a tailwheel airplane without prior experience, you must receive and log flight training from an authorized instructor in a tailwheel airplane and have your instructor endorse your logbook stating that you are proficient in the operation of a tailwheel airplane.
Answer (A) is incorrect because, to act as pilot in command of a tailwheel airplane without prior experience, you must receive and log flight training from an authorized instructor. There is no requirement to log ground training. Answer (B) is incorrect because, to act as pilot in command of a tailwheel airplane without prior experience, you must receive and log flight training and receive a logbook endorsement from an authorized instructor. There is no requirement to pass a competency check.

61.51 Pilot Logbooks

18.
5025. What flight time may a pilot log as second in command?

A— All flight time while acting as second in command in aircraft configured for more than one pilot.
B— Only that flight time during which the second in command is the sole manipulator of the controls.
C— All flight time when qualified and occupying a crewmember station in an aircraft that requires more than one pilot.

Answer (C) is correct (5025). *(FAR 61.51)*
A person may log second-in-command flight time only for that flight time during which that person is qualified in accordance with FAR 61.55 and occupies a crewmember station in an aircraft that requires more than one pilot by the aircraft's type certificate.
Answer (A) is incorrect because a pilot may log second-in-command flight time only if (s)he is qualified and the aircraft or regulations required more than one pilot, not if the aircraft is configured for more than one pilot. Answer (B) is incorrect because a pilot may log all second-in-command flight time if (s)he is qualified and the aircraft requires more than one pilot, not just when the pilot is the sole manipulator of the controls. If the pilot is rated in that aircraft, (s)he can log PIC when (s)he is the sole manipulator of the controls.

19.
5026. What flight time must be documented and recorded by a pilot exercising the privileges of a commercial certificate?

A— All flight time flown for compensation or hire.
B— Only flight time for compensation or hire with passengers aboard which is necessary to meet the recent flight experience requirements.
C— Flight time showing training and aeronautical experience to meet requirements for a certificate, rating, or flight review.

Answer (C) is correct (5026). *(FAR 61.51)*
Flight time showing training and aeronautical experience used to meet the requirements for a certificate, rating, or flight review must be documented and recorded in a reliable record (logbook). Additionally, the aeronautical experience required for meeting the recent flight experience requirements must also be recorded in your logbook.
Answer (A) is incorrect because you must log the training and aeronautical experience used to meet the requirements for a certificate, rating, or flight review and the recent flight experience requirements, not all flight time for compensation or hire. Answer (B) is incorrect because, while you are required to log the experience required for meeting the recent flight experience requirements, it can be done at any time, not only when a flight is for compensation or hire with passengers on board.

61.55 Second-in-Command Qualifications

20.
5108. To serve as second in command of an airplane that is certificated for more than one pilot crewmember, and operated under part 91, a person must

A— receive and log flight training from an authorized flight instructor in the type of airplane privileges are requested.
B— hold at least a commercial pilot certificate with an airplane category rating.
C— within the last 12 months become familiar with the required information, and perform and log pilot time in the type of airplane for which privileges are requested.

Answer (C) is correct (5108). *(FAR 61.55)*
To serve as second in command of an airplane type certificated for more than one required pilot flight crewmember and operated under Part 91, a person, within the previous 12 calendar months, must become familiar with the required information (system operations, performance and limitations, normal and emergency operations, and the flight manual and placards) and have logged pilot time in the type of airplane for which privileges are requested.
Answer (A) is incorrect because, to serve as second in command of an airplane that is certificated for more than one pilot flight crewmember, a person, within the previous 12 calendar months, must become familiar with the required information and must have performed and logged pilot time, not just received and logged flight training, in the type of airplane for which privileges are requested. Answer (B) is incorrect because, to serve as second in command of an airplane that is certificated for more than one pilot flight crewmember under Part 91, a person must hold at least a private pilot certificate, not a commercial pilot certificate, with an airplane and appropriate class rating.

61.56 Flight Review

21.
5031. To act as pilot in command of an aircraft under 14 CFR Part 91, a commercial pilot must have satisfactorily accomplished a flight review or completed a proficiency check within the preceding

A— 24 calendar months.
B— 12 calendar months.
C— 6 calendar months.

Answer (A) is correct (5031). *(FAR 61.56)*
No person may act as pilot in command of an aircraft unless, within the preceding 24 calendar months, (s)he has accomplished a flight review; a pilot proficiency check for a certificate, rating, or operating privilege; or one or more phases of the FAA Wings program.
Answer (B) is incorrect because a flight review or a proficiency check must have been accomplished within the preceding 24 months, not 12 months. Answer (C) is incorrect because a flight review or a proficiency check must have been accomplished within the preceding 24 months, not 6 months.

61.57 Recent Flight Experience: Pilot in Command

22.
5027. If a pilot does not meet the recency of experience requirements for night flight and official sunset is 1900 CST, the latest time passengers should be carried is

A— 1900 CST.
B— 1800 CST.
C— 1959 CST.

Answer (C) is correct (5027). *(FAR 61.57)*
   If a pilot does not meet the recent night experience requirements, (s)he may not carry passengers during the period from 1 hr. after sunset to 1 hr. before sunrise. If sunset is 1900 CST, the latest that passengers may be carried is 1959 CST.
   Answer (A) is incorrect because, without recent night experience, a pilot may not carry passengers beginning 1 hr. after sunset, not at sunset. At sunset, the airplane must have lighted position lights. Answer (B) is incorrect because, without recent night experience, a pilot may not carry passengers beginning 1 hr. after, not before, sunset.

23.
5028. Prior to carrying passengers at night, the pilot in command must have accomplished the required takeoffs and landings in

A— any category aircraft.
B— the same category and class of aircraft to be used.
C— the same category, class, and type of aircraft (if a type rating is required).

Answer (C) is correct (5028). *(FAR 61.57)*
   No person may act as pilot in command of an aircraft carrying passengers at night unless that person has made at least three takeoffs and landings to a full stop within the preceding 90 days; that person was the sole manipulator of the controls; and the takeoffs and landings were performed in the same category, class, and type (if a type rating is required) of aircraft.
   Answer (A) is incorrect because the takeoffs and landings must be in the same category, class, and type (if a type rating is required) of aircraft, not just the same category. Answer (B) is incorrect because, if a type rating is required in a particular aircraft, then the takeoffs and landings must also be done in the same type of aircraft, not only the same category and class.

23a.
0601-35. No pilot may act as pilot in command of an aircraft under IFR or in weather conditions less than the minimums prescribed for VFR unless that pilot has, within the past 6 months, performed and logged under actual or simulated instrument conditions, at least

A— six instrument approaches, holding procedures, intercepting and tracking courses, or passed an instrument proficiency check in an aircraft that is appropriate to the aircraft category.
B— six instrument flights and six approaches.
C— three instrument approaches and logged 3 hours of instruments.

Answer (A) is correct (0601-35). *(FAR 61.57a)*
   No pilot may act as pilot in command when operating under IFR or in weather conditions less than the minimums prescribed for VFR unless (s)he has, within the past 6 months, logged instrument time under actual or simulated IFR conditions in the category of aircraft involved or in an appropriate flight simulator or flight training device and has performed at least six instrument approaches, holding procedures, and intercepting and tracking courses through the use of navigation systems. An alternative way to remain current is to pass an instrument proficiency check in the category of aircraft involved.
   Answer (B) is incorrect because only 6 approaches, not 6 instrument flights, are required, and holding procedures and intercepting and tracking courses must also be performed. Answer (C) is incorrect because 6, not 3, instrument approaches are required, and there is no instrument time requirement.

61.58 Pilot-in-Command Proficiency Check: Operation of Aircraft Requiring More than One Pilot Flight Crewmember

24.
5107. To serve as pilot in command of an airplane that is certified for more than one pilot crewmember, and operated under Part 91, a person must

A— complete a flight review within the preceding 24 calendar months.
B— receive and log ground and flight training from an authorized flight instructor.
C— complete a pilot-in-command proficiency check within the preceding 12 calendar months in an airplane that is type certificated for more than one pilot.

Answer (C) is correct (5107). *(FAR 61.58)*
   To serve as pilot in command of an aircraft that is type certificated for more than one required pilot flight crewmember and operated under Part 91, a person must have completed a pilot-in-command proficiency check within the preceding 12 calendar months in an airplane that is type certificated for more than one required pilot flight crewmember. Additionally, that person must also have completed a pilot-in-command proficiency check within the preceding 24 calendar months in the particular type of aircraft in which that person will serve as pilot in command.
   Answer (A) is incorrect because, to serve as pilot in command of an airplane that is certified for more than one pilot crewmember, a person must complete a pilot-in-command proficiency check in an appropriate airplane every 12 calendar months, which meets the flight review requirement. Answer (B) is incorrect because, to serve as pilot in command of an airplane that is certified for more than one pilot crewmember, a person must have completed a pilot proficiency check within the preceding 12 calendar months in an airplane that is type certificated for more than one pilot, not just receive and log ground and flight training from an authorized flight instructor.

61.60 Change of Address

25.
5032. Pilots who change their permanent mailing address and fail to notify the FAA Airmen Certification Branch of this change, are entitled to exercise the privileges of their pilot certificate for a period of

A— 30 days.
B— 60 days.
C— 90 days.

Answer (A) is correct (5032). *(FAR 61.60)*
    The holder of a pilot or flight instructor certificate who has made a change in his/her permanent mailing address may not, after 30 days from the date (s)he moved, exercise the privileges of the certificate unless (s)he has notified the FAA in writing.
    Note: While you must notify the FAA if your address changes, you are not required to carry a certificate that shows your current address. The FAA will not issue a new certificate upon receipt of your new address unless you also send a written request and a $2 fee.
    Answer (B) is incorrect because the FAA must be notified within 30, not 60, days of moving. Answer (C) is incorrect because the FAA must be notified within 30, not 90, days of moving.

61.69 Glider Towing: Experience and Training Requirements

26.
5034. To act as pilot in command of an airplane towing a glider, a pilot must have accomplished, within the preceding 12 months, at least

A— three actual glider tows under the supervision of a qualified tow pilot.
B— three actual or simulated glider tows while accompanied by a qualified tow pilot.
C— ten flights as pilot in command of an aircraft while towing a glider.

Answer (B) is correct (5034). *(FAR 61.69)*
    To act as pilot in command of an airplane towing a glider, a pilot must have accomplished, within the preceding 12 months, at least three actual or simulated glider tows while accompanied by a qualified tow pilot or must have made at least three flights as pilot in command of a glider towed by an aircraft.
    Answer (A) is incorrect because the glider tows may be actual or simulated and the pilot must be accompanied by, not just under the supervision of, a qualified tow pilot. Answer (C) is incorrect because 10 flights as pilot in command of an aircraft while towing a glider is a requirement for a person to be authorized to endorse the logbook of a pilot seeking glider-towing privileges. This does not meet the 12-month requirement of three actual or simulated glider tows while accompanied by another qualified tow pilot.

27.
5033. To act as pilot in command of an airplane towing a glider, the tow pilot is required to have

A— at least a private pilot certificate with a category rating for powered aircraft, and made and logged at least three flights as pilot or observer in a glider being towed by an airplane.
B— a logbook endorsement from an authorized glider instructor certifying receipt of ground and flight training in gliders, and be proficient with techniques and procedures for safe towing of gliders.
C— a logbook record of having made at least three flights as sole manipulator of the controls of a glider being towed by an airplane.

Answer (B) is correct (5033). *(FAR 61.69)*
    No person may act as a pilot in command of an aircraft towing a glider unless (s)he has a logbook endorsement in his/her pilot logbook from an authorized glider instructor certifying that (s)he has received ground and flight training in gliders and is proficient in the techniques and procedures essential for safe towing of gliders.
    Answer (A) is incorrect because, to act as pilot in command of an airplane towing a glider, the pilot must have logged at least three flights as the sole manipulator of the controls of an airplane towing a glider, not as a pilot or an observer in a glider being towed by an airplane. Answer (C) is incorrect because, to act as pilot in command of an airplane towing a glider, the tow pilot must have made at least three flights as pilot in command of a glider towed by an aircraft within the preceding 12 months, not just have logged three flights as sole manipulator of the controls of a glider towed by an airplane.

61.133 Commercial Pilot Privileges and Limitations

28.
5039. What limitation is imposed on a newly certificated commercial pilot-airplane, if that person does not hold an instrument rating? The carriage of passengers

A— or property for hire on cross-country flights at night is limited to a radius of 50 NM.
B— for hire on cross-country flights is limited to 50 NM for night flights, but not limited for day flights.
C— for hire on cross-country flights in excess of 50 NM, or for hire at night is prohibited.

Answer (C) is correct (5039). *(FAR 61.133)*
    If a commercial airplane pilot does not hold an instrument rating, his/her certificate will carry a limitation prohibiting the carriage of passengers for hire in airplanes on cross-country flights of more than 50 NM or at night.
    Answer (A) is incorrect because the carriage of property is not restricted. Answer (B) is incorrect because the carriage of passengers is prohibited at night and is limited to 50 NM during the day.

29.
5126a. A person with a Commercial Pilot certificate may act as pilot in command of an aircraft for compensation or hire, if that person

A— is qualified in accordance with 14 CFR part 61 and with the applicable parts that apply to the operation.
B— is qualified in accordance with 14 CFR part 61 and has passed a pilot competency check given by an authorized check pilot.
C— holds appropriate category, class ratings, and meets the recent flight experience requirements of 14 CFR part 61.

Answer (A) is correct (5126a). *(FAR 61.133)*
A person who holds a commercial pilot certificate may act as pilot in command of an airplane for compensation or hire, provided that person is qualified in accordance with FAR Part 61 and any other FAR Parts that apply to the operation.
Answer (B) is incorrect because a commercial pilot may act as pilot in command of an airplane operating for compensation or hire, if that person is qualified in accordance with Part 61 and any other FAR Parts that apply to the operation, not if that person passes a competency check given by an authorized check pilot.
Answer (C) is incorrect because a commercial pilot may act as pilot in command of an airplane operating for compensation or hire, if that person is qualified in accordance with Part 61 and any other FAR Parts that apply to the operation, not only if that person holds the appropriate category and class ratings and meets the recent flight experience requirements.

30.
5126b. A person with a commercial pilot certificate may act as pilot in command of an aircraft carrying persons or property for compensation or hire, if that person

A— holds appropriate category, class ratings, and meets the recent flight experience requirements of 14 CFR part 61.
B— is qualified in accordance with 14 CFR part 61 and with the applicable parts that apply to the operation.
C— is qualified in accordance with 14 CFR part 61 and has passed a pilot competency check given by an authorized check pilot.

Answer (B) is correct (5126b). *(FAR 61.133)*
A person who holds a commercial pilot certificate may act as pilot in command of an airplane carrying persons or property for compensation or hire, provided that person is qualified in accordance with FAR Part 61 and any other FAR Parts that apply to the operation.
Answer (A) is incorrect because a commercial pilot may act as pilot in command of an airplane carrying persons or property for compensation or hire, if that person is qualified in accordance with Part 61 and any other FAR Parts that apply to the operation, not only if that person holds appropriate category and class ratings and meets the recent flight experience. Answer (C) is incorrect because a commercial pilot may act as pilot in command of an airplane carrying persons or property for compensation or hire, if that person is qualified in accordance with Part 61 and any other FAR Parts that apply to the operation, not if that person passes a pilot competency check given by an authorized check pilot.

4.4 FAR PART 91
91.3 Responsibility and Authority of the Pilot in Command

31.
5044. What action must be taken when a pilot in command deviates from any rule in 14 CFR Part 91?

A— Upon landing, report the deviation to the nearest FAA Flight Standards District Office.
B— Advise ATC of the pilot in command's intentions.
C— Upon the request of the Administrator, send a written report of that deviation to the Administrator.

Answer (C) is correct (5044). *(FAR 91.3)*
If a pilot in command deviates from any rule in FAR Part 91 (due to an in-flight emergency requiring immediate action), (s)he must submit a written report to the Administrator (FAA), if requested.
Answer (A) is incorrect because the pilot in command must submit a written report of any rule deviation only when requested by the FAA, not upon landing.
Answer (B) is incorrect because the pilot in command must inform ATC of any deviation of an ATC clearance or instruction and should advise ATC of his/her intentions, even if no rule in FAR Part 91 was violated.

32.
5109. What person is directly responsible for the final authority as to the operation of the airplane?

A— Certificate holder.
B— Pilot in command.
C— Airplane owner/operator.

Answer (B) is correct (5109). *(FAR 91.3)*
The pilot in command of an airplane is directly responsible for, and is the final authority as to, the operation of that airplane.
Answer (A) is incorrect because the pilot in command, not the certificate holder, is directly responsible for, and is the final authority as to, the operation of that airplane.
Answer (C) is incorrect because the pilot in command, not the airplane owner or operator, is directly responsible for, and the final authority as to, the operation of that airplane.

91.7 Civil Aircraft Airworthiness

33.
5045. Who is responsible for determining if an aircraft is in condition for safe flight?

A— A certificated aircraft mechanic.
B— The pilot in command.
C— The owner or operator.

Answer (B) is correct (5045). *(FAR 91.7)*
     The pilot in command is directly responsible for determining whether the airplane is in condition for safe flight.
     Answer (A) is incorrect because the pilot in command, not a certificated aircraft mechanic, is responsible for determining if an airplane is in condition for safe flight. Answer (C) is incorrect because the pilot in command (who is considered the operator when piloting an airplane), not the owner, is directly responsible for determining if an airplane is in condition for safe flight.

91.9 Civil Aircraft Flight Manual, Marking, and Placard Requirements

34.
5046. When operating a U.S.-registered civil aircraft, which document is required by regulation to be available in the aircraft?

A— A manufacturer's Operations Manual.
B— A current, approved Airplane Flight Manual.
C— An Owner's Manual.

Answer (B) is correct (5046). *(FAR 91.9)*
     No person may operate a U.S.-registered civil aircraft unless there is available in the aircraft a current, approved Airplane Flight Manual.
     Answer (A) is incorrect because anyone operating a U.S.-registered civil aircraft is required by regulation to have available in the aircraft a current, approved Airplane Flight Manual, not a manufacturer's Operations Manual. Answer (C) is incorrect because anyone operating a U.S.-registered civil aircraft is required by regulation to have available in the aircraft a current, approved Airplane Flight Manual, not an Owner's Manual.

91.15 Dropping Objects

35.
5047. A pilot in command (PIC) of a civil aircraft may not allow any object to be dropped from that aircraft in flight

A— if it creates a hazard to persons and property.
B— unless the PIC has permission to drop any object over private property.
C— unless reasonable precautions are taken to avoid injury to property.

Answer (A) is correct (5047). *(FAR 91.15)*
     A pilot in command of a civil aircraft may not allow any object to be dropped from that aircraft in flight if it creates a hazard to persons or property. However, an object may be dropped from an aircraft if reasonable precautions are taken to avoid injury or damage to persons or property.
     Answer (B) is incorrect because an object may be dropped from an aircraft if reasonable precautions are taken to avoid injury or damage to persons or property. Permission from a property owner is not required. Answer (C) is incorrect because an object may be dropped from an aircraft if reasonable precautions are taken to avoid injury or damage to persons or property, not only damage to property.

91.21 Portable Electronic Devices

36.
5056a. Portable electronic devices which may cause interference with the navigation or communication system may not be operated on a U.S.-registered civil aircraft being flown

A— along Federal airways.
B— within the U.S.
C— in air carrier operations.

Answer (C) is correct (5056a). *(FAR 91.21)*
     Portable electronic devices which may cause interference with the navigation or communication system may not be operated on a U.S.-registered civil aircraft being flown in air carrier operations or other operations requiring an operating certificate, or on any aircraft while it is operated under IFR.
     Answer (A) is incorrect because portable electronic devices which may cause interference with the navigation or communication system may be operated on an aircraft being flown along Federal airways, as long as the aircraft is not an air carrier or an aircraft operating under IFR. Answer (B) is incorrect because portable electronic devices which may cause interference with the navigation or communication system may be operated within the U.S., as long as the aircraft is not an air carrier or an aircraft operating under IFR.

37.
5056b. Portable electronic devices which may cause interference with the navigation or communication system may not be operated on U.S.-registered civil aircraft being operated

A— under IFR.
B— in passenger carrying operations.
C— along Federal airways.

Answer (A) is correct (5056b). *(FAR 91.21)*
Portable electronic devices which may cause interference with the navigation or communication system may not be operated on a U.S.-registered civil aircraft being operated under IFR or an aircraft being operated under an air carrier operating certificate or other operating certificate.
Answer (B) is incorrect because portable electronic devices which may cause interference with the navigation or communication system may be operated on an aircraft in passenger-carrying operations, as long as the aircraft is not operated under an air carrier or other operating certificate or under IFR. Answer (C) is incorrect because portable electronic devices which may cause interference with the navigation or communication system may be operated on an aircraft operating along Federal airways, as long as the airplane is not operated under IFR.

91.23 Truth in Leasing Clause Requirement in Leases and Conditional Sales Contracts

38.
5071. No person may operate a large civil aircraft of U.S.-registry which is subject to a lease, unless the lessee has mailed a copy of the lease to the FAA Aircraft Registration Branch, Oklahoma City, OK, within how many hours of its execution?

A— 24.
B— 48.
C— 72.

Answer (A) is correct (5071). *(FAR 91.23)*
A copy of the lease or contract to a large civil aircraft must be mailed to the FAA within 24 hr. of its execution.
Answer (B) is incorrect because the lease must be mailed within 24 hr., not 48 hr. Answer (C) is incorrect because the lease must be mailed within 24 hr., not 72 hr.

91.103 Preflight Action

39.
5049a. When is preflight action required, relative to alternatives available, if the planned flight cannot be completed?

A— IFR flights only.
B— Any flight not in the vicinity of an airport.
C— Any flight conducted for hire or compensation.

Answer (B) is correct (5049a). *(FAR 91.103)*
Each pilot in command shall, before beginning a flight, familiarize him/herself with all available information concerning that flight. This information must include, for a flight under IFR or a flight not in the vicinity of an airport, weather reports and forecasts, fuel requirements, alternatives available if the planned flight cannot be completed, and any known traffic delays of which (s)he has been advised by ATC. For any flight, runway lengths at airports of intended use and certain takeoff and landing distance information should be obtained.
Answer (A) is incorrect because preflight action relative to alternate airports is required for all flights not in the vicinity of an airport, not just IFR flights. Answer (C) is incorrect because preflight action relative to alternate airports is required for all flights not in the vicinity of an airport, not just commercial flights.

40.
5049b. The required preflight action relative to weather reports and fuel requirements is applicable to

A— any flight conducted for compensation or hire.
B— any flight not in the vicinity of an airport.
C— IFR flights only.

Answer (B) is correct (5049b). *(FAR 91.103)*
A required preflight action by the pilot in command of a flight not in the vicinity of an airport or a flight under IFR is to become familiar with all available information concerning that flight, including weather reports and forecasts and fuel requirements. Additional preflight information for the flight includes alternatives available, runway length at airports of intended use, and takeoff and landing distance information.
Answer (A) is incorrect because preflight action relative to weather reports and fuel requirements is applicable to a flight under IFR or a flight not in the vicinity of an airport, not just any flight conducted for compensation or hire. Answer (C) is incorrect because preflight action relative to weather reports and fuel requirements is applicable to a flight under IFR or a flight not in the vicinity of an airport, not IFR flights only.

41.
5050a. Before beginning any flight under IFR, the pilot in command must become familiar with all available information concerning that flight. In addition, the pilot must

A— be familiar with all instrument approaches at the destination airport.
B— list an alternate airport on the flight plan, and confirm adequate takeoff and landing performance at the destination airport.
C— be familiar with the runway lengths at airports of intended use, and the alternatives available, if the flight cannot be completed.

Answer (C) is correct (5050a). *(FAR 91.103)*
Each pilot in command shall, before beginning a flight, familiarize him/herself with all available information concerning that flight. For a flight under IFR or a flight not in the vicinity of an airport, this information should include weather reports and forecasts, fuel requirements, alternatives available if the planned flight cannot be completed, and any known traffic delays of which (s)he has been advised by ATC. For any flight, the preflight information should include runway lengths at airports of intended use and takeoff and landing distance information.
Answer (A) is incorrect because IFR pilots should carry instrument approach charts for their destination airports and possible alternates. Answer (B) is incorrect because an alternate is not always required.

42.
5050b. Before beginning any flight under IFR, the pilot in command must become familiar with all available information concerning that flight. In addition, the pilot must

A— list an alternate airport on the flight plan, and confirm adequate takeoff and landing performance at the destination airport.
B— be familiar with all instrument approaches at the destination airport.
C— be familiar with the runway lengths at airports of intended use, weather reports, fuel requirements, and alternatives available, if the planned flight cannot be completed.

Answer (C) is correct (5050b). *(FAR 91.103)*
Before beginning any flight under IFR, the pilot in command must become familiar with all available information concerning the flight. This information must include the runway lengths at airports of intended use, weather reports and forecasts, alternatives available if the planned flight cannot be completed, and any known traffic delays that have been advised by ATC.
Answer (A) is incorrect because an alternate airport may not be required for the flight, based on the weather reports and forecast at the destination. Answer (B) is incorrect because, while the pilot in command should be familiar with the instrument approaches at the destination airport (especially if (s)he should expect to conduct an instrument approach), it is not a required preflight action for any flight under IFR.

91.105 Flight Crewmembers at Stations

43.
5051a. Required flight crewmembers' seatbelts must be fastened

A— only during takeoff and landing.
B— while the crewmembers are at their stations.
C— only during takeoff and landing when passengers are aboard the aircraft.

Answer (B) is correct (5051a). *(FAR 91.105)*
During takeoff and landing, and while en route, each required flight crewmember shall keep his/her seatbelt fastened while at his/her station.
Answer (A) is incorrect because crewmembers are required to keep their seatbelts fastened while at their stations, not only during takeoff and landing. Answer (C) is incorrect because crewmembers are required to keep their seatbelts fastened while at their stations, not only during takeoff and landing when passengers are aboard.

44.
5051b. Each required flight crewmember is required to keep his or her shoulder harness fastened

A— during takeoff and landing only when passengers are aboard the aircraft.
B— while the crewmembers are at their stations, unless he or she is unable to perform required duties.
C— during takeoff and landing, unless he or she is unable to perform required duties.

Answer (C) is correct (5051b). *(FAR 91.105)*
Each required flight crewmember is required to keep his/her shoulder harness fastened during takeoff or landing while at his/her assigned duty station, unless (s)he would be unable to perform required duties or the seat is not equipped with a shoulder harness.
Answer (A) is incorrect because a required flight crewmember is required to keep his/her shoulder harness fastened during takeoff and landing, regardless of whether or not passengers are aboard the airplane. Answer (B) is incorrect because each required flight crewmember is required to keep his/her shoulder harness fastened during takeoff and landing while at their stations, not all the time while at their stations.

91.107 Use of Safety Belts, Shoulder Harnesses, and Child Restraint Systems

45.
5052. With U.S.-registered civil airplanes, the use of safety belts is required during movement on the surface, takeoffs, and landings for

A— safe operating practice, but not required by regulations.
B— each person over 2 years of age on board.
C— commercial passenger operations only.

Answer (B) is correct (5052). *(FAR 91.107)*
Each person over 2 years of age on a U.S.-registered civil airplane must occupy an approved seat or berth with a safety belt and, if installed, shoulder harness properly secured about him/her during movement on the surface, takeoff, and landing.
Answer (A) is incorrect because, while the use of safety belts is a safe operating practice, it is also required by regulations during movement on the surface, takeoffs, and landings for each person over 2 years of age on board. Answer (C) is incorrect because the use of safety belts is required on all U.S.-registered civil airplanes, not only commercial passenger airplanes, during movement on the surface, takeoffs, and landings for each person over 2 years of age on board.

46.
5110a. Operating regulations for U.S.-registered civil airplanes require that during movement on the surface, takeoffs, and landings, a seat belt and shoulder harness (if installed) must be properly secured about each

A— flight crewmember only.
B— person on board.
C— flight and cabin crewmembers.

Answer (B) is correct (5110a). *(FAR 91.107)*
Each person on board a U.S.-registered civil airplane must occupy an approved seat or berth with a safety belt and, if installed, shoulder harness properly secured about him/her during movement on the surface, takeoffs, and landings.
Answer (A) is incorrect because each person on board, not only the flight crewmembers, must have a safety belt and, if installed, shoulder harness properly secured about him/her during movement on the surface, takeoffs, and landings. Answer (C) is incorrect because each person on board, not only the flight and cabin crewmembers, must have a safety belt and, if installed, a shoulder harness properly secured about him/her during movement on the surface, takeoffs, and landings.

91.109 Flight Instruction; Simulated Instrument Flight and Certain Flight Tests

47.
5111. No person may operate an aircraft in simulated instrument flight conditions unless the

A— other control seat is occupied by at least an appropriately rated commercial pilot.
B— pilot has filed an IFR flight plan and received an IFR clearance.
C— other control seat is occupied by a safety pilot, who holds at least a private pilot certificate and is appropriately rated.

Answer (C) is correct (5111). *(FAR 91.109)*
No person may operate an aircraft in simulated instrument flight conditions unless the other control seat is occupied by a safety pilot who possesses at least a private pilot certificate with category and class ratings appropriate to the aircraft being flown.
Answer (A) is incorrect because the safety pilot must hold at least a private, not commercial, pilot certificate with the category and class ratings appropriate to the aircraft being flown. Answer (B) is incorrect because there is no requirement that a person file an IFR flight plan and receive an IFR clearance to operate in simulated flight conditions. Normally, a person will be operating under VFR while operating in simulated instrument flight conditions.

91.111 Operating near Other Aircraft

48.
5073a. Which is true with respect to formation flights? Formation flights are

A— authorized when carrying passengers for hire, with prior arrangement with the pilot in command of each aircraft in the formation.
B— not authorized when visibilities are less than 3 SM.
C— not authorized when carrying passengers for hire.

Answer (C) is correct (5073a). *(FAR 91.111)*
No person may operate an aircraft carrying passengers for hire in formation flight.
Answer (A) is incorrect because formation flights are prohibited when carrying passengers for hire. Answer (B) is incorrect because formation flights are authorized when visibility is less than 3 SM.

49.
5073b. Which is true with respect to operating near other aircraft in flight? They are

A— not authorized, when operated so close to another aircraft they can create a collision hazard.
B— not authorized, unless the pilot in command of each aircraft is trained and found competent in formation.
C— authorized when carrying passengers for hire, with prior arrangement with the pilot in command of each aircraft in the formation.

50.
5073c. Which is true with respect to formation flights? Formation flights are

A— not authorized, except by arrangement with the pilot in command of each aircraft.
B— not authorized, unless the pilot in command of each aircraft is trained and found competent in formation.
C— authorized when carrying passengers for hire, with prior arrangement with the pilot in command of each aircraft in the formation.

91.113 Right-of-Way Rules: Except Water Operations

51.
5076c. Airplane A is overtaking airplane B. Which airplane has the right-of-way?

A— Airplane A; the pilot should alter course to the right to pass.
B— Airplane B; the pilot should expect to be passed on the right.
C— Airplane B; the pilot should expect to be passed on the left.

52.
5076d. An airplane is overtaking a helicopter. Which aircraft has the right-of-way?

A— Helicopter; the pilot should expected to be passed on the right.
B— Airplane; the airplane pilot should alter course to the left to pass.
C— Helicopter; the pilot should expect to be passed on the left.

53.
5075. Two aircraft of the same category are approaching an airport for the purpose of landing. The right-of-way belongs to the aircraft

A— at the higher altitude.
B— at the lower altitude, but the pilot shall not take advantage of this rule to cut in front of or to overtake the other aircraft.
C— that is more maneuverable, and that aircraft may, with caution, move in front of or overtake the other aircraft.

Answer (A) is correct (5073b). *(FAR 91.111)*
No person may operate an aircraft so close to another aircraft as to create a collision hazard.
Answer (B) is incorrect because formation flights are authorized when an arrangement is made with the pilot in command of each aircraft in the formation. There is no regulatory requirement for any type of training in formation flying. Answer (C) is incorrect because formation flight is not authorized when carrying passengers for hire.

Answer (A) is correct (5073c). *(FAR 91.111)*
Formation flights are not authorized, except by arrangement with the pilot in command of each aircraft in the formation.
Answer (B) is incorrect because formation flights are not authorized, except by arrangement with the pilot in command of each aircraft in the formation. There is no regulatory requirement for any specific training in formation flying. Answer (C) is incorrect because formation flights are not authorized when carrying passengers for hire.

Answer (B) is correct (5076c). *(FAR 91.113)*
Each aircraft that is being overtaken has the right-of-way, and each pilot of an overtaking aircraft shall alter course to the right to pass well clear.
Answer (A) is incorrect because the airplane being overtaken has the right-of-way. Answer (C) is incorrect because, when overtaking another aircraft, you pass to the right, not left.

Answer (A) is correct (5076d). *(FAR 91.113)*
Each aircraft that is being overtaken (the helicopter) has the right-of-way, and each pilot of an overtaking aircraft (the airplane) shall alter course to the right to pass well clear.
Answer (B) is incorrect because the helicopter has the right-of-way because it is being overtaken and the airplane should alter course to the right, not left, to pass well clear. Answer (C) is incorrect because the airplane should alter course to the right, not left, to pass well clear.

Answer (B) is correct (5075). *(FAR 91.113)*
When two or more aircraft are approaching an airport for the purpose of landing, the aircraft at the lower altitude has the right-of-way, but it shall not take advantage of this rule to cut in front of another that is on final approach to land, or to overtake that aircraft.
Answer (A) is incorrect because the right-of-way belongs to the aircraft at the lower, not higher, altitude. Answer (C) is incorrect because the right-of-way belongs to the aircraft at the lower altitude, not to the more maneuverable aircraft.

54.
5076a. During a night operation, the pilot of aircraft #1 sees only the green light of aircraft #2. If the aircraft are converging, which pilot has the right-of-way? The pilot of aircraft

A— #2; aircraft #2 is to the left of aircraft #1.
B— #2; aircraft #2 is to the right of aircraft #1.
C— #1; aircraft #1 is to the right of aircraft #2.

Answer (C) is correct (5076a). (FAR 91.113)
When aircraft of the same category are converging at approximately the same altitude (except head-on or nearly so), the aircraft to the other's right has the right-of-way. Since the green position light is on aircraft #2's right wing, aircraft #1 is to the right of aircraft #2 and thus has the right-of-way.
Answer (A) is incorrect because, when two aircraft are converging, the aircraft to the right, not left, has the right-of-way. Since aircraft #2 is to the left of aircraft #1, aircraft #1 has the right-of-way. Answer (B) is incorrect because the green position light is on the right wing of aircraft #2. Since aircraft #1 can see only the green position light, aircraft #1 is to the right, not left, of aircraft #2, and aircraft #1 has the right-of-way.

55.
5076b. A pilot flying a single-engine airplane observes a multiengine airplane approaching from the left. Which pilot should give way?

A— The pilot of the multiengine airplane should give way; the single-engine airplane is to its right.
B— The pilot of the single-engine airplane should give way; the other airplane is to the left.
C— Each pilot should alter course to the right.

Answer (A) is correct (5076b). (FAR 91.113)
When aircraft of the same category are converging at the same altitude (except head-on, or nearly so), the aircraft to the other's right has the right-of-way. Since the single-engine airplane is to the right of the multiengine airplane, the pilot of the multiengine airplane should give way to the single-engine airplane.
Answer (B) is incorrect because the airplane to the right, not left, has the right-of-way. Thus, the pilot of the multiengine airplane should give way to the single-engine airplane. Answer (C) is incorrect because each pilot should alter course to the right if the airplanes are approaching each other head-on, not converging.

56.
5074. While in flight a helicopter and an airplane are converging at a 90° angle, and the helicopter is located to the right of the airplane. Which aircraft has the right-of-way, and why?

A— The helicopter, because it is to the right of the airplane.
B— The helicopter, because helicopters have the right-of-way over airplanes.
C— The airplane, because airplanes have the right-of-way over helicopters.

Answer (A) is correct (5074). (FAR 91.113)
When aircraft are converging at approximately the same altitude, the aircraft to the other's right has the right-of-way. Since the helicopter is to the airplane's right, it has the right-of-way. Since helicopters and airplanes are considered equally maneuverable, neither has the right-of-way over the other.
Answer (B) is incorrect because helicopters do not have the right-of-way over airplanes. Answer (C) is incorrect because airplanes do not have the right-of-way over helicopters.

91.121 Altimeter Settings

57.
5114. What altimeter setting is required when operating an aircraft at 18,000 feet MSL?

A— Current reported altimeter setting of a station along the route.
B— 29.92" Hg.
C— Altimeter setting at the departure or destination airport.

Answer (B) is correct (5114). (FAR 91.121)
When operating an airplane at or above 18,000 ft. MSL, the altimeter should be set to 29.92 in. Hg.
Answer (A) is incorrect because the altimeter is set to the current reported altimeter setting of a station along the route when below 18,000 ft. MSL, not at or above 18,000 ft. MSL. Answer (C) is incorrect because the altimeter is set to 29.92 in. Hg when operating at or above 18,000 ft. MSL, not to the altimeter setting at the departure or destination airport.

91.123 Compliance with ATC Clearances and Instructions

58.
5115. After an ATC clearance has been obtained, a pilot may not deviate from that clearance, unless the pilot

A— requests an amended clearance.
B— is operating VFR on top.
C— receives an amended clearance or has an emergency.

Answer (C) is correct (5115). *(FAR 91.123)*
After an ATC clearance has been obtained, a pilot may not deviate from that clearance unless an amended clearance is obtained, an emergency exists, or the deviation is in response to a traffic alert and collision avoidance system (TCAS) resolution advisory.
Answer (A) is incorrect because a pilot may not deviate from an ATC clearance until an amended clearance has been received, not when the pilot requests an amended clearance. Answer (B) is incorrect because operating VFR-on-top is an IFR clearance; thus, a pilot may not deviate from VFR-on-top unless an amended clearance is received or an emergency exists.

91.144 Temporary Restriction on Flight Operations During Abnormally High Barometric Pressure Conditions

59.
5121. When weather information indicates that abnormally high barometric pressure exists, or will be above ___ inches of mercury, flight operations will not be authorized contrary to the requirements published in NOTAMs.

A— 31.00
B— 32.00
C— 30.50

Answer (A) is correct (5121). *(FAR 91.144)*
When weather information indicates that barometric pressure on the route of flight exceeds 31.00 in. of mercury, no person may operate an aircraft or initiate a flight contrary to the requirements published in NOTAMs.
Answer (B) is incorrect because flight operations will not be authorized contrary to the requirements published in NOTAMs when barometric pressure exceeds, or will exceed, 31.00 in., not 32.00 in., of mercury. Answer (C) is incorrect because flight operations will not be authorized contrary to the requirements published in NOTAMs when barometric pressure exceeds, or will exceed, 31.00 in., not 30.50 in., of mercury.

91.155 Basic VFR Weather Minimums

60.
5085. What is the minimum flight visibility and proximity to cloud requirements for VFR flight, at 6,500 feet MSL, in Class C, D, and E airspace?

A— 1 mile visibility; clear of clouds.
B— 3 miles visibility; 1,000 feet above and 500 feet below.
C— 5 miles visibility; 1,000 feet above and 1,000 feet below.

Answer (B) is correct (5085). *(FAR 91.155)*
At 6,500 ft. MSL in Class C, D, or E airspace, the basic VFR flight visibility requirement is 3 SM. The distance from clouds requirement is 500 ft. below, 1,000 ft. above, and 2,000 ft. horizontal.
Answer (A) is incorrect because 1 SM visibility and clear of clouds is the basic VFR weather minimums when at or below 1,200 ft. AGL (regardless of MSL altitude) in Class G airspace during the day, not at 6,500 ft. MSL in Class C, D, or E airspace. Answer (C) is incorrect because 5 SM visibility and a distance from clouds of 1,000 ft. above or below is the basic VFR weather minimums in Class E airspace at or above, not below, 10,000 ft. MSL.

61.
5083. The minimum flight visibility for VFR flight increases to 5 statute miles beginning at an altitude of

A— 14,500 feet MSL.
B— 10,000 feet MSL if above 1,200 feet AGL.
C— 10,000 feet MSL regardless of height above ground.

Answer (B) is the best answer (5083). *(FAR 91.155)*
The minimum flight visibility for VFR flight increases to 5 SM beginning at an altitude of 10,000 ft. MSL if above 1,200 ft. AGL in Class G airspace. In Class E airspace, the minimum flight visibility for VFR flight increases to 5 SM beginning at an altitude of 10,000 ft. MSL regardless of height above ground. Answer (B) is the best answer because it includes both Class E and Class G airspace.
Answer (A) is incorrect because 14,500 ft. MSL is not an altitude associated with basic VFR minimums. Answer (C) is incorrect because, while the minimum flight visibility for VFR flight increases to 5 SM at an altitude of 10,000 ft. MSL regardless of the height above ground for Class E airspace, it does not include that in Class G airspace. The minimum flight visibility increases to 5 SM when at 10,000 ft. MSL and above 1,200 ft. AGL.

Chapter 4: Federal Aviation Regulations

91.159 VFR Cruising Altitude or Flight Level

62.
5091. VFR cruising altitudes are required to be maintained when flying

A— at 3,000 feet or more AGL; based on true course.
B— more than 3,000 feet AGL; based on magnetic course.
C— at 3,000 feet or more above MSL; based on magnetic heading.

Answer (B) is correct (5091). *(FAR 91.159)*
    VFR cruising altitudes are prescribed for level flight above 3,000 ft. AGL and are based on magnetic course.
    Answer (A) is incorrect because VFR cruising altitudes are based upon magnetic (not true) course. Answer (C) is incorrect because VFR cruising altitudes apply for flight above 3,000 ft. AGL (not MSL) and are based on magnetic course (not heading).

91.167 Fuel Requirements for Flight in IFR Conditions

63.
5059. If weather conditions are such that it is required to designate an alternate airport on your IFR flight plan, you should plan to carry enough fuel to arrive at the first airport of intended landing, fly from that airport to the alternate airport, and fly thereafter for

A— 30 minutes at slow cruising speed.
B— 45 minutes at normal cruising speed.
C— 1 hour at normal cruising speed.

Answer (B) is correct (5059). *(FAR 91.167)*
    No person may operate a civil aircraft in IFR conditions unless it carries enough fuel (considering weather reports, forecasts, and conditions) to complete the flight to the first airport of intended landing; fly from that airport to the alternate airport; and fly after that for 45 min. at normal cruising speed.
    Answer (A) is incorrect because enough fuel must be carried to fly for 45 (not 30) min. at normal (not slow) cruising speed after reaching the alternate airport. Answer (C) is incorrect because enough fuel must be carried to fly for 45 min. (not 1 hr.) at normal cruising speed after reaching the alternate airport.

91.169 IFR Flight Plan: Information Required

64.
5123a. For an airport with an approved instrument approach procedure to be listed as an alternate airport on an IFR flight plan, the forecasted weather conditions at the time of arrival must be at or above the following weather minimums.

A— Ceiling 600 feet and visibility 2 NM for precision.
B— Ceiling 800 feet and visibility 2 SM for nonprecision.
C— Ceiling 800 feet and visibility 2 NM for nonprecision.

Answer (B) is correct (5123a). *(FAR 91.169)*
    For an airport with an approved instrument approach procedure to be listed as an alternate airport on an IFR flight plan, the forecasted weather conditions at the time of arrival for a nonprecision approach must be at or above a ceiling of 800 ft. and visibility of 2 SM.
    Answer (A) is incorrect because, for a precision approach, the weather minimums are a ceiling of 600 ft. and visibility of 2 SM, not 2 NM. Answer (C) is incorrect because, for a nonprecision approach, the weather minimums are a ceiling of 800 ft. and visibility of 2 SM, not 2 NM.

65.
5123b. For an airport without an approved instrument approach procedure to be listed as an alternate airport on an IFR flight plan, the forecasted weather conditions at the time of arrival must have at least a

A— ceiling of 2,000 feet and visibility 3 SM.
B— ceiling and visibility that allows for a descent, approach, and landing under basic VFR.
C— ceiling of 1,000 feet and visibility 3 NM.

Answer (B) is correct (5123b). *(FAR 91.169)*
    For an airport without an approved instrument approach procedure to be listed as an alternate airport on an IFR flight plan, the forecasted weather conditions at the time of arrival must have ceiling and visibility minimums that allow for descent from the MEA, approach, and landing under basic VFR.
    Answer (A) is incorrect because the weather minimums for an alternate airport without an approved instrument approach must allow for a descent from the MEA, approach, and landing under basic VFR, not a ceiling of 2,000 ft. and visibility of 3 SM. Answer (C) is incorrect because the weather minimums for an alternate airport without an approved instrument approach must allow for a descent from the MEA, approach, and landing under basic VFR, not a ceiling of 1,000 ft. and visibility of 3 SM.

91.171 VOR Equipment Check for IFR Operations

66.

5122a. When must an operational check on the aircraft VOR equipment be accomplished to operate under IFR? Within the preceding

A— 30 days or 30 hours of flight time.
B— 10 days or 10 hours of flight time.
C— 30 days.

Answer (C) is correct (5122a). *(FAR 91.171)*
To use the aircraft VOR equipment under IFR, the VOR equipment must have been operationally checked within the preceding 30 days.

Answer (A) is incorrect because, prior to operating under IFR, an operational check of the VOR must have been accomplished within the preceding 30 days, regardless of the flight time. Answer (B) is incorrect because, prior to operating under IFR, an operational check of the VOR must have been accomplished within the preceding 30 days, not 10 days, regardless of the flight time.

67.

5062. What is the maximum bearing error (+ or −) allowed for an operational VOR equipment check when using an FAA-approved ground test signal?

A— 4 degrees.
B— 6 degrees.
C— 8 degrees.

Answer (A) is correct (5062). *(FAR 91.171)*
When using an FAA-approved ground test signal (such as a VOT) for an operational VOR equipment check, the maximum allowable bearing error is ±4°.

Answer (B) is incorrect because ±6° is the permissible bearing error when using an airborne checkpoint, not a ground test signal. Answer (C) is incorrect because ±8° is not a permissible bearing error on VOR checks.

68.

5122b. Which data must be recorded in the aircraft logbook or other record by a pilot making a VOR operational check for IFR operations?

A— VOR name or identification, place of operational check, amount of bearing error, and date of check.
B— Date of check, place of operational check, bearing error, and signature.
C— VOR name or identification, amount of bearing error, date of check, and signature.

Answer (B) is correct (5122b). *(FAR 91.171)*
When you make a VOR operational check, you must enter the date of check, place of operational check, and bearing error, and sign the airplane logbook or other record.

Answer (A) is incorrect because, when you make a VOR operational check, you must enter in the airplane logbook or other record the date, place, and bearing error. The VOR name or identification is not required, but you must sign the airplane logbook or other record. Answer (C) is incorrect because, when you make a VOR operational check, you must enter in the airplane logbook or other record the date, bearing error, and your signature. Additionally, the place of the operational check, not the VOR name or identification, must be entered.

91.175 Takeoff and Landing under IFR

69.

5124b. On an instrument approach where a DH or MDA is applicable, the pilot may not operate below, or continue the approach unless the

A— aircraft is continuously in a position from which a descent to a normal landing, on the intended runway, can be made.
B— approach and runway lights are distinctly visible to the pilot.
C— flight visibility and ceiling are at, or above, the published minimums for that approach.

Answer (A) is correct (5124b). *(FAR 91.175)*
On an instrument approach when a DH or MDA is applicable, the pilot may not operate below the DH or MDA, or continue the approach, unless (among other items) the airplane is continuously in a position from which a descent to a landing on the intended runway can be made at a normal rate of descent using normal maneuvers.

Answer (B) is incorrect because, to operate below the DH or MDA, or to continue the approach, a pilot needs only to (among other requirements) maintain visual reference to either the approach lights or the runway lights, not both. Answer (C) is incorrect because a pilot may not operate below the DH or MDA, or continue the approach, unless the flight visibility, not the ceiling, is at or above the published minimums for that approach.

70.
5124a. Pilots are not authorized to land an aircraft from an instrument approach unless the

A— flight visibility is at, or exceeds, the visibility prescribed in the approach procedure being used.
B— flight visibility and ceiling are at, or exceed, the minimums prescribed in the approach being used.
C— visual approach slope indicator and runway references are distinctly visible to the pilot.

Answer (A) is correct (5124a). *(FAR 91.175)*
    Pilots are not authorized to land an airplane from an instrument approach unless the flight visibility is at, or exceeds, the visibility prescribed in the instrument approach procedure being used.
    Answer (B) is incorrect because a pilot may not land an airplane from an instrument approach unless the flight visibility, not the ceiling, is at, or exceeds, the visibility prescribed for that instrument approach. Answer (C) is incorrect because a pilot may not descend below the DH or MDA unless runway references or the VASI is available. To land, the flight visibility must be at, or must exceed, the visibility minimum prescribed in the instrument approach procedure being used.

71.
5124c. A pilot performing a published instrument approach is not authorized to perform a procedure turn when

A— receiving a radar vector to a final approach course or fix.
B— maneuvering at minimum safe altitudes.
C— maneuvering at radar vectoring altitudes.

Answer (A) is correct (5124c). *(FAR 91.175)*
    In the case of a radar vector to a final approach or fix, a timed approach from a holding fix, or an approach for which the procedure specifies "No PT," a pilot may not make a procedure turn unless cleared to do so by ATC.
    Answer (B) is incorrect because a pilot performing a published instrument approach is not authorized to perform a procedure turn when receiving a radar vector to a final approach course or fix, rather than when maneuvering at minimum safe altitudes. Answer (C) is incorrect because a pilot performing a published instrument approach is not authorized to perform a procedure turn when receiving a radar vector to a final approach course or fix, rather than when maneuvering at minimum radar vector altitudes.

91.177 Minimum Altitudes for IFR Operations

72.
5092. Except when necessary for takeoff or landing or unless otherwise authorized by the Administrator, the minimum altitude for IFR flight is

A— 2,000 feet over all terrain.
B— 3,000 feet over designated mountainous terrain; 2,000 feet over terrain elsewhere.
C— 2,000 feet above the highest obstacle over designated mountainous terrain; 1,000 feet above the highest obstacle over terrain elsewhere.

Answer (C) is correct (5092). *(FAR 91.177)*
    No one may operate an aircraft under IFR below the published minimum altitudes or, if none are prescribed, below an altitude of 2,000 ft. above the highest obstacle in a mountainous area or an altitude of 1,000 ft. above the highest obstacle over terrain elsewhere.
    Answer (A) is incorrect because 2,000 ft. is the minimum altitude for IFR operations over mountainous terrain; elsewhere the minimum altitude is 1,000 ft. Answer (B) is incorrect because the minimum altitude is 2,000 ft., not 3,000 ft., over mountainous terrain and 1,000 ft., not 2,000 ft., over terrain elsewhere.

91.183 IFR Radio Communications

73.
5125a. The pilot in command of an aircraft operated under IFR, in controlled airspace, not in radar contact, shall report by radio as soon as possible when

A— passing FL 180.
B— passing each designated reporting point, to include time and altitude.
C— changing control facilities.

Answer (B) is correct (5125a). *(FAR 91.183)*
    The pilot in command of an airplane operated under IFR in controlled airspace and not in radar contact shall report by radio as soon as possible the time and altitude of passing each designated reporting point.
    Answer (A) is incorrect because, when operating under IFR in controlled airspace and not in radar contact, the pilot must report passing each designated reporting point, not passing FL 180. Answer (C) is incorrect because, when operating under IFR in controlled airspace and not in radar contact, the pilot must report passing each designated reporting point, not changing control facilities. When changing control facilities, the pilot will check in with the new facility whether operating in radar contact or not.

91.187 Operation under IFR in Controlled Airspace: Malfunction Reports

74.
5125b. The pilot in command of an aircraft operated under IFR, in controlled airspace, shall report as soon as practical to ATC when

A— climbing or descending to assigned altitudes.
B— experiencing any malfunctions of navigational, approach, or communications equipment, occurring in flight.
C— requested to contact a new controlling facility.

Answer (B) is correct (5125b). *(FAR 91.187)*
    The pilot in command of an airplane operated under IFR in controlled airspace shall report as soon as practicable to ATC any malfunctions of navigational, approach, or communication equipment occurring in flight.
    Answer (A) is incorrect because a pilot should inform ATC that (s)he is climbing or descending to an assigned altitude only on initial contact with an ATC facility, not at all times. Answer (C) is incorrect because, as a general procedure (found in the *AIM*), the pilot should, not shall (i.e., must), acknowledge and select the new frequency as soon as possible and make the initial call as soon as practical.

91.205 Powered Civil Aircraft with Standard Category U.S. Airworthiness Certificates: Instrument and Equipment Requirements

75.
5066. Which is required equipment for powered aircraft during VFR night flights?

A— Flashlight with red lens, if the flight is for hire.
B— An electric landing light, if the flight is for hire.
C— Sensitive altimeter adjustable for barometric pressure.

Answer (B) is correct (5066). *(FAR 91.205)*
    For VFR flights at night, the required equipment includes one electric landing light if the aircraft is operated for hire.
    Answer (A) is incorrect because no specific requirement concerns flashlights and the color of the lens. Answer (C) is incorrect because sensitive altimeters are required only for IFR flight.

76.
5065. Which is required equipment for powered aircraft during VFR night flights?

A— Anticollision light system.
B— Gyroscopic direction indicator.
C— Gyroscopic bank-and-pitch indicator.

Answer (A) is correct (5065). *(FAR 91.205)*
    For VFR flight at night, the required instruments and equipment include an approved aviation red or aviation white anticollision light system on all U.S.-registered civil aircraft.
    Answer (B) is incorrect because a gyroscopic direction indicator is required for IFR, not VFR night, flight. Answer (C) is incorrect because a gyroscopic bank-and-pitch indicator is required for IFR, not VFR night, flight.

77.
5067b. Approved flotation gear, readily available to each occupant, is required on each airplane if it is being flown for hire over water,

A— in amphibious aircraft beyond 50 NM from shore.
B— beyond power-off gliding distance from shore.
C— more than 50 statute miles from shore.

Answer (B) is correct (5067b). *(FAR 91.205)*
    If an airplane is operated for hire over water and beyond power-off gliding distance from shore, approved flotation gear, readily available to each occupant, and at least one pyrotechnic signaling device are required.
    Answer (A) is incorrect because the flotation gear requirement applies to all aircraft operated for hire when flying beyond power-off gliding distance, not 50 NM, from shore. Answer (C) is incorrect because flotation gear is required for each occupant if the airplane is flown beyond the power-off gliding distance from shore, not more than 50 SM from shore.

77a.
0601-79. Approved flotation gear, readily available to each occupant, is required on each aircraft if it is being flown for hire over water,

A— in amphibious aircraft beyond 50 NM from shore.
B— more than 50 statute miles from shore.
C— beyond power-off gliding distance from shore.

Answer (C) is correct (0601-79). *(FAR 61.205)*
    If an aircraft is operated for hire over water and beyond power-off gliding distance from shore, approved flotation gear readily available to each occupant and at least one pyrotechnic signaling device are required.
    Answer (A) is incorrect because the 50 NM requirement applies to large and turbine-powered multi-engine airplanes. Answer (B) is incorrect because the requirement for hire on an aircraft is beyond power-off gliding distance from shore, not 50 statute miles from shore.

91.207 Emergency Locator Transmitters

78.
5070. The maximum cumulative time that an emergency locator transmitter may be operated before the rechargeable battery must be recharged is

A— 30 minutes.
B— 45 minutes.
C— 60 minutes.

Answer (C) is correct (5070). *(FAR 91.207)*
    ELT batteries must be replaced or recharged when the transmitter has been in use for more than 1 cumulative hr. or when 50% of their useful life (or useful life of charge) has expired.
    Answer (A) is incorrect because an ELT battery must be replaced or recharged after 1 hr. (not 30 min.) of cumulative use. Answer (B) is incorrect because an ELT battery must be replaced or recharged after 1 hr. (not 45 min.) of cumulative use.

91.209 Aircraft Lights

79.
5080a. If not equipped with required position lights, an aircraft must terminate flight

A— at sunset.
B— 30 minutes after sunset.
C— 1 hour after sunset.

Answer (A) is correct (5080a). *(FAR 91.209)*
   No person may, during the period from sunset to sunrise, operate an aircraft unless it has lighted position lights.
   Answer (B) is incorrect because position lights are required at, not 30 min. after, sunset. Answer (C) is incorrect because position lights are required at, not 1 hr. after, sunset.

80.
5080b. If an aircraft is not equipped with an electrical or anticollision light system, no person may operate that aircraft

A— after dark.
B— 1 hour after sunset.
C— after sunset to sunrise.

Answer (C) is correct (5080b). *(FAR 91.209)*
   If an aircraft is not equipped with an electrical or anticollision light system, you may not operate that aircraft during the period from sunset to sunrise.
   Answer (A) is incorrect because you may not operate an aircraft that is not equipped with an electrical or anticollision light system after sunset, not after dark. Answer (B) is incorrect because you may not operate an aircraft that is not equipped with an electrical or anticollision light system after sunset, not 1 hr. after sunset. The logging of night flight time begins 1 hr. after sunset.

91.211 Supplemental Oxygen

81.
5064. What are the oxygen requirements when operating at cabin pressure altitudes above 15,000 feet MSL?

A— Oxygen must be available for the flightcrew.
B— Oxygen is not required at any altitude in a balloon.
C— The flightcrew and passengers must be provided with supplemental oxygen.

Answer (C) is correct (5064). *(FAR 91.211)*
   No person may operate a civil aircraft of U.S. registry at cabin pressure altitudes above 15,000 ft. MSL unless each occupant of the aircraft is provided with supplemental oxygen.
   Answer (A) is incorrect because the flight crew must use oxygen (not just have it available) above 14,000 ft. MSL. Answer (B) is incorrect because each occupant, not only the flightcrew, must be provided with supplemental oxygen at cabin pressure altitudes above 15,000 ft. MSL.

82.
5063. In accordance with 14 CFR Part 91, supplemental oxygen must be used by the required minimum flightcrew for that time exceeding 30 minutes while at cabin pressure altitudes of

A— 10,500 feet MSL up to and including 12,500 feet MSL.
B— 12,000 feet MSL up to and including 18,000 feet MSL.
C— 12,500 feet MSL up to and including 14,000 feet MSL.

Answer (C) is correct (5063). *(FAR 91.211)*
   No one may operate a U.S. civil aircraft at cabin pressure altitudes above 12,500 ft. MSL up to and including 14,000 ft. MSL, unless the required minimum flight crew is provided with and uses supplemental oxygen for that part of the flight at those altitudes that is of more than 30 min. duration.
   Answer (A) is incorrect because supplemental oxygen is not required below 12,500 ft. MSL. Answer (B) is incorrect because supplemental oxygen is not required below 12,500 ft. MSL and is required at all times above 14,000 ft. MSL.

91.215 ATC Transponder and Altitude Reporting Equipment and Use

83.
5060. A coded transponder equipped with altitude reporting equipment is required for

A— Class A, Class B, and Class C airspace areas.
B— all airspace of the 48 contiguous U.S. and the District of Columbia at and above 10,000 feet MSL (including airspace at and below 2,500 feet above the surface).
C— both answer A and B.

Answer (A) is correct (5060). *(FAR 91.215)*
   An operable coded transponder with altitude reporting capability (i.e., Mode C) is required in Class A, Class B, and Class C airspace areas.
   Answer (B) is incorrect because an operable coded transponder equipped with altitude reporting capability is required in all airspace of the 48 contiguous U.S. and the District of Columbia at and above 10,000 ft. MSL excluding, not including, airspace at and below 2,500 ft. AGL. Answer (C) is incorrect because an operable coded transponder equipped with altitude reporting capability is required in all airspace of the 48 contiguous U.S. and the District of Columbia at and above 10,000 ft. MSL excluding, not including, airspace at and below 2,500 ft. AGL.

84.
5061. In the contiguous U.S., excluding the airspace at and below 2,500 feet AGL, an operable coded transponder equipped with Mode C capability is required in all airspace above

A— 10,000 feet MSL.
B— 12,500 feet MSL.
C— 14,500 feet MSL.

Answer (A) is correct (5061). *(FAR 91.215)*
An operable transponder with altitude reporting capability (i.e., Mode C) is required for all operations above 10,000 ft. MSL, excluding the airspace at and below 2,500 ft. AGL.
Answer (B) is incorrect because 12,500 ft. MSL is the altitude above which crewmembers are required to use oxygen after 30 min. in an unpressurized aircraft. Answer (C) is incorrect because 14,500 ft. MSL is the base of Class E airspace.

91.303 Aerobatic Flight

85.
5079. What is the minimum altitude and flight visibility required for acrobatic flight?

A— 1,500 feet AGL and 3 miles.
B— 2,000 feet MSL and 2 miles.
C— 3,000 feet AGL and 1 mile.

Answer (A) is correct (5079). *(FAR 91.303)*
No person may operate an aircraft in acrobatic flight below an altitude of 1,500 ft. AGL or with flight visibility of less than 3 SM.
Answer (B) is incorrect because the minimum altitude and visibility are 1,500 ft. AGL, not 2,000 ft. MSL, and 3 SM, not 2 SM. Answer (C) is incorrect because the minimum altitude and visibility are 1,500 ft. AGL, not 3,000 ft., AGL and 3 SM, not 1 SM.

91.311 Towing: Other Than under Sec. 91.309

86.
5055. Which is required to operate an aircraft towing an advertising banner?

A— Approval from ATC to operate in Class E airspace.
B— A certificate of waiver issued by the Administrator.
C— A safety link at each end of the towline which has a breaking strength not less than 80 percent of the aircraft's gross weight.

Answer (B) is correct (5055). *(FAR 91.311)*
No pilot of a civil aircraft may tow anything with that aircraft (other than a glider) except in accordance with the terms of a certificate of waiver issued by the Administrator of the FAA.
Answer (A) is incorrect because ATC approval for flight in Class E airspace is required only during IFR conditions. Answer (C) is incorrect because the breaking strength of the safety link applies to towing gliders, not banners.

91.313 Restricted Category Civil Aircraft: Operating Limitations

87.
5068b. Which is true with respect to operating limitations of a "restricted" category airplane?

A— A pilot of a "restricted" category airplane is required to hold a commercial pilot certificate.
B— A "restricted" category airplane is limited to an operating radius of 25 miles from its home base.
C— No person may operate a "restricted" category airplane carrying passengers or property for compensation or hire.

Answer (C) is correct (5068b). *(FAR 91.313)*
Persons or property cannot be transported for compensation or hire in a restricted category airplane.
Answer (A) is incorrect because, with respect to operating limitations of a restricted category airplane, there is no minimum pilot certification level. If the pilot is receiving compensation, then, due to that type of operation, a commercial pilot certificate may be required. Answer (B) is incorrect because, with respect to operating limitations of a restricted category airplane, there is no limitation as to how far from the airplane's home base it may be operated.

91.315 Limited Category Civil Aircraft: Operating Limitations

88.
5069. The carriage of passengers for hire by a commercial pilot is

A— not authorized in limited category aircraft.
B— not authorized in utility category airplane.
C— authorized in restricted category aircraft.

Answer (A) is correct (5069). *(FAR 91.315)*
Persons or property cannot be transported for compensation or hire in a limited category civil aircraft.
Answer (B) is incorrect because carriage of passengers for hire is permitted in utility category aircraft. Answer (C) is incorrect because carriage of passengers for hire is not permitted in restricted category aircraft.

91.319 Aircraft Having Experimental Certificates: Operating Limitations

89.
5129. No person may operate an aircraft that has an experimental airworthiness certificate

A— under instrument flight rules (IFR).
B— when carrying property for hire.
C— when carrying persons or property for hire.

Answer (C) is correct (5129). *(FAR 91.319)*
No person may operate an aircraft that has an experimental airworthiness certificate when carrying persons or property for hire.
Answer (A) is incorrect because, while an experimental aircraft is to be flown only VFR-day weather conditions, the FAA may specifically authorize IFR operations. Answer (B) is incorrect because no person may operate an aircraft that has an experimental certificate when carrying persons or property for hire, not only property.

91.325 Primary Category Aircraft: Operating Limitations

90.
5068c. Which is true with respect to operating limitations of a "primary" category airplane?

A— A "primary" category airplane is limited to a specified operating radius from its home base.
B— No person may operate a "primary" category airplane carrying passengers or property for compensation or hire.
C— A pilot of a "primary" category airplane must hold a commercial pilot certificate when carrying passengers for compensation or hire.

Answer (B) is correct (5068c). *(FAR 91.325)*
With respect to operating limitations of a primary category airplane, no person may operate a primary category airplane carrying persons or property for compensation or hire.
Answer (A) is incorrect because, with respect to operating limitations of a primary category airplane, there is no limitation as to how far from the airplane's home base it may be operated. Answer (C) is incorrect because, with respect to operating limitations of a primary category airplane, there is no minimum level of pilot certification required.

91.403 General

91.
5094. Assuring compliance with an Airworthiness Directive is the responsibility of the

A— pilot in command and the FAA certificated mechanic assigned to that aircraft.
B— pilot in command of that aircraft.
C— owner or operator of that aircraft.

Answer (C) is correct (5094). *(FAR 91.403)*
The owner or operator of an aircraft is primarily responsible for maintaining that aircraft in an airworthy condition, including compliance with all Airworthiness Directives. The term "operator" includes the pilot in command.
Answer (A) is incorrect because, although a mechanic will perform the maintenance required to comply with an Airworthiness Directive, assuring compliance is the responsibility of the owner or operator. Answer (B) is incorrect because the owner or operator, not only the pilot in command, is responsible for assuring compliance with all Airworthiness Directives.

92.
5093. Who is primarily responsible for maintaining an aircraft in an airworthy condition?

A— The lead mechanic responsible for that aircraft.
B— Pilot in command or operator.
C— Owner or operator of the aircraft.

Answer (C) is correct (5093). *(FAR 91.403)*
The owner or operator of an aircraft is primarily responsible for maintaining that aircraft in an airworthy condition. The term "operator" includes the pilot in command.
Answer (A) is incorrect because mechanics work at the direction of the owner or operator. Answer (B) is incorrect because the owner or operator, not only the operator, of an aircraft is primarily responsible for an aircraft's airworthiness. The term "operator" includes the pilot in command.

91.405 Maintenance Required

93.
5095. After an annual inspection has been completed and the aircraft has been returned to service, an appropriate notation should be made

A— on the airworthiness certificate.
B— in the aircraft maintenance records.
C— in the FAA-approved flight manual.

Answer (B) is correct (5095). *(FAR 91.405)*
   Each owner or operator shall ensure that maintenance personnel make appropriate entries in the aircraft maintenance records indicating that an annual inspection has been completed and that the aircraft has been approved for return to service.
   Answer (A) is incorrect because annual inspections are recorded in maintenance records, not on the Airworthiness Certificate. Answer (C) is incorrect because annual inspections are recorded in maintenance records, not in the flight manual.

94.
5096. A standard airworthiness certificate remains in effect as long as the aircraft receives

A— required maintenance and inspections.
B— an annual inspection.
C— an annual inspection and a 100-hour inspection prior to their expiration dates.

Answer (A) is correct (5096). *(FAR 91.405)*
   A standard airworthiness certificate remains in effect as long as the aircraft receives the required maintenance and inspections. This includes compliance with Airworthiness Directives, annual inspections, 100-hr. inspections, repairs between inspections, etc.
   Answer (B) is incorrect because a standard airworthiness certificate remains in effect as long as the aircraft receives the required maintenance and inspections. An annual inspection is just one part of the inspections and maintenance requirements, and some aircraft have an inspection program, which means an annual inspection is not required. Answer (C) is incorrect because a standard airworthiness certificate remains in effect as long as the aircraft receives the required maintenance and inspections. Not all aircraft require an annual and a 100-hr. inspection.

91.407 Operation after Maintenance, Preventive Maintenance, Rebuilding, or Alteration

95.
5097. If an aircraft's operation in flight was substantially affected by an alteration or repair, the aircraft documents must show that it was test flown and approved for return to service by an appropriately-rated pilot prior to being operated

A— under VFR or IFR rules.
B— with passengers aboard.
C— for compensation or hire.

Answer (B) is correct (5097). *(FAR 91.407)*
   No person may carry any person (other than crewmembers) in an altered aircraft that may have appreciably changed its flight characteristics or substantially affected its operation in flight until an appropriately rated pilot with at least a private pilot certificate flies the aircraft, makes an operational check of the maintenance performed or alteration made, and logs the flight in the aircraft records.
   Answer (A) is incorrect because an altered aircraft must be test flown before passengers are carried. A maintenance logbook entry by an appropriate maintenance person returns the aircraft to service, which allows the airplane to be flown under VFR or IFR. Answer (C) is incorrect because an altered aircraft must be test flown before passengers are carried regardless of whether the flight is for compensation or hire.

91.409 Inspections

96.
5100. Which is true concerning required maintenance inspections?

A— A 100-hour inspection may be substituted for an annual inspection.
B— An annual inspection may be substituted for a 100-hour inspection.
C— An annual inspection is required even if a progressive inspection system has been approved.

Answer (B) is correct (5100). *(FAR 91.409)*
   No person may operate an aircraft within the preceding 12 calendar months unless it has had an annual inspection. If the aircraft is required to have a 100-hr. inspection, an annual inspection may be substituted for a 100-hr. inspection.
   Answer (A) is incorrect because an annual inspection may be substituted for a 100-hr. inspection (not vice versa). Answer (C) is incorrect because an annual inspection is not required if a progressive inspection system has been approved.

97.
5099. An aircraft carrying passengers for hire has been on a schedule of inspection every 100 hours of time in service. Under which condition, if any, may that aircraft be operated beyond 100 hours without a new inspection?

A— The aircraft may be flown for any flight as long as the time in service has not exceeded 110 hours.
B— The aircraft may be dispatched for a flight of any duration as long as 100 hours has not been exceeded at the time it departs.
C— The 100-hour limitation may be exceeded by not more than 10 hours if necessary to reach a place at which the inspection can be done.

Answer (C) is correct (5099). *(FAR 91.409)*
The 100-hr. limitation may be exceeded by not more than 10 hr. if necessary to reach a place at which the inspection can be done. The excess time, however, is included in computing the next 100 hr. of time in service.
Answer (A) is incorrect because the 10-hr. leeway is applicable only if necessary to reach a place to perform the 100-hr. inspection. Answer (B) is incorrect because there is a 10-hr. leeway in excess of the 100-hr. limitation, and the 10-hr. leeway is applicable only if necessary to reach a place to perform the 100-hr. inspection.

91.413 ATC Transponder Tests and Inspections

98.
5105. If an ATC transponder installed in an aircraft has not been tested, inspected, and found to comply with regulations within a specified period, what is the limitation on its use?

A— Its use is not permitted.
B— It may be used when in Class G airspace.
C— It may be used for VFR flight only.

Answer (A) is correct (5105). *(FAR 91.413)*
No person may use an ATC transponder unless, within the preceding 24 calendar months, that ATC transponder has been tested and inspected and found to comply with the appropriate regulations.
Answer (B) is incorrect because there are no exceptions. Answer (C) is incorrect because there are no exceptions.

99.
5101. An ATC transponder is not to be used unless it has been tested, inspected, and found to comply with regulations within the preceding

A— 30 days.
B— 12 calendar months.
C— 24 calendar months.

Answer (C) is correct (5101). *(FAR 91.413)*
No person may use an ATC transponder unless, within the preceding 24 calendar months, that ATC transponder has been tested and inspected and found to comply with the appropriate regulations.
Answer (A) is incorrect because a VOR (not a transponder) must be checked every 30 days.
Answer (B) is incorrect because a transponder must be inspected every 24 (not 12) calendar months.

91.417 Maintenance Records

100.
5102. Aircraft maintenance records must include the current status of the

A— applicable airworthiness certificate.
B— life-limited parts of only the engine and airframe.
C— life-limited parts of each airframe, engine, propeller, rotor, and appliance.

Answer (C) is correct (5102). *(FAR 91.417)*
Each owner or operator must keep certain records for each airplane:

1. Records of maintenance, preventive maintenance, and alteration, and of the 100-hr., annual, progressive, and other required or approved inspections for each aircraft
2. Records containing total time in service of the airframe, each engine, and each propeller; current status of life-limited parts of each airframe, engine, propeller, rotor, and appliance; all items which are required to be overhauled on a specified time basis; the current inspection of the aircraft; airworthiness directives; and copies of forms prescribed for major alterations

Answer (A) is incorrect because airworthiness certificates are issued only at the time of manufacture. Answer (B) is incorrect because the current status of the life-limited parts of the propeller, rotor, and appliance is required as well.

101.
5098. Which is correct concerning preventive maintenance, when accomplished by a pilot?

A— A record of preventive maintenance is not required.
B— A record of preventive maintenance must be entered in the maintenance records.
C— Records of preventive maintenance must be entered in the FAA-approved flight manual.

Answer (B) is correct (5098). *(FAR 91.417)*
Each owner or operator must keep certain records for each airplane:

1. Records of maintenance, preventive maintenance, and alteration, and of the 100-hr., annual, progressive, and other required or approved inspections for each aircraft
2. Records containing total time in service of the airframe, each engine, and each propeller; current status of life-limited parts of each airframe, engine, propeller, rotor, and appliance; all items which are required to be overhauled on a specified time basis; the current inspection of the aircraft; airworthiness directives; and copies of forms prescribed for major alterations

Answer (A) is incorrect because preventive maintenance records are required. Answer (C) is incorrect because maintenance must be recorded in the maintenance records, not the flight manual.

102.
5103. Which is true relating to Airworthiness Directives (AD's)?

A— AD's are advisory in nature and are, generally, not addressed immediately.
B— Noncompliance with AD's renders an aircraft unairworthy.
C— Compliance with AD's is the responsibility of maintenance personnel.

Answer (B) is correct (5103). *(FAR 91.417)*
FAR 91.405 requires annual inspections with appropriate entries in the airplane maintenance records. FAR 91.417 requires that the current status of applicable Airworthiness Directives (ADs) and the method of compliance be specified. Noncompliance means the airplane is unairworthy and may not be flown.
Answer (A) is incorrect because ADs are regulatory in nature, i.e., mandatory. Answer (C) is incorrect because compliance with ADs as well as maintenance is the responsibility of the operator/owner, not maintenance personnel.

91.421 Rebuilt Engine Maintenance Records

103.
5104. A new maintenance record being used for an aircraft engine rebuilt by the manufacturer must include previous

A— operating hours of the engine.
B— annual inspections performed on the engine.
C— changes as required by Airworthiness Directives.

Answer (C) is correct (5104). *(FAR 91.421)*
Each manufacturer or agency that grants zero time to an engine rebuilt by it shall enter, in the new record, a signed statement of the date the engine was rebuilt; each change made as required by AD; and each change made in compliance with manufacturer's service bulletins, if the entry is specifically requested in that bulletin.
Answer (A) is incorrect because a rebuilt engine is considered to have zero operating hours. Answer (B) is incorrect because a record of previous inspections is not required on a rebuilt engine.

4.5 FAR PART 119
119.1 Applicability

103a.
1001-170. In what type of operation, not regulated by 14 CFR part 119, may a commercial pilot act as pilot in command and receive compensation for services?

A— Part-time contract pilot.
B— Nonstop flights within a 25 SM radius of an airport to carry persons for intentional parachute jumps.
C— Nonstop flights within a 25 SM radius of an airport to carry cargo only.

Answer (B) is correct (1001-170). *(FAR 119.1)*
14 CFR Part 119 regulates the certification of air carriers and commercial operators. FAR 119.1 lists several types of operations to which Part 119 does not apply, including nonstop flights within a 25 SM radius of an airport to carry persons for intentional parachute jumps.
Answer (A) is incorrect because Part 119 regulates the types of operations which need an operating certificate, not how a pilot is employed. A commercial pilot may act as PIC (and receive compensation for services) as a part-time contract pilot for any of the operations regulated or not regulated under Part 119, provided the pilot complies with all applicable regulations for those operations. Answer (C) is incorrect because operators conducting nonstop cargo-only flights within a 25 SM radius of an airport are regulated by Part 119.

103b.
1001-171. In what type of operation, not regulated by 14 CFR part 119, may a commercial pilot act as pilot in command and receive compensation for services?

A— Crop dusting, spraying, and bird chasing.
B— On-demand, nine or less passenger, charter flights.
C— On-demand cargo flights.

Answer (A) is correct (1001-171). *(FAR 119.1)*
FAR Part 119 regulates the certification of air carriers and commercial operators. FAR 119.1 lists several types of operations to which Part 119 does not apply, including crop dusting, seeding, spraying, and bird-chasing.
Answer (B) is incorrect because operators of on-demand charter flights are regulated by Part 119. Answer (C) is incorrect because operators of on-demand cargo flights are regulated by Part 119.

4.6 NTSB PART 830
830.2 Definitions

103c.
1001-11. What period of time must a person be hospitalized before an injury may be defined by the NTSB as a "serious injury"?

A— 10 days, with no other extenuating circumstances.
B— 48 hours; commencing within 7 days after date of the injury.
C— 72 hours; commencing within 10 days after date of the injury.

Answer (B) is correct (1001-11). *(NTSB 830.2)*
A serious injury is defined as an injury which: requires hospitalization for more than 48 hours, commencing within 7 days from the date of the injury; results in the fracture of any bone, other than simple fractures of the fingers, toes, or nose; causes severe hemorrhages, nerve, muscle, or tendon damage; involves any internal organ; or involves second- or third-degree burns, or any burns affecting more than 5 percent of the body surface.
Answer (A) is incorrect because, for an injury to be considered a serious injury on the basis of hospitalization, the injury must require hospitalization for more than 48 hours, not 10 days, commencing within 7 days from the date of the injury, not without other extenuating circumstances or requirements. Answer (C) is incorrect because, for an injury to be considered a serious injury on the basis of hospitalization, the injury must require hospitalization for more than 48 hours, not 72 hours, commencing within 7 days, not 10 days, from the date of the injury.

830.5 Immediate Notification

104.
5006. When should notification of an aircraft accident be made to the NTSB if there was substantial damage and no injuries?

A— Immediately.
B— Within 10 days.
C— Within 30 days.

Answer (A) is correct (5006). *(NTSB 830.5)*
An accident is an occurrence associated with the operation of an aircraft that takes place between the time any person boards the aircraft with the intention of flight and all such persons have disembarked, and in which any person suffers death or serious injury, or in which the aircraft receives substantial damage. The operator of an aircraft must immediately notify the nearest NTSB field office when an accident occurs.
Answer (B) is incorrect because 10 days is the time specified to file a detailed aircraft accident report with the NTSB. Answer (C) is incorrect because 30 days is not a deadline specified in NTSB Part 830.

105.
5002. NTSB Part 830 requires an immediate notification as a result of which incident?

A— Engine failure for any reason during flight.
B— Damage to the landing gear as a result of a hard landing.
C— Any required flight crewmember being unable to perform flight duties because of illness.

Answer (C) is correct (5002). *(NTSB 830.5)*
Immediate notification is required when an aircraft accident or any of the following listed incidents occurs: flight control system malfunction or failure; inability of any required flight crewmember to perform normal flight duties as a result of injury or illness; failure of structural components of a turbine engine excluding compressor and turbine blades and vanes; in-flight fire; or aircraft collision in flight. Immediate notice is also required when an aircraft is overdue and is believed to have been involved in an accident.
Answer (A) is incorrect because engine failure, in itself, is not considered "substantial damage" requiring immediate notification. Answer (B) is incorrect because damage to landing gear is not considered "substantial damage" requiring immediate notification.

106.
5003a. Which incident would require that the nearest NTSB field office be notified immediately?

A— In-flight fire.
B— Ground fire resulting in fire equipment dispatch.
C— Fire of the primary aircraft while in a hangar which results in damage to other property of more than $25,000.

107.
5003b. Which airborne incident would require that the nearest NTSB field office be notified immediately?

A— Cargo compartment door malfunction or failure.
B— Cabin door opened in-flight.
C— Flight control systems malfunction or failure.

108.
5004a. While taxiing for takeoff, a small fire burned the insulation from a transceiver wire. What action would be required to comply with NTSB Part 830?

A— No notification or report is required.
B— A report must be filed with the avionics inspector at the nearest FAA field office within 48 hours.
C— An immediate notification must be filed by the operator of the aircraft with the nearest NTSB field office.

109.
5004b. While taxiing on the parking ramp, the landing gear, wheel, and tire are damaged by striking ground equipment. What action would be required to comply with NTSB Part 830?

A— An immediate notification must be filed by the operator of the aircraft with the nearest NTSB field office.
B— A report must be filed with the nearest FAA field office within 7 days.
C— No notification or report is required.

Answer (A) is correct (5003a). *(NTSB 830.5)*
Immediate notification is required when an aircraft accident or any of the following listed incidents occurs: flight control system malfunction or failure; inability of any required flight crewmember to perform normal flight duties as a result of injury or illness; failure of structural components of a turbine engine excluding compressor and turbine blades and vanes; in-flight fire; or aircraft collision in flight. Immediate notice is also required when an aircraft is overdue and is believed to have been involved in an accident.
Answer (B) is incorrect because only in-flight incidents require immediate notification. Answer (C) is incorrect because only in-flight incidents require immediate notification.

Answer (C) is correct (5003b). *(NTSB 830.5)*
Immediate notification is required when an aircraft accident or any of the following listed incidents occurs: flight control system malfunction or failure; inability of any required flight crewmember to perform normal flight duties as a result of an injury or illness; failure of structural components of a turbine engine excluding compressor and turbine blades and vanes; in-flight fire; or aircraft collision in flight. Immediate notification is also required when an aircraft is overdue and believed to have been involved in an accident.
Answer (A) is incorrect because a flight control system, not a cargo compartment door, malfunction or failure requires immediate notification. Answer (B) is incorrect because a cabin door that comes open in flight is not considered an incident that requires immediate notification.

Answer (A) is correct (5004). *(NTSB 830.5)*
An in-flight fire is an incident that requires immediate notification. The minor fire described did not occur in flight, however. Moreover, it did not cause substantial damage and was thus not classifiable as an accident. No report or notification is required unless an accident or a specified incident has occurred or unless an aircraft is overdue and believed to have been in an accident.
Answer (B) is incorrect because an immediate report is required only if certain items occur such as an in-flight fire. Also, the reports are to go to the NTSB, not the FAA offices. Answer (C) is incorrect because an immediate report is required only if certain items occur such as an in-flight fire.

Answer (C) is correct (5004b). *(NTSB 830.5)*
No report or notification is required unless an accident or a specified incident has occurred or unless an aircraft is overdue and believed to have been in an accident. The described incident is not one specified that requires notification or a report, and it is not considered an accident under NTSB Part 830. One requirement of an accident is substantial damage. Under NTSB Part 830.2, damage to landing gear, wheels, and tires is not considered "substantial damage."
Answer (A) is incorrect because immediate notification is required only for accidents or certain incidents. Damage to the landing gear, wheel, and tire is not considered an accident or an incident that requires immediate notification under NTSB Part 830. Answer (B) is incorrect because no report is required to be filed under NTSB Part 830. Additionally, NTSB Part 830 deals with notification and reports to the NTSB only, not the FAA.

110.

5001. Notification to the NTSB is required when there has been substantial damage

A— which requires repairs to landing gear.
B— to an engine caused by engine failure in flight.
C— which adversely affects structural strength or flight characteristics.

Answer (C) is correct (5001). *(NTSB 830.5)*
An accident is an occurrence associated with the operation of an aircraft that takes place between the time any person boards the aircraft with the intention of flight and all such persons have disembarked, and in which any person suffers death or serious injury, or in which the aircraft receives substantial damage. Substantial damage means damage or failure that adversely affects the structural strength, performance, or flight characteristics of the aircraft and that would normally require major repair or replacement of the affected component. An accident causing substantial damage requires immediate notification to the NTSB.
Answer (A) is incorrect because damage to landing gear is not considered "substantial damage" requiring immediate notification. Answer (B) is incorrect because damage to an engine caused by engine failure is not considered "substantial damage" requiring immediate notification.

111.

5005. During flight a fire, which was extinguished, burned the insulation from a transceiver wire. What action is required by regulations?

A— No notification or report is required.
B— A report must be filed with the avionics inspector at the nearest FAA Flight Standards District Office within 48 hours.
C— An immediate notification by the operator of the aircraft to the nearest NTSB field office.

Answer (C) is correct (5005). *(NTSB 830.5)*
Immediate notification is required when an aircraft accident or any of the following listed incidents occurs: flight control system malfunction or failure; inability of any required flight crewmember to perform normal flight duties as a result of injury or illness; failure of structural components of a turbine engine excluding compressor and turbine blades and vanes; in-flight fire; or aircraft collision in flight. Immediate notice is also required when an aircraft is overdue and is believed to have been involved in an accident.
Answer (A) is incorrect because an in-flight fire (in contrast to an on-ground fire) does require immediate notification. Answer (B) is incorrect because no report to the avionics inspector is required.

830.15 Reports and Statements to Be Filed

112.

5008. How many days after an accident is a report required to be filed with the nearest NTSB field office?

A— 2.
B— 7.
C— 10.

Answer (C) is correct (5008). *(NTSB 830.15)*
The operator of an aircraft must file a report within 10 days after an accident, or after 7 days if an overdue aircraft is still missing. A report on an incident for which notification is required should be filed only as requested by an authorized representative of the NTSB.
Answer (A) is incorrect because 2 days is not a reporting requirement in NTSB Part 830. Answer (B) is incorrect because 7 days is the limitation with respect to an overdue aircraft that is missing.

113.

5007. The operator of an aircraft that has been involved in an incident is required to submit a report to the nearest field office of the NTSB

A— within 7 days.
B— within 10 days.
C— only if requested to do so.

Answer (C) is correct (5007). *(NTSB 830.15)*
The operator of an aircraft must file a report within 10 days after an accident, or after 7 days if an overdue aircraft is still missing. A report on an incident for which notification is required shall be filed only as requested by an authorized representative of the Board.
Answer (A) is incorrect because 7 days is the time limitation for reporting overdue (missing) aircraft. Answer (B) is incorrect because 10 days is the limitation on filing a report for accidents.

END OF CHAPTER

CHAPTER FIVE
AIRPLANE PERFORMANCE AND
WEIGHT AND BALANCE

This chapter contains outlines of major concepts tested, all FAA test questions and answers regarding airplane performance and weight and balance, and an explanation of each answer. Each module, or subtopic, within this chapter is listed above with the number of questions from the FAA pilot knowledge test pertaining to that particular module. For each module, the first number following the parentheses is the page number on which the outline begins, and the next number is the page number on which the questions begin.

CAUTION: Recall that the **sole purpose** of this book is to expedite your passing the FAA pilot knowledge test for the commercial pilot certificate. Accordingly, all extraneous material (i.e., topics or regulations not directly tested on the FAA pilot knowledge test) is omitted, even though much more information and knowledge are necessary to become a proficient commercial pilot. This additional material is presented in *Commercial Pilot Flight Maneuvers and Practical Test Prep* and *Pilot Handbook*, available from Gleim Publications, Inc. See the order form on page 284.

5.1 DENSITY ALTITUDE (Questions 1-3)

1. Density altitude is a measurement of the density of the air in terms of altitude on a standard day.

    a. Air density varies inversely with altitude and temperature, and directly with barometric pressure.

        1) Humidity also affects air density.

    b. The scale of air density to altitude was made using a constant (standard) temperature and barometric pressure.

        1) Standard temperature at sea level is 15°C.
        2) Standard pressure at sea level is 29.92" Hg.

    c. Pressure altitude is the height above the standard pressure plane.

        1) To determine pressure altitude, the altimeter is set to 29.92 and the altimeter indication is noted.

    d. Density altitude is pressure altitude corrected for nonstandard temperature.

2. The performance tables of an aircraft are based on pressure/density altitude.

    a. High density altitude reduces an airplane's performance.

        1) Climb performance is lower.

        2) Takeoff distance is longer.

        3) Propellers also have less efficiency because there is less air for the propeller to grip.

    b. However, the same indicated airspeed is used for takeoffs and landings regardless of altitude or air density because the airspeed indicator is also directly affected by air density.

5.2 DENSITY ALTITUDE COMPUTATIONS (Questions 4-7)

1. Density altitude is determined by finding the pressure altitude (indicated altitude when your altimeter is set to 29.92) and adjusting for the temperature.

    a. This adjustment is made using your flight computer or a density altitude chart. This part of the FAA knowledge test requires you to use your flight computer.

    b. On your flight computer, set the air temperature (°C) over the pressure altitude in the center right.

        1) In the adjacent density altitude window, read the density altitude.

    c. Note that humidity affects air density and aircraft performance slightly but is not taken into account on performance charts.

2. To convert °F to °C, you may use a conversion chart (on most flight computers) or calculate by using the formula:

$$°C = \frac{5}{9} \times (°F - 32)$$

3. EXAMPLE: Pressure altitude   12,000 ft.
             True air temperature   +50°F

From the conditions given, the approximate density altitude is 14,130 ft. This is determined as follows:

   a. Convert +50°F to °C by using the formula:

$$°C = \frac{5}{9} \times (°F - 32)$$

$$\text{Thus, } \frac{5}{9} \times (50 - 32) = +10°C$$

   b. Under the "True Airspeed and Density Altitude" window on your flight computer, put the pressure altitude of 12,000 ft. under the true air temperature of +10°C.

   c. In the window above ("Density Altitude"), read the density altitude above the index mark to be approximately 14,130 ft.

5.3 TAKEOFF DISTANCE (Questions 8-12)

1. Takeoff distance is displayed in the airplane operating manual in graph form or on a chart. The variables are

   a. Pressure altitude and temperature
   b. Airplane weight
   c. Headwind component

2. In either case, it is usually presented in terms of pressure altitude and temperature. Thus, one must first adjust the airport elevation for barometric pressure. Associated conditions are often listed in legends, e.g., paved runway, sloping runway, etc.

   a. An upslope runway increases takeoff distance.

3. In the graph used on this exam (see Figure 32 on page 123), the first section on the left uses outside air temperature and pressure altitude to obtain density altitude.

   a. The line labeled "ISA" is standard atmosphere, which you use when the question calls for standard temperature.

   b. The second section of the graph, to the right of the first reference line, takes the weight in pounds into account.

   c. The third section of the graph, to the right of the second reference line, takes the headwind into account.

4. EXAMPLE: Given an outside air temperature of 75°F, an airport pressure altitude of 4,000 ft., a takeoff weight of 3,100 lb., and a headwind component of 20 kt., find the ground roll.

   a. The solution to the example problem is marked with arrows on the graph. Move straight up from 75°F to the pressure altitude of 4,000 ft. and then horizontally to the right. From the first reference line (2,400 lb.), you must proceed up and to the right, parallel to the guide lines, to 3,100 lb. From that point, continue horizontally to the right to the second reference line. The headwind component of 20 kt. requires you to move down and to the right parallel to the guide lines to the 20-kt. point. Finally, moving horizontally to the right gives the total takeoff distance over a 50-ft. obstacle of 1,350 ft.

    b.   A note above the graph states that the ground roll is approximately 73% of the total takeoff distance over a 50-ft. obstacle. Thus, the ground roll is 986 ft. (1,350 x .73).

    c.   You may be asked the maximum weight that may be carried under specified conditions to meet a certain takeoff distance requirement.

       1)   To solve this, simply work backwards on the chart to find the maximum weight.

5.4 TIME, FUEL, AND DISTANCE TO CLIMB (Questions 13-22)

1.   Performance data concerning time, fuel, and distance to climb are often presented in operating handbooks for both normal conditions (Fig. 14 on page 126) and maximum rate of climb (Fig. 13 on page 125). The variables involved are

    a.   Airplane weight
    b.   Pressure altitude and temperature
    c.   Climb speed (indicated airspeed)
    d.   Rate of climb in ft. per min. (fpm)
    e.   Data from sea level

       1)   Time in minutes
       2)   Pounds of fuel used
       3)   Distance in nautical miles

2.   See Fig. 13 on page 125.

    a.   EXAMPLE: At 4,000 lb., to climb from sea level to a pressure altitude of 8,000 ft., the indicated climb speed is 100 kt., and the average rate of climb is 845 fpm, requiring 9 min. using 24 lb. of fuel and covering a distance of 16 NM.

       1)   Note that, frequently, one starts at a pressure altitude other than sea level, so the computation must be done twice, and the difference is the time, fuel, and distance to climb. For example, if you depart with a pressure altitude of 4,000 ft. and are going to cruise at a pressure altitude of 8,000 ft., you must compute the values for both and then subtract the values at 4,000 ft. from those at 8,000 ft. to determine the time, fuel, and distance for climbing from a pressure altitude of 4,000 ft. to 8,000 ft.

    b.   Adjust for differences from standard temperature, if necessary.

       1)   Recall that the formula for computing standard temperature at altitude is 15°C − (N x 2°C), where N is the altitude divided by 1,000.

       2)   EXAMPLE: At 8,000 ft. MSL, standard temperature is −1°C [15 − (8 x 2)].

    c.   Note 1 states that you must add 16 lb. of fuel for engine start, taxi, and takeoff allowance.

    d.   You may need to interpolate to find the values for an altitude that is not specifically shown in the table.

3.   As an alternate to a table, the fuel, time, and distance to climb may be presented in graph form, as in Fig. 15 on page 128. The same variables are involved.

    a.   Note the example on Fig. 15 for computing fuel, time, and distance for departing an airport with a pressure altitude of 1,400 ft. with an OAT of 15°C to a cruise pressure altitude of 12,000 ft. that has an OAT of 0°C.

       1)   Here again, note that the solution is the difference between calculations at the airport elevation and at the desired cruise altitude.

5.5 MAXIMUM RATE OF CLIMB (Questions 23-24)

1. The rate of climb for maximum climb is dependent upon

    a. Pressure altitude and temperature
    b. Airplane weight
    c. Use of the best rate of climb speed

2. The maximum rate of climb can be presented in a table such as Fig. 33, page 134.

    a. EXAMPLE: At 3,700 lb., the rate of climb at an 8,000-ft. pressure altitude at +20°C is 815 fpm.

    b. You may need to interpolate to find the value for an altitude that is not specifically shown in the table.

5.6 CRUISE AND RANGE PERFORMANCE (Questions 25-39)

1. Cruise performance is based upon the pressure altitude and temperature, the manifold pressure, and the engine RPM setting.

2. Given these variables, charts provide the following information:

    a. The percentage of brake horsepower (%BHP)
    b. True airspeed (TAS)
    c. Pounds of fuel per hour (PPH) or gallons of fuel per hour (GPH)

3. Also used is a cruise and range performance chart, as in Fig. 11 on page 136.

    a. Note that the range assumes a zero wind component.

    b. Note each of the nine columns in the chart (Fig. 11).

    c. Given altitude and RPM in the first two columns, the last seven columns are the results.

    d. EXAMPLE: At a gross weight of 2,300 lb., 5,000 ft. pressure altitude, and 2300 RPM, you are operating at 55% power and will achieve a true airspeed of 108 mph, burn 6.5 GPH, and have a range with a 38-gal. tank of 5.9 hr., or 635 SM.

4. See the cruise performance chart, Fig. 12, on page 138.

    a. Note each of the columns in the chart.

    b. Given the pressure altitude of 18,000 ft. and the manifold pressure (MP) and RPM, the last nine columns are the results.

    c. EXAMPLE: At 2500 RPM, 28" MP, −41°C, you are using 80% power, will achieve a true airspeed of 184 kt., and will burn 105 PPH.

        1) If you have 315 lb. of usable fuel on board, you have a total available flight time of 3 hr. (315 ÷ 105).

        2) Allowing for day-VFR reserve, your maximum endurance is 2 hr. 30 min. (3 hr. − 30 min.).

5. Finally, a fuel consumption versus brake horsepower graph is sometimes available. It relates the fuel flow in GPH (vertical scale) to brake horsepower (horizontal scale) based upon various power settings at various altitudes, as illustrated in Fig. 8 on page 142.

   a. EXAMPLE: If you want to determine the amount of fuel consumed when climbing at 75% power for 10 min., find the intersection of the takeoff and climb curve with the 75% brake horsepower line, and from that intersection proceed horizontally to the left to the margin to read a fuel flow of 18.3 GPH.

     1) Since 10 min. is 1/6 hr., divide 18.3 by 6 to determine the amount consumed in 10 min.

6. As gross weight decreases, maximum range airspeed decreases.

5.7 CROSSWIND/HEADWIND COMPONENT (Questions 40-43)

1. Many airplanes have an upper limit as to the amount of direct crosswind in which they can land. Crosswinds of less than 90° (i.e., direct) can be converted into a 90° component by the use of charts. Variables on the crosswind component charts are

   a. Angle between wind and runway
   b. Knots of total wind velocity

2. The variables are plotted on the graph; tracing the coordinates to the vertical and horizontal axes indicates the headwind and crosswind components of a quartering headwind.

3. An example crosswind component chart appears below.

a.   Note the example on the chart of a 40-kt. wind at a 30° angle.

b.   Find the 30° wind angle line. This is the angle between the wind direction and runway direction, e.g., runway 16 and wind from 190°.

c.   Find the 40-kt. wind velocity arc. Note the intersection of the wind arc and the 30° angle line (point B).

d.   Drop straight down from point B to determine the crosswind component of 20 kt.; i.e., landing in this situation is like having a direct crosswind of 20 kt.

e.   Move horizontally to the left from point B to determine the headwind component of 35 kt.; i.e., landing in this situation is like having a headwind component of 35 kt.

f.   Note whether you are being asked for the headwind or the crosswind component.

4.   An airplane's crosswind capability may be expressed in terms of a fraction of its V_{S0}.

a.   EXAMPLE: Given a .2 V_{S0} crosswind capability and V_{S0} of 65 kt., the crosswind capability is 13 kt. (65 x .2).

5.8 LANDING DISTANCE (Questions 44-47)

1.   Required landing distances differ at various altitudes and temperatures due to changes in air density.

a.   However, indicated airspeed for landing is the same at all altitudes.

2.   Landing distance information is given in airplane operating manuals in chart or graph form to adjust for headwind, temperature, and dry grass runways.

3.   You must distinguish between the distance for clearing a 50-ft. obstacle and the distance without a 50-ft. obstacle at the beginning of the runway (the latter is described as the ground roll).

4.   A landing distance graph is used on this exam (see Fig. 35 on page 146).

a.   The first section on the left uses outside air temperature and pressure altitude to obtain density altitude.

b.   The second section of the graph, to the right of the first reference line, takes the weight in pounds into account.

c.   The third section of the graph, to the right of the second reference line, takes the headwind into account.

d.   A note above the graph states that the ground roll is approximately 53% of the total landing distance over a 50-ft. obstacle.

e.   EXAMPLE: Given an outside air temperature of 75°F, a pressure altitude of 4,000 ft., a landing weight of 3,200 lb., and a headwind component of 10 kt., find the ground roll for landing.

1)   The solution to the example problem is marked with the dotted arrows on the graph. Move straight up from 75°F to the pressure altitude of 4,000 ft. and then horizontally to the right. Then move up and to the right, parallel to the guide lines, to 3,200 lb. and then horizontally to the next reference line. Continuing to the right, the headwind component of 10 kt. means moving down and to the right (parallel to the guide lines to 10 kt.). Finally, moving to the right horizontally gives the total landing distance over a 50-ft. obstacle of 1,475 ft. Ground roll is 53% of this amount, or 782 ft. (1,475 x .53).

5.9 WEIGHT AND BALANCE (Questions 48-51)

1. Empty weight consists of the airframe, the engine, and all installed optional equipment, including fixed ballast, unusable fuel, full operating fluids, and full oil.

2. The center of gravity (CG) by definition is total moments divided by total weight.

    a. Total moment is the position of weight (measured in index units) from some fixed point (called the datum) times that weight.

3. If all index units (arms) are positive when computing weight and balance, the location of the datum is at the nose or out in front of the airplane.

5.10 WEIGHT AND MOMENT COMPUTATIONS (Questions 52-59)

1. Airplanes must be loaded in a manner such that the CG is in front of the center of lift. This placement provides airplane stability about the lateral axis (for pitch).

2. The CG is a point of balance in an airplane determined in relation to the weight of objects put into the airplane times their distance from a specified point in the airplane (either positive or negative). This distance is called the arm. The CG determination can be made by calculation or by chart.

3. The basic formula for weight and balance is

    $$\text{Weight} \times \text{Arm} = \text{Moment}$$

    a. Arm is the distance from the datum (a fixed position on the longitudinal axis of the airplane).

    b. The weight/arm/moment calculation computes the location of the CG.

        1) Multiply the weight of each item loaded into the airplane by its arm (distance from datum) to determine "moment."

        2) Add moments.

        3) Divide total weight into total moments to obtain CG (expressed in distance from the datum).

    c. EXAMPLE: You have placed items A, B, and C into the airplane. Note that the airplane's empty weight is given as 1,500 lb. with a 20-in. arm.

	Weight		Arm		Moment
Empty airplane	1,500	×	20	=	30,000
A (pilot and passenger?)	300	×	25	=	7,500
B (25 gal. of fuel?)	150	×	30	=	4,500
C (baggage?)	100	×	40	=	4,000
	2,050				46,000

    The total loaded weight of the airplane is 2,050 lb. Divide the total moments of 46,000 in.-lb. by the total weight of 2,050 lb. to obtain the CG of 22.44 in. Then check to see whether the weight and the CG are within allowable limits.

4. Some manufacturers provide a loading graph (see Fig. 38 on page 150) that is used to plot weight vs. moment of various items. The graph can save you the steps of multiplying and dividing to obtain moments and CG.

    a. The load weight in pounds is listed on the left side. Using Fig. 38 on page 150, move horizontally to the right across the chart from the amount of weight to intersect the line indicating where the weight is located; e.g., different diagonal lines usually exist for fuel, baggage, pilot and front seat passengers, and center seat and back seat passengers.

b. From the point of intersection of the weight with the appropriate diagonal line, drop straight down to the bottom of the chart where the moments are located.

1) Note that you may have to estimate some moments when it is not clear exactly where the diagonal line intersects. For instance, the pilot and copilot diagonal at 300 lb. on Fig. 38 intersects somewhere between 27.0 and 28.0 in.-lb. of moment. Do not let this worry you, as using 27.0 in.-lb. will be close enough.

c. Total the weights and moments.

d. EXAMPLE: Determine the center of gravity moment/1,000 in.-lb. given the following situation. The "/1,000" reduces the number to manageable proportions by eliminating a lot of zeros. First, set up a schedule of what you are given and what you must find (see below).

	Weight (lb.)	Moment/1000 in.-lb.
Empty weight	1,271	102.04
Pilot and copilot	340	?
Rear-seat passengers	140	?
Cargo	60	?
Fuel (25 gal. × 6 lb./gal.)	150	?

1) Compute the moment of the pilot and copilot by referring to the loading graph (Fig. 38, page 150). Locate 340 lb. on the weight scale. Move horizontally across the graph to intersect the diagonal line representing the pilot and front passenger. Then move vertically to the bottom scale, which indicates a moment of approximately 31.0 in.-lb.

2) Locate 140 lb. on the weight scale for the rear-seat passengers. Move horizontally across the graph to intersect the diagonal line that represents rear-seat passengers. Then move down vertically to the bottom scale, which indicates a moment of approximately 18.0 in.-lb.

3) Use the graph in the same manner to locate moments for cargo and fuel.

4) Now add the weights and the moments.

	Weight (lb.)	Moment/1000 in.-lb.
Empty weight	1,271	102.04
Pilot and copilot	340	31.0
Rear-seat passengers	140	18.0
Cargo	60	7.0
Fuel (25 gal. × 6 lb./gal.)	150	13.5
	1,961	171.54

5) Use the center-of-gravity envelope graph to see whether the total weight and the CG are within acceptable limits.

6) Find the total weight of 1,961 lb. on the weight scale (left margin) and draw a horizonal line from it across the graph.

7) Find the total moment of 171.54 in.-lb. on the moment scale (bottom of graph) and draw a vertical line from it up the graph.

8) Because the lines intersect inside the normal-category envelope, the airplane is loaded within acceptable limits for normal-category operations.

5.11 WEIGHT CHANGE AND WEIGHT SHIFT COMPUTATIONS (Questions 60-63)

1. Author's note: The following is an effective, intuitively appealing handout used by Dr. Melville R. Byington at Embry-Riddle Aeronautical University (used with permission).

   a. **Background** -- Center of gravity shift problems can be intimidating when an organized approach is not followed. If one goes to the usual texts for assistance, the result is often either

      1) "Just plug this/these formulas" (without adequate rationale), or
      2) Follow a set of (up to six) formulas to solve the problems, or
      3) Follow a tabular approach, which is often lengthy and tedious.

   b. **Basic theory** -- The foregoing "methods" obscure what can and should be a logical, straightforward approach. The standard question is, **"If the CG started out there, and certain changes occurred, where is it now?"** It can be answered directly using a SINGLE, UNIVERSAL, UNCOMPLICATED FORMULA.

      1) At **any** time, the CG is simply the sum of all moments (ΣM) divided by the sum of all weights (ΣW).

      $$CG = \frac{\Sigma M}{\Sigma W}$$

      2) Since CG was known at some previous (#1) loading condition (with moment = M_1 and weight = W_1), it is logical that this become the point of departure. Due to weight addition, removal, or shift, the moment has changed by some amount, ΔM. The total weight has also changed **if**, and only if, weight has been added or removed. Therefore, the current CG is merely the current total moment divided by the current total weight. In equation format,

      $$CG = \text{Current Moment/Current Weight} \quad \text{becomes} \quad CG = \frac{M_1 \pm \Delta M}{W_1 \pm \Delta W}$$

   c. **Application** -- This UNIVERSAL FORMULA will accommodate ANY CG SHIFT PROBLEM! Before proceeding, certain conventions deserve review:

      1) Any weight added causes a + moment change (Weight removed is –).
      2) Weight **shifted** rearward causes a + moment change (Forward is –).
      3) A weight **shift** changes only the moment ($\Delta W = 0$).

   d. **Example 1** -- An airplane takes off at 3,000 lb. with CG at station 60. Since takeoff 25 gal. (150 lb.) of fuel has been consumed. Fuel cell CG is station 65. Find the new CG.

   $$CG = \frac{M_1 \pm \Delta M}{W_1 \pm \Delta W} = \frac{(3,000 \times 60) - (150 \times 65)}{3,000 - 150} = 59.74 \text{ in.}$$

   e. **Example 2** -- An airplane has a gross weight of 10,000 lb. 500 lb. of cargo is shifted 50″. How far does the CG shift? (Note original CG and direction of shift are unspecified. Since datum is undefined, why not define it, temporarily, as the initial CG location, even though it is unknown? This causes M_1 to become zero! Incidentally, the **direction** of CG shift corresponds precisely to the **direction** of the weight shift.)

   $$CG = \frac{M_1 \pm \Delta M}{W_1 \pm \Delta W} = \frac{500 \times 50}{10,000} = 2.5″$$

QUESTIONS AND ANSWER EXPLANATIONS

All the FAA questions from the pilot knowledge test for the commercial pilot certificate relating to airplane performance and weight and balance and the material outlined previously are reproduced on the following pages in the same modules as the outlines. To the immediate right of each question are the correct answer and answer explanation. You should cover these answers and answer explanations while responding to the questions. (A bookmark for this purpose has been provided in the back of the book.) Refer to the general discussion in the Introduction on how to take the FAA pilot knowledge test.

Remember that the questions from the FAA pilot knowledge test bank have been reordered by topic, and the topics have been organized into a meaningful sequence. Accordingly, the first line of the answer explanation gives the FAA question number and the citation of the authoritative source for the answer.

5.1 Density Altitude

1.
5234. The performance tables of an aircraft for takeoff and climb are based on

A— pressure/density altitude.
B— cabin altitude.
C— true altitude.

Answer (A) is correct (5234). *(FTH Chap 17)*
Performance tables of an aircraft for takeoff climb, cruise, and landing are based on pressure and/or density altitude. They are an index to the efficiency of airplane performance at various air densities. Pressure altitude is the indicated altitude when the altimeter is set to 29.92 (the standard datum plane). Density altitude is pressure altitude adjusted for nonstandard temperature.
Answer (B) is incorrect because cabin altitude is the altitude that corresponds to the pressure within the cabin of a pressurized airplane. Answer (C) is incorrect because true altitude is the height above sea level. Airport, terrain, and obstacle elevations found on aeronautical charts are true altitudes.

2.
5740. To determine pressure altitude prior to takeoff, the altimeter should be set to

A— the current altimeter setting.
B— 29.92" Hg and the altimeter indication noted.
C— the field elevation and the pressure reading in the altimeter setting window noted.

Answer (B) is correct (5740). *(FTH Chap 17)*
Pressure altitude can be determined by either of two methods: (1) Set the barometric scale of the altimeter to 29.92 and read the indicated altitude, or (2) apply a correction factor to the airport elevation according to the reported altimeter setting.
Answer (A) is incorrect because, with the current altimeter setting in the altimeter, the altimeter should indicate the airport elevation (i.e., true altitude), not pressure altitude. Answer (C) is incorrect because the pressure reading in the altimeter setting window should be the current altimeter setting, which should indicate the airport elevation (i.e., true, not pressure, altitude).

3.

5208. At higher elevation airports the pilot should know that indicated airspeed

A— will be unchanged, but groundspeed will be faster.
B— will be higher, but groundspeed will be unchanged.
C— should be increased to compensate for the thinner air.

Answer (A) is correct (5208). *(FTH Chap 17)*
   If an airplane of given weight and configuration is operated at greater heights above standard sea level, the airplane will still require the same dynamic pressure to become airborne at the takeoff lift coefficient. Thus, the airplane at altitude will take off at the same indicated airspeed as at sea level, but because of the reduced air density, the true airspeed (and groundspeed) will be greater.
   Answer (B) is incorrect because the indicated airspeed will remain the same, not higher, and the groundspeed will be higher, not unchanged. Answer (C) is incorrect because the true, not indicated, airspeed will increase at higher elevation airports due to the thinner (i.e., reduced air density) air.

5.2 Density Altitude Computations

4.

5306. GIVEN:

Pressure altitude . . . . 12,000 ft
True air temperature . . . . +50 °F

From the conditions given, the approximate density altitude is

A— 11,900 feet.
B— 14,130 feet.
C— 18,150 feet.

Answer (B) is correct (5306). *(FTH Chap 17)*
   To convert from °F to °C, use the formula:

$$°C = \frac{5}{9} \times (°F - 32)$$

Thus, convert +50°F to °C as follows:

$$\frac{5}{9} \times (50 - 32) = 10°C$$

   On the center of the computer side of your flight computer, put the pressure altitude of 12,000 ft. under the true air temperature of +10°C. The density altitude is indicated in the window as 14,130 ft.
   Answer (A) is incorrect because 11,900 ft. is the density altitude for −10°C, not +10°C. Answer (C) is incorrect because 18,150 ft. is the density for +50°C, not +50°F.

5.

5307. GIVEN:

Pressure altitude . . . . 5,000 ft
True air temperature . . . . +30 °C

From the conditions given, the approximate density altitude is

A— 7,800 feet.
B— 7,200 feet.
C— 9,000 feet.

Answer (A) is correct (5307). *(FTH Chap 17)*
   On the center of the computer side of your flight computer, put the pressure altitude of 5,000 ft. under the true air temperature of +30°C. The density altitude is indicated in the window as 7,800 ft.
   Answer (B) is incorrect because 7,200 ft. is the approximate density altitude at a temperature of 25°C, not 30°C. Answer (C) is incorrect because 9,000 ft. is the approximate density altitude at a temperature of 42°C, not 30°C.

6.

5308. GIVEN:

Pressure altitude . . . . 6,000 ft
True air temperature . . . . +30 °F

From the conditions given, the approximate density altitude is

A— 9,000 feet.
B— 5,500 feet.
C— 5,000 feet.

Answer (B) is correct (5308). *(FTH Chap 17)*
   To convert from °F to °C, use the formula:

$$°C = \frac{5}{9} \times (°F - 32)$$

Thus, convert +30°F to °C as follows:

$$\frac{5}{9} \times (30 - 32) = -1°C$$

   On the center of the computer side of your flight computer, put the pressure altitude of 6,000 ft. under the true air temperature of −1°C. The density altitude is indicated in the window as 5,500 ft.
   Answer (A) is incorrect because 9,000 ft. is the density altitude for +30°C, not +30°F. Answer (C) is incorrect because 5,000 ft. is the density altitude for −5°C, not −1°C.

7.
5309. GIVEN:

Pressure altitude . . . . 7,000 ft
True air temperature . . . . +15 °C

From the conditions given, the approximate density
altitude is

A— 5,000 feet.
B— 8,500 feet.
C— 9,500 feet.

5.3 Takeoff Distance

8.
5614. What effect does an uphill runway slope have on
takeoff performance?

A— Increases takeoff speed.
B— Increases takeoff distance.
C— Decreases takeoff distance.

9.
5622. (Refer to figure 32 on page 123.)

GIVEN:

Temperature . . . . 30 °F
Pressure altitude . . . . 6,000 ft
Weight . . . . 3,300 lb
Headwind . . . . 20 kts

What is the total takeoff distance over a 50-foot obstacle?

A— 1,100 feet.
B— 1,300 feet.
C— 1,500 feet.

Answer (B) is correct (5309). *(FTH Chap 17)*
On the center of the computer side of your flight
computer, put the pressure altitude of 7,000 ft. under the
true air temperature of +15°C. The density altitude is
indicated in the window as 8,500 ft.
Answer (A) is incorrect because 5,000 ft. is the density
altitude for –15°C, not +15°C. Answer (C) is incorrect
because 9,500 ft. is the density altitude for +23°C, not
+15°C.

Answer (B) is correct (5614). *(PHAK Chap 4)*
The upslope or downslope of the runway (runway
gradient) is quite important when runway length and
takeoff distance are critical. Upslope provides a retarding
force which impedes acceleration because the engine
has to overcome gravity as well as surface friction and
drag, resulting in a longer ground run or takeoff.
Answer (A) is incorrect because the indicated takeoff
speed is the same on a level, downhill, or uphill runway at
a given density altitude. Answer (C) is incorrect because
a downhill, not an uphill, runway slope will decrease the
takeoff distance.

Answer (C) is correct (5622). *(PHAK Chap 4)*
Fig. 32 presents the takeoff distance graph. Find the
total takeoff distance over a 50-ft. obstacle as follows:

1. Move up vertically from 30°F to the 6,000-ft. pressure
   altitude line.
2. Move to the right horizontally to the first reference line.
3. Move up and to the right parallel to the guideline to
   the weight of 3,300 lb.
4. Move to the right horizontally to the second reference
   line.
5. Move down and to the right parallel to the guideline to
   the headwind of 20 kt.
6. Move to the right horizontally to the right margin of the
   graph and read the distance, which is 1,500 ft.

Answer (A) is incorrect because 1,100 ft. (73% of
1,500 ft.) is the approximate ground roll, not total takeoff,
distance. Answer (B) is incorrect because 1,300 ft. is
required for an aircraft weighing 3,000 lb., not 3,300 lb.

10.

5621. (Refer to figure 32 on page 123.)

GIVEN:

```
Temperature ............................ 100 °F
Pressure altitude ..................... 4,000 ft
Weight ............................... 3,200 lb
Wind ................................. Calm
```

What is the ground roll required for takeoff over a 50-foot obstacle?

A— 1,180 feet.
B— 1,350 feet.
C— 1,850 feet.

11.

5620. (Refer to figure 32 on page 123.)

GIVEN:

```
Temperature .......................... 50 °F
Pressure altitude .................... 2,000 ft.
Weight .............................. 2,700 lb
Wind ................................ Calm
```

What is the total takeoff distance over a 50-foot obstacle?

A— 800 feet.
B— 650 feet.
C— 1,050 feet.

12.

5619. (Refer to figure 32 on page 123.)

GIVEN:

```
Temperature .......................... 75 °F
Pressure altitude .................... 6,000 ft
Weight .............................. 2,900 lb
Headwind ............................ 20 kts
```

To safely take off over a 50-foot obstacle in 1,000 feet, what weight reduction is necessary?

A— 50 pounds.
B— 100 pounds.
C— 300 pounds.

Answer (B) is correct (5621). *(PHAK Chap 4)*
Fig. 32 presents the takeoff distance graph. Find the ground roll required for takeoff over a 50-ft. obstacle as follows:

1. Move up vertically from 100°F to the 4,000-ft. pressure altitude line.
2. Move to the right horizontally to the first reference line.
3. Move up and to the right parallel to the guideline to the weight of 3,200 lb.
4. Since the wind is calm, move right horizontally to the right margin to determine the total takeoff distance of 1,850 ft.
5. Ground roll is approximately 73% of the total takeoff distance (as stated in the note below the Associated Conditions). Thus, the ground roll is approximately 1,350 ft. (1,850 x .73).

Answer (A) is incorrect because 1,180 ft. is the required ground roll for a 2,950-lb., not 3,200-lb., aircraft. Answer (C) is incorrect because 1,850 ft. is the total takeoff, not ground roll, distance to clear a 50-ft. obstacle.

Answer (A) is correct (5620). *(PHAK Chap 4)*
Fig. 32 presents the takeoff distance graph. Find the total takeoff distance over a 50-ft. obstacle as follows:

1. Move up vertically from 50°F to the 2,000-ft. pressure altitude line.
2. Move to the right horizontally to the first reference line.
3. Move up and to the right parallel to the guideline to the weight of 2,700 lb.
4. Since the wind is calm, move right horizontally to the right margin of the graph to determine the total takeoff distance, which is 800 ft.

Answer (B) is incorrect because 650 ft. is required for a pressure altitude of sea level, not 2,000 ft. Answer (C) is incorrect because 1,050 ft. is required for an aircraft weighing 2,900 lb., not 2,700 lb.

Answer (C) is correct (5619). *(PHAK Chap 4)*
Fig. 32 presents the takeoff distance graph. Find the weight reduction necessary to safely take off over a 50-ft. obstacle in 1,000 ft. as follows:

1. Move up vertically from 75°F to the 6,000-ft. pressure altitude line.
2. Move to the right horizontally to the first reference line.
3. Move up and to the right parallel to the guideline to the weight of 2,900 lb.
4. Move to the right horizontally to the second reference line.
5. Move down and to the right parallel to the guideline to the headwind of 20 kt.
6. Move to the right horizontally to the margin of the graph to indicate a total takeoff distance of 1,400 ft. This exceeds the 1,000-ft. limit by 400 ft., or 2 grid squares on the graph.
7. Return to the weight segment of the graph.
8. From the original point of 2,900 lb., move down and to the left, parallel to the guideline, to a point that is 2 grid squares less than 2,900 lb. This would be 2,600 lb.
9. The total weight reduction required is 300 lb. (2,900 – 2,600).

Answer (A) is incorrect because a 50-lb. reduction requires a takeoff distance of 1,350 ft., not 1,000 ft. Answer (B) is incorrect because a 100-lb. reduction requires a takeoff distance of 1,300 ft., not 1,000 ft.

ASSOCIATED CONDITIONS:

POWER   TAKEOFF POWER
             SET BEFORE
             BRAKE RELEASE
FLAPS   20*
RUNWAY   PAVED, LEVEL,
             DRY SURFACE
TAKEOFF
SPEED   IAS AS TABULATED

NOTE: GROUND ROLL IS APPROX. 73%
        OF TOTAL TAKEOFF DISTANCE
        OVER A 50 FT OBSTACLE

EXAMPLE:

OAT	75 °F
PRESSURE ALTITUDE	4000 FT
TAKEOFF WEIGHT	3100 LB
HEADWIND	20 KNOTS
TOTAL TAKEOFF DISTANCE OVER A 50 FT OBSTACLE	1350 FT
GROUND ROLL (73% OF 1350)	986 FT
IAS TAKEOFF SPEED LIFT–OFF	74 MPH
AT 50 FT	74 MPH

WEIGHT POUNDS	IAS TAKEOFF SPEED (ASSUMES ZERO INSTR. ERROR)			
	LIFT–OFF		50 FEET	
	MPH	KNOTS	MPH	KNOTS
3400	77	67	77	67
3200	75	65	75	65
3000	72	63	72	63
2800	69	60	69	60
2600	66	57	66	57
2400	63	55	63	55

FIGURE 32.—Obstacle Take-off Chart.

5.4 Time, Fuel, and Distance to Climb

13.
5482. (Refer to figure 13 on page 125.)

GIVEN:

Aircraft weight . . . . 3,400 lb
Airport pressure altitude . . . . 6,000 ft
Temperature at 6,000 ft . . . . 10 °C

Using a maximum rate of climb under the given
conditions, how much fuel would be used from engine
start to a pressure altitude of 16,000 feet?

A— 43 pounds.
B— 45 pounds.
C— 49 pounds.

Answer (A) is correct (5482). *(PHAK Chap 4)*
    The procedure is to note the difference on Fig. 13
between fuel usage on a climb to 16,000 ft. and on a
climb to 6,000 ft. Also note that the temperature is not
standard. Standard temperature at sea level is 15°C, and
there is a lapse rate of 2°C per 1,000 ft., so the standard
temperature at 6,000 ft. would be 3°C [15°C – (6 x 2°C)].
On a climb from sea level to 16,000 ft. with an aircraft
weight of 3,400 lb., the amount of fuel used is 39 lb. For
a climb from sea level to 6,000 ft., interpolate to find a fuel
burn of 14 lb. The difference between the two altitudes is
25 lb. (39 – 14), but this difference must be increased by
7%, which is 1.75 lb., to allow for the 7°C above standard.
Do not forget the 16 lb. for engine start, taxi, and takeoff.
Thus, the total fuel used is approximately 43 lb. (25 +
1.75 + 16).
    Answer (B) is incorrect because 45 lb. of fuel is
required to climb from approximately 5,000 ft., not
6,000 ft., to 16,000 ft. Answer (C) is incorrect because
49 lb. of fuel is required to climb from approximately
3,000 ft., not 6,000 ft., to 16,000 ft.

14.
5483. (Refer to figure 13 on page 125.)

GIVEN:

Aircraft weight . . . . 4,000 lb
Airport pressure altitude . . . . 2,000 ft
Temperature at 2,000 ft . . . . 32 °C

Using a maximum rate of climb under the given
conditions, how much time would be required to climb to
a pressure altitude of 8,000 feet?

A— 7 minutes.
B— 8.4 minutes.
C— 11.2 minutes.

Answer (B) is correct (5483). *(PHAK Chap 4)*
    The time to climb from 2,000 ft. to 8,000 ft. at an
aircraft weight of 4,000 lb. is computed using Fig. 13 as
follows: The time required to climb from sea level to
8,000 ft. (9 min.) minus the time required to climb from
sea level to 2,000 ft. (2 min., interpolated) equals 7 min.
Standard temperature is 11°C [15°C – (2°C x 2)], so the
temperature is 21°C above standard. Thus, the total time
required to climb from 2,000 ft. to 8,000 ft. is 8.4 min.
(7 x 1.21).
    Answer (A) is incorrect because 7 min. is the time
required for the climb at standard temperature.
Answer (C) is incorrect because 11.2 min. is the time
required to climb from sea level, not 2,000 ft., to 8,000 ft.

MAXIMUM RATE OF CLIMB

CONDITIONS:
Flaps Up
Gear Up
2600 RPM
Cowl Flaps Open
Standard Temperature

PRESS ALT	MP	PPH
S.L. TO 17,000	35	162
18,000	34	156
20,000	32	144
22,000	30	132
24,000	28	120

NOTES:
1. Add 16 pounds of fuel for engine start, taxi and takeoff allowance.
2. Increase time, fuel and distance by 10% for each 10 °C above standard temperature.
3. Distances shown are based on zero wind.

WEIGHT LBS	PRESS ALT FT	CLIMB SPEED KIAS	RATE OF CLIMB FPM	FROM SEA LEVEL		
				TIME MIN	FUEL USED POUNDS	DISTANCE NM
4000	S.L.	100	930	0	0	0
	4000	100	890	4	12	7
	8000	100	845	9	24	16
	12,000	100	790	14	38	25
	16,000	100	720	19	52	36
	20,000	99	515	26	69	50
	24,000	97	270	37	92	74
3700	S.L.	99	1060	0	0	0
	4000	99	1020	4	10	6
	8000	99	975	8	21	13
	12,000	99	915	12	33	21
	16,000	99	845	17	45	30
	20,000	97	630	22	59	42
	24,000	95	370	30	77	60
3400	S.L.	97	1205	0	0	0
	4000	97	1165	3	9	5
	8000	97	1120	7	19	12
	12,000	97	1060	11	29	18
	16,000	97	985	15	39	26
	20,000	96	760	19	51	36
	24,000	94	485	26	65	50

FIGURE 13.—Fuel, Time, and Distance to Climb.

NORMAL CLIMB – 110 KIAS

CONDITIONS:
Flaps Up
Gear Up
2500 RPM
30 Inches Hg
120 PPH Fuel Flow
Cowl Flaps Open
Standard Temperature

NOTES:
1. Add 16 pounds of fuel for engine start, taxi and takeoff allowance.
2. Increase time, fuel and distance by 10% for each 7 °C above standard temperature.
3. Distances shown are based on zero wind.

WEIGHT LBS	PRESS ALT FT	RATE OF CLIMB FPM	FROM SEA LEVEL		
			TIME MIN	FUEL USED POUNDS	DISTANCE NM
4000	S.L.	605	0	0	0
	4000	570	7	14	13
	8000	530	14	28	27
	12,000	485	22	44	43
	16,000	430	31	62	63
	20,000	365	41	82	87
3700	S.L.	700	0	0	0
	4000	665	6	12	11
	8000	625	12	24	23
	12,000	580	19	37	37
	16,000	525	26	52	53
	20,000	460	34	68	72
3400	S.L.	810	0	0	0
	4000	775	5	10	9
	8000	735	10	21	20
	12,000	690	16	32	31
	16,000	635	22	44	45
	20,000	565	29	57	61

FIGURE 14.—Fuel, Time, and Distance to Climb.

15.
5484. (Refer to figure 14 on page 126.)

GIVEN:

Aircraft weight .... 3,700 lb
Airport pressure altitude .... 4,000 ft
Temperature at 4,000 ft .... 21 °C

Using a normal climb under the given conditions, how much fuel would be used from engine start to a pressure altitude of 12,000 feet?

A— 30 pounds.
B— 37 pounds.
C— 46 pounds.

16.
5485. (Refer to figure 14 on page 126.)

GIVEN:

Aircraft weight .... 3,400 lb
Airport pressure altitude .... 4,000 ft
Temperature at 4,000 ft .... 14 °C

Using a normal climb under the given conditions, how much time would be required to climb to a pressure altitude of 8,000 feet?

A— 4.8 minutes.
B— 5 minutes.
C— 5.5 minutes.

Answer (C) is correct (5484). *(PHAK Chap 4)*
The amount of fuel needed to climb from 4,000 ft. (airport pressure altitude) to 12,000 ft. pressure altitude with a weight of 3,700 lb. is calculated as the amount needed to climb from sea level to 12,000 ft. (37 lb.) minus the amount to climb to 4,000 ft. (12 lb.). The difference is 25 lb. However, you must adjust (add) 10% for every 7°C above standard. Here, standard temperature at the 4,000-ft. pressure altitude is 7°C [15°C − (2°C x 4)], so OAT of 21°C is 14°C above standard. If you increase time, fuel, and distance by 10% for each 7°C above standard, multiply standard conditions usage by 120% for 14°C over standard. Fuel needed to climb is thus 30 lb. (25 lb. x 1.20). Finally, you must add 16 lb. for engine start, taxi, and takeoff. Total fuel needed to climb from engine start is thus 46 lb. (30 + 16).
Answer (A) is incorrect because 30 lb. is the fuel required for the climb without taking into consideration the 16 lb. for engine start, taxi, and takeoff. Answer (B) is incorrect because 37 lb. is the fuel required for a climb from sea level to 12,000 ft. at standard temperature.

Answer (C) is correct (5485). *(PHAK Chap 4)*
The time to climb to 8,000 ft. from 4,000 ft. with a weight of 3,400 lb. is calculated as the time to climb from sea level to 8,000 ft. (10 min.) minus the time to climb to 4,000 ft. (5 min.). The difference is 5 min. However, you must adjust (add) 10% for every 7°C above standard. Here, standard temperature at the 4,000-ft. pressure altitude is 7°C [15°C − (2°C x 4)], so OAT of 14°C at 4,000 ft. is 7°C above standard. Time to climb is thus 5.5 min. (5 min. x 1.10).
Answer (A) is incorrect because 4.8 min. was not arrived at by subtracting the climb from sea level to 4,000 ft. from the climb from sea level to 8,000 ft. and factoring in nonstandard temperature. Answer (B) is incorrect because 5 min. would be the time required for the climb before the correction for nonstandard temperature is made.

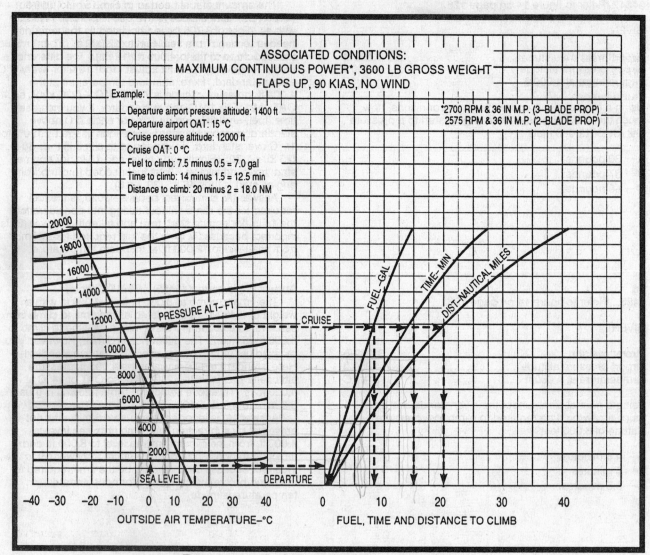

ASSOCIATED CONDITIONS:
MAXIMUM CONTINUOUS POWER*, 3600 LB GROSS WEIGHT
FLAPS UP, 90 KIAS, NO WIND

Example:

Departure airport pressure altitude: 1400 ft
Departure airport OAT: 15 °C
Cruise pressure altitude: 12000 ft
Cruise OAT: 0 °C
Fuel to climb: 7.5 minus 0.5 = 7.0 gal
Time to climb: 14 minus 1.5 = 12.5 min
Distance to climb: 20 minus 2 = 18.0 NM

*2700 RPM & 36 IN M.P. (3–BLADE PROP)
2575 RPM & 36 IN M.P. (2–BLADE PROP)

FIGURE 15.—Fuel, Time, and Distance to Climb.

17.
5486. (Refer to figure 15 on page 128.)

GIVEN:

Airport pressure altitude . . . . 4,000 ft
Airport temperature . . . . 12 °C
Cruise pressure altitude . . . . 9,000 ft
Cruise temperature . . . . −4 °C

What will be the distance required to climb to cruise
altitude under the given conditions?

A— 6 miles.
B— 8.5 miles.
C— 11 miles.

18.
5487. (Refer to figure 15 on page 128.)

GIVEN:

Airport pressure altitude . . . . 2,000 ft
Airport temperature . . . . 20 °C
Cruise pressure altitude . . . . 10,000 ft
Cruise temperature . . . . 0 °C

What will be the fuel, time, and distance required to climb
to cruise altitude under the given conditions?

A— 5 gallons, 9 minutes, 13 NM.
B— 6 gallons, 11 minutes, 16 NM.
C— 7 gallons, 12 minutes, 18 NM.

Answer (B) is correct (5486). *(PHAK Chap 4)*
Start at the lower left corner of Fig. 15. Go up from
−4°C cruise temperature to the 9,000-ft. cruise pressure
altitude. From there proceed horizontally to the right to
the intersection of the third curve (distance). Then
proceed down to the bottom of the chart, which is at
14 NM. Note that this is the distance from sea level to
9,000 ft.
Since the airport pressure altitude is 4,000 ft., go back
to the left lower corner and go up from the airport
temperature of 12°C to the pressure altitude line of
4,000 ft. Then proceed horizontally to the third curve
(distance) and move downward to determine the distance
of 5.5 NM to climb to 4,000 ft. from sea level. Thus, the
distance to climb from 4,000 ft. to 9,000 ft. is 8.5 NM
(14 − 5.5).
Answer (A) is incorrect because 6 NM is approximately the distance required to climb from sea level to
4,000 ft., not from 4,000 ft. to 9,000 ft. Answer (C) is
incorrect because the distance required to climb from
4,000 ft. to 9,000 ft. is 8.5 NM, not 11 NM.

Answer (A) is correct (5487). *(PHAK Chap 4)*
Start at the lower left corner of Fig. 15., Go up from
0°C cruise temperature to the 10,000-ft. cruise pressure
altitude. From there proceed horizontally to the right to
the intersection of each of the curves (fuel, time, and
distance). From there proceed down to 6 gal., 11 min.,
and 16 NM. Note that these are the fuel, time, and
distance from sea level to 10,000 ft.
Since the airport pressure altitude is 2,000 ft., go back
to the left lower corner and go up from the airport temperature of 20°C to the pressure altitude line of 2,000 ft.
Then proceed horizontally to each of the curves and
move downward to determine the fuel of 1 gal., time of
2 min., and distance of 3 NM to cllmb to 2,000 ft. from sea
level.
Thus, to climb from 2,000 ft. to 10,000 ft. requires
5 gal. (6 − 1), 9 min. (11 − 2), and 13 NM (16 − 3).
Answer (B) is incorrect because 6 gal., 11 min., and
16 NM are required for a climb from sea level, not
2,000 ft., to 10,000 ft. Answer (C) is incorrect because to
climb from 2,000 ft. to 10,000 ft. requires 5 gal., not 7 gal.;
9 min., not 12 min.; and 13 NM, not 18 NM.

NORMAL CLIMB – 100 KIAS

CONDITIONS:
Flaps Up
Gear Up
2550 RPM
25 Inches MP or Full Throttle
Cowl Flaps Open
Standard Temperature

MIXTURE SETTING	
PRESS ALT	PPH
S.L. to 4000	108
8000	96
12,000	84

NOTES:
1. Add 12 pounds of fuel for engine start, taxi and takeoff allowance.
2. Increase time, fuel and distance by 10% for each 10 °C above standard temperature.
3. Distances shown are based on zero wind.

WEIGHT LBS	PRESS ALT FT	RATE OF CLIMB FPM	FROM SEA LEVEL		
			TIME MIN	FUEL USED POUNDS	DISTANCE NM
3800	S.L.	580	0	0	0
	2000	580	3	6	6
	4000	570	7	12	12
	6000	470	11	19	19
	8000	365	16	27	28
	10,000	265	22	37	40
	12,000	165	32	51	59
3500	S.L.	685	0	0	0
	2000	685	3	5	5
	4000	675	6	11	10
	6000	565	9	16	16
	8000	455	13	23	23
	10,000	350	18	31	33
	12,000	240	25	41	46
3200	S.L.	800	0	0	0
	2000	800	2	4	4
	4000	795	5	9	8
	6000	675	8	14	13
	8000	560	11	19	19
	10,000	445	15	25	27
	12,000	325	20	33	37

FIGURE 9.—Fuel, Time, and Distance to Climb.

19.

5456. (Refer to figure 9 on page 130.) Using a normal climb, how much fuel would be used from engine start to 12,000 feet pressure altitude?

Aircraft weight . . . . 3,800 lb
Airport pressure altitude . . . . 4,000 ft
Temperature . . . . 26 °C

A— 46 pounds.
B— 51 pounds.
C— 58 pounds.

Answer (C) is correct (5456). *(PHAK Chap 4)*
At 3,800 lb., 51 lb. of fuel is required to climb from sea level to 12,000 ft., according to Fig. 9. From sea level to 4,000 ft., only 12 lb. is required. The net difference is 39 lb. to climb from 4,000 ft. pressure altitude to 12,000 ft. pressure altitude. The air temperature of 26°C, however, is 19°C over standard temperature (standard at 4,000 ft. is 7°C, which is 15°C at sea level minus 8°C for the lapse rate). Note that there is an increase of 1% for each 1°C above standard. Accordingly, you must increase the 39 lb. by 19% (39 x 1.19) to get 46.41 lb. Then add 12 lb. to taxi, takeoff, etc., which is approximately 58 lb.
Answer (A) is incorrect because 46 lb. is the fuel required to make the climb without factoring in the 12 lb. required for engine start, taxi, and takeoff. Answer (B) is incorrect because 51 lb. of fuel is required for the climb from sea level to 12,000 ft. before adjustments are made for nonstandard temperature; the 4,000-ft. airport altitude; and engine start, taxi, and takeoff.

20.

5457. (Refer to figure 9 on page 130.) Using a normal climb, how much fuel would be used from engine start to 10,000 feet pressure altitude?

Aircraft weight . . . . 3,500 lb
Airport pressure altitude . . . . 4,000 ft
Temperature . . . . 21 °C

A— 23 pounds.
B— 31 pounds.
C— 35 pounds.

Answer (C) is correct (5457). *(PHAK Chap 4)*
At 3,500 lb., 31 lb. of fuel is required to climb from sea level to 10,000 ft., per Fig. 9. From sea level to 4,000 ft., only 11 lb. is required. The net difference is 20 lb. to climb from 4,000 ft. pressure altitude to 10,000 ft. pressure altitude. The air temperature of 21°C, however, is 14°C over standard temperature (standard at 4,000 ft. is 7°C, which is 15°C at sea level minus 8°C for the lapse rate). Note that there is an increase of 1% for each 1° above standard. Accordingly, you must increase the 20 lb. by 14% (20 x 1.14) to get 22.8 lb. Then add 12 lb. to taxi, takeoff, etc., which is approximately 35 lb.
Answer (A) is incorrect because 23 lb. of fuel is required for the climb itself. The fuel required for engine start, taxi, and takeoff must be factored in. Answer (B) is incorrect because 31 lb. of fuel is required to climb from sea level to 10,000 ft. Adjustments must be made for nonstandard temperature; a 4,000-ft. airport altitude; and the engine start, taxi, and takeoff.

$(1.14)(31 - 11) + 12 = 34.8$ or 35 lbs.

MAXIMUM RATE OF CLIMB

CONDITIONS:
Flaps Up
Gear Up
2700 RPM
Full Throttle
Mixture Set at Placard Fuel Flow
Cowl Flaps Open
Standard Temperature

MIXTURE SETTING	
PRESS ALT	PPH
S.L.	138
4000	126
8000	114
12,000	102

NOTES:
1. Add 12 pounds of fuel for engine start, taxi and takeoff allowance.
2. Increase time, fuel and distance by 10% for each 10 °C above standard temperature.
3. Distances shown are based on zero wind.

WEIGHT LBS	PRESS ALT FT	CLIMB SPEED KIAS	RATE OF CLIMB FPM	FROM SEA LEVEL		
				TIME MIN	FUEL USED POUNDS	DISTANCE NM
3800	S.L.	97	860	0	0	0
	2000	95	760	2	6	4
	4000	94	660	5	12	9
	6000	93	565	9	18	14
	8000	91	465	13	26	21
	10,000	90	365	18	35	29
	12,000	89	265	24	47	41
3500	S.L.	95	990	0	0	0
	2000	94	885	2	5	3
	4000	93	780	5	10	7
	6000	91	675	7	16	12
	8000	90	570	11	22	17
	10,000	89	465	15	29	24
	12,000	87	360	20	38	32
3200	S.L.	94	1135	0	0	0
	2000	92	1020	2	4	3
	4000	91	910	4	9	6
	6000	90	800	6	14	10
	8000	88	685	9	19	14
	10,000	87	575	12	25	20
	12,000	86	465	16	32	26

FIGURE 10.—Fuel, Time, and Distance to Climb.

21.
5458. (Refer to figure 10 on page 132.) Using a maximum rate of climb, how much fuel would be used from engine start to 6,000 feet pressure altitude?

Aircraft weight . . . . 3,200 lb
Airport pressure altitude . . . . 2,000 ft
Temperature . . . . 27 °C

A— 10 pounds.
B— 14 pounds.
C— 24 pounds.

$$(1.2)(14-4)+12$$
$$10 \quad \boxed{24}$$

22.
5459. (Refer to figure 10 on page 132.) Using a maximum rate of climb, how much fuel would be used from engine start to 10,000 feet pressure altitude?

Aircraft weight . . . . 3,800 lb
Airport pressure altitude . . . . 4,000 ft
Temperature . . . . 30 °C

A— 28 pounds.
B— 35 pounds.
C— 40 pounds.

$$(1.23)(35-12)+12$$
$$23 \qquad = 40.29$$

oh yeah

Answer (C) is correct (5458). (PHAK Chap 4)
At 3,200 lb., 14 lb. of fuel is required to climb from sea level to 6,000 ft. per Fig. 10. From sea level to 2,000 ft., only 4 lb. is required. The net difference is 10 lb. to climb from 2,000 ft. pressure altitude to 6,000 ft. pressure altitude. The air temperature of 27°C, however, is 16°C over standard temperature (standard at 2,000 ft. is 11°C, which is 15°C at sea level minus 4°C for the lapse rate). Note that there is an increase of 1% for each 1° above standard. Accordingly, you must increase the 10 lb. by 16% (10 x 1.16) to get 11.6 lb. Then add 12 lb. to taxi, takeoff, etc., which is approximately 24 lb.
Answer (A) is incorrect because 10 lb. is required for the climb from 2,000 ft. to 6,000 ft. without factoring in nonstandard temperature or the fuel required for the engine start, taxi, and takeoff adjustment. Answer (B) is incorrect because 14 lb. is required for a climb from sea level, not 2,000 ft., to 6,000 ft.

Answer (C) is correct (5459). (PHAK Chap 4)
At 3,800 lb., 35 lb. of fuel is required to climb from sea level to 10,000 ft., per Fig. 10. From sea level to 4,000 ft., only 12 lb. is required. The net difference is 23 lb. to climb from 4,000 ft. pressure altitude to 10,000 ft. pressure altitude. The air temperature of 30°C, however, is 23°C over standard temperature (standard at 4,000 ft. is 7°C, which is 15°C at sea level minus 8°C for the lapse rate). Note that there is an increase of 1% for each 1° above standard. Accordingly, you must increase the 23 lb. by 23% (23 x 1.23) to get 28.29 lb. Then add 12 lb. to taxi, takeoff, etc., which is approximately 40 lb.
Answer (A) is incorrect because 28 lb. of fuel is required to climb from 4,000 ft. to 10,000 ft., but the 12 lb. of fuel required for engine start, taxi, and takeoff has not been added to the total. Answer (B) is incorrect because 35 lb. of fuel is required to climb from sea level, not 4,000 ft., to 10,000 ft.

CONDITIONS:
Flaps Up
Gear Up
2600 RPM
Cowl Flaps Open

PRESS ALT	MP	PPH
S.L. TO 17,000	35	162
18,000	34	156
20,000	32	144
22,000	30	132
24,000	28	120

WEIGHT LBS	PRESS ALT FT	CLIMB SPEED KIAS	RATE OF CLIMB – FPM			
			-20 °C	0 °C	20 °C	40 °C
4000	S.L.	100	1170	1035	895	755
	4000	100	1080	940	800	655
	8000	100	980	840	695	555
	12,000	100	870	730	590	---
	16,000	100	740	605	470	---
	20,000	99	485	355	---	---
	24,000	97	190	70	---	---
3700	S.L.	99	1310	1165	1020	875
	4000	99	1215	1070	925	775
	8000	99	1115	965	815	670
	12,000	99	1000	855	710	---
	16,000	99	865	730	590	---
	20,000	97	600	470	---	---
	24,000	95	295	170	---	---
3400	S.L.	97	1465	1320	1165	1015
	4000	97	1370	1220	1065	910
	8000	97	1265	1110	955	795
	12,000	97	1150	995	845	---
	16,000	97	1010	865	725	---
	20,000	96	730	595	---	---
	24,000	94	405	275	---	---

FIGURE 33.—Maximum Rate-of-Climb Chart.

5.5 Maximum Rate of Climb

23.
5623. (Refer to figure 33 on page 134.)

GIVEN:

Weight . . . . 4,000 lb
Pressure altitude . . . . 5,000 ft
Temperature . . . . 30 °C

What is the maximum rate of climb under the given conditions?

A— 655 ft/min.
B— 702 ft/min.
C— 774 ft/min.

Answer (B) is correct (5623). *(PHAK Chap 4)*
The maximum rate of climb at a pressure altitude of 5,000 ft., temperature of 30°C, and 4,000 lb. is found by using the 4,000 lb. weight section of Fig. 33. Note that you must interpolate for both 5,000 ft. and 30°C.
First, interpolate for 5,000 ft. At 20°C, the difference between 4,000 ft. and 8,000 ft. is 105 fpm (800 – 695). 5,000 ft. is 1/4 of the way between 4,000 ft. and 8,000 ft. 105 x .25 = 26.25. 800 – 26.25 = 773.75. At 40°C, the difference is 100 (655 – 555). Subtracting one-fourth of 100 from 655 gives 630 (655 – 25).
Using these values, interpolate for 30°C between 773.75 at 20° and 630 at 40°. The difference is 143.75 fpm (773.75 – 630). Subtracting one-half of 143.75 (about 72) from 773.75 to split the difference between 40° and 30° gives about 702 fpm.
Answer (A) is incorrect because 655 fpm is the maximum rate of climb at 4,000 ft., not 5,000 ft., at 40°C, not 30°C. Answer (C) is incorrect because 774 fpm is the maximum rate of climb at 5,000 ft. at 20°C, not 30°C.

24.
5624. (Refer to figure 33 on page 134.)

GIVEN:

Weight . . . . 3,700 lb
Pressure altitude . . . . 22,000 ft
Temperature . . . . –10 °C

What is the maximum rate of climb under the given conditions?

A— 305 ft/min.
B— 320 ft/min.
C— 384 ft/min.

Answer (C) is correct (5624). *(PHAK Chap 4)*
The maximum rate of climb at a pressure altitude of 22,000 ft., temperature of –10°C, and 3,700 lb. is found by using the 3,700 lb. weight section of Fig. 33. Note that you must interpolate for both 22,000 ft. and –10°C.
First, interpolate for 22,000 ft. At 0°C, the difference between 20,000 ft. and 24,000 ft. is 300 fpm (470 – 170). One-half of 300 added to 170 is 320 (170 + 150).
At –20°C, the difference is 305 (600 – 295). Adding one-half of 305 to 295 is 447.5 (295 + 152.5).
The next step is to interpolate the 22,000 ft. values for –10°C: 320 at 0° and 447.5 at –20°. The difference is 127.5 (447.5 – 320). Adding one-half of 127.5 to 320 to split the difference between 0° and –20° gives 384 fpm (320 + 64).
Answer (A) is incorrect because 305 fpm is the difference in rate of climb between 20,000 ft. and 24,000 ft. at –20°C. Answer (B) is incorrect because 320 fpm is the maximum rate of climb at 22,000 ft. and a temperature of 0°C, not –10°C.

Gross Weight- 2300 Lbs.
Standard Conditions
Zero Wind Lean Mixture

NOTE: Maximum cruise is normally limited to 75% power.

ALT.	RPM	% BHP	TAS MPH	GAL/ HOUR	38 GAL (NO RESERVE)		48 GAL (NO RESERVE)	
					ENDR. HOURS	RANGE MILES	ENDR. HOURS	RANGE MILES
2500	2700	86	134	9.7	3.9	525	4.9	660
	2600	79	129	8.6	4.4	570	5.6	720
	2500	72	123	7.8	4.9	600	6.2	760
	2400	65	117	7.2	5.3	620	6.7	780
	2300	58	111	6.7	5.7	630	7.2	795
	2200	52	103	6.3	6.1	625	7.7	790
5000	2700	82	134	9.0	4.2	565	5.3	710
	2600	75	128	8.1	4.7	600	5.9	760
	2500	68	122	7.4	5.1	625	6.4	790
	2400	61	116	6.9	5.5	635	6.9	805
	2300	55	108	6.5	5.9	635	7.4	805
	2200	49	100	6.0	6.3	630	7.9	795
7500	2700	78	133	8.4	4.5	600	5.7	755
	2600	71	127	7.7	4.9	625	6.2	790
	2500	64	121	7.1	5.3	645	6.7	810
	2400	58	113	6.7	5.7	645	7.2	820
	2300	52	105	6.2	6.1	640	7.7	810
10,000	2650	70	129	7.6	5.0	640	6.3	810
	2600	67	125	7.3	5.2	650	6.5	820
	2500	61	118	6.9	5.5	655	7.0	830
	2400	55	110	6.4	5.9	650	7.5	825
	2300	49	100	6.0	6.3	635	8.0	800

FIGURE 11.—Cruise and Range Performance.

5.6 Cruise and Range Performance

25.
5460. (Refer to figure 11 on page 136.) If the cruise altitude is 7,500 feet, using 64 percent power at 2,500 RPM, what would be the range with 48 gallons of usable fuel?

A— 635 miles.
B— 645 miles.
C— 810 miles.

Answer (C) is correct (5460). *(PHAK Chap 4)*
On Fig. 11 at 7,500 ft. and 2500 RPM, which is 64% power, go to the far right-hand column to determine range of 810 mi. with 48 gal. of usable fuel.
Answer (A) is incorrect because the range at 7,500 ft. and 2500 RPM is found in the far right column to be 810 mi., not 635 mi. Answer (B) is incorrect because 645 mi. is the range at 7,500 ft. and 2,500 RPM with 38 gal., not 48 gal., of usable fuel.

26.
5461. (Refer to figure 11 on page 136.) What would be the endurance at an altitude of 7,500 feet, using 52 percent power?

NOTE: (With 48 gallons fuel—no reserve.)

A— 6.1 hours.
B— 7.7 hours.
C— 8.0 hours.

Answer (B) is correct (5461). *(PHAK Chap 4)*
On Fig. 11 at 7,500 ft. and 2300 RPM, which is 52% power, go to the endurance column at 48 gal. of usable fuel to determine 7.7 hr.
Answer (A) is incorrect because 6.1 hr. is the endurance for 38 gal., not 48 gal., of usable fuel. Answer (C) is incorrect because 8.0 hr. is the endurance at 10,000 ft., not 7,500 ft., and 49%, not 52%, power.

27.
5462. (Refer to figure 11 on page 136.) What would be the approximate true airspeed and fuel consumption per hour at an altitude of 7,500 feet, using 52 percent power?

A— 103 MPH TAS, 6.3 GPH.
B— 105 MPH TAS, 6.6 GPH.
C— 105 MPH TAS, 6.2 GPH.

Answer (C) is correct (5462). *(PHAK Chap 4)*
On Fig. 11 at 7,500 ft. and 2300 RPM, which is 52% power, the TAS is 105 mph and the fuel consumption is 6.2 GPH.
Answer (A) is incorrect because, at 52% power, a TAS of 103 mph and a fuel consumption of 6.3 GPH are for an altitude of 2,500 ft., not 7,500 ft. Answer (B) is incorrect because 6.6 is not a performance value (i.e., fuel consumption or endurance) that appears on the chart.

PRESSURE ALTITUDE 18,000 FEET

CONDITIONS:
4000 Pounds
Recommended Lean Mixture
Cowl Flaps Closed

NOTE
For best fuel economy at 70% power or less, operate at 6 PPH leaner than shown in this chart or at peak EGT.

RPM	MP	20 °C BELOW STANDARD TEMP -41 °C			STANDARD TEMPERATURE -21 °C			20 °C ABOVE STANDARD TEMP -1 °C		
		% BHP	KTAS	PPH	% BHP	KTAS	PPH	% BHP	KTAS	PPH
2500	30	---	---	---	81	188	106	76	185	100
	28	80	184	105	76	182	99	71	178	93
	26	75	178	99	71	176	93	67	172	88
	24	70	171	91	66	168	86	62	164	81
	22	63	162	84	60	159	79	56	155	75
2400	30	81	185	107	77	183	101	72	180	94
	28	76	179	100	72	177	94	67	173	88
	26	71	172	93	67	170	88	63	166	83
	24	66	165	87	62	163	82	58	159	77
	22	61	158	80	57	155	76	54	150	72
2300	30	79	182	103	74	180	97	70	176	91
	28	74	176	97	70	174	91	65	170	86
	26	69	170	91	65	167	86	61	163	81
	24	64	162	84	60	159	79	56	155	75
	22	58	154	77	55	150	73	51	145	65
2200	26	66	166	87	62	163	82	58	159	77
	24	61	158	80	57	154	76	54	150	72
	22	55	148	73	51	144	69	48	138	66
	20	49	136	66	46	131	63	43	124	59

FIGURE 12.—Cruise Performance.

28.
5463. (Refer to figure 12 on page 138.)

GIVEN:

Pressure altitude . . . . 18,000 ft
Temperature . . . . –21 °C
Power . . . . 2,400 RPM – 28″ MP
Recommended lean mixture
   usable fuel . . . . 425 lb

What is the approximate flight time available under the
given conditions? (Allow for VFR day fuel reserve.)

A— 3 hours 46 minutes.
B— 4 hours 1 minute.
C— 4 hours 31 minutes.

29.
5464. (Refer to figure 12 on page 138.)

GIVEN:

Pressure altitude . . . . 18,000 ft
Temperature . . . . –41 °C
Power . . . . 2,500 RPM – 26″ MP
Recommended lean mixture
   usable fuel . . . . 318 lb

What is the approximate flight time available under the
given conditions? (Allow for VFR night fuel reserve.)

A— 2 hours 27 minutes.
B— 3 hours 12 minutes.
C— 3 hours 42 minutes.

30.
5465. (Refer to figure 12 on page 138.)

GIVEN:

Pressure altitude . . . . 18,000 ft
Temperature . . . . –1 °C
Power . . . . 2,200 RPM – 20″ MP
Best fuel economy
   usable fuel . . . . 344 lb

What is the approximate flight time available under the
given conditions? (Allow for VFR day fuel reserve.)

A— 4 hours 50 minutes.
B— 5 hours 20 minutes.
C— 5 hours 59 minutes.

Answer (B) is correct (5463). *(PHAK Chap 4)*
   Given 2400 RPM and manifold pressure of 28″, use
Fig. 12 to find 94 lb. of fuel per hr. at –21°C. Since you
have 425 lb. of usable fuel, you can cruise for 4 hr.
31 min. less the 30-min. VFR-day fuel reserve, or 4 hr.
1 min. The time is calculated as 425 lb. of fuel divided by
94 lb./hr. equals 4.52 hr. 60 min./hr. times .52 hr. equals
31 min.
   Alternatively, you can use your flight computer. Put
94 over 60 min. on the time index (dark triangle). Then
look to 425 on the outer scale and find that it corresponds
to 4 hr. 31 min. on the inner scale. Note that the question
asks for the flight time, not flight time plus VFR-day
reserve; i.e., compute 4 hr. 31 min. and subtract 30 min.
to get 4 hr. 1 min.
   Answer (A) is incorrect because 3 hr. 46 min. is the
flight time available with a VFR-night, not VFR-day, fuel
reserve of 45 min. Answer (C) is incorrect because 4 hr.
31 min. is the flight time available with no reserve.

Answer (A) is correct (5464). *(PHAK Chap 4)*
   Given 2500 RPM and manifold pressure of 26″, use
Fig. 12 to find 99 lb. of fuel per hr. at –41°C. Since you
have 318 lb. of usable fuel, you can cruise for 3 hr.
12 min. less the 45 min. VFR-night fuel reserve, or 2 hr.
27 min.
   Calculate the time as 318 lb. of fuel divided by
99 lb./hr. equals 3.21 hr. 60 min./hr. times .21 hr. equals
about 12 min.
   Answer (B) is incorrect because 3 hr. 12 min. is the
flight time available with no fuel reserve. Answer (C) is
incorrect because 3 hr. 42 min. is the flight time with no
reserve at a fuel consumption of 86 PPH, not 99 PPH.

Answer (C) is correct (5465). *(PHAK Chap 4)*
   Given 2200 RPM and manifold pressure of 20″, use
Fig. 12 to find 59 lb. of fuel per hr. at –1°C. The "Note"
indicates to use 6 lb./hr. less for "best fuel economy."
Thus, use 53 lb./hr. (59 – 6). Since you have 344 lb. of
usable fuel, you can cruise for 6 hr. 29 min. (344 lb./53 lb.
per hr.) less the 30 min. VFR-day fuel reserve, or 5 hr.
59 min.
   Answer (A) is incorrect because, using 53 PPH, the
flight time available is 5 hr. 59 min., not 4 hr. 50 min.
Answer (B) is incorrect because 5 hr. 20 min. is the
endurance, with a VFR-day reserve, using the
recommended lean mixture, not the best fuel economy,
fuel flow.

32

PRESSURE ALTITUDE 6,000 FEET

CONDITIONS:
Recommended Lean Mixture
3800 Pounds
Cowl Flaps Closed

RPM	MP	20 °C BELOW STANDARD TEMP -17 °C			STANDARD TEMPERATURE 3 °C			20 °C ABOVE STANDARD TEMP 23 °C		
		% BHP	KTAS	PPH	% BHP	KTAS	PPH	% BHP	KTAS	PPH
2550	24	---	---	---	78	173	97	75	174	94
	23	76	167	96	74	169	92	71	171	89
	22	72	164	90	69	166	87	67	167	84
	21	68	160	85	65	162	82	63	163	80
2500	24	78	169	98	75	171	95	73	172	91
	23	74	166	93	71	167	90	69	169	87
	22	70	162	88	67	164	85	65	165	82
	21	66	158	83	63	160	80	61	160	77
2400	24	73	165	91	70	166	88	68	167	85
	23	69	161	87	67	163	84	64	164	81
	22	65	158	82	63	159	79	61	160	77
	21	61	154	77	59	155	75	57	155	73
2300	24	68	161	86	66	162	83	64	163	80
	23	65	158	82	62	159	79	60	159	76
	22	61	154	77	59	155	75	57	155	72
	21	57	150	73	55	150	71	53	150	68
2200	24	63	156	80	61	157	77	59	158	75
	23	60	152	76	58	153	73	56	154	71
	22	57	149	72	54	149	70	53	149	67
	21	53	144	68	51	144	66	49	143	64
	20	50	139	64	48	138	62	46	137	60
	19	46	133	60	44	132	58	43	131	57

FIGURE 34.—Cruise Performace Chart.

31.
5625. (Refer to figure 34 on page 140.)

GIVEN:

Pressure altitude . . . . 6,000 ft
Temperature . . . . +3 °C
Power . . . . 2,200 RPM - 22″ MP
Usable fuel available . . . . 465 lb

What is the maximum available flight time under the
conditions stated?

A— 6 hours 27 minutes.
B— 6 hours 39 minutes.
C— 6 hours 56 minutes.

32.
5626. (Refer to figure 34 on page 140.)

GIVEN:

Pressure altitude . . . . 6,000 ft
Temperature . . . . −17 °C
Power . . . . 2,300 RPM - 23″ MP
Usable fuel available . . . . 370 lb

What is the maximum available flight time under the
conditions stated?

A— 4 hours 20 minutes.
B— 4 hours 30 minutes.
C— 4 hours 50 minutes.

33.
5627. (Refer to figure 34 on page 140.)

GIVEN:

Pressure altitude . . . . 6,000 ft
Temperature . . . . +13 °C
Power . . . . 2,500 RPM - 23″ MP
Usable fuel available . . . . 460 lb

What is the maximum available flight time under the
conditions stated?

A— 4 hours 58 minutes.
B— 5 hours 7 minutes.
C— 5 hours 12 minutes.

34.
5505. Which maximum range factor decreases as weight
decreases?

A— Altitude.
B— Airspeed.
C— Angle of attack.

Answer (B) is correct (5625). *(PHAK Chap 4)*
Using Fig. 34 at 2,200 RPM, find the 22″ MP line.
Then go across to the PPH column in the middle section
for standard temperatures and find 70 PPH. Divide
465 lb. of usable fuel by 70 PPH to determine a time of
6.64 hr., which translates to about 6 hr. 39 min.
Alternatively, use your flight computer. Put 70 PPH on
the outer scale over the time index on the inner scale.
Then find 465 on the outer scale and read about 6 hr.
40 min. on the inner scale.
Answer (A) is incorrect because the maximum
available flight time at 2,200 RPM, 22″ MP, and −17°C,
not +3°C, is 6 hr. 27 min. Answer (C) is incorrect
because the maximum available flight time at 2,200 RPM,
22″ MP, and +23°C, not +3°C, is 6 hr. 56 min.

Answer (B) is correct (5626). *(PHAK Chap 4)*
Using Fig. 34 at 2300 RPM, find the 23″ MP line. Then
go across to the PPH column in the section for 20° below
standard temperature and find 82 PPH. Divide 370 lb. of
usable fuel by 82 PPH to determine a time of 4.51 hr.,
which translates to about 4 hr. 30 min.
Alternatively, use your flight computer. Put 82 PPH on
the outer scale over the time index on the inner scale.
Then find 370 on the outer scale and find about 4 hr.
30 min. on the inner scale.
Answer (A) is incorrect because the maximum
available flight time of 4 hr. 20 min. is achieved by using
an MP of 24 in., not 23 in. Answer (C) is incorrect
because the maximum flight time of 4 hr. 50 min. is
achieved by using an MP of 22 in., not 23 in.

Answer (C) is correct (5627). *(PHAK Chap 4)*
Using Fig. 34 at 2500 RPM, find the 23″ MP line.
Then, notice that 13°C, 10° above standard temperature
(ST), is not given. You must interpolate between
standard temperature and 20° above ST. At standard
temperature, fuel flow equals 90 PPH; at 20° above ST,
fuel flow equals 87 PPH, a difference of 3 PPH. Since the
required 10° above ST is exactly halfway between ST and
ST + 20°, half of 3 PPH, or 1.5, should be added to the
value of 87 PPH, giving 88.5 PPH. Divide 460 lb. of
usable fuel by 88.5 PPH to determine a time of 5.19 hr.,
which translates to about 5 hr. 12 min.
Answer (A) is incorrect because the maximum flight
time of 4 hr. 58 min. is at a temperature of −17°C, not
+13°C. Answer (B) is incorrect because the maximum
flight time of 5 hr. 7 min. is at a temperature of +3°C, not
+13°C.

Answer (B) is correct (5505). *(FTH Chap 17)*
As weight decreases, the maximum range is achieved
when the airplane is flown at the airspeed which maxi-
mizes the lift/drag ratio. As weight decreases, the L/D$_{MAX}$
airspeed decreases.
Answer (A) is incorrect because maximum range
altitude may increase, not decrease, with weight
decrease. Answer (C) is incorrect because angle of
attack is not a maximum range factor (as are weight,
altitude, and power setting).

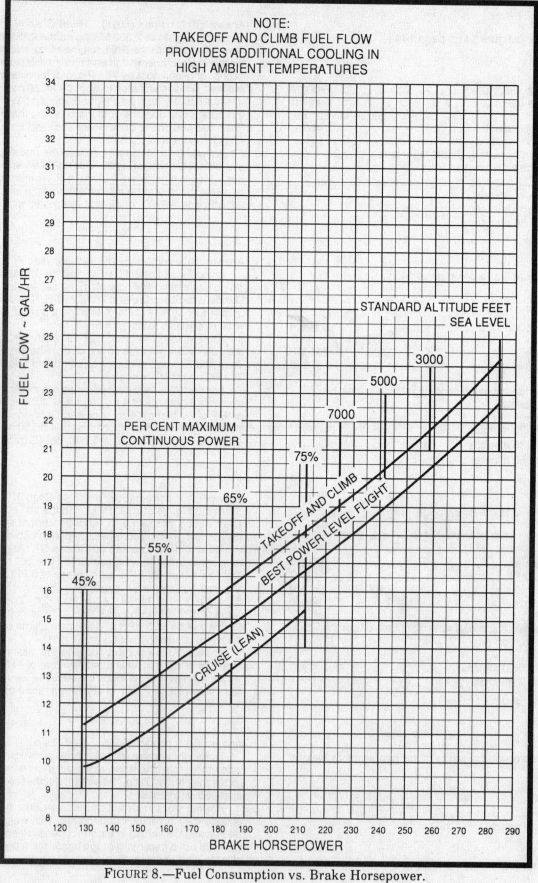

FIGURE 8.—Fuel Consumption vs. Brake Horsepower.

35.

5451. (Refer to figure 8 on page 142.)

GIVEN:

Fuel quantity . . . . 47 gal
Power-cruise (lean) . . . . 55 percent

Approximately how much flight time would be available with a night VFR fuel reserve remaining?

A— 3 hours 8 minutes.
B— 3 hours 22 minutes.
C— 3 hours 43 minutes.

Answer (B) is correct (5451). *(PHAK Chap 4)*

Given 47 gal. of fuel available at cruise power (55%), how much time is available, not counting a 45-min. fuel reserve? On Fig. 8, find the intersection of the cruise (lean) curve and 55% power. From the intersection, proceed horizontally to the left to determine 11.4 GPH. Divide 47 gal. usable fuel by 11.4 GPH to determine 4.122 hr., which translates to 4 hr. 7 min. Subtract 45 min. to determine 3 hr. 22 min.

Alternatively, use your flight computer. Put 11.4 over the true index. Then on the outer scale find 47, which gives you about 4 hr. 7 min. Subtract 45 min. to get 3 hr. 22 min.

Answer (A) is incorrect because 3 hr. 8 min. is the flight time at best power, not cruise, and with a VFR-day, not VFR-night (i.e., 45 min.), reserve. Answer (C) is incorrect because the flight time with a VFR-night reserve (45 min.) at cruise (lean) power is 3 hr. 22 min., not 3 hr. 43 min.

36.

5452. (Refer to figure 8 on page 142.)

GIVEN:

Fuel quantity . . . . 65 gal
Best power (level flight) . . . . 55 percent

Approximately how much flight time would be available with a day VFR fuel reserve remaining?

A— 4 hours 17 minutes.
B— 4 hours 30 minutes.
C— 5 hours 4 minutes.

Answer (B) is correct (5452). *(PHAK Chap 4)*

Given 65 gal. of fuel available at best power (55%), how much time is available, not counting a 30-min. fuel reserve? On Fig. 8, find the intersection of the level flight curve and 55% power. From the intersection, proceed horizontally to the left to determine 13 GPH. Divide 65 gal. usable fuel by 13 GPH to determine 5 hr. Subtract 30 min. to determine 4 hr. 30 min.

Answer (A) is incorrect because 4 hr. 17 min. is the approximate flight time with a VFR-night, not VFR-day, fuel reserve. Answer (C) is incorrect because 5 hr. 4 min. is the approximate flight time with no fuel reserve.

37.

5453. (Refer to figure 8 on page 142.) Approximately how much fuel would be consumed when climbing at 75 percent power for 7 minutes?

A— 1.82 gallons.
B— 1.97 gallons.
C— 2.15 gallons.

Answer (C) is correct (5453). *(PHAK Chap 4)*

To determine the amount of fuel to be burned in 7 min., on Fig. 8 find the intersection of the takeoff and climb curve with 75% power. From the intersection, proceed horizontally to the left to determine about 18.2 GPH. Multiply this times 7/60 to determine 2.12 gal.

Answer (A) is incorrect because 1.8 gal. is used with a fuel flow of 15.6 GPH, not 18.2 GPH. Answer (B) is incorrect because 1.97 gal. is used with a fuel flow of 16.8 GPH, not 18.2 GPH.

38.

5454. (Refer to figure 8 on page 142.) Determine the amount of fuel consumed during takeoff and climb at 70 percent power for 10 minutes.

A— 2.66 gallons.
B— 2.88 gallons.
C— 3.2 gallons.

Answer (B) is correct (5454). *(PHAK Chap 4)*

To determine the amount of fuel to be burned in 10 min., on Fig. 8 find the intersection of the takeoff and climb curve with 70% power (the 70% power line is approximately one-half of the way between 65% and 75%), which is about 17.3 GPH. One-sixth of this is 2.88 gal.

Answer (A) is incorrect because 2.66 gal. is used with a fuel flow of 16 GPH, not 17.3 GPH. Answer (C) is incorrect because 3.2 gal. is used with a fuel flow of 19.2 GPH, not 17.3 GPH.

39.
5455. (Refer to figure 8 on page 142.) With 38 gallons of fuel aboard at cruise power (55 percent), how much flight time is available with night VFR fuel reserve still remaining?

A— 2 hours 34 minutes.
B— 2 hours 49 minutes.
C— 3 hours 18 minutes.

Answer (A) is correct (5455). *(PHAK Chap 4)*
On Fig. 8, find the intersection of the cruise (lean) curve and 55% power. From the intersection, proceed horizontally to the left to determine 11.4 GPH. Divide 38 gal. usable fuel by 11.4 GPH to determine 3 hr. 19 min. Subtract 45 min. to determine 2 hr. 34 min.
Answer (B) is incorrect because 2 hr. 49 min. requires a fuel flow of 10.7 GPH, not 11.4 GPH. Answer (C) is incorrect because 3 hr. 18 min. is the approximate flight time without considering the 45-min. VFR-night fuel reserve.

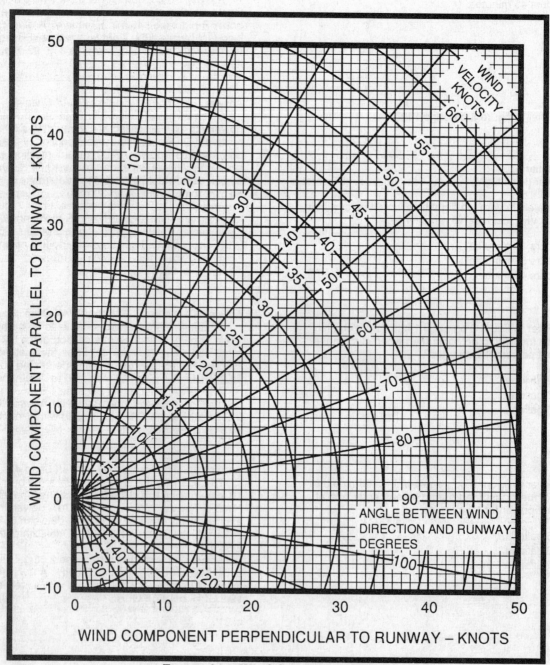

FIGURE 31.—Wind Component Chart.

5.7 Crosswind/Headwind Component

40.

5615. (Refer to figure 31 on page 144.) Rwy 30 is being used for landing. Which surface wind would exceed the airplane's crosswind capability of 0.2 V_{so}, if V_{so} is 60 knots?

A— 260° at 20 knots.
B— 275° at 25 knots.
C— 315° at 35 knots.

Answer (A) is correct (5615). *(PHAK Chap 4)*

The crosswind capability of .2 V_{so} with a V_{so} of 60 kt. means a crosswind capability of 12 kt. (60 x .2). Thus, you must go through each of the situations to determine which crosswind component is in excess of 12 kt.

With a wind of 260° and a landing on Rwy 30 (i.e., at 300°), the crosswind angle is 40° (300° – 260°). Go out to the 20-kt. arc and then down vertically to determine a 13-kt. crosswind component, which exceeds the 12-kt. capability.

Answer (B) is incorrect because the crosswind angle is 25° (300° – 275°). Go out to the 25-kt. arc and then down vertically to determine a 10.5-kt. crosswind component, which is less than the airplane's 12-kt. crosswind capability. Answer (C) is incorrect because the crosswind angle is 15° (315° – 300°). Go out to the 35-kt. arc and then down vertically to determine a 9-kt. crosswind component, which is less than the airplane's 12-kt. crosswind capability.

41.

5617. (Refer to figure 31 on page 144.) The surface wind is 180° at 25 knots. What is the crosswind component for a Rwy 13 landing?

A— 19 knots.
B— 21 knots.
C— 23 knots.

Answer (A) is correct (5617). *(PHAK Chap 4)*

When landing on Rwy 13 with a surface wind of 180°, the crosswind will be at 50° (180° – 130°). On Fig. 31, go out the 50° line to the 25-kt. wind arc. From that intersection go vertically down to the horizontal scale at the bottom of the graph and find a 19-kt. crosswind component.

Answer (B) is incorrect because a 21-kt. crosswind component requires a surface wind of 180° at 28 kt., not 25 kt. Answer (C) is incorrect because a 23-kt. crosswind component requires a surface wind of 180° at 30 kt., not 25 kt.

42.

5618. (Refer to figure 31 on page 144.) What is the headwind component for a Rwy 13 takeoff if the surface wind is 190° at 15 knots?

A— 7 knots.
B— 13 knots.
C— 15 knots.

Answer (A) is correct (5618). *(PHAK Chap 4)*

When landing on Rwy 13 with a surface wind of 190°, the crosswind will be at 60° (190° – 130°). On Fig. 31, go out the 60° line to the 15-kt. wind arc. From that intersection go horizontally across to the left to the vertical scale at the side of the graph and find a 7-kt. headwind component.

Answer (B) is incorrect because 13 kt. is the crosswind, not headwind, component. Answer (C) is incorrect because 15 kt. is the surface wind, not headwind, component.

43.

5616. (Refer to figure 31 on page 144.) If the tower-reported surface wind is 010° at 18 knots, what is the crosswind component for a Rwy 08 landing?

A— 7 knots.
B— 15 knots.
C— 17 knots.

Answer (C) is correct (5616). *(PHAK Chap 4)*

When landing on Rwy 08 with a surface wind of 10° the crosswind will be at 70° (80° – 10°). On Fig. 31, go out the 70° line to the 18-kt. wind arc. From that intersection go vertically down to the horizontal scale at the bottom of the graph and find a 17-kt. crosswind component.

Answer (A) is incorrect because a 7-kt. crosswind component requires a 7-kt., not an 18-kt., surface wind at 010°. Answer (B) is incorrect because a 15-kt. crosswind component requires a 16-kt., not an 18-kt., surface wind at 010°.

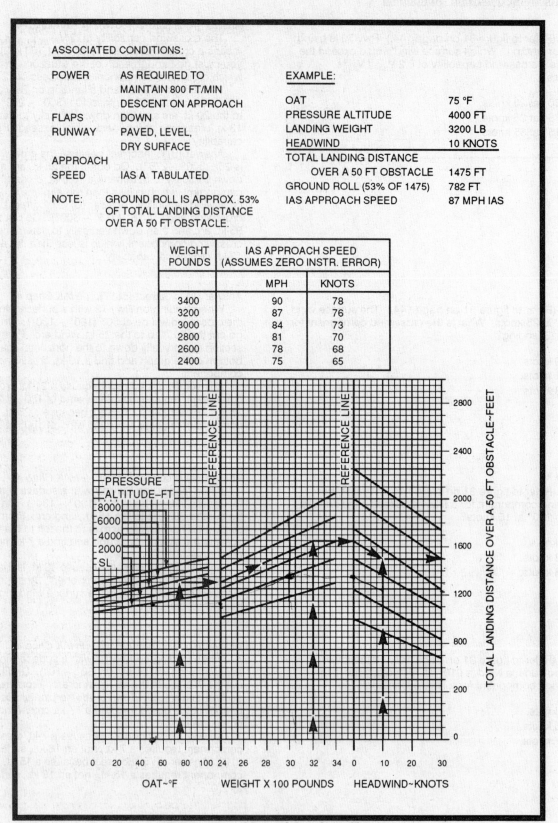

ASSOCIATED CONDITIONS:

POWER	AS REQUIRED TO MAINTAIN 800 FT/MIN DESCENT ON APPROACH
FLAPS	DOWN
RUNWAY	PAVED, LEVEL, DRY SURFACE
APPROACH SPEED	IAS A TABULATED

NOTE: GROUND ROLL IS APPROX. 53% OF TOTAL LANDING DISTANCE OVER A 50 FT OBSTACLE.

EXAMPLE:

OAT	75 °F
PRESSURE ALTITUDE	4000 FT
LANDING WEIGHT	3200 LB
HEADWIND	10 KNOTS
TOTAL LANDING DISTANCE OVER A 50 FT OBSTACLE	1475 FT
GROUND ROLL (53% OF 1475)	782 FT
IAS APPROACH SPEED	87 MPH IAS

WEIGHT POUNDS	IAS APPROACH SPEED (ASSUMES ZERO INSTR. ERROR)	
	MPH	KNOTS
3400	90	78
3200	87	76
3000	84	73
2800	81	70
2600	78	68
2400	75	65

FIGURE 35.—Normal Landing Chart.

5.8 Landing Distance

44.
5630. (Refer to figure 35 on page 146.)

GIVEN:

Temperature . . . . 50 °F
Pressure altitude . . . . Sea level
Weight . . . . 3,000 lb
Headwind . . . . 10 kts

Determine the approximate ground roll.

A— 425 feet.
B— 636 feet.
C— 836 feet.

45.
5631. (Refer to figure 35 on page 146.)

GIVEN:

Temperature . . . . 80 °F
Pressure altitude . . . . 4,000 ft
Weight . . . . 2,800 lb
Headwind . . . . 24 kts

What is the total landing distance over a 50-foot obstacle?

A— 1,125 feet.
B— 1,250 feet.
C— 1,325 feet.

46.
5628. (Refer to figure 35 on page 146.)

GIVEN:

Temperature . . . . 70 °F
Pressure altitude . . . . Sea level
Weight . . . . 3,400 lb
Headwind . . . . 16 kts

Determine the approximate ground roll.

A— 689 feet.
B— 716 feet.
C— 1,275 feet.

Answer (B) is correct (5630). *(PHAK Chap 4)*
Determine the ground roll on Fig. 35 by computing 53% of the total landing distance over a 50-ft. obstacle, which is listed on the right-hand side of the figure. Begin with the temperature of 50°F at the lower left. Proceed upward to the sea-level line. From that intersection, proceed horizontally to the right to the first reference line. From that point, proceed up and to the right parallel to the guidelines to the 3,000-lb. point, as shown at the bottom of the graph. From that point, proceed horizontally to the second reference line. Then proceed to the right and down parallel to the headwind guidelines until you intersect the 10-kt. line. From that point, proceed horizontally to the right to determine about 1,200 ft. to clear a 50-ft. obstacle. Multiply this amount by .53 to get the ground roll of 636 ft.
Answer (A) is incorrect because 425 ft. is the ground roll for a total landing distance over a 50-ft. obstacle of 802 ft. Answer (C) is incorrect because 836 ft. is the ground roll for a total landing distance over a 50-ft. obstacle of 1,577 ft.

Answer (A) is correct (5631). *(PHAK Chap 4)*
Begin with the temperature of 80°F at the lower left on Fig. 35. Proceed upward to the 4,000-ft. line. From that intersection, proceed horizontally to the right to the first reference line. From that point, proceed up and to the right parallel to the guidelines to the 2,800-lb. point, as shown at the bottom of the graph. From that point, proceed horizontally to the second reference line. From that point on the second reference line, proceed to the right and down parallel to the headwind guidelines until you intersect the 24-kt. line. From that point, proceed horizontally to the right to determine about 1,125 ft. to clear a 50-ft. obstacle.
Answer (B) is incorrect because 1,250 ft. requires a headwind of 16 kt., not 24 kt. Answer (C) is incorrect because 1,325 ft. requires a headwind of 10 kt., not 24 kt.

Answer (A) is correct (5628). *(PHAK Chap 4)*
Determine the ground roll on Fig. 35 by computing 53% of the total landing distance over a 50-ft. obstacle, which is listed on the right-hand side of the figure. Begin with the temperature of 70°F at the lower left. Proceed upward to the sea-level line. From that intersection, proceed horizontally to the right to the first reference line. From that point, proceed up and to the right parallel to the guidelines to the 3,400-lb. point, as shown at the bottom of the graph. From that point, proceed horizontally to the second reference line. Then proceed to the right and down parallel to the headwind guidelines until you intersect the 16-kt. line. From that point, proceed horizontally to the right to determine a total landing distance of 1,300 ft. to clear a 50-ft. obstacle. Multiply this amount by .53 to get the ground roll of 689 ft.
Answer (B) is incorrect because a ground roll of 716 ft. requires a headwind of 14 kt., not 16 kt. Answer (C) is incorrect because 1,275 ft. is the total landing distance over a 50-ft. obstacle, not ground roll, with a 19-kt., not-16 kt., headwind.

47.
5629. (Refer to figure 35 on page 146.)

GIVEN:

Temperature . . . . 85 °F
Pressure altitude . . . . 6,000 ft
Weight . . . . 2,800 lb
Headwind . . . . 14 kts

Determine the approximate ground roll.

A— 742 feet.
B— 1,280 feet.
C— 1,480 feet.

Answer (A) is correct (5629). *(PHAK Chap 4)*
    Determine the ground roll on Fig. 35 by computing 53% of the total landing distance over a 50-ft. obstacle, which is listed on the right-hand side of the figure. Begin with the temperature of 85°F at the lower left. Proceed upward to the 6,000-ft. line. From that intersection, proceed horizontally to the right to the first reference line. From that point, proceed up and to the right parallel to the guidelines to the 2,800-lb. point, as shown at the bottom of the graph. From that point, proceed horizontally to the second reference line. Then proceed to the right and down parallel to the headwind guidelines until you intersect the 14-kt. line. From that point, proceed horizontally to the right to determine about 1,400 ft. to clear a 50-ft. obstacle. Multiply this amount by .53 to get the ground roll of 742 ft.
    Answer (B) is incorrect because a 1,280-ft. ground roll requires a 2,415-ft. total landing distance. Answer (C) is incorrect because 1,480 ft. is the total landing distance, not the ground roll, with a 10-kt., not 14-kt., headwind.

5.9 Weight and Balance

48.
5632. When computing weight and balance, the basic empty weight includes the weight of the airframe, engine(s), and all installed optional equipment. Basic empty weight also includes

A— the unusable fuel, full operating fluids, and full oil.
B— all usable fuel, full oil, hydraulic fluid, but does not include the weight of pilot, passengers, or baggage.
C— all usable fuel and oil, but does not include any radio equipment or instruments that were installed by someone other than the manufacturer.

Answer (A) is correct (5632). *(PHAK Chap 4)*
    Empty weight consists of the airframe, the engine, and all installed optional equipment, including fixed ballast, unusable fuel, full operating fluids, and full oil.
    Answer (B) is incorrect because empty weight does not include usable fuel. Answer (C) is incorrect because empty weight does not include usable fuel, but it does include all installed equipment.

49.
5634. The CG of an aircraft can be determined by which of the following methods?

A— Dividing total arms by total moments.
B— Multiplying total arms by total weight.
C— Dividing total moments by total weight.

Answer (C) is correct (5634). *(PHAK Chap 4)*
    The center of gravity, by definition, is the total moment of the airplane divided by its total weight. Moment is the position of weight from some fixed point (called the datum) multiplied by that weight.
    Answer (A) is incorrect because arms are the distances of weight from the datum; each arm is individually multiplied by its respective weight to determine an individual moment. Answer (B) is incorrect because arms are the distances of weight from the datum; each arm is individually multiplied by its respective weight to determine an individual moment.

50.
5635. The CG of an aircraft may be determined by

A— dividing total arms by total moments.
B— dividing total moments by total weight.
C— multiplying total weight by total moments.

51.
5633. If all index units are positive when computing weight and balance, the location of the datum would be at the

A— centerline of the main wheels.
B— nose, or out in front of the airplane.
C— centerline of the nose or tailwheel, depending on the type of airplane.

Answer (B) is correct (5635). *(PHAK Chap 4)*
The center of gravity, by definition, is the total moment of the airplane divided by its total weight. Moment is the position of weight from some fixed point (called the datum) multiplied by that weight.
Answer (A) is incorrect because arms are the distances of weight from the datum; each arm is individually multiplied by its respective weight to determine an individual moment. Answer (C) is incorrect because you must divide total moments by total weight (not vice versa).

Answer (B) is correct (5633). *(PWBH Chap 4)*
Index units refer to arms. If all the arms are positive in computing weight and balance, the datum (or starting point) must be at the nose or out in front of the nose of the airplane. If it is somewhere between the nose and the tail, some items (those between the datum and the nose) would be negative.
Answer (A) is incorrect because, if the datum were at the centerline of the main wheels, the engine would have a negative arm (or index unit). Answer (C) is incorrect because, if the datum were at the centerline of the nose or tailwheel, at least the propeller would have a negative arm (or index unit).

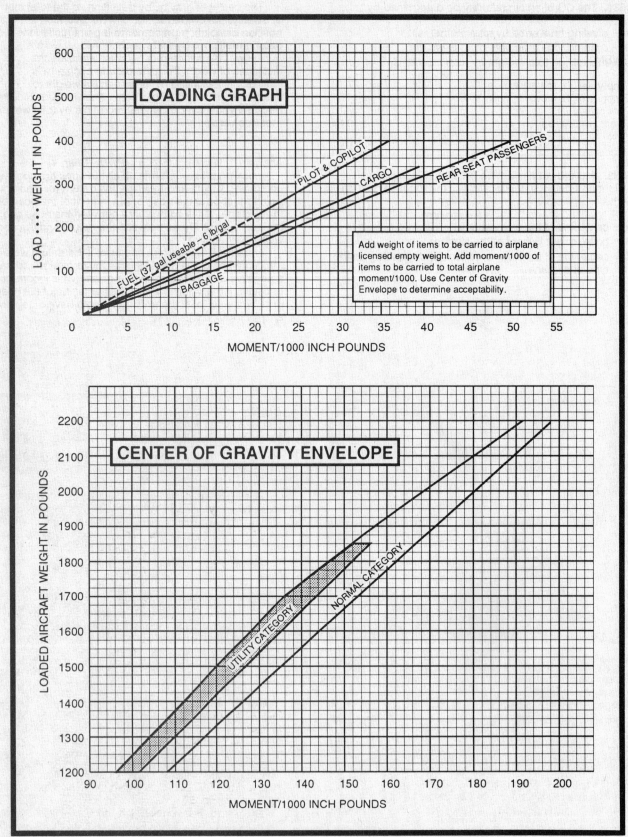

FIGURE 38.—Loading Graph and Center-of-Gravity Envelope.

5.10 Weight and Moment Computations

52.
5650. (Refer to figure 38 on page 150.)

GIVEN:

Empty weight (oil is included) . . . . 1,271 lb
Empty weight moment (in-lb/1,000) 102.04
Pilot and copilot . . . . 400 lb
Rear seat passenger . . . . 140 lb
Cargo . . . . 100 lb
Fuel . . . . 37 gal

Is the airplane loaded within limits?

A— Yes, the weight and CG is within limits.
B— No, the weight exceeds the maximum allowable.
C— No, the weight is acceptable, but the CG is aft of the aft limit.

53.
5651. (Refer to figure 38 on page 150.)

GIVEN:

Empty weight (oil is included) . . . . 1,271 lb
Empty weight moment (in-lb/1,000) 102.04
Pilot and copilot . . . . 260 lb
Rear seat passenger . . . . 120 lb
Cargo . . . . 60 lb
Fuel . . . . 37 gal

Under these conditions, the CG is determined to be located

A— within the CG envelope.
B— on the forward limit of the CG envelope.
C— within the shaded area of the CG envelope.

54.
5652. (Refer to figure 38 on page 150.)

GIVEN:

Empty weight (oil is included) . . . . 1,271 lb
Empty weight moment (in-lb/1,000) 102.04
Pilot and copilot . . . . 360 lb
Cargo . . . . 340 lb
Fuel . . . . 37 gal

Will the CG remain within limits after 30 gallons of fuel has been used in flight?

A— Yes, the CG will remain within limits.
B— No, the CG will be located aft of the aft CG limit.
C— Yes, but the CG will be located in the shaded area of the CG envelope.

Answer (A) is correct (5650). *(PWBH Chap 6)*
Use the loading graph at the top of Fig. 38 to determine the moment for each individual weight.

	Weight	Moment/ 1,000 in.-lb.
Empty weight	1,271	102.04
Pilot and copilot	400	36.0
Rear-seat passenger	140	18.0
Cargo	100	11.5
Fuel (37 gal. × 6 lb./gal.)	222	20.0
	2,133	187.54

The intersection of total weight of 2,133 lb. and total moment of 187.54 in.-lb. is within the CG moment envelope in Fig. 38.
Answer (B) is incorrect because 2,133 lb. is less than the maximum allowable weight of 2,200 lb. Answer (C) is incorrect because 187.54 in.-lb. is less than the aft limit at 2,133 lb. of 193 in.-lb.

Answer (A) is correct (5651). *(PWBH Chap 6)*
Use the loading graph at the top of Fig. 38 to determine the moment for each individual weight.

	Weight	Moment/ 1,000 in.-lb.
Empty weight	1,271	102.04
Pilot and copilot	260	23.5
Rear-seat passenger	120	15.0
Cargo	60	7.0
Fuel (37 gal. × 6 lb./gal.)	222	20.0
	1,933	167.54

The intersection of total weight of 1,933 lb. and total moment of 167.54 in.-lb. is within the CG moment envelope in Fig. 38.
Answer (B) is incorrect because a total moment of approximately 160.5 in.-lb., not 167.54 in.-lb., would put the CG at the forward limit of the CG envelope at a weight of 1,933 lb. Answer (C) is incorrect because both the weight and the moment are outside the shaded (utility category) area.

Answer (A) is correct (5652). *(PWBH Chap 6)*
Use the loading graph at the top of Fig. 38 to determine the moment for each individual weight. Fuel remaining is determined by 37 gal. to start – 30 gal. burned = 7 gal. left x 6 lb. per gal.

	Weight	Moment/ 1,000 in.-lb.
Empty weight	1,271	102.04
Pilot and copilot	360	32.5
Cargo	340	39.5
Fuel (7 gal. × 6 lb./gal.)	42	4.0
	2,013	178.04

The intersection of total weight of 2,013 lb. and total moment of 178.04 in.-lb. is within the CG moment envelope in Fig. 38.
Answer (B) is incorrect because 178.04 in.-lb. is less than the aft CG limit at 2,013 lb. of 180 in.-lb. Answer (C) is incorrect because both the weight and the moment are outside the shaded (utility category) area.

55.
5636. GIVEN:

Weight A — 155 pounds at 45 inches aft of datum
Weight B — 165 pounds at 145 inches aft of datum
Weight C — 95 pounds at 185 inches aft of datum

Based on this information, where would the CG be located aft of datum?

A— 86.0 inches.
B— 116.8 inches.
C— 125.0 inches.

Answer (B) is correct (5636). *(PWBH Chap 6)*
    To determine the CG, use a three-step process:

1. First, multiply the individual weights by their arms to get the individual moments.

	W	×	A	=	M
A =	155	×	45	=	6,975
B =	165	×	145	=	23,925
C =	95	×	185	=	17,575
	415				48,475

2. Compute total weight and total moments.
3. Divide total moments by total weight to get the CG.

$$CG = \frac{48,475}{415} = 116.8 \; in.$$

Answer (A) is incorrect because the CG is 116.8 in., not 86.0 in. Answer (C) is incorrect because the CG is 116.8 in., not 125.0 in.

56.
5637. GIVEN:

Weight A — 140 pounds at 17 inches aft of datum
Weight B — 120 pounds at 110 inches aft of datum
Weight C — 85 pounds at 210 inches aft of datum

Based on this information, the CG would be located how far aft of datum?

A— 89.11 inches.
B— 96.89 inches.
C— 106.92 inches.

Answer (B) is correct (5637). *(PWBH Chap 6)*
    To determine the CG, use a three-step process:

1. First, multiply the individual weights by their arms to get the individual moments.

	W	×	A	=	M
A =	140	×	17	=	2,380
B =	120	×	110	=	13,200
C =	85	×	210	=	17,850
	345				33,430

2. Compute total weight and total moments.
3. Divide total moments by total weight to get the CG.

$$CG = \frac{33,430}{345} = 96.89 \; in.$$

Answer (A) is incorrect because the CG is 96.89 in., not 89.11 in. Answer (C) is incorrect because the CG is 96.89 in., not 106.92 in.

57.
5643. GIVEN:

	WEIGHT	ARM	MOMENT
Empty weight	957	29.07	?
Pilot (fwd seat)	140	−45.30	?
Passenger (aft seat)	170	+1.60	?
Ballast	15	−45.30	?
TOTALS	?	?	?

The CG is located at station

A— −6.43.
B— +16.43.
C— +27.38.

Answer (B) is correct (5643). *(PWBH Chap 6)*
    To determine the CG, use a three-step process:

1. Multiply the individual weights by individual arms to get individual moments.

	W	×	A	=	M
A =	957	×	29.07	=	27,819.99
B =	140	×	−45.30	=	−6,342.00
C =	170	×	1.60	=	272.00
D =	15	×	−45.30	=	−679.50
	1,282				21,070.49

2. Compute total weight and total moments.
3. Divide total moments by total weight to get the CG.

$$CG = \frac{21,070.49}{1,282} = +16.43$$

Answer (A) is incorrect because the CG is +16.43, not −6.43. Answer (C) is incorrect because the CG is +16.43, not +27.38.

58.
5638. GIVEN:

Weight A — 135 pounds at 15 inches aft of datum
Weight B — 205 pounds at 117 inches aft of datum
Weight C — 85 pounds at 195 inches aft of datum

Based on this information, the CG would be located how far aft of datum?

A— 100.2 inches.
B— 109.0 inches.
C— 121.7 inches.

Answer (A) is correct (5638). *(PWBH Chap 6)*
    To determine the CG, use a three-step process:

1. Multiply the individual weights by their arms to get the individual moments.

W	×	A	=	M
A = 135	×	15	=	2,025
B = 205	×	117	=	23,985
C = 85	×	195	=	16,575
425				42,585

2. Compute total weight and total moments.
3. Divide total moments by total weight to get the CG.

$$CG = \frac{42,585}{425} = 100.2 \ in.$$

    Answer (B) is incorrect because the CG is 100.2 in., not 109.0 in. Answer (C) is incorrect because the CG is 100.2 in., not 121.7 in.

59.
5639. GIVEN:

Weight A — 175 pounds at 135 inches aft of datum
Weight B — 135 pounds at 115 inches aft of datum
Weight C — 75 pounds at 85 inches aft of datum

The CG for the combined weights would be located how far aft of datum?

A— 91.76 inches.
B— 111.67 inches.
C— 118.24 inches.

Answer (C) is correct (5639). *(PWBH Chap 6)*
    To determine the CG, use a three-step process:

1. Multiply the individual weights by their arms to get the individual moments.

W	×	A	=	M
A = 175	×	135	=	23,625
B = 135	×	115	=	15,525
C = 75	×	85	=	6,375
385				45,525

2. Compute total weight and total moments.
3. Divide total moments by total weight to get the CG.

$$CG = \frac{45,525}{385} = 118.24 \ in.$$

    Answer (A) is incorrect because the CG is 118.24 in., not 91.76 in. Answer (B) is incorrect because the CG is 118.24 in., not 111.67 in.

5.11 Weight Change and Weight Shift Computations

60.
5646. GIVEN:

Total weight .... 4,137 lb
CG location .... station 67.8
Fuel consumption .... 13.7 GPH
Fuel CG .... station 68.0

After 1 hour 30 minutes of flight time, the CG would be located at station

A— 67.79.
B— 68.79.
C— 70.78.

Answer (A) is correct (5646). *(PWBH Chap 5)*
    To determine the new CG, complete the following steps:

1. Weight change = Fuel consumption (GPH) × flight time × 6 lb./gal.
        = 13.7 × 1.5 × 6
        = 123.3 lb.

2. Use the following formula to determine the new CG:

$$New \ CG = \frac{M_1 \pm \Delta M}{W_1 \pm \Delta W}$$

where M_1 = original moment and W_1 = original weight.

$$New \ CG = \frac{(4,137 \times 67.8) - (123.3 \times 68.0)}{4,137 - 123.3}$$

$$= \frac{280,488.6 - 8,384.4}{4,013.7} = \frac{272,104.2}{4,013.7} = 67.79$$

    Answer (B) is incorrect because the new CG is 67.79, not 68.79. Answer (C) is incorrect because the new CG is 67.79, not 70.78.

61.
5649. GIVEN:

Total weight	3,037 lb
CG location	station 68.8
Fuel consumption	12.7 GPH
Fuel CG	station 68.0

After 1 hour 45 minutes of flight time, the CG would be located at station

A— 68.77.
B— 68.83.
C— 69.77.

Answer (B) is correct (5649). *(PWBH Chap 5)*
  To determine the new CG, complete the following steps:

1. Weight change = Fuel consumption (GPH) ×
           flight time × 6 lb./gal.
        = 12.7 × 1.75 × 6
        = 133.35 lb.

2. Use the following formula to determine the new CG:

$$New\ CG = \frac{M_1 \pm \Delta M}{W_1 \pm \Delta W}$$

where M_1 = original moment and W_1 = original weight.

$$New\ CG = \frac{(3,037 \times 68.8) - (133.35 \times 68.0)}{3,037 - 133.35}$$

$$= \frac{208,945.6 - 9,067.8}{2,903.65} = \frac{199,877.8}{2,903.65} = 68.83$$

  Answer (A) is incorrect because the new CG is 68.83, not 68.77. Answer (C) is incorrect because the new CG is 68.83, not 69.77.

62.
5648. An airplane is loaded to a gross weight of 4,800 pounds, with three pieces of luggage in the rear baggage compartment. The CG is located 98 inches aft of datum, which is 1 inch aft of limits. If luggage which weighs 90 pounds is moved from the rear baggage compartment (145 inches aft of datum) to the front compartment (45 inches aft of datum), what is the new CG?

A— 96.13 inches aft of datum.
B— 95.50 inches aft of datum.
C— 99.87 inches aft of datum.

Answer (A) is correct (5648). *(PWBH Chap 5)*
  To determine the new CG, use the following formula:

$$New\ CG = \frac{M_1 \pm \Delta M}{W_1 \pm \Delta W}$$

where M_1 = original moment and W_1 = original weight.

  Since there is no change in weight, $\Delta W = 0$ and weight shifted forward causes a "–" moment change.

$$New\ CG = \frac{(4,800 \times 98) - 90(145 - 45)}{4,800}$$

$$= \frac{470,400 - 9,000}{4,800} = \frac{461,400}{4,800} = 96.13$$

  Answer (B) is incorrect because the new CG is 96.13, not 95.50. Answer (C) is incorrect because the new CG is 96.13, not 99.87.

63.
5647. An aircraft is loaded with a ramp weight of 3,650 pounds and having a CG of 94.0, approximately how much baggage would have to be moved from the rear baggage area at station 180 to the forward baggage area at station 40 in order to move the CG to 92.0?

A— 52.14 pounds.
B— 62.24 pounds.
C— 78.14 pounds.

Answer (A) is correct (5647). *(PWBH Chap 5)*
  To determine how much weight needs to be shifted forward (causing a "–" moment change), use the following formula:

$$New\ CG = \frac{M_1 \pm \Delta M}{W_1 \pm \Delta W}$$

where M_1 = original moment, W_1 = original weight, and since there is no change in weight, $\Delta W = 0$.

$$92.0 = \frac{(3,650 \times 94.0) - x(180 - 40)}{3,650}$$

$$335,800 = 343,100 - 140x$$
$$140x = 343,100 - 335,800$$
$$140x = 7,300$$
$$x = 52.14\ lb.$$

  Answer (B) is incorrect because only 52.14 lb., not 62.24 lb., of baggage needs to be shifted. Answer (C) is incorrect because only 52.14 lb., not 78.14 lb., of baggage needs to be shifted.

CHAPTER SIX
AEROMEDICAL FACTORS AND
AERONAUTICAL DECISION MAKING (ADM)

This chapter contains outlines of major concepts tested, all FAA test questions and answers regarding aeromedical factors and aeronautical decision making (ADM), and an explanation of each answer. Each module, or subtopic, within this chapter is listed above with the number of questions from the FAA pilot knowledge test pertaining to that particular module. For each module, the first number following the parentheses is the page number on which the outline begins, and the next number is the page number on which the questions begin.

CAUTION: Recall that the **sole purpose** of this book is to expedite your passing the FAA pilot knowledge test for the commercial pilot certificate. Accordingly, all extraneous material (i.e., topics or regulations not directly tested on the FAA pilot knowledge test) is omitted, even though much more information and knowledge are necessary to become a proficient commercial pilot. This additional material is presented in *Commercial Pilot Flight Maneuvers and Practical Test Prep* and *Pilot Handbook*, available from Gleim Publications, Inc. See the order form on page 284.

6.1 HYPOXIA AND ALCOHOL (Questions 1-3)

1. Hypoxia is a state of oxygen deficiency in the body sufficient to impair functions of the brain and other organs.

2. Hypoxia susceptibility due to inhalation of carbon monoxide increases as altitude increases.

3. Even small amounts of alcohol in the body adversely affect judgment and decision making abilities.

6.2 HYPERVENTILATION (Questions 4-7)

1. Hyperventilation occurs when an excessive amount of air is breathed in and out of the lungs; e.g., when you become excited, undergo stress, tension, fear, or anxiety.

    a. This results in insufficient carbon dioxide in the body.

    b. Symptoms include lightheadedness, suffocation, drowsiness, tingling in the extremities, and coolness. Incapacitation and finally unconsciousness can occur.

    c. To overcome hyperventilation, a pilot should slow the breathing rate.

6.3 SPATIAL DISORIENTATION (Question 8)

1. To best overcome spatial disorientation, a pilot should rely on aircraft instrument indications.

6.4 PILOT VISION (Question 9)

1. To scan for other aircraft during the day, use a series of short, regularly spaced eye movements that bring successive areas of the sky into the center of your vision field.

    a. Each movement should not exceed 10°, and each area should be observed for at least 1 second.

6.5 AERONAUTICAL DECISION MAKING (ADM) (Questions 10-32)

1. **Aeronautical decision making (ADM)** is a systematic approach to the mental process used by pilots to consistently determine the best course of action in response to a given set of circumstances.

2. **Risk management** is the part of the ADM process which relies on situational awareness, problem recognition, and good judgment to reduce risks associated with each flight.

3. The ADM process addresses all aspects of decision making in the cockpit and identifies the steps involved in good decision making.

    a. One of the steps for good decision making is for you to identify personal hazardous attitudes to safe flight.

        1) This is accomplished by taking a Self-Assessment Hazardous Attitude Inventory Test.

4. There are a number of classical behavioral traps into which pilots have been known to fall.

    a. Experienced pilots, as a rule, always try to complete a flight as planned, please passengers, meet schedules, and generally demonstrate that they have the "right stuff."

    b. The basic drive to demonstrate the "right stuff" can have an adverse effect on safety and can impose an unrealistic assessment of piloting skills under stressful conditions.

        1) These tendencies ultimately may lead to practices that are dangerous and often illegal and that may result in a mishap.

5. Most pilots have fallen prey to dangerous tendencies or behavioral problems at some time. Some of these dangerous tendencies or behavioral patterns, which must be identified and eliminated, include

    a. Peer pressure
    b. Get-there-itis
    c. Loss of positional or situational awareness
    d. Operating without adequate fuel reserves

6. ADM addresses the following five hazardous attitudes:

    a. Antiauthority -- "Do not tell me!"

        1) EXAMPLE: The passengers for a charter flight have arrived almost an hour late for a flight that requires a reservation. An antiauthority attitude (reaction) by the pilot would be to think that those reservation rules do not apply to this flight.

    b. Impulsivity -- "Do something quickly without thinking!"

        1) EXAMPLE: The pilot and the passengers are anxious to get to their destination for a business presentation, but level 4 thunderstorms are reported to be in a line across their intended route of flight. An impulsivity attitude (reaction) would be for the pilot to "hurry and get going" before things get worse.

    c. Invulnerability -- "It will not happen to me."

        1) EXAMPLE: During an operational check of the cabin pressurization system, the pilot discovers that the rate control feature is inoperative. Since the pilot knows that (s)he can manually control the system, the pilot elects to disregard the discrepancy and departs on the trip. An invulnerability attitude (reaction) would be to think, "What is the worst that could happen? (Problems happen to other people.)"

    d. Macho -- "I can do it!"

        1) EXAMPLE: While on an IFR flight, a pilot emerges from a cloud to find himself within 300 ft. of a helicopter. A macho attitude (reaction) by the pilot would be to fly a little closer to the helicopter, just to "show" the other pilot.

    e. Resignation -- "What is the use?"

        1) EXAMPLE: A pilot and friends are going to fly to an out-of-town football game. When the passengers arrive, the pilot determines that the loaded airplane will be over the maximum gross weight for takeoff with the existing fuel load. A resignation attitude (reaction) by the pilot would be to think, "Well, nobody told me about the extra weight."

7. Hazardous attitudes that contribute to poor pilot judgment can be effectively counteracted by redirecting those hazardous attitudes so that appropriate action can be taken.

8. Recognition of hazardous thoughts is the first step in neutralizing them in the ADM process.

9. When you recognize a hazardous thought, you should label it as hazardous and then correct it by stating the corresponding antidote.

10. The hazardous attitude antidotes, shown below, should be learned thoroughly and practiced.

Hazardous Attitude	Antidote
Antiauthority: *Don't tell me!*	Follow the rules. They are usually right.
Impulsivity: *Do something quickly!*	Not so fast. Think first.
Invulnerability: *It won't happen to me.*	It could happen to me.
Macho: *I can do it.*	Taking chances is foolish.
Resignation: *What's the use?*	I'm not helpless. I can make a difference.

11. Good cockpit stress management begins with good life stress management.

   a.   Since many of the stress coping techniques practiced for life stress management are not usually practiced in flight, you must condition yourself to relax and think rationally when stress occurs.

12. The Decide Model is comprised of a six-step process to provide pilots with a logical way of approaching ADM. The six steps (in order) are

   a.   **D**etect. The decision maker detects the fact that change has occurred.

   b.   **E**stimate. The decision maker estimates the need to counter or react to the change.

   c.   **C**hoose. The decision maker chooses a desirable outcome (in terms of success) for the flight.

   d.   **I**dentify. The decision maker identifies actions which could successfully control the change.

   e.   **D**o. The decision maker takes the necessary action.

   f.   **E**valuate. The decision maker evaluates the effect(s) of his action countering the change.

QUESTIONS AND ANSWER EXPLANATIONS

  All the FAA questions from the pilot knowledge test for the commercial pilot certificate relating to aeromedical factors and the material outlined previously are reproduced on the following pages in the same modules as the outlines. To the immediate right of each question are the correct answer and answer explanation. You should cover these answers and answer explanations while responding to the questions. (A bookmark for this purpose has been provided in the back of the book.) Refer to the general discussion in the Introduction on how to take the FAA pilot knowledge test.

  Remember that the questions from the FAA pilot knowledge test bank have been reordered by topic, and the topics have been organized into a meaningful sequence. Accordingly, the first line of the answer explanation gives the FAA question number and the citation of the authoritative source for the answer.

6.1 Hypoxia and Alcohol

1.
5764. Hypoxia susceptibility due to inhalation of carbon monoxide increases as

A— humidity decreases.
B— altitude increases.
C— oxygen demand increases.

Answer (B) is correct (5764). *(AIM Para 8-1-2)*
  Carbon monoxide inhaled during smoking or from exhaust fumes can reduce the oxygen-carrying capacity of the blood to a degree that the amount of oxygen provided to body tissues will be equivalent to the oxygen provided to the tissues when exposed to a cabin pressure altitude of several thousand feet. Thus, hypoxia (i.e., oxygen deficiency) susceptibility due to inhalation of carbon monoxide increases as altitude increases.
  Answer (A) is incorrect because the humidity level has no bearing on either the carbon monoxide or the oxygen level. Answer (C) is incorrect because oxygen demand stays the same. The availability of oxygen changes.

2.
5761. Hypoxia is the result of which of these conditions?

A— Excessive oxygen in the bloodstream.
B— Insufficient oxygen reaching the brain.
C— Excessive carbon dioxide in the bloodstream.

Answer (B) is correct (5761). *(AIM Para 8-1-2)*
  Hypoxia is a state of oxygen deficiency in the bloodstream sufficient to impair function of the brain and other organs.
  Answer (A) is incorrect because the problem is insufficient oxygen, not excessive oxygen. Answer (C) is incorrect because it is a nonsense answer. Insufficient, not excessive, carbon dioxide in the bloodstream is the result of hyperventilation, not hypoxia.

3.
5763. Which is true regarding the presence of alcohol within the human body?

A— A small amount of alcohol increases vision acuity.
B— An increase in altitude decreases the adverse effect of alcohol.
C— Judgment and decision-making abilities can be adversely affected by even small amounts of alcohol.

Answer (C) is correct (5763). *(AIM Para 8-1-1)*
  As little as 1 ounce of liquor, 12 ounces of beer, or 4 ounces (one glass) of wine can impair flying skills, with the alcohol consumed in these drinks being detectable in the breath and blood for at least 3 hr.
  Answer (A) is incorrect because any amount of alcohol decreases, not increases, virtually all mental and physical activities. Answer (B) is incorrect because increases in altitude increase, not decrease, the adverse effects of alcohol.

6.2 Hyperventilation

4.
5759. Which is a common symptom of hyperventilation?

A— Drowsiness.
B— Decreased breathing rate.
C— Euphoria – sense of well-being.

Answer (A) is correct (5759). *(AIM Para 8-1-3)*
Hyperventilation is an abnormal increase in breathing, which can occur subconsciously when a stressful situation is encountered. It can cause lightheadedness, drowsiness, suffocation, tingling in the extremities, and coolness.
Answer (B) is incorrect because hyperventilation usually occurs from an increased, not a decreased, breathing rate. Answer (C) is incorrect because euphoria is a potential symptom of hypoxia, not hyperventilation.

5.
5757. As hyperventilation progresses a pilot can experience

A— decreased breathing rate and depth.
B— heightened awareness and feeling of well-being.
C— symptoms of suffocation and drowsiness.

Answer (C) is correct (5757). *(AIM Para 8-1-3)*
Hyperventilation is an abnormal increase in breathing, which can occur subconsciously when a stressful situation is encountered. It can cause lightheadedness, drowsiness, suffocation, tingling in the extremities, and coolness.
Answer (A) is incorrect because hyperventilation is an increase, not a decrease, of the breathing rate and depth. Answer (B) is incorrect because heightened awareness and euphoria are potential symptoms of hypoxia, not hyperventilation.

6.
5762. To overcome the symptoms of hyperventilation, a pilot should

A— swallow or yawn.
B— slow the breathing rate.
C— increase the breathing rate.

Answer (B) is correct (5762). *(AIM Para 8-1-3)*
Hyperventilation is an abnormal increase in breathing, which can occur subconsciously when a stressful situation is encountered. To counteract hyperventilation, you should slow the breathing rate.
Answer (A) is incorrect because swallowing and yawning are used to relieve ear block, not hyperventilation. Answer (C) is incorrect because you should slow, not increase, the breathing rate to increase the amount of carbon dioxide in the blood.

7.
5760. Which would most likely result in hyperventilation?

A— Insufficient oxygen.
B— Excessive carbon monoxide.
C— Insufficient carbon dioxide.

Answer (C) is correct (5760). *(AIM Para 8-1-3)*
Hyperventilation occurs when an excessive amount of carbon dioxide is passed out of the body and too much oxygen is retained.
Answer (A) is incorrect because it describes hypoxia. Answer (B) is incorrect because it describes carbon monoxide poisoning.

6.3 Spatial Disorientation

8.
5765. To best overcome the effects of spatial disorientation, a pilot should

A— rely on body sensations.
B— increase the breathing rate.
C— rely on aircraft instrument indications.

Answer (C) is correct (5765). *(AIM Para 8-1-5)*
Various complex motions and forces and certain visual scenes encountered in flight can create illusions of motion and position. Spatial disorientation from these illusions can be prevented only by visual reference to reliable fixed points on the ground or to flight instruments.
Answer (A) is incorrect because you must ignore, not rely on, body sensations. Answer (B) is incorrect because breathing rates relate to hyperventilation, not spatial disorientation.

6.4 Pilot Vision

9.
5758. To scan properly for traffic, a pilot should

A— slowly sweep the field of vision from one side to the other at intervals.
B— concentrate on any peripheral movement detected.
C— use a series of short, regularly spaced eye movements that bring successive areas of the sky into the central visual field.

Answer (C) is correct (5758). *(AIM Para 8-1-6)*
The most effective way to scan for other aircraft during the day is to use a series of short, regularly spaced eye movements that bring successive areas of the sky into your central vision. Each movement should not exceed 10°, and each area should be observed for at least 1 second to facilitate detection.
Answer (A) is incorrect because you must concentrate on different segments systematically. Answer (B) is incorrect because peripheral movement will not be detected easily, especially under adverse conditions such as haze.

6.5 Aeronautical Decision Making

10.
5942. Aeronautical Decision Making (ADM) is a

A— systematic approach to the mental process used by pilots to consistently determine the best course of action for a given set of circumstances.
B— decision making process which relies on good judgment to reduce risks associated with each flight.
C— mental process of analyzing all information in a particular situation and making a timely decision on what action to take.

Answer (A) is correct (5942). *(AC 60-22)*
ADM is a systematic approach to the mental process used by pilots to consistently determine the best course of action in response to a given set of circumstances.
Answer (B) is incorrect because risk management, not ADM, is the part of the decision-making process which relies on situational awareness, problem recognition, and good judgment to reduce risks associated with each flight. Answer (C) is incorrect because judgment, not ADM, is the mental process of recognizing and analyzing all pertinent information in a particular situation, rationally evaluating alternative actions in response to it, and making a timely decision on which action to take.

11.
5941. Risk management, as part of the Aeronautical Decision Making (ADM) process, relies on which features to reduce the risks associated with each flight?

A— The mental process of analyzing all information in a particular situation and making a timely decision on what action to take.
B— Application of stress management and risk element procedures.
C— Situational awareness, problem recognition, and good judgment.

Answer (C) is correct (5941). *(AC 60-22)*
Risk management is the part of the ADM process which relies on situational awareness, problem recognition, and good judgment to reduce risks associated with each flight.
Answer (A) is incorrect because judgment, not risk management, is the mental process of recognizing and analyzing all pertinent information in a particular situation, rationally evaluating alternative actions in response to it, and making a timely decision on what action to take. Answer (B) is incorrect because risk management relies on situational awareness, problem recognition, and good judgment, not the application of stress management and risk element procedures, to reduce the risks associated with each flight.

12.
5943. The Aeronautical Decision Making (ADM) process identifies the steps involved in good decision making. One of these steps includes a pilot

A— making a rational evaluation of the required actions.
B— developing the "right stuff" attitude.
C— identifying personal attitudes hazardous to safe flight.

Answer (C) is correct (5943). *(AC 60-22)*
The ADM process addresses all aspects of decision making in the cockpit and identifies the steps involved in good decision making. One step in good decision making is to identify personal attitudes hazardous to safe flight.
Answer (A) is incorrect because making a rational evaluation of the required actions is a part of judgment, not a step in good decision making. Answer (B) is incorrect because a step in the ADM process is to identify, not develop, a behavioral trap.

13.
5947. An early part of the Aeronautical Decision Making (ADM) process involves

A— taking a self-assessment hazardous attitude inventory test.
B— understanding the drive to have the "right stuff."
C— obtaining proper flight instruction and experience during training.

Answer (A) is correct (5947). *(AC 60-22)*
An early part of the ADM process includes identifying personal attitudes hazardous to safe flight by taking a self-assessment hazardous attitude inventory test.
Answer (B) is incorrect because taking a self-assessment hazardous attitude inventory test, not just understanding the drive to have the "right stuff," is an early part of the ADM process. Answer (C) is incorrect because obtaining proper flight instruction and experience during training is critical in the development of a safe pilot but is not a part of the ADM process itself.

14.
5944. Examples of classic behavioral traps that experienced pilots may fall into are: trying to

A— assume additional responsibilities and assert PIC authority.
B— promote situational awareness and then necessary changes in behavior.
C— complete a flight as planned, please passengers, meet schedules, and demonstrate the "right stuff."

Answer (C) is correct (5944). *(AC 60-22)*
There are a number of classic behavioral traps into which pilots have been known to fall. Pilots, particularly those with considerable experience, as a rule always try to complete a flight as planned, please passengers, meet schedules, and generally demonstrate that they have the "right stuff."
Answer (A) is incorrect because classical behavioral traps include trying to complete a flight as planned, please passengers, meet schedules, and demonstrate the "right stuff," not trying to assume additional responsibilities and assert PIC authority. Answer (B) is incorrect because classical behavioral traps include trying to complete a flight as planned, please passengers, meet schedules, and demonstrate the "right stuff," not trying to promote situational awareness and then necessary changes in behavior.

15.
5945. The basic drive for a pilot to demonstrate the "right stuff" can have an adverse effect on safety, by

A— a total disregard for any alternative course of action.
B— generating tendencies that lead to practices that are dangerous, often illegal, and may lead to a mishap.
C— allowing events, or the situation, to control his or her actions.

Answer (B) is correct (5945). *(AC 60-22)*
The basic drive to demonstrate the "right stuff" can have an adverse effect on safety and can impose an unrealistic assessment of piloting skills under stressful conditions. These tendencies ultimately may lead to practices that are dangerous and often illegal and that may result in a mishap.
Answer (A) is incorrect because get-there-itis, not a basic drive to demonstrate the "right stuff," has an adverse effect on safety when a pilot totally disregards any alternative course of action. Answer (C) is incorrect because getting behind the aircraft, not a basic drive to demonstrate the "right stuff," has an adverse effect on safety by allowing events, or the situation, to control the pilot's actions.

16.
5946. Most pilots have fallen prey to dangerous tendencies or behavior problems at some time. Some of these dangerous tendencies or behavior patterns which must be identified and eliminated include:

A— Deficiencies in instrument skills and knowledge of aircraft systems or limitations.
B— Performance deficiencies from human factors such as fatigue, illness, or emotional problems.
C— Peer pressure, get-there-itis, loss of positional or situational awareness, and operating without adequate fuel reserves.

Answer (C) is correct (5946). *(AC 60-22)*
Peer pressure, get-there-itis, loss of positional or situational awareness, operating without an adequate fuel reserve, and others are dangerous tendencies or behavior patterns which must be identified and eliminated.
Answer (A) is incorrect because deficiencies in skills and/or knowledge may be overcome by conventional training and do not represent dangerous tendencies or behavior problems. Answer (B) is incorrect because performance deficiencies caused by fatigue may be overcome by rest, and those caused by illness or emotional problems may be overcome by medical intervention. These deficiencies are physiological; they do not result from dangerous tendencies or behavior patterns.

17.
5949. What are some of the hazardous attitudes dealt with in Aeronautical Decision Making (ADM)?

A— Antiauthority (don't tell me), impulsivity (do something quickly without thinking), macho (I can do it).
B— Risk management, stress management, and risk elements.
C— Poor decision making, situational awareness, and judgment.

Answer (A) is correct (5949). *(AC 60-22)*
ADM addresses five hazardous attitudes: antiauthority ("Don't tell me"), impulsivity ("Do something quickly without thinking"), invulnerability ("It won't happen to me"), macho ("I can do it"), and resignation ("What's the use?").
Answer (B) is incorrect because risk management, stress management, and risk elements are all part of the ADM process, not hazardous attitudes dealt with in ADM. Answer (C) is incorrect because situational awareness and judgment are part of the mental process in ADM to prevent or stop poor judgment, not hazardous attitudes in ADM.

18.
5955. The passengers for a charter flight have arrived almost an hour late for a flight that requires a reservation. Which of the following alternatives best illustrates the ANTIAUTHORITY reaction?

A— Those reservation rules do not apply to this flight.
B— If the pilot hurries, he or she may still make it on time.
C— The pilot can't help it that the passengers are late.

Answer (A) is correct (5955). *(AC 60-22)*
By demonstrating the attitude that rules do not apply to his/her flight, the pilot is illustrating the antiauthority hazardous attitude.
Answer (B) is incorrect because, if the pilot chooses the alternative to hurry in the belief that (s)he may make it on time, the pilot is illustrating the impulsivity reaction, not the antiauthority reaction. Answer (C) is incorrect because, if the pilot feels that (s)he cannot help that the passengers are late, (s)he is illustrating the resignation reaction, not the antiauthority reaction.

19.
5957. The pilot and passengers are anxious to get to their destination for a business presentation. Level IV thunderstorms are reported to be in a line across their intended route of flight. Which of the following alternatives best illustrates the IMPULSIVITY reaction?

A— They want to hurry and get going, before things get worse.
B— A thunderstorm won't stop them.
C— They can't change the weather, so they might as well go.

Answer (A) is correct (5957). *(AC 60-22)*
The pilot and passengers are anxious to get to their destination for a business presentation, but level 4 thunderstorms are reported to be in a line across their intended route of flight. An impulsivity hazardous attitude ("Act now; there is no time") would be to "hurry and get going" before things get worse.
Answer (B) is incorrect because a thought of "a thunderstorm will not stop them" is an invulnerability, not impulsivity, hazardous attitude. Answer (C) is incorrect because a thought of "they cannot change the weather, so they might as well go" is a resignation, not impulsivity, hazardous attitude.

20.
5956. While conducting an operational check of the cabin pressurization system, the pilot discovers that the rate control feature is inoperative. He knows that he can manually control the cabin pressure, so he elects to disregard the discrepancy and departs on his trip. He will just handle the system himself. Which of the following alternatives best illustrates the INVULNERABILITY reaction?

A— What is the worst that could happen?
B— He can handle a little problem like this.
C— It's too late to fix it now.

Answer (A) is correct (5956). *(AC 60-22)*
A pilot discovers that the rate control feature is inoperative on the cabin pressurization system, elects to disregard the discrepancy, and departs on the trip since he knows he can manually control the pressurization. An invulnerability ("Nothing bad will happen") reaction would be, "What is the worst that could happen?"
Answer (B) is incorrect because "He can handle a little problem like this" is a macho reaction, not an invulnerability reaction. Answer (C) is incorrect because "It is too late to fix it now" is an impulsivity reaction, not an invulnerability reaction.

21.
5958. While on an IFR flight, a pilot emerges from a cloud to find himself within 300 feet of a helicopter. Which of the following alternatives best illustrates the "MACHO" reaction?

A— He is not too concerned; everything will be alright.
B— He flies a little closer, just to show him.
C— He quickly turns away and dives, to avoid collision.

Answer (B) is correct (5958). *(AC 60-22)*
While on an IFR flight, a pilot emerges from a cloud to find himself within 300 ft. of a helicopter. A hazardous macho reaction would be to fly a little closer, just to "show" the other pilot. Macho hazardous thoughts include "I will show you."
Answer (A) is incorrect because a reaction of "not too concerned; everything will be all right" is one of invulnerability, not macho. Answer (C) is incorrect because a reaction of quickly turning away and diving to avoid a collision is an impulsivity reaction, not a macho reaction.

22.
5960. A pilot and friends are going to fly to an out-of-town football game. When the passengers arrive, the pilot determines that they will be over the maximum gross weight for takeoff with the existing fuel load. Which of the following alternatives best illustrates the RESIGNATION reaction?

A— Well, nobody told him about the extra weight.
B— Weight and balance is a formality forced on pilots by the FAA.
C— He can't wait around to de-fuel, they have to get there on time.

Answer (A) is correct (5960). *(AC 60-22)*
A pilot and his friends are going on a flight, but when the passengers arrive, the pilot determines the loaded airplane will be over maximum gross weight for takeoff with the existing fuel load. A resignation reaction by the pilot would be that nobody told him about the extra weight. When the responsibility is assumed to be someone else's, a pilot is in the hazardous thinking pattern of resignation.
Answer (B) is incorrect because considering weight and balance to be a formality forced on pilots by the FAA (ignoring the rules) is a hazardous attitude of antiauthority, not resignation. Answer (C) is incorrect because the pilot who cannot wait around to defuel because of a need to get somewhere on time illustrates the impulsivity ("I must act now; there is no time"), not the resignation, hazardous attitude.

23.
5948. Hazardous attitudes which contribute to poor pilot judgment can be effectively counteracted by

A— early recognition of hazardous thoughts.
B— taking meaningful steps to be more assertive with attitudes.
C— redirecting that hazardous attitude so that appropriate action can be taken.

Answer (C) is correct (5948). *(AC 60-22)*
Hazardous attitudes that contribute to poor pilot judgment can be effectively counteracted by redirecting those hazardous attitudes so that appropriate action can be taken.
Answer (A) is incorrect because, while early recognition of hazardous thoughts is important as an initial step in dealing with hazardous attitudes, they can be effectively counteracted only by redirecting them so that appropriate action can be taken. Answer (B) is incorrect because being more assertive with attitudes, if those attitudes are hazardous, would be counterproductive to safety, while redirecting the hazardous attitudes will allow appropriate action to be taken in dealing with them.

24.
5951. What is the first step in neutralizing a hazardous attitude in the ADM process?

A— Recognition of invulnerability in the situation.
B— Dealing with improper judgment.
C— Recognition of hazardous thoughts.

Answer (C) is correct (5951). *(AC 60-22)*
Recognition of hazardous thoughts is the first step in neutralizing them in the ADM process.
Answer (A) is incorrect because recognition of hazardous thoughts, not recognition of invulnerability in the situation, is the first step in neutralizing them.
Answer (B) is incorrect because recognition of hazardous thoughts, not dealing with improper judgment, is the first step in neutralizing them.

25.
5952. What should a pilot do when recognizing a thought as hazardous?

A— Avoid developing this hazardous thought.
B— Develop this hazardous thought and follow through with modified action.
C— Label that thought as hazardous, then correct that thought by stating the corresponding learned antidote.

26.
5959. When a pilot recognizes a hazardous thought, he or she then should correct it by stating the corresponding antidote. Which of the following is the antidote for ANTIAUTHORITY?

A— Not so fast. Think first.
B— It won't happen to me. It could happen to me.
C— Don't tell me. Follow the rules. They are usually right.

27.
5950. When a pilot recognizes a hazardous thought, he or she then should correct it by stating the corresponding antidote. Which of the following is the antidote for MACHO?

A— Follow the rules. They are usually right.
B— Not so fast. Think first.
C— Taking chances Is foolish.

28.
5954. What does good cockpit stress management begin with?

A— Knowing what causes stress.
B— Eliminating life and cockpit stress issues.
C— Good life stress management.

29.
5953. To help manage cockpit stress, pilots must

A— be aware of life stress situations that are similar to those in flying.
B— condition themselves to relax and think rationally when stress appears.
C— avoid situations that will degrade their abilities to handle cockpit responsibilities.

Answer (C) is correct (5952). *(AC 60-22)*
When a pilot recognizes a hazardous thought, the pilot should label it as hazardous and then correct it by stating the corresponding learned antidote.
Answer (A) is incorrect because, once a hazardous thought is recognized, it is too late to avoid developing the thought. The pilot should label the thought as hazardous and then correct it by stating the corresponding learned antidote. Answer (B) is incorrect because, once a hazardous thought is recognized, it should not be developed. Instead, the pilot should label the thought as hazardous and then correct it by stating the corresponding learned antidote.

Answer (C) is correct (5959). *(AC 60-22)*
When you recognize a hazardous thought, you should then correct it by stating the corresponding antidote. The antidote for an antiauthority ("Do not tell me") attitude is "Follow the rules; they are usually right."
Answer (A) is incorrect because "Not so fast; think first" is the antidote for the impulsivity, not the antiauthority, attitude. Answer (B) is incorrect because "It could happen to me" is the antidote for the invulnerability ("It will not happen to me"), not the antiauthority, attitude.

Answer (C) is correct (5950). *(AC 60-22)*
The antidote for the macho hazardous attitude is: "Taking chances is foolish."
Answer (A) is incorrect because "Taking chances is foolish" is the antidote for macho, not "Follow the rules. They are usually right," which is the antidote for antiauthority. Answer (B) is incorrect because "Taking chances is foolish" is the antidote for macho, rather than "Not so fast. Think first," which is the antidote for impulsivity.

Answer (C) is correct (5954). *(AC 60-22)*
Good cockpit stress management begins with good life stress management, since you will bring the stress in your life into the cockpit with you.
Answer (A) is incorrect because knowing what causes stress is required to reduce stress associated with crisis management in the air, but it is not the beginning of cockpit stress management. Answer (B) is incorrect because eliminating life and cockpit stress issues is impossible. In fact, stress is a necessary part of life that adds motivation to life and heightens your response to meet a challenge.

Answer (B) is correct (5953). *(AC 60-22)*
To help manage cockpit stress, pilots must condition themselves to relax and think rationally when stress occurs.
Answer (A) is incorrect because pilots must condition themselves to relax and think rationally when stress occurs since many of the stress coping techniques practiced for life stress management are not usually practical in flight. Answer (C) is incorrect because pilots must condition themselves to relax and think rationally when unavoidable situations occur that could increase stress and degrade their abilities.

30.
5963. The Decide Model is comprised of a 6-step process to provide a pilot a logical way of approaching Aeronautical Decision Making. These steps are:

A— Detect, estimate, choose, identify, do, and evaluate.
B— Determine, evaluate, choose, identify, do, and eliminate.
C— Determine, eliminate, choose, identify, detect, and evaluate.

Answer (A) is correct (5963). *(AC 60-22)*
     The Decide Model, comprised of a six-step process, is intended to provide you with a logical way of approaching decision making. The six steps (in order) are detect, estimate, choose, identify, do, and evaluate.
     Answer (B) is incorrect because detect, not determine, and estimate, not eliminate, are steps in the Decide Model. Answer (C) is incorrect because do, not determine, and estimate, not eliminate, are steps in the Decide Model.

31.
5962. Which of the following is the first step of the Decide Model for effective risk management and Aeronautical Decision Making?

A— Detect.
B— Identify.
C— Evaluate.

Answer (A) is correct (5962). *(AC 60-22)*
     The Decide Model, comprised of a six-step process, is intended to provide you with a logical way of approaching decision making. The six steps (in order) are detect, estimate, choose, identify, do, and evaluate.
     Answer (B) is incorrect because identify is the fourth step, not the first step, in the Decide Model. Answer (C) is incorrect because evaluate is the final step, not the first step, in the Decide Model.

32.
5961. Which of the following is the final step of the Decide Model for effective risk management and Aeronautical Decision Making?

A— Estimate.
B— Evaluate.
C— Eliminate.

Answer (B) is correct (5961). *(AC 60-22)*
     The Decide Model, comprised of a six-step process, is intended to provide you with a logical way of approaching decision making. The six steps (in order) are detect, estimate, choose, identify, do, and evaluate.
     Answer (A) is incorrect because estimate is the second step, not the final step, in the Decide Model. Answer (C) is incorrect because eliminate is not a step in the Decide Model.

END OF CHAPTER

CHAPTER SEVEN
AVIATION WEATHER

This chapter contains outlines of major concepts tested, all FAA test questions and answers regarding aviation weather, and an explanation of each answer. Each module, or subtopic, within this chapter is listed above with the number of questions from the FAA pilot knowledge test pertaining to that particular module. For each module, the first number following the parentheses is the page number on which the outline begins, and the next number is the page number on which the questions begin.

CAUTION: Recall that the **sole purpose** of this book is to expedite your passing the FAA pilot knowledge test for the commercial pilot certificate. Accordingly, all extraneous material (i.e., topics or regulations not directly tested on the FAA pilot knowledge test) is omitted, even though much more information and knowledge are necessary to become a proficient commercial pilot. This additional material is presented in *Commercial Pilot Flight Maneuvers and Practical Test Prep* and *Pilot Handbook*, available from Gleim Publications, Inc. See the order form on page 284.

7.1 CAUSES OF WEATHER (Questions 1-7)

1. Every physical process of weather is accompanied by, or is a result of, heat exchange.

2. Moisture is added to a parcel of air by evaporation and sublimation.

3. Wind is caused by pressure differences with wind flowing from high-pressure areas to low-pressure areas.

   a. When the isobars are close together, the pressure gradient force is greater, which results in a stronger wind.

4. The Coriolis force deflects wind to the right in the Northern Hemisphere.

   a. Coriolis force tends to counterbalance the horizontal pressure gradient, causing wind to flow parallel to the isobars.

5. A cold front occlusion occurs when the air ahead of the warm front is warmer than the air behind the overtaking cold front.

7.2 HIGH/LOW PRESSURE AREAS (Questions 8-14)

1.   A high-pressure area or ridge is an area of descending air.

   a.   The general circulation of air in a high-pressure area in the Northern Hemisphere is outward, downward, and clockwise.

2.   A low-pressure area or trough is an area of rising air.

   a.   The circulation of air (wind system) in a low-pressure area in the Northern Hemisphere is cyclonic, i.e., counterclockwise.

   b.   Thus, when flying into such a low-pressure area, the wind direction and velocity will be from the left and increasing.

   c.   A low-pressure area is generally an area of unfavorable weather conditions.

3.   The Coriolis force prevents wind from flowing directly from high-pressure areas to low-pressure areas and produces the associated circulations.

7.3 JET STREAM (Questions 15-21)

1.   In the middle latitudes during the winter months, the jet stream shifts south and the wind speed increases.

   a.   It is normally weaker and farther north in the summer.

2.   Clear air turbulence (CAT) is typically found in an upper trough on the polar side of the jet stream.

3.   The jet stream and associated CAT can sometimes be visually identified by long streaks of cirrus clouds.

4.   Strong wind shears can be expected on the low-pressure side of a jet stream core where the wind speed at the core is greater than 110 kt.

5.   A curving jet stream means there are abrupt weather system changes which lend themselves to more violent turbulence.

6.   The tropopause is the layer of air above the troposphere and is characterized by an abrupt change in the temperature lapse rate.

7.4 TEMPERATURE (Questions 22-25)

1.   Standard temperature is 15°C (59°F) at sea level; the standard lapse rate is 2°C per 1,000 ft.

   a.   Thus, the standard temperature at any altitude is 15°C minus (2 times the altitude in thousands of feet).

   b.   EXAMPLE: Standard temperature at 20,000 ft. is 15°C − (2 x 20) = −25°C.

2.   Standard sea level pressure is 29.92 in. Hg or 1013.2 mb.

3.   The temperature/dew point spread decreases as relative humidity increases.

7.5 CLOUDS (Questions 26-32)

1. When air is being forced to ascend, the stability of air before lifting occurs determines the structure or type of clouds which will form.

2. When a cold air mass moves over a warm surface, the result is unstable air.

   a. Unstable conditions, moist air, and a lifting action provide cumuliform clouds, good visibility, showery rain, and possible clear icing in clouds.

   b. Towering cumulus clouds indicate convective turbulence.

3. The altitude of cumuliform cloud bases can be estimated using surface temperature/dew point spread.

   a. Unsaturated air in a convective current cools at about 3.0°C per 1,000 ft., and dew point decreases about 0.5°C per 1,000 ft.

   b. Thus, temperature and dew point converge at about 2.5°C per 1,000 ft.

   c. Cloud bases are at the altitude where the temperature and dew point are the same.

4. Standing lenticular altocumulus clouds are a good indication of very strong turbulence.

5. Virga describes streamers of precipitation trailing beneath clouds but evaporating before reaching the ground.

7.6 FOG (Questions 33-40)

1. Evaporation or precipitation-induced fog arises from drops of warm rain or drizzle falling through cool air.

   a. This kind of fog is produced by frontal activity.

   b. Precipitation-induced fog is an in-flight hazard most commonly associated with warm fronts.

2. A situation in which advection fog forms is when an air mass moves inland from the coastline during winter.

   a. It is most common along coastal areas.

   b. Wind stronger than 15 kt. dissipates or lifts the fog into low stratus clouds.

   c. It is usually more persistent than radiation fog and can appear suddenly during day or night.

3. Radiation fog is the result of a surface-based temperature inversion which occurs on clear, cool nights with calm or light wind.

   a. It is restricted to land areas.

4. Steam fog occurs when cold air moves over relatively warm water or wet ground.

7.7 STABILITY (Questions 41-57)

1. The stability of the atmosphere is determined by the ambient lapse rate, which is the decrease in temperature with altitude.

2. Warming from below decreases the stability of an air mass.

   a. Cooling from below increases the stability of an air mass.

3. The formation of either predominantly stratiform or cumuliform clouds is dependent upon the stability of the air being lifted.

   a. If clouds form as a result of stable, moist air ascending a mountain slope, the clouds will be stratus type.

4. The lifted index is computed as if a parcel of air near the surface were lifted to the 500-mb level (18,000 ft. MSL).

5. Convective circulation is caused by unequal heating of air by the Earth's surface.

 a. An example is sea and land breezes created by land absorbing and radiating heat faster than water.

 b. Cool air sinks because it is denser and gravity is stronger than less dense air. The sinking cool air displaces the warmer less dense air which rises.

Characteristics of Stable and Unstable Air

	Stable	Unstable
Temperature decrease as altitude increases	Little or none	More than normal so air rises as soon as lifting action occurs
Clouds	Stratiform Flat, layered	Cumuliform Billowy, cumulus
Turbulence	Relatively little	Turbulent, strong updrafts
Visibility	Poor	Good
Precipitation	Steady	Showery, intermittent

7.8 THUNDERSTORMS AND ICING (Questions 58-76)

1. Extreme turbulence in a thunderstorm is indicated by very frequent lightning and roll clouds on the leading edge of cumulonimbus clouds.

 a. A lifting action and unstable, moist air are necessary for the formation of cumulonimbus clouds.

2. The life of a thunderstorm can be divided into three stages:

 a. The cumulus stage is associated with continuous updraft.
 b. The mature stage is indicated by the start of rain at the Earth's surface.
 c. The dissipating stage is characterized predominantly by downdrafts.

3. Outside thunderstorm clouds, shear turbulence can be encountered 20 NM laterally from severe storms.

4. A squall line is a non-frontal, narrow band of active thunderstorms.

 a. It often contains severe steady-state thunderstorms and presents the single most intense weather hazard to aircraft.

 b. It is also associated with destructive winds, heavy hail, and tornadoes.

5. Airborne weather avoidance radar is designed to identify areas of precipitation, especially heavy precipitation, which may signify an active thunderstorm.

 a. Instrument weather conditions can be caused by clouds which are not indicated on radar screens.

 b. Intense radar echoes should be avoided by at least 20 NM.

 1) Thus, 40 NM should exist between intense echoes before you attempt to fly between them.

6.   Hail, an in-flight hazard, is likely to be associated with cumulonimbus clouds.

a.   Hailstones may be encountered in clear air several miles from a thunderstorm.

7.   When a warm front (or a cold front) is about to pass, any rain freezes as it falls from the warmer air into air having a temperature of 32°F or less.

a.   As the freezing rain continues to fall, it turns into ice pellets.
b.   Thus, ice pellets indicate freezing rain at a higher altitude.

7.9 TURBULENCE (Questions 77-84)

1.   Light turbulence momentarily causes slight, erratic changes in altitude and/or attitude.

2.   Moderate turbulence causes changes in altitude and/or attitude, but aircraft control remains positive.

a.   Moderate turbulence should be expected where vertical wind shear exceeds 6 kt. per 1,000 ft.

3.   Clear air turbulence (CAT) is a higher-level phenomenon, i.e., above 15,000 ft. AGL, not associated with cumuliform cloudiness.

4.   When wind flows over ridges or mountain ranges, it flows up the windward side and down the leeward side.

a.   A pilot who approaches mountainous terrain from the leeward side may be forced into the side of the mountain by the downward-flowing air.

b.   Wave formation should be expected with stable air at mountaintop altitude and winds of at least 20 kt. across the mountaintop.

1)   The most dangerous feature of mountain waves is the turbulent areas in and below rotor clouds.

5.   Convective currents are most active on warm summer afternoons when winds are light.

7.10 WIND SHEAR (Questions 85-92)

1.   Wind shear is a change in wind direction and/or speed within a very short distance in the atmosphere.

a.   It can be present at any level and can exist in both a horizontal and vertical direction.

2.   Hazardous wind shear is commonly encountered during periods of strong temperature inversion and near thunderstorms.

a.   Low-level wind shear may occur when there is a low-level temperature inversion with strong winds above the inversion.

3.   During an approach, possible wind shear is indicated by changes in the power and vertical velocity required to remain on the proper glide path.

a.   A sudden decrease in headwind results in a loss of indicated airspeed equal to the decrease in wind velocity.

4.   While approaching for landing when either possible wind shear or convective turbulence is indicated, you should increase approach airspeed slightly above normal to avoid stalling.

QUESTIONS AND ANSWER EXPLANATIONS

All the FAA questions from the pilot knowledge test for the commercial pilot certificate relating to aviation weather and the material outlined previously are reproduced on the following pages in the same modules as the outlines. To the immediate right of each question are the correct answer and answer explanation. You should cover these answers and answer explanations while responding to the questions. (A bookmark for this purpose has been provided in the back of the book.) Refer to the general discussion in the Introduction on how to take the FAA pilot knowledge test.

Remember that the questions from the FAA pilot knowledge test bank have been reordered by topic, and the topics have been organized into a meaningful sequence. Accordingly, the first line of the answer explanation gives the FAA question number and the citation of the authoritative source for the answer.

7.1 Causes of Weather

1.
5301. Every physical process of weather is accompanied by or is the result of

A— a heat exchange.
B— the movement of air.
C— a pressure differential.

Answer (A) is correct (5301). *(AvW Chap 1)*
Every physical process of weather is accompanied by, or is the result of, a heat exchange. A heat differential (difference between the temperatures of two air masses) causes a differential in pressure, which in turn causes movement of air. Heat exchanges occur constantly, e.g., melting, cooling, evaporation, condensation, updrafts, downdrafts, wind, etc.
Answer (B) is incorrect because movement of air is caused by heat exchanges. Answer (C) is incorrect because pressure differentials are caused by heat exchanges.

2.
5323. Moisture is added to a parcel of air by

A— sublimation and condensation.
B— evaporation and condensation.
C— evaporation and sublimation.

Answer (C) is correct (5323). *(AvW Chap 5)*
Moisture is added to a parcel of air when liquid water or ice are changed into water vapor. Evaporation is the change from liquid water to water vapor. Sublimation is the change from ice directly to water vapor, without the intervening liquid stage.
Answer (A) is incorrect because condensation is the changing of water vapor into liquid water, which removes (not adds) moisture from the air. Answer (B) is incorrect because condensation is the changing of water vapor into liquid water, which removes (not adds) moisture from the air.

3.
5311. In the Northern Hemisphere, the wind is deflected to the

A— right by Coriolis force.
B— right by surface friction.
C— left by Coriolis force.

Answer (A) is correct (5311). *(AvW Chap 4)*
Coriolis force, caused by the Earth's rotation, deflects air movements to the right in the Northern Hemisphere and to the left in the Southern Hemisphere. Coriolis force is at a right angle to wind direction, and is directly proportional to wind speed.
Answer (B) is incorrect because surface friction slows wind speed, which lessens the deflection to the right caused by Coriolis force. Answer (C) is incorrect because wind is deflected to the left by Coriolis force in the Southern (not Northern) Hemisphere.

4.

5312. Why does the wind have a tendency to flow parallel to the isobars above the friction level?

A— Coriolis force tends to counterbalance the horizontal pressure gradient.
B— Coriolis force acts perpendicular to a line connecting the highs and lows.
C— Friction of the air with the Earth deflects the air perpendicular to the pressure gradient.

Answer (A) is correct (5312). *(AvW Chap 4)*
Normally wind flows from areas of high pressure to areas of low pressure. Wind is deflected by the Coriolis force, however. This force, which is the result of the Earth's rotation, deflects wind to the right in the Northern Hemisphere, counterbalancing the horizontal pressure gradient. Its effects are lessened by friction with the Earth's surface at altitudes closer to the surface.
Answer (B) is incorrect because the Coriolis force acts at a right angle to wind direction in direct proportion to wind speed. Also, the Coriolis force varies with latitude from zero at the equator to maximum at the poles. Answer (C) is incorrect because surface friction tends to diminish the Coriolis force and permits the wind to follow the pressure gradient force.

5.

5314. With regard to windflow patterns shown on surface analysis charts; when the isobars are

A— close together, the pressure gradient force is slight and wind velocities are weaker.
B— not close together, the pressure gradient force is greater and wind velocities are stronger.
C— close together, the pressure gradient force is greater and wind velocities are stronger.

Answer (C) is correct (5314). *(AvW Chap 4)*
Pressure differences create a force, the pressure gradient force, which drives the wind from higher pressure to lower pressure. This force is perpendicular to isobars, or pressure contours. The closer the spacing of isobars, the stronger the pressure gradient force and the stronger the wind.
Answer (A) is incorrect because when the isobars are close together, the pressure gradient force and wind are stronger (not weaker). Answer (B) is incorrect because when the isobars are not close together, the pressure gradient force and wind are weaker (not stronger).

6.

5310. What causes wind?

A— The Earth's rotation.
B— Air mass modification.
C— Pressure differences.

Answer (C) is correct (5310). *(AvW Chap 4)*
Wind is caused by pressure differences with wind flowing from high-pressure areas to low-pressure areas. These pressure differences arise from the different heating of the Earth's surface.
Answer (A) is incorrect because the Earth's rotation results in Coriolis force which deflects wind but does not cause wind. It deflects it to the right in the Northern Hemisphere. Answer (B) is incorrect because air mass modification refers to air masses taking on the properties of the underlying region(s) after it leaves its source region.

7.

5347. Which is true regarding a cold front occlusion? The air ahead of the warm front

A— is colder than the air behind the overtaking cold front.
B— is warmer than the air behind the overtaking cold front.
C— has the same temperature as the air behind the overtaking cold front.

Answer (B) is correct (5347). *(AvW Chap 8)*
An occluded front, or occlusion, occurs when a cold front overtakes a warm front. A cold front occlusion occurs when the cool air ahead of the warm front is warmer than the cold air behind the overtaking cold front, lifting the warm front aloft.
Answer (A) is incorrect because when the cool air ahead of the warm front is colder than that behind the cold front, a warm front (not cold front) occlusion occurs. Answer (C) is incorrect because when the cool air ahead of the warm front has the same temperature as that behind the cold front, a temperature inversion (not a cold front occlusion) is likely to occur.

7.2 High/Low Pressure Areas

8.
5317. Which is true with respect to a high- or low-pressure system?

A— A high-pressure area or ridge is an area of rising air.
B— A low-pressure area or trough is an area of descending air.
C— A high-pressure area or ridge is an area of descending air.

Answer (C) is correct (5317). *(AvW Chap 4)*
    High-pressure air descends because it is heavier than low-pressure air. Ridge refers to an elongated area of high pressure.
    Answer (A) is incorrect because high-pressure air descends, not rises. Answer (B) is incorrect because low-pressure air rises, not descends.

9.
5318. Which is true regarding high- or low-pressure systems?

A— A high-pressure area or ridge is an area of rising air.
B— A low-pressure area or trough is an area of rising air.
C— Both high- and low-pressure areas are characterized by descending air.

Answer (B) is correct (5318). *(AvW Chap 4)*
    Low-pressure air rises because it weighs less than high-pressure air. Trough refers to an elongated area of low pressure.
    Answer (A) is incorrect because high-pressure air descends, not rises. Answer (C) is incorrect because high-pressure air descends and low-pressure air rises, not descends.

10.
5319. When flying into a low-pressure area in the Northern Hemisphere, the wind direction and velocity will be from the

A— left and decreasing.
B— left and increasing.
C— right and decreasing.

Answer (B) is correct (5319). *(AvW Chap 4)*
    When flying into a low-pressure area, the wind is flowing counterclockwise and thus will be from the left. Also, winds tend to be greater in low-pressure systems than in high-pressure systems, so the velocity will increase as you fly into the area.
    Answer (A) is incorrect because the wind is usually increasing, not decreasing, as you fly into a low-pressure area. Answer (C) is incorrect because the wind will be from the left, not right, and the wind is usually increasing, not decreasing, as you fly into a low pressure area.

11.
5316. While flying cross-country, in the Northern Hemisphere, you experience a continuous left crosswind which is associated with a major wind system. This indicates that you

A— are flying toward an area of generally unfavorable weather conditions.
B— have flown from an area of unfavorable weather conditions.
C— cannot determine weather conditions without knowing pressure changes.

Answer (A) is correct (5316). *(AvW Chap 4)*
    Due to the counterclockwise circulation around a low pressure area in the Northern Hemisphere, a continuous left crosswind indicates that you are flying into such an area. Low pressure areas are areas of rising air which are conducive to cloudiness and precipitation -- generally unfavorable weather conditions.
    Answer (B) is incorrect because, when flying away from unfavorable weather, you are generally flying out of a low, which means you should have a right, not left, crosswind. Answer (C) is incorrect because the wind can give you a general indication of pressure changes, and thus, weather.

12.
5315. What prevents air from flowing directly from high-pressure areas to low-pressure areas?

A— Coriolis force.
B— Surface friction.
C— Pressure gradient force.

Answer (A) is correct (5315). *(AvW Chap 4)*
    Coriolis force, caused by the Earth's rotation, deflects air movements to the right in the Northern Hemisphere and to the left in the Southern Hemisphere. Coriolis force is at a right angle to wind direction, and is directly proportional to wind speed. Thus, air is deflected to the right as it flows from high-pressure areas to low-pressure areas.
    Answer (B) is incorrect because surface friction encourages air movement directly from highs to lows by decreasing wind speed, which decreases the Coriolis force effect. Answer (C) is incorrect because the pressure gradient force causes the initial movement from high-pressure areas to low-pressure areas.

13.

5321. The general circulation of air associated with a high-pressure area in the Northern Hemisphere is

A— outward, downward, and clockwise.
B— outward, upward, and clockwise.
C— inward, downward, and clockwise.

14.

5313. The wind system associated with a low-pressure area in the Northern Hemisphere is

A— an anticyclone and is caused by descending cold air.
B— a cyclone and is caused by Coriolis force.
C— an anticyclone and is caused by Coriolis force.

7.3 Jet Stream

15.

5384. During the winter months in the middle latitudes, the jet stream shifts toward the

A— north and speed decreases.
B— south and speed increases.
C— north and speed increases.

16.

5385. The strength and location of the jet stream is normally

A— weaker and farther north in the summer.
B— stronger and farther north in the winter.
C— stronger and farther north in the summer.

17.

5382. A common location of clear air turbulence is

A— in an upper trough on the polar side of a jet stream.
B— near a ridge aloft on the equatorial side of a high-pressure flow.
C— south of an east/west oriented high-pressure ridge in its dissipating stage.

18.

5383. The jet stream and associated clear air turbulence can sometimes be visually identified in flight by

A— dust or haze at flight level.
B— long streaks of cirrus clouds.
C— a constant outside air temperature.

Answer (A) is correct (5321). *(AvW Chap 4)*
Air flows outward from a high-pressure area, causing a descending column of air within the high. As the air moves outward, it is deflected to the right by Coriolis force, resulting in a clockwise rotation.
Answer (B) is incorrect because air flows downward (not upward) in a high. Answer (C) is incorrect because air flows outward (not inward) from a high.

Answer (B) is correct (5313). *(AvW Chap 4)*
Air flowing into a low-pressure area is deflected to the right in the Northern Hemisphere, resulting in a counterclockwise (or cyclonic) circulation.
Answer (A) is incorrect because an anticyclone and descending air describes a high- (not low-) pressure area. Answer (C) is incorrect because an anticyclone caused by Coriolis force describes a high- (not low-) pressure area.

Answer (B) is correct (5384). *(AvW Chap 13)*
The jet stream is a narrow band of strong winds meandering through the atmosphere at an altitude near the tropopause. In the mid-latitudes, the wind speed in the jet stream is considerably stronger in winter than in summer. Also, the jet stream shifts farther south in winter than in summer.
Answer (A) is incorrect because the jet stream shifts south (not north) and speed increases (not decreases) in the winter months. Answer (C) is incorrect because the jet stream shifts south (not north) in the winter months.

Answer (A) is correct (5385). *(AvW Chap 13)*
The jet stream is a narrow band of strong winds meandering through the atmosphere at an altitude near the tropopause. In the mid-latitudes, the wind speed in the jet stream is considerably stronger in winter than in summer. Also, the jet stream shifts farther south in winter than in summer.
Answer (B) is incorrect because the jetstream is normally farther south (not north) in the winter.
Answer (C) is incorrect because the jetstream is normally weaker (not stronger) in the summer.

Answer (A) is correct (5382). *(AvW Chap 13)*
The typical location of clear air turbulence is an upper trough on the cold (polar) side of the jet stream.
Answer (B) is incorrect because most clear air turbulence is on the northern or polar (not equatorial) side of contrasting air masses. Answer (C) is incorrect because most clear air turbulence is on the northern or polar (not southern) side of contrasting air masses.

Answer (B) is correct (5383). *(AvW Chap 13)*
Streamlined, windswept cirrus clouds always indicate very strong upper winds.
Answer (A) is incorrect because the presence of dust or haze means there is not much wind or air movement to dissipate the particles. Answer (C) is incorrect because clear air turbulence is caused by mixing cold and warm air at different pressure levels.

19.
5448. A strong wind shear can be expected

A— in the jetstream front above a core having a speed of 60 to 90 knots.

B— if the 5 °C isotherms are spaced between 7° to 10° of latitude.

C— on the low-pressure side of a jetstream core where the speed at the core is stronger than 110 knots.

Answer (C) is correct (5448). *(AC00-30A)*
When the speed of the jet stream is in excess of 110 kt., strong wind shears can be expected on the lower-pressure side.
Answer (A) is incorrect because wind speeds of less than 100 kt. are not dramatic in the jet stream. Also, the turbulence is usually to the sides or beneath the core. Answer (B) is incorrect because this does not indicate abrupt temperature or wind changes (which cause wind shear).

20.
5447. Which type of jetstream can be expected to cause the greater turbulence?

A— A straight jetstream associated with a low-pressure trough.

B— A curving jetstream associated with a deep low-pressure trough.

C— A jetstream occurring during the summer at the lower latitudes.

Answer (B) is correct (5447). *(AvW Chap 13)*
A curving jet stream indicates abrupt weather system changes which lend themselves to more violent turbulence. In general, the more pronounced the difference in weather systems, the greater the potential for very strong turbulence.
Answer (A) is incorrect because a straight jet stream normally produces less turbulence than a curving jet stream. Answer (C) is incorrect because the jet stream is weaker in the summer, when it usually does not get to the lower latitudes.

21.
5381. Which feature is associated with the tropopause?

A— Constant height above the Earth.

B— Abrupt change in temperature lapse rate.

C— Absolute upper limit of cloud formation.

Answer (B) is correct (5381). *(AvW Chap 13)*
The tropopause is the transition layer of atmosphere between the troposphere and the stratosphere. Height of the tropopause varies from about 65,000 ft. over the Equator to 20,000 ft. or lower over the poles. A characteristic of the tropopause is an abrupt change in the temperature lapse rate, i.e., the rate at which temperature decreases with height.
Answer (A) is incorrect because the tropopause is considerably closer to the Earth's surface at the poles than at the equator. Answer (C) is incorrect because clouds may form above the tropopause.

7.4 Temperature

22.
5302. What is the standard temperature at 10,000 feet?

A— –5 °C.

B— –15 °C.

C— +5 °C.

Answer (A) is correct (5302). *(AvW Chap 2)*
Standard temperature is 15°C at sea level and the standard lapse rate is 2°C per 1,000 ft. Thus, at 10,000 ft., the standard temperature would be 20°C colder than at sea level, or –5°C (15°C – 20°C).
Answer (B) is incorrect because –15°C is the standard temperature at 15,000 ft. (not 10,000 ft.). Answer (C) is incorrect because +5°C is the standard temperature at 5,000 ft. (not 10,000 ft.).

23.
5305. What are the standard temperature and pressure values for sea level?

A— 15 °C and 29.92" Hg.

B— 59 °F and 1013.2" Hg.

C— 15 °C and 29.92 Mb.

Answer (A) is correct (5305). *(AvW Chap 1)*
Standard temperature at sea level is defined as 15°C or 59°F. Standard sea-level pressure is 29.92 in. Hg or 1013.2 mb.
Answer (B) is incorrect because standard sea-level pressure is 1013.2 mb (not in. Hg). Answer (C) is incorrect because standard sea-level pressure is 29.92 in. Hg (not mb).

24.
5303. What is the standard temperature at 20,000 feet?

A— –15 °C.

B— –20 °C.

C— –25 °C.

Answer (C) is correct (5303). *(AvW Chap 2)*
Standard temperature is 15°C at sea level and the standard lapse rate is 2°C per 1,000 ft. Thus, at 20,000 ft., the standard temperature would be 40°C colder than at sea level, or –25°C (15°C – 40°C).
Answer (A) is incorrect because –15°C is the standard temperature at 15,000 ft. (not 20,000 ft.). Answer (B) is incorrect because –20°C is the standard temperature at 17,500 ft. (not 20,000 ft.).

25.

5320. Which is true regarding actual air temperature and dew point temperature spread? The temperature spread

A— decreases as the relative humidity decreases.
B— decreases as the relative humidity increases.
C— increases as the relative humidity increases.

Answer (B) is correct (5320). *(AvW Chap 5)*
Dew point refers to the temperature to which air must be cooled to become saturated by the water vapor already present in the air. Thus, as the relative humidity increases, the dew point-temperature spread decreases. As relative humidity increases to 100%, the dew point approaches the temperature and the spread approaches zero.
Answer (A) is incorrect because, as relative humidity decreases, the temperature/dew point spread increases (not decreases). Answer (C) is incorrect because the temperature/dew point spread decreases (not increases) as relative humidity increases.

7.5 Clouds

26.

5338. Which cloud types would indicate convective turbulence?

A— Cirrus clouds.
B— Nimbostratus clouds.
C— Towering cumulus clouds.

Answer (C) is correct (5338). *(AvW Chap 7)*
Towering cumulus clouds signify a relatively deep layer of unstable air, thus indicating very strong convective turbulence.
Answer (A) is incorrect because cirrus clouds are high, thin, feathery ice crystal clouds in patches and narrow bands which are not generated by any convective activity. Answer (B) is incorrect because nimbostratus are gray or dark, massive clouds, usually producing continuous rain or ice pellets. They form in stable air and do not produce convective activity or turbulence.

27.

5341. Which combination of weather-producing variables would likely result in cumuliform-type clouds, good visibility, and showery rain?

A— Stable, moist air and orographic lifting.
B— Unstable, moist air and orographic lifting.
C— Unstable, moist air and no lifting mechanism.

Answer (B) is correct (5341). *(AvW Chap 8)*
Unstable, moist air accompanied by lifting usually results in showery rain, good visibility, and cumuliform clouds. Orographic lifting is caused by mountain forces, mountain winds, etc.
Answer (A) is incorrect because, if air is stable, stratiform rather than cumuliform type clouds will form, and the rain will be steady (not showery). Answer (C) is incorrect because cumuliform clouds and showery rain cannot exist without a lifting mechanism.

28.

5348. Which are characteristics of a cold air mass moving over a warm surface?

A— Cumuliform clouds, turbulence, and poor visibility.
B— Cumuliform clouds, turbulence, and good visibility.
C— Stratiform clouds, smooth air, and poor visibility.

Answer (B) is correct (5348). *(AvW Chap 6)*
When a cold air mass moves over a warm surface, the warm air near the surface rises and creates an unstable condition. These convective currents give rise to cumuliform clouds, turbulence, and good visibility.
Answer (A) is incorrect because unstable air lifts and blows haze away, resulting in good (not poor) visibility. Answer (C) is incorrect because unstable conditions produce cumuliform (not stratiform) clouds.

29.

5328. What is the approximate base of the cumulus clouds if the temperature at 2,000 feet MSL is 10°C and the dew point is 1°C?

A— 3,000 feet MSL.
B— 4,000 feet MSL.
C— 6,000 feet MSL.

Answer (C) is correct (5328). *(AvW Chap 6)*
The height of cumuliform cloud bases can be estimated using the surface temperature/dew point spread. Unsaturated air in a convective current cools at about 3°C per 1,000 ft., and dew point decreases about 0.5°C per 1,000 ft. Thus, temperature and dew point converge at about 2.5°C per 1,000 ft. Since the temperature/dew point spread was 9°C (10-1), temperature and dew point will converge at 3,600 ft. AGL (9 ÷ 2.5 = 3.6 or 3,600). The base of the cumulus clouds is approximately 5,600 ft. MSL (3,600 + 2,000).
Answer (A) is incorrect because 3,000 ft. MSL is the approximate base of the cumulus clouds if the dew point of 1°C, not the temperature/dew point spread of 9°C, is divided by 2.5. Answer (B) is incorrect because the base of the cumulus clouds is approximately 4,000 ft. AGL, not 4,000 ft. MSL.

30.
5330. What determines the structure or type of clouds which will form as a result of air being forced to ascend?

A— The method by which the air is lifted.
B— The stability of the air before lifting occurs.
C— The relative humidity of the air after lifting occurs.

Answer (B) is correct (5330). *(AvW Chap 6)*
   The structure of cloud types which form as a result of air being forced to ascend is determined by the stability of the air before lifting occurs. The difference between the existing lapse rate (the actual decrease in temperature with altitude) and the adiabatic rate of cooling in upward-moving air (cooling of air as a result of expansion as it ascends) determines the stability of the air. If the upward-moving air remains warmer than the surrounding air, the air is accelerated upward as a convective current. The air is considered unstable, and these conditions provide for the vertical development of cumulus clouds. If, on the other hand, the upward- moving air becomes colder than the surrounding air, it sinks. The air is considered stable, and stratiform clouds will form.
   Answer (A) is incorrect because the stability of the air (not the lifting method) determines the type of clouds that will form. Answer (C) is incorrect because the relative humidity of the air determines the amount (not type) of clouds that will form.

31.
5339. The presence of standing lenticular altocumulus clouds is a good indication of

A— lenticular ice formation in calm air.
B— very strong turbulence.
C— heavy icing conditions.

Answer (B) is correct (5339). *(AvW Chaps 7, 9)*
   When stable air crosses a mountain barrier, turbulence usually results. Air flowing up the windward side is relatively smooth. Windflow across the barrier is laminar; i.e., it tends to flow in layers. The barrier may set up waves in these layers much as waves develop on a disturbed water surface. Wave crests extend well above the highest mountain tops. Under each wave crest is a rotary circulation, in which turbulence can be quite violent. Updrafts and downdrafts in the waves can also create very violent turbulence.
   Answer (A) is incorrect because standing lenticular clouds indicate turbulence (not calm air). Answer (C) is incorrect because standing lenticular clouds indicate turbulence (not icing conditions).

32.
5322. Virga is best described as

A— streamers of precipitation trailing beneath clouds which evaporates before reaching the ground.
B— wall cloud torrents trailing beneath cumulonimbus clouds which dissipate before reaching the ground.
C— turbulent areas beneath cumulonimbus clouds.

Answer (A) is correct (5322). *(AvW Chap 5)*
   Virga is streamers of precipitation, either water or ice particles, falling from a cloud in wisps or streaks, and evaporating before reaching the ground.
   Answer (B) is incorrect because virga is generally thin and wispy (not a torrential wall). Answer (C) is incorrect because virga is precipitation (not turbulence).

7.6 Fog

33.
5350. Fog produced by frontal activity is a result of saturation due to

A— nocturnal cooling.
B— adiabatic cooling.
C— evaporation of precipitation.

Answer (C) is correct (5350). *(AvW Chap 12)*
   Fog produced by frontal activity is known as precipitation-induced fog. It arises from drops of warm rain or drizzle falling through cool air. The evaporation from the precipitation saturates the cool air and forms fog.
   Answer (A) is incorrect because nocturnal cooling forms radiation (not precipitation-induced) fog.
Answer (B) is incorrect because adiabatic cooling forms upslope (not precipitation-induced) fog.

34.

5374. Which in-flight hazard is most commonly associated with warm fronts?

A— Advection fog.
B— Radiation fog.
C— Precipitation-induced fog.

Answer (C) is correct (5374). *(AvW Chap 6)*
Precipitation-induced fog arises from drops of warm rain or drizzle evaporating as it falls through cool air. This evaporation saturates the cool air and forms fog. This kind of fog can become quite dense and continue for an extended period of time. It is most commonly associated with warm fronts.
Answer (A) is incorrect because advection fog results from the movement of warm, humid air over a cold water surface. Answer (B) is incorrect because radiation fog results from terrestrial cooling of the Earth's surface on calm, clear nights.

35.

5376. A situation most conducive to the formation of advection fog is

A— a light breeze moving colder air over a water surface.
B— an air mass moving inland from the coastline during the winter.
C— a warm, moist air mass settling over a cool surface under no-wind conditions.

Answer (B) is correct (5376). *(AvW Chap 12)*
Advection fog forms when moist air moves over colder ground or water. This type of fog is common when comparatively warm, moist oceanic air moves inland from the coastline during winter.
Answer (A) is incorrect because a light breeze moving colder air over a warmer water surface describes steam fog. Answer (C) is incorrect because a warm, moist air mass settling over a cool surface under no-wind conditions describes radiation fog.

36.

5377. Advection fog has drifted over a coastal airport during the day. What may tend to dissipate or lift this fog into low stratus clouds?

A— Nighttime cooling.
B— Surface radiation.
C— Wind 15 knots or stronger.

Answer (C) is correct (5377). *(AvW Chap 12)*
Advection fog deepens as wind speed increases up to 15 kt. Wind much stronger than 15 kt. will lift the fog into a layer of low stratus or stratocumulus.
Answer (A) is incorrect because nighttime cooling forms radiation fog (not low stratus clouds). Answer (B) is incorrect because surface radiation forms radiation fog (not low stratus clouds).

37.

5379. In what ways do advection fog, radiation fog, and steam fog differ in their formation or location?

A— Radiation fog is restricted to land areas; advection fog is most common along coastal areas; steam fog forms over a water surface.
B— Advection fog deepens as windspeed increases up to 20 knots; steam fog requires calm or very light wind; radiation fog forms when the ground or water cools the air by radiation.
C— Steam fog forms from moist air moving over a colder surface; advection fog requires cold air over a warmer surface; radiation fog is produced by radiational cooling of the ground.

Answer (A) is correct (5379). *(AvW Chap 12)*
Radiation fog is restricted to land because water surfaces cool little from nighttime radiation. Advection fog forms when moist air moves over colder ground or water. It is most common along coastal areas. Steam fog occurs when cold air moves over relatively warm water or wet ground.
Answer (B) is incorrect because advection fog breaks up (not deepens) when wind speed increases to 15 kt. or more; steam fog requires wind to move cold air over warm, moist surfaces; and radiation fog does not form over water. Answer (C) is incorrect because steam fog occurs when cold air moves over warm, moist surfaces, and advection fog is caused by warm air moving over a cool surface.

38.

5378. What lifts advection fog into low stratus clouds?

A— Nighttime cooling.
B— Dryness of the underlying land mass.
C— Surface winds of approximately 15 knots or stronger.

Answer (C) is correct (5378). *(AvW Chap 12)*
Advection fog deepens as wind speed increases up to 15 kt. Wind much stronger than 15 kt. lifts the fog into a layer of low stratus or stratocumulus.
Answer (A) is incorrect because nighttime cooling forms radiation fog (not low stratus clouds). Answer (B) is incorrect because dryness of the underlying land mass forms radiation fog (not low stratus clouds).

39.
5304. Which conditions are favorable for the formation of a surface based temperature inversion?

A— Clear, cool nights with calm or light wind.
B— Area of unstable air rapidly transferring heat from the surface.
C— Broad areas of cumulus clouds with smooth, level bases at the same altitude.

40.
5380. With respect to advection fog, which statement is true?

A— It is slow to develop, and dissipates quite rapidly.
B— It forms almost exclusively at night or near daybreak.
C— It can appear suddenly during day or night, and it is more persistent than radiation fog.

7.7 Stability

41.
5332. What are the characteristics of stable air?

A— Good visibility; steady precipitation; stratus clouds.
B— Poor visibility; steady precipitation; stratus clouds.
C— Poor visibility; intermittent precipitation; cumulus clouds.

42.
5333. Which would decrease the stability of an air mass?

A— Warming from below.
B— Cooling from below.
C— Decrease in water vapor.

43.
5336. Which would increase the stability of an air mass?

A— Warming from below.
B— Cooling from below.
C— Decrease in water vapor.

44.
5342. What is a characteristic of stable air?

A— Stratiform clouds.
B— Fair weather cumulus clouds.
C— Temperature decreases rapidly with altitude.

Answer (A) is correct (5304). *(AvW Chap 12)*
A temperature inversion occurs when warm air exists over cooler air. When ground heat radiates out on clear nights, the cool ground surface cools still air at the surface to a temperature below the air above it.
Answer (B) is incorrect because the air near the surface must be stable both horizontally and vertically to permit the cool ground to cool the air near the surface. Answer (C) is incorrect because cumulus clouds are well above the surface.

Answer (C) is correct (5380). *(AvW Chap 12)*
Advection fog is usually more extensive and much more persistent than radiation fog. Advection fog can move in rapidly regardless of the time of day or night.
Answer (A) is incorrect because advection fog can move in rapidly regardless of the time of day or night and is persistent. Answer (B) is incorrect because it describes radiation fog.

Answer (B) is correct (5332). *(AvW Chap 8)*
Stable air is still or moving horizontally but without vertical movement. As a result, the pollutants in the air are not swept away and visibility is poor. Also, stable air forms layer-like clouds since the air is moving in layers. Relatedly, precipitation spreads over a wide area and is relatively steady and the air is smooth.
Answer (A) is incorrect because the visibility is poor (not good) in stable air. Answer (C) is incorrect because the precipitation is steady (not intermittent) and the clouds are stratiform (not cumulus) in stable air.

Answer (A) is correct (5333). *(AvW Chap 8)*
When air is warmed from below, it tends to rise, resulting in instability; i.e., vertical movement occurs.
Answer (B) is incorrect because cooling from below keeps the air from rising, resulting in increased (not decreased) stability. Answer (C) is incorrect because a decrease in water vapor lowers the dew point of the air, which does not affect the stability.

Answer (B) is correct (5336). *(AvW Chap 8)*
When air is cooled from below, it does not rise, resulting in stability, i.e., no vertical movement.
Answer (A) is incorrect because warming from below causes the air to rise, resulting in decreased (not increased) stability. Answer (C) is incorrect because a decrease in water vapor lowers the dew point of the air, which does not affect stability.

Answer (A) is correct (5342). *(AvW Chap 6)*
Stable air is still or moving horizontally but without vertical movement. As a result, the pollutants in the air are not swept away and visibility is poor. Also, stable air forms layer-like clouds since the air is moving in layers. Relatedly, precipitation spreads over a wide area and is relatively steady and the air is smooth.
Answer (B) is incorrect because cumulus clouds are a characteristic of unstable (not stable) air. Answer (C) is incorrect because a rapid temperature decrease with altitude (high lapse rate) is a characteristic of unstable (not stable) air.

45.
5345. Which is a characteristic of stable air?

A— Cumuliform clouds.
B— Excellent visibility.
C— Restricted visibility.

Answer (C) is correct (5345). *(AvW Chap 6)*
Stable air is still or moving horizontally but without vertical movement. As a result, the pollutants in the air are not swept away and visibility is poor. Also, stable air forms layer-like clouds since the air is moving in layers. Relatedly, precipitation spreads over a wide area and is relatively steady and the air is smooth.
Answer (A) is incorrect because cumuliform clouds are a characteristic of unstable (not stable) air.
Answer (B) is incorrect because excellent visibility is a characteristic of unstable (not stable) air.

46.
5346. Which is a characteristic typical of a stable air mass?

A— Cumuliform clouds.
B— Showery precipitation.
C— Continuous precipitation.

Answer (C) is correct (5346). *(AvW Chap 6)*
Stable air is still or moving horizontally but without vertical movement. As a result, the pollutants in the air are not swept away and visibility is poor. Also, stable air forms layer-like clouds since the air is moving in layers. Relatedly, precipitation spreads over a wide area and is relatively steady and the air is smooth.
Answer (A) is incorrect because cumuliform clouds are a characteristic of unstable (not stable) air.
Answer (B) is incorrect because showery precipitation is a characteristic of unstable (not stable) air.

47.
5335. What type weather can one expect from moist, unstable air, and very warm surface temperature?

A— Fog and low stratus clouds.
B— Continuous heavy precipitation.
C— Strong updrafts and cumulonimbus clouds.

Answer (C) is correct (5335). *(AvW Chap 8)*
Unstable air is air that is being heated from below, producing updrafts. As a result, pollutants in the air are swept away and visibility is good. Also, unstable air forms cumulus clouds because the air is moving vertically. Relatedly, precipitation is showery and turbulence may be present.
Answer (A) is incorrect because fog and stratus clouds are characteristics of stable (not unstable) air.
Answer (B) is incorrect because continuous precipitation is a characteristic of stable (not unstable) air.

48.
5343. A moist, unstable air mass is characterized by

A— poor visibility and smooth air.
B— cumuliform clouds and showery precipitation.
C— stratiform clouds and continuous precipitation.

Answer (B) is correct (5343). *(AvW Chap 8)*
Unstable air is air that is being heated from below, producing updrafts. As a result, pollutants in the air are swept away and visibility is good. Also, unstable air forms cumulus clouds because the air is moving vertically. Relatedly, precipitation is showery and turbulence may be present.
Answer (A) is incorrect because poor visibility and smooth air are characteristics of stable (not unstable) air.
Answer (C) is incorrect because stratiform clouds and continuous precipitation are characteristics of stable (not unstable) air.

49.
5329. If clouds form as a result of very stable, moist air being forced to ascend a mountain slope, the clouds will be

A— cirrus type with no vertical development or turbulence.
B— cumulus type with considerable vertical development and turbulence.
C— stratus type with little vertical development and little or no turbulence.

Answer (C) is correct (5329). *(AvW Chap 8)*
Moist, stable air flowing upslope produces stratified clouds as it cools. Stable air resists upward movement.
Answer (A) is incorrect because cirrus are high clouds, usually consisting of ice crystals. Answer (B) is incorrect because there would be vertical development only if the air were unstable. Also, there is little or no turbulence in stable air.

50.

5340. The formation of either predominantly stratiform or predominantly cumuliform clouds is dependent upon the

A— source of lift.
B— stability of the air being lifted.
C— temperature of the air being lifted.

Answer (B) is correct (5340). *(AvW Chap 6)*

The structure of cloud types which form as a result of air being forced to ascend is determined by the stability of the air before lifting occurs. Stability refers to the relationship of the lapse rate to the adiabatic cooling rate. If the temperature that decreases with altitude (lapse rate) is warmer than the adiabatic cooling rate (cooling of air as a result of expansion as it ascends), the air that is lifted will continue to rise, which provides for the vertical development of cumulus clouds. That is, unstable conditions exist. If, on the other hand, the lapse rate is less than (cooler than) the adiabatic rate, the air that is lifted will be as cool as or cooler than the air around it, will not lift further, and stratiform clouds will form; i.e., stable conditions exist.

Answer (A) is incorrect because the stability of the air (not the source of lift) determines the type of clouds that will form. Answer (C) is incorrect because the temperature of the air (along with the dew point) determines the altitude (not type) of cloud formation.

51.

5344. When an air mass is stable, which of these conditions are most likely to exist?

A— Numerous towering cumulus and cumulonimbus clouds.
B— Moderate to severe turbulence at the lower levels.
C— Smoke, dust, haze, etc., concentrated at the lower levels with resulting poor visibility.

Answer (C) is correct (5344). *(AvW Chap 8)*

Stable air is still or moving horizontally but without vertical movement. As a result, the pollutants in the air are not swept away and visibility is poor. Also, stable air forms layer-like clouds since the air is moving in layers. Relatedly, precipitation spreads over a wide area and is relatively steady and the air is smooth.

Answer (A) is incorrect because towering cumulus and cumulonimbus clouds are characteristics of unstable (not stable) air. Answer (B) is incorrect because turbulence is a characteristic of unstable (not stable) air.

52.

5388. Which is true regarding the development of convective circulation?

A— Cool air must sink to force the warm air upward.
B— Warm air is less dense and rises on its own accord.
C— Warmer air covers a larger surface area than the cool air; therefore, the warmer air is less dense and rises.

Answer (A) is correct (5388). *(AvW Chap 4)*

When two surfaces are heated unequally, they heat the overlying air unevenly. The warmer air expands and becomes lighter or less dense than the cool air. The more dense, cool air is drawn to the ground by its greater gravitational force lifting or forcing the warm air upward much as oil is forced to the top of water when the two are mixed.

Answer (B) is incorrect because cool air sinking forces the warm air up (without the cool air, the warm air would be stationary). Answer (C) is incorrect because convective circulation is based on unequal heating of the Earth's surface, not the relative size of surface.

53.

5327. When conditionally unstable air with high-moisture content and very warm surface temperature is forecast, one can expect what type of weather?

A— Strong updrafts and stratonimbus clouds.
B— Restricted visibility near the surface over a large area.
C— Strong updrafts and cumulonimbus clouds.

Answer (C) is correct (5327). *(AvW Chap 8)*

Unstable air is air that is being heated from below, producing updrafts. As a result, pollutants in the air are swept away and visibility is good. Also, unstable air forms cumulus clouds because the air is moving vertically. Relatedly, precipitation is showery and turbulence may be present.

Answer (A) is incorrect because stratonimbus clouds are a characteristic of stable (not unstable) air.
Answer (B) is incorrect because restricted visibility is a characteristic of stable (not unstable) air.

54.
5392. Convective circulation patterns associated with sea breezes are caused by

A— water absorbing and radiating heat faster than the land.
B— land absorbing and radiating heat faster than the water.
C— cool and less dense air moving inland from over the water, causing it to rise.

55.
5334. From which measurement of the atmosphere can stability be determined?

A— Atmospheric pressure.
B— The ambient lapse rate.
C— The dry adiabatic lapse rate.

56.
5439. The difference found by subtracting the temperature of a parcel of air theoretically lifted from the surface to 500 millibars and the existing temperature at 500 millibars is called the

A— lifted index.
B— negative index.
C— positive index.

57.
5337. The conditions necessary for the formation of stratiform clouds are a lifting action and

A— unstable, dry air.
B— stable, moist air.
C— unstable, moist air.

7.8 Thunderstorms and Icing

58.
5369. What visible signs indicate extreme turbulence in thunderstorms?

A— Base of the clouds near the surface, heavy rain, and hail.
B— Low ceiling and visibility, hail, and precipitation static.
C— Cumulonimbus clouds, very frequent lightning, and roll clouds.

Answer (B) is correct (5392). *(AvW Chap 4)*
Sea breezes are caused by cool and denser air moving inland off of the water. Once over the warmer land, the air heats up and rises. Currents push the hot air over the water where it cools and descends, starting the cycle over again. The temperature differential between land and water is caused by land absorbing and radiating heat faster than water.
Answer (A) is incorrect because water absorbs and radiates heat slower (not faster) than land. Answer (C) is incorrect because the cool air moving inland is more (not less) dense, and it rises after it is warmed, not while it is cool.

Answer (B) is correct (5334). *(AvW Chap 6)*
The stability of the atmosphere is determined by vertical movements of air. Warm air rises when the air above is cooler. The lapse rate, which is the decrease of temperature with altitude, is therefore a measure of stability.
Answer (A) is incorrect because, while atmospheric pressure may have some effect on temperature changes and air movements, it is the actual lapse rate that determines the stability of the atmosphere. Answer (C) is incorrect because the dry adiabatic lapse rate is a constant rate.

Answer (A) is correct (5439). *(AWS Sect 10)*
The lifted index is computed as if a parcel of air near the surface were lifted to 500 mb (18,000 ft. MSL). As the air is lifted, it cools by expansion. The temperature the parcel would have at 500 mb is then subtracted from the environmental 500-mb temperature. The difference is the lifted index, which may be positive, zero, or negative. Thus, the lifted index indicates stability at 500 mb (18,000 ft. MSL).
Answer (B) is incorrect because a positive index means that a parcel of air, if lifted, would be colder than existing air at 500 mb, and thus the air is stable. Answer (C) is incorrect because a negative index means that a parcel of air, if lifted, would be warmer than existing air at 500 mb, and thus the air is unstable.

Answer (B) is correct (5337). *(AvW Chap 6)*
Stable, moist air and adiabatic cooling, e.g., upslope flow or lifting over colder air, are needed to form stratiform clouds.
Answer (A) is incorrect because stable (not unstable), moist (not dry) air is required. Answer (C) is incorrect because stable (not unstable) air is required.

Answer (C) is correct (5369). *(AvW Chap 11)*
Cumulonimbus clouds are thunderstorms by definition. Their intensity can be gauged by the presence of roll clouds on the lower leading edge of the storm, which mark the eddies in the shear. Roll clouds are prevalent with cold frontal or squall line thunderstorms and signify an extremely turbulent zone. Also, the more frequent the lightning, the more severe the storm.
Answer (A) is incorrect because cloud bases and precipitation are not, in themselves, definite indicators of extreme turbulence. Answer (B) is incorrect because low ceilings, hail, and precipitation static are not, in themselves, definite indicators of extreme turbulence.

59.
5371. What feature is normally associated with the cumulus stage of a thunderstorm?

A— Roll cloud.
B— Continuous updraft.
C— Beginning of rain at the surface.

Answer (B) is correct (5371). (AvW Chap 11)
The cumulus stage of a thunderstorm has continuous updrafts which build the cloud up. The water droplets are carried up until they become too heavy. Once they begin falling and creating downdrafts, the storm changes from the cumulus to the mature stage.
Answer (A) is incorrect because the roll cloud is the cloud near the ground which is formed by the downrushing cold air pushing out from below the thunderstorm usually in the mature stage. Answer (C) is incorrect because the beginning of rain at the surface indicates the start of the mature stage, which follows the cumulus stage.

60.
5349. The conditions necessary for the formation of cumulonimbus clouds are a lifting action and

A— unstable, dry air.
B— stable, moist air.
C— unstable, moist air.

Answer (C) is correct (5349). (AvW Chap 6)
Unstable, moist air and a lifting action, i.e., convective activity, are needed to form cumulonimbus clouds.
Answer (A) is incorrect because moist (not dry) air is required. Answer (B) is incorrect because unstable (not stable) air is required.

61.
5363. The most severe weather conditions, such as destructive winds, heavy hail, and tornadoes, are generally associated with

A— slow-moving warm fronts which slope above the tropopause.
B— squall lines.
C— fast-moving occluded fronts.

Answer (B) is correct (5363). (AvW Chap 11)
A squall line is a non-frontal, narrow band of thunderstorms that often develops ahead of a cold front. It often contains severe steady-state thunderstorms and presents the single most intense weather hazard to aircraft.
Answer (A) is incorrect because warm fronts generally do not produce severe weather. Answer (C) is incorrect because, although occluded fronts have some associated instability, the weather they produce is not nearly as severe as a squall line.

62.
5364. Of the following, which is accurate regarding turbulence associated with thunderstorms?

A— Outside the clouds, shear turbulence can be encountered 50 miles laterally from a severe storm.
B— Shear turbulence is encountered only inside cumulonimbus clouds or within a 5-mile radius of them.
C— Outside the cloud, shear turbulence can be encountered 20 miles laterally from a severe storm.

Answer (C) is correct (5364). (AvW Chap 11)
Hazardous turbulence is present in and around all thunderstorms. Outside the cloud, shear turbulence has been encountered several thousand feet above and 20 NM laterally from a severe storm. The roll cloud signifies an extremely turbulent zone.
Answer (A) is incorrect because shear turbulence can be encountered to 20 NM (not 50 NM) laterally from a severe storm. Answer (B) is incorrect because shear turbulence can be encountered above and 20 NM (not 5 NM) laterally (not just inside) severe thunderstorms.

63.
5367. Which statement is true concerning squall lines?

A— They form slowly, but move rapidly.
B— They are associated with frontal systems only.
C— They offer the most intense weather hazards to aircraft.

Answer (C) is correct (5367). (AvW Chap 11)
A squall line is a non-frontal narrow band of active thunderstorms. It often contains severe steady-state thunderstorms and presents the single most intense weather hazard to aircraft.
Answer (A) is incorrect because squall lines usually form rapidly, generally reaching maximum intensity during the late afternoon and the first few hours of darkness. Answer (B) is incorrect because while it may develop ahead of a cold front in moist and unstable air, it may develop in unstable air far removed from any front.

64.
5366. Which statement is true regarding squall lines?

A— They are always associated with cold fronts.
B— They are slow in forming, but rapid in movement.
C— They are nonfrontal and often contain severe, steady-state thunderstorms.

65.
5368. Select the true statement pertaining to the life cycle of a thunderstorm.

A— Updrafts continue to develop throughout the dissipating stage of a thunderstorm.
B— The beginning of rain at the Earth's surface indicates the mature stage of the thunderstorm.
C— The beginning of rain at the Earth's surface indicates the dissipating stage of the thunderstorm.

66.
5375. Which is true regarding the use of airborne weather-avoidance radar for the recognition of certain weather conditions?

A— The radarscope provides no assurance of avoiding instrument weather conditions.
B— The avoidance of hail is assured when flying between and just clear of the most intense echoes.
C— The clear area between intense echoes indicates that visual sighting of storms can be maintained when flying between the echoes.

67.
5370. Which weather phenomenon signals the beginning of the mature stage of a thunderstorm?

A— The start of rain.
B— The appearance of an anvil top.
C— Growth rate of cloud is maximum.

68.
5372. During the life cycle of a thunderstorm, which stage is characterized predominately by downdrafts?

A— Mature.
B— Developing.
C— Dissipating.

Answer (C) is correct (5366). *(AvW Chap 11)*
A squall line is a non-frontal, narrow band of active thunderstorms that frequently develops ahead of a cold front. It can, however, occur in any area of moist, unstable air. It often contains severe steady-state thunderstorms and presents the single most intense weather hazard to aircraft.
Answer (A) is incorrect because while squall lines usually precede cold fronts, they can form in any area of unstable air. Answer (B) is incorrect because squall lines usually form rapidly.

Answer (B) is correct (5368). *(AvW Chap 11)*
Thunderstorms have three stages in their life cycle: cumulus, mature, and dissipating. The beginning of rain at the Earth's surface indicates the mature stage which is characterized by numerous updrafts and downdrafts.
Answer (A) is incorrect because updrafts do not continue during the dissipating stage of the thunderstorm; only downdrafts are present. Answer (C) is incorrect because the beginning of rain at the Earth's surface is the beginning of the mature (not dissipating) stage.

Answer (A) is correct (5375). *(AvW Chap 11)*
Airborne weather avoidance radar is designed to identify areas of precipitation, especially heavy precipitation which may signify an active thunderstorm. Instrument weather conditions are restricted visibility due to clouds or fog which are not indicated on radar screens.
Answer (B) is incorrect because hail is often thrown from the tops of thunderstorms for several miles away from the cloud itself. Answer (C) is incorrect because clouds without precipitation may exist between the intense echoes.

Answer (A) is correct (5370). *(AvW Chap 11)*
Thunderstorms have three stages in their life cycle: cumulus, mature, and dissipating. The beginning of rain at the Earth's surface indicates the mature stage which is characterized by numerous updrafts and downdrafts.
Answer (B) is incorrect because the anvil top generally appears during (not necessarily at the beginning of) the mature stage. Answer (C) is incorrect because maximum cloud growth rate occurs further into the mature stage of a thunderstorm (not at the beginning).

Answer (C) is correct (5372). *(AvW Chap 11)*
Thunderstorms have three stages in their life cycle: cumulus, mature, and dissipating. In the dissipating stage, the storm is characterized by downdrafts as the storm rains itself out.
Answer (A) is incorrect because the mature stage has both updrafts and downdrafts, which creates tremendous wind shears. Answer (B) is incorrect because cumulus is the developing stage when there are primarily updrafts.

69.
5373. What minimum distance should exist between intense radar echoes before any attempt is made to fly between these thunderstorms?

A— 20 miles.
B— 30 miles.
C— 40 miles.

Answer (C) is correct (5373). *(AvW Chap 11)*
Wind shear turbulence has been encountered as far as 20 NM laterally from a severe thunderstorm. Thus, a minimum distance of 40 NM should exist between intense radar echoes before any attempt is made to fly between them.
Answer (A) is incorrect because shear turbulence may be encountered 20 NM (not 10 NM) laterally from intense echoes. Answer (B) is incorrect because shear turbulence may be encountered 20 NM (not 15 NM) laterally from intense echoes.

70.
5365. If airborne radar is indicating an extremely intense thunderstorm echo, this thunderstorm should be avoided by a distance of at least

A— 20 miles.
B— 10 miles.
C— 5 miles.

Answer (A) is correct (5365). *(AvW Chap 11)*
Wind shear turbulence has been encountered as far as 20 NM laterally from a severe thunderstorm.
Answer (B) is incorrect because the danger of shear turbulence exists 20 NM (not 10 NM) laterally from a severe storm. Answer (C) is incorrect because the danger of shear turbulence exists 20 NM (not 5 NM) laterally from a severe storm.

71.
5360. Which situation would most likely result in freezing precipitation? Rain falling from air which has a temperature of

A— 32 °F or less into air having a temperature of more than 32 °F.
B— 0 °C or less into air having a temperature of 0 °C or more.
C— more than 32 °F into air having a temperature of 32 °F or less.

Answer (C) is correct (5360). *(AvW Chap 10)*
A condition favorable for rapid accumulation of clear icing is freezing rain. Rain forms at temperatures warmer than freezing, then falls through air at temperatures below freezing and becomes supercooled. The supercooled drops freeze on impact with an aircraft surface.
Answer (A) is incorrect because the rain must begin in temperatures of 32°F or warmer and fall through a layer of below-freezing temperatures. Answer (B) is incorrect because the rain must begin in temperatures of 0°C or warmer and fall through a layer of below-freezing temperatures.

72.
5361. Which statement is true concerning the hazards of hail?

A— Hail damage in horizontal flight is minimal due to the vertical movement of hail in the clouds.
B— Rain at the surface is a reliable indication of no hail aloft.
C— Hailstones may be encountered in clear air several miles from a thunderstorm.

Answer (C) is correct (5361). *(AvW Chap 11)*
Hail competes with turbulence as the greatest thunderstorm hazard to aircraft. Hail has been observed in clear air several miles from the parent thunderstorm. You should anticipate possible hail with any thunderstorm, especially beneath the anvil of a large cumulonimbus cloud.
Answer (A) is incorrect because hail, along with turbulence, presents one of the greatest hazards to aircraft in thunderstorms; hail damages the leading edges and windshields of aircraft. Answer (B) is incorrect because rain at the surface does not mean the absence of hail aloft, i.e., hail vs. rain is a function of temperature.

73.
5362. Hail is most likely to be associated with

A— cumulus clouds.
B— cumulonimbus clouds.
C— stratocumulus clouds.

Answer (B) is correct (5362). *(AvW Chap 11)*
Hail competes with turbulence as the greatest thunderstorm hazard to aircraft. Hail has been observed in clear air several miles from the parent thunderstorm. You should anticipate possible hail with any thunderstorm, especially beneath the anvil of a large cumulonimbus cloud.
Answer (A) is incorrect because hail is usually associated with cumulonimbus (not cumulus) clouds. Answer (C) is incorrect because hail is usually associated with cumulonimbus (not stratocumulus) clouds.

74.
5324. Ice pellets encountered during flight normally are evidence that

A— a warm front has passed.
B— a warm front is about to pass.
C— there are thunderstorms in the area.

Answer (B) is correct (5324). *(AvW Chap 10)*
Ice pellets form as a result of rain freezing at a higher altitude. This indicates that there is a layer of warm air above in which it is raining and the rain freezes as it falls through the colder air. Thus, either a warm front or a cold front is about to pass.
Answer (A) is incorrect because the layer of warm air above cold air necessary for the formation of ice pellets occurs when a warm front is about to pass (not after it has passed). Answer (C) is incorrect because ice pellets are a result of rain freezing at a higher altitude (not necessarily from a thunderstorm).

75.
5326. Ice pellets encountered during flight are normally evidence that

A— a cold front has passed.
B— there are thunderstorms in the area.
C— freezing rain exists at higher altitude.

Answer (C) is correct (5326). *(AvW Chap 10)*
Rain falling through subfreezing cold air may become supercooled, freezing on impact as freezing rain; or it may freeze during its descent, falling as ice pellets. Ice pellets always indicate freezing rain at higher altitude.
Answer (A) is incorrect because ice pellets may indicate that either a warm front is about to pass OR a cold front has passed, not only that a cold front has passed. Answer (B) is incorrect because ice pellets always indicate freezing rain at higher altitudes (not necessarily that a thunderstorm is in the area).

76.
5325. What is indicated if ice pellets are encountered at 8,000 feet?

A— Freezing rain at higher altitude.
B— You are approaching an area of thunderstorms.
C— You will encounter hail if you continue your flight.

Answer (A) is correct (5325). *(AvW Chap 10)*
Ice pellets form as a result of rain freezing at a higher altitude. There is a layer of warm air above in which it is raining and the rain freezes as it falls through the colder air. Thus, either a warm front is about to pass, or a cold front has passed.
Answer (B) is incorrect because freezing rain can be encountered even where there are no thunderstorms. Answer (C) is incorrect because ice pellets are a form of hail.

7.9 Turbulence

77.
5444. A pilot reporting turbulence that momentarily causes slight, erratic changes in altitude and/or attitude should report it as

A— light chop.
B— light turbulence.
C— moderate turbulence.

Answer (B) is correct (5444). *(AWS Sect 14)*
Light turbulence momentarily causes slight, erratic changes in altitude and/or attitude.
Answer (A) is incorrect because light chop is rapid, somewhat rhythmic bumpiness. Answer (C) is incorrect because moderate turbulence causes changes in altitude and/or attitude, and variations in indicated airspeed.

78.
5445. When turbulence causes changes in altitude and/or attitude, but aircraft control remains positive, that should be reported as

A— light.
B— severe.
C— moderate.

Answer (C) is correct (5445). *(AWS Sect 14)*
Moderate turbulence is similar to light turbulence but of greater intensity. Changes in altitude and/or attitude occur, but the aircraft remains in positive control at all times.
Answer (A) is incorrect because light turbulence momentarily causes slight, erratic changes in altitude and/or attitude. Answer (B) is incorrect because severe turbulence causes large, abrupt changes in altitude and/or attitude and the aircraft may be momentarily out of control.

79.
5446. Turbulence that is encountered above 15,000 feet AGL not associated with cumuliform cloudiness, including thunderstorms, should be reported as

A— severe turbulence.
B— clear air turbulence.
C— convective turbulence.

Answer (B) is correct (5446). *(AWS Sect 14)*
CAT (clear air turbulence) is turbulence encountered in air where no clouds (or only occasional cirrus clouds) are present. The name is properly applied to high-level turbulence associated with wind shear, i.e., above 15,000 ft. AGL.
Answer (A) is incorrect because severe is a degree of turbulence not related to altitude. CAT may be light, moderate, or severe. Answer (C) is incorrect because convective turbulence refers to cumulus clouds and the lifting action related to turbulence.

80.
5443. The minimum vertical wind shear value critical for probable moderate or greater turbulence is

A— 4 knots per 1,000 feet.
B— 6 knots per 1,000 feet.
C— 8 knots per 1,000 feet.

Answer (B) is correct (5443). *(AWS Sect 14)*
Moderate or greater turbulence should be expected where vertical wind shears exceed 6 kt. per 1,000 ft.
Answer (A) is incorrect because moderate or greater turbulence should be expected where vertical wind shears exceed 6 kt. (not 4 kt.) per 1,000 ft. Answer (C) is incorrect because moderate or greater turbulence should be expected where vertical wind shears exceed 6 kt. (not 8 kt.) per 1,000 ft.

81.
5450. One of the most dangerous features of mountain waves is the turbulent areas in and

A— below rotor clouds.
B— above rotor clouds.
C— below lenticular clouds.

Answer (A) is correct (5450). *(AvW Chap 16)*
When stable air flows across a mountain range, large waves occur downwind from the mountains. Underneath each wave crest is a rotary circulation called a rotor. Turbulence is most frequent and most severe in and below the rotor clouds.
Answer (B) is incorrect because the turbulent areas of a mountain wave are in and below (not above) the rotor clouds. Answer (C) is incorrect because the most turbulent areas of a mountain wave are in and below the rotor (not lenticular) clouds.

82.
5393. The conditions most favorable to wave formation over mountainous areas are a layer of

A— stable air at mountaintop altitude and a wind of at least 20 knots blowing across the ridge.
B— unstable air at mountaintop altitude and a wind of at least 20 knots blowing across the ridge.
C— moist, unstable air at mountaintop altitude and a wind of less than 5 knots blowing across the ridge.

Answer (A) is correct (5393). *(AvW Chap 16)*
A mountain wave requires a layer of stable air at mountaintop altitude and a wind of at least 20 kt. blowing across the ridge.
Answer (B) is incorrect because the air at the mountaintop must be stable (not unstable). Unstable air tends to deter wave formation. Answer (C) is incorrect because the air at the mountaintop must be stable (not unstable). Unstable air tends to deter wave formation. Also, a wind of at least 20 kt. (not 5 kt.) must be blowing across the ridge.

83.
5357. When flying low over hilly terrain, ridges, or mountain ranges, the greatest potential danger from turbulent air currents will usually be encountered on the

A— leeward side when flying with a tailwind.
B— leeward side when flying into the wind.
C— windward side when flying into the wind.

Answer (B) is correct (5357). *(AvW Chap 9)*
When wind flows over ridges or mountain ranges, it flows up the windward side and down the leeward side. Thus, a pilot who approaches mountainous terrain from the leeward side may be forced into the side of the mountain by the downward-flowing air.
Answer (A) is incorrect because you are flying away from the mountain when you fly with the wind.
Answer (C) is incorrect because you are flying in air rising up the mountain on the windward side.

84.
5356. Convective currents are most active on warm summer afternoons when winds are

A— light.
B— moderate.
C— strong.

7.10 Wind Shear

85.
5359. During departure, under conditions of suspected low-level wind shear, a sudden decrease in headwind will cause

A— a loss in airspeed equal to the decrease in wind velocity.
B— a gain in airspeed equal to the decrease in wind velocity.
C— no change in airspeed, but groundspeed will decrease.

86.
5358. During an approach, the most important and most easily recognized means of being alerted to possible wind shear is monitoring the

A— amount of trim required to relieve control pressures.
B— heading changes necessary to remain on the runway centerline.
C— power and vertical velocity required to remain on the proper glidepath.

87.
5351. What is an important characteristic of wind shear?

A— It is present at only lower levels and exists in a horizontal direction.
B— It is present at any level and exists in only a vertical direction.
C— It can be present at any level and can exist in both a horizontal and vertical direction.

88.
5353. Low-level wind shear may occur when

A— surface winds are light and variable.
B— there is a low-level temperature inversion with strong winds above the inversion.
C— surface winds are above 15 knots and there is no change in wind direction and windspeed with height.

Answer (A) is correct (5356). *(AvW Chap 9)*
Convective currents are localized vertical air movements, both ascending and descending. They are most active on warm summer afternoons when winds are light. Heated air at the surface creates a shallow, unstable layer, and the warm air is forced upward. Convection increases in strength and to greater heights as surface heating increases.
Answer (B) is incorrect because moderate wind disrupts the vertical movement of convective currents. Answer (C) is incorrect because strong wind disrupts the vertical movement of convective currents.

Answer (A) is correct (5359). *(AvW Chap 9)*
In such low-airspeed operations, wind shears causing a sudden decrease in headwind are critical. A sudden decrease in headwind will decrease airspeed equal to the decrease in the wind velocity.
Answer (B) is incorrect because there is a loss (not gain) in airspeed. Answer (C) is incorrect because initially there is a loss of airspeed, followed by an increase (not decrease) of groundspeed.

Answer (C) is correct (5358). *(AvW Chap 9)*
If substantial power and vertical speed adjustments are required to remain on the proper glidepath during an approach, wind shear factors exist.
Answer (A) is incorrect because trim adjustments are a function of power settings, airspeeds, and flap-gear configurations. Answer (B) is incorrect because heading changes necessary to remain on the runway centerline are related to crosswind direction rather than headwind/tailwind wind shears.

Answer (C) is correct (5351). *(AvW Chap 9)*
Wind shear occurs because of changes in wind direction and wind velocity, both horizontal and vertical. It may be present at any flight level.
Answer (A) is incorrect because wind shear occurs at all altitudes and can be both vertical and horizontal. Answer (B) is incorrect because wind shear occurs at all altitudes and can be both vertical and horizontal.

Answer (B) is correct (5353). *(AvW Chap 9)*
A low-level temperature inversion forms on a clear night with calm or light surface winds. When the wind just above the inversion is relatively strong, a wind shear zone develops between the calm and the stronger winds above.
Answer (A) is incorrect because light surface winds alone would not cause wind shear. Answer (C) is incorrect because, by definition, wind shear refers to abrupt changes in wind speed and/or direction.

89.
5352. Hazardous wind shear is commonly encountered

A— near warm or stationary frontal activity.
B— when the wind velocity is stronger than 35 knots.
C— in areas of temperature inversion and near thunderstorms.

90.
5354. If a temperature inversion is encountered immediately after takeoff or during an approach to a landing, a potential hazard exists due to

A— wind shear.
B— strong surface winds.
C— strong convective currents.

91.
5355. GIVEN:

Winds at 3,000 feet AGL . . . . 30 kts
Surface winds . . . . Calm

While on approach for landing, under clear skies with convective turbulence a few hours after sunrise, one should

A— increase approach airspeed slightly above normal to avoid stalling.
B— keep the approach airspeed at or slightly below normal to compensate for floating.
C— not alter the approach airspeed, these conditions are nearly ideal.

92.
5449. The Low Level Wind Shear Alert System (LLWAS) provides wind data and software process to detect the presence of a

A— rotating column of air extending from a cumulonimbus cloud.
B— change in wind direction and/or speed within a very short distance above the airport.
C— downward motion of the air associated with continuous winds blowing with an easterly component due to the rotation of the Earth.

Answer (C) is correct (5352). *(AvW Chap 9)*
    Hazardous wind shear is found near thunderstorms and also near strong temperature inversions.
    Answer (A) is incorrect because, although frontal activity implies a change in wind, i.e., wind shear, the most hazardous wind shear is found specifically near inversions and thunderstorms. Answer (B) is incorrect because a strong wind does not by itself result in wind shears; only if there are strong winds in another direction.

Answer (A) is correct (5354). *(AvW Chap 9)*
    A wind shear develops in a zone between cold, calm air covered by warm air with a strong wind. This often occurs during a temperature inversion.
    Answer (B) is incorrect because strong surface winds by themselves do not create the potential hazard that wind shear does. Answer (C) is incorrect because temperature inversion precludes (not generates) strong convective currents.

Answer (A) is correct (5355). *(AvW Chap 9)*
    When landing in calm wind under clear skies within a few hours after sunrise, you should be prepared for a temperature inversion near the ground. Wind shear can be expected if the winds at 2,000 to 4,000 ft. are 25 kt. or more (30 kt. at 3,000 ft. in this question). Additionally, the convective turbulence on approach can cause abrupt changes in airspeed and may result in a stall at a low altitude. The corrective action for both of these conditions is to increase approach airspeed slightly above normal to avoid stalling.
    Answer (B) is incorrect because the danger in this situation is low-level wind shear and convective turbulence, both of which may cause an abrupt loss of airspeed during the approach. Thus, you should slightly increase, not maintain or reduce airspeed, above the normal approach speed. Answer (C) is incorrect because low-level wind shear and convective turbulence are not ideal landing conditions. Thus, you should increase approach airspeed slightly above normal to avoid stalling.

Answer (B) is correct (5449). *(Aim Para 7-1-23)*
    The LLWAS provides wind data and software process to detect the presence of hazardous wind shear and microbursts in the vicinity of the airport. Wind sensors mounted on poles as high as 150 ft., are located 2,000 to 3,500 ft. from the runway centerline.
    Wind shear is defined as a change in wind speed and/or direction in a short distance and can exist in either, or both, horizontal or vertical direction.
    Answer (A) is incorrect because a rotating column of air extending from a cumulonimbus cloud describes a funnel cloud or tornado, which is a phenomenon which the LLWAS cannot detect. Answer (C) is incorrect because the downward motion of air associated with continuous winds blowing with an easterly component due to the rotation of the Earth is describing a general circulation pattern of air in the north polar region, not something a LLWAS is designed to detect.

END OF CHAPTER

CHAPTER EIGHT
AVIATION WEATHER SERVICES

This chapter contains outlines of major concepts tested, all FAA test questions and answers regarding aviation weather services, and an explanation of each answer. Each module, or subtopic, within this chapter is listed above with the number of questions from the FAA pilot knowledge test pertaining to that particular module. For each module, the first number following the parentheses is the page number on which the outline begins, and the next number is the page number on which the questions begin.

CAUTION: The **sole purpose** of this book is to expedite your passing the pilot knowledge test for the commercial pilot certificate. Topics or regulations not directly tested are omitted, even though much more information and knowledge are necessary to become a proficient commercial pilot. This additional material is presented in *Commercial Pilot Flight Maneuvers and Practical Test Prep* and *Pilot Handbook*, available from Gleim Publications, Inc. See the order form on page 284.

8.1 SOURCES OF WEATHER INFORMATION (Questions 1-7)

1. Current en route and destination flight information for an IFR flight should be obtained from an Automated FSS (AFSS).

    a. Weather report forecasts which are not routinely available at the AFSS can best be obtained by contacting an NWS weather forecast office (WFO).

2. En Route Flight Advisory Service (EFAS) is available by contacting flight watch by using the name of the ARTCC facility in your area, your airplane identification, and the name of the nearest VOR on 122.0 MHz, when operating below 17,500 ft. MSL.

3. Telephone Information Briefing Service (TIBS), provided by an AFSS, is a continuous recording of meteorological and aeronautical information available by telephone.

4. Hazardous Inflight Weather Advisory Service (HIWAS) is a continuous broadcast over selected VORs of convective SIGMETs, SIGMETs, AIRMETs, severe weather forecast alerts (AWW), and center weather advisories (CWA).

5. Transcribed weather broadcasts (TWEBs) are continuous transcribed weather briefings, including winds aloft and route forecasts, monitored on certain VOR and NDB frequencies.

6. Weather advisory broadcasts, including AWWs, convective SIGMETs, and SIGMETs, are provided by ARTCCs on all frequencies, except emergency, when any part of the area described is within 150 mi. of the airspace under their jurisdiction.

8.2 AVIATION ROUTINE WEATHER REPORT (METAR) (Questions 8-12)

1. Aviation routine weather reports (METARs) are actual weather observations at the time indicated on the report. There are two types of reports.

    a. METAR is an hourly routine observation (scheduled).
    b. SPECI is a special METAR observation (unscheduled).

2. Following the type of report are the elements listed below:

    a. The four-letter ICAO station identifier
    b. Date and time of report
    c. Modifier (if required)
    d. Wind
    e. Visibility
    f. Runway visual range
    g. Weather phenomena

        1) **RA** means rain.
        2) **BR** means mist.

    h. Sky conditions

        1) Cloud bases are reported with three digits in hundreds of feet AGL.

            a) EXAMPLE: **OVC005** means overcast cloud layer at 500 ft. AGL.

        2) To determine the thickness of a cloud layer, first add the field elevation to the reported cloud base to determine the height of the cloud base in feet MSL and then subtract this from the reported cloud layer top.

    i. Temperature/dew point
    j. Altimeter
    k. Remarks (RMK)

        1) **RAB12** means rain began at 12 min. past the hour.

            a) If the time of the observation was at 1854 UTC, the rain began at 1812 UTC.

        2) **WSHFT 30 FROPA** means wind shift, 30 min. past the hour, due to frontal passage.

3. EXAMPLE: METAR KAUS 301651Z 12008KT 4SM –RA HZ BKN010 BKN023 OVC160 21/17 A3005 RMK RAB25

    a. METAR is a routine weather observation.

    b. KAUS is Austin, TX.

    c. 301651Z is the date (30th day) and time (1651 UTC) of the observation.

    d. 12008KT means the wind is from 120° true at 8 kt.

    e. 4SM means the visibility is 4 statute miles.

    f. –RA HZ means light rain and haze.

    g. BKN010 BKN023 OVC160 means ceiling 1,000 ft. broken, 2,300 ft. broken, 16,000 ft. overcast.

    h. 21/17 means the temperature is 21°C and the dew point is 17°C.

    i. A3005 means the altimeter setting is 30.05 in. of Hg.

    j. RMK RAB25 means remarks, rain began at 25 min. past the hour.

4. **Pilot Report (PIREP).** In a PIREP, reported sky cover begins with **/SK**, followed by

   a. Height of cloud base in hundreds of feet MSL

   b. Cloud cover contraction

   c. Height of cloud tops in hundreds of feet MSL

   d. Cloud layers separated by a solidus (/)

   e. EXAMPLE: **/SK OVC 025/045 OVC 090** means the top of the lower overcast cloud layer is 2,500 ft. MSL and the base and top of the second overcast cloud layer is 4,500 ft. MSL and 9,000 ft. MSL, respectively.

5. To determine the bases of convective-type cumulus clouds in thousands of feet is to divide the temperature/dew point spread by 2.5.

8.3 RADAR WEATHER REPORT (SD) (Question 13)

1. Thunderstorms and general areas of precipitation can be observed by radar. An SD may be transmitted as a separate report, or it may be included in a scheduled weather broadcast by Flight Service Stations.

2. EXAMPLE:

   LZK 1133 AREA 4TRW +/+ 22/100 88/170 196/180 220/115 C2425 MT 310 AT 162/110

   Little Rock (Arkansas) radar weather observation at 1133 UTC. An area of echoes, four-tenths coverage, containing thunderstorms and heavy rainshowers, increasing in intensity.

   The AREA is defined by points (referenced from LZK radar site) at 22°, 100 NM; 88°, 170 NM; 196°, 180 NM; and 220°, 115 NM. Cells moving from 240° at 25 kt. (These points are plotted on a map. Connecting the points with straight lines outlines the area of echoes.)

   Maximum top (MT) is 31,000 ft. MSL located at 162° and 110 NM from LZK.

8.4 SURFACE ANALYSIS CHART (Questions 14-18)

1. The Surface Analysis Chart, often referred to as a surface weather map, is the basic observed weather chart.

   a. It provides a ready means of locating observed frontal positions and pressure centers.

   b. The Surface Analysis Chart displays weather information such as

      1) Surface wind direction and speed
      2) Temperature
      3) Dew point
      4) Position of fronts
      5) Areas of high or low pressure
      6) Obstructions to vision

   c. It does not show cloud heights and coverage.

2. Solid lines depicting the pressure pattern are called isobars. They denote lines of equal pressure.

   a. Isobars are placed at 4-mb intervals.

   b. When the pressure gradient is weak, dashed isobars are sometimes inserted at 2-mb intervals to more clearly define the pressure pattern.

   c. Close spacing of isobars indicates a strong pressure gradient.

8.5 CONSTANT PRESSURE CHARTS (Questions 19-21)

1. Constant pressure charts provide information about the observed temperature, wind, and temperature/dew point spread at a specified altitude.

2. Areas of strong winds (70 to 110 kt.) are denoted by hatching.

8.6 TERMINAL AERODROME FORECAST (TAF) (Questions 22-26)

1. A terminal aerodrome forecast (TAF) is a concise statement of the expected meteorological conditions at an airport during a specified period.

   a. TAFs are issued four times daily and are usually valid for a 24-hr. period.

2. The elements of a TAF are listed below:

   a. Type of report

      1) TAF is a routine forecast.
      2) TAF AMD is an amended forecast.

   b. ICAO station identifier
   c. Date and time the forecast is actually prepared
   d. Valid period of the forecast
   e. Forecast meteorological conditions -- the body of the forecast, which includes

      1) Wind

         a) **VRB** means a variable wind direction.

      2) Visibility

         a) **P6SM** means the forecast visibility is greater than 6 SM.

      3) Weather
      4) Sky condition

         a) **SKC** means no clouds or less than 1/8 cloud coverage, i.e., sky clear.

3. A PROB40 group in a TAF indicates a 40% probability of occurrence of thunderstorms or other precipitation events.

   a. EXAMPLE: **PROB40 2102 +TSRA** means there is a 40% probability between 2100Z and 0200Z of thunderstorms with heavy rain.

8.7 AVIATION AREA FORECAST (FA) (Questions 27-29)

1. An aviation area forecast (FA) is a forecast of general weather conditions over an area the size of several states. It is used to determine forecast en route weather and to interpolate conditions at airports which do not have TAFs issued.

   a. FAs are issued three times a day by the Aviation Weather Center.

2. The FA is comprised of four sections.

   a. Product header
   b. Precautionary statements
   c. Synopsis
   d. VFR clouds and weather (VFR CLDS/WX)

3.   VFR CLDS/WX section contains a 12-hr. specific forecast, followed by a 6-hr. categorical outlook.

   a.   The specific forecast section gives a general description of clouds and weather which cover an area greater than 3,000 square miles and are significant to VFR operations.

      1)   Surface visibility and obstructions to vision are included when the forecast visibility is 6 SM or less.

      2)   Precipitation, thunderstorms, and sustained winds of 20 kt. or greater are always included when forecast.

8.8 IN-FLIGHT WEATHER ADVISORIES (Questions 30-35)

1.   In-flight aviation weather advisories, designated as severe weather forecast alerts (AWW), convective SIGMETs, SIGMETs, AIRMETs, and center weather advisories (CWA), are forecasts to advise en route aircraft of development of potentially hazardous weather.

   a.   A SIGMET contains information regarding a volcanic eruption that is occurring or expected to occur.

   b.   AIRMETs and CWAs are issued for the possibility of moderate icing, moderate turbulence, sustained surface winds of 30 kt. or more, and extensive mountain obscurement.

2.   SIGMET advisories are issued as a warning of weather phenomena which are potentially hazardous to all aircraft.

3.   Convective SIGMETs contain both an observation and a forecast or just a forecast for

   a.   Tornadoes

   b.   Lines of thunderstorms

   c.   Embedded thunderstorms

   d.   Thunderstorm areas greater than or equal to thunderstorm intensity level 4 with an area coverage of 40% or more

   e.   Hail greater than or equal to 3/4 in. in diameter

4.   A squall is a sudden increase in wind speed of at least 16 kt. to a sustained speed of 22 kt. or more and lasting for at least 1 min.

8.9 LOW-LEVEL AND HIGH-LEVEL PROGNOSTIC CHARTS (Questions 36-39)

1.   Low-Level Significant Weather Prognostic Charts depict conditions expected to exist 12 and 24 hr. in the future.

   a.   The upper limit of the Low-Level Significant Weather Prognostic Chart is 24,000 ft. MSL.

2.   High-Level Significant Weather Prognostic Charts are also published.

   a.   They forecast significant weather between 24,000 ft. MSL and 63,000 ft. MSL.

   b.   Small scalloped lines are used in high-level significant weather prognostic charts to indicate cumulonimbus clouds.

      1)   The presence of these clouds automatically implies moderate or greater turbulence and icing.

8.10 OTHER CHARTS AND FORECASTS (Questions 40-46)

1. To best determine observed weather conditions between weather reporting stations, the pilot should refer to pilot reports.

2. The Weather Depiction Chart provides a graphic display of both VFR and IFR weather.

   a. When the sky cover is few or scattered, the height on the chart is the base of the lowest layer.

3. The Radar Summary Chart shows lines and cells of significant thunderstorms.

4. The freezing level panel found on the Composite Moisture Stability Chart is an analysis of observed freezing level data from upper air observations.

5. In the Winds Aloft Forecast, the winds are given in true direction and in knots.

6. The TWEB Route Forecast is similar to the Area Forecast except that information is contained in a route format. For a corridor 25 NM either side of the route, it forecasts

   a. Sky cover
   b. Height and amount of cloud bases
   c. Cloud tops
   d. Visibility
   e. Weather
   f. Obstructions to vision

QUESTIONS AND ANSWER EXPLANATIONS

All the FAA questions from the pilot knowledge test for the commercial pilot certificate relating to aviation weather services and the material outlined previously are reproduced on the following pages in the same modules as the outlines. To the immediate right of each question are the correct answer and answer explanation. You should cover these answers and answer explanations while responding to the questions. (A bookmark for this purpose has been provided in the back of this book.) Refer to the general discussion in the Introduction on how to take the FAA pilot knowledge test.

Remember that the questions from the FAA pilot knowledge test bank have been reordered by topic, and the topics have been organized into a meaningful sequence. Accordingly, the first line of the answer explanation gives the FAA question number and the citation of the authoritative source for the answer.

8.1 Sources of Weather Information

1.
5399. The most current en route and destination weather information for an instrument flight should be obtained from the

A— AFSS.
B— ATIS broadcast.
C— Notices to Airmen Publications.

Answer (A) is correct (5399). *(AWS Sect 1)*
   Automated FSS (AFSS) are the primary source for obtaining preflight briefings and in-flight weather information.
   Answer (B) is incorrect because the ATIS broadcast includes information pertaining only to landing and departing operations at one airport and is thus not sufficient for en route information. Answer (C) is incorrect because the Notices to Airmen Publication contains the published NOTAM (D) and FDC NOTAMs, which is not weather information.

2.

5401. The Telephone Information Briefing Service (TIBS) provided by AFSSs includes

A— weather information service on a common frequency (122.0 mHz).
B— recorded weather briefing service for the local area, usually within 50 miles and route forecasts.
C— continuous recording of meteorological and/or aeronautical information available by telephone.

Answer (C) is correct (5401). *(AWS Sect 1)*
Telephone Information Briefing Service (TIBS) is provided by automated FSSs and provides continuous telephone recordings of meteorological and/or aeronautical information. Specifically, TIBS provides area and/or route briefings, airspace procedures, and special announcements, if applicable, concerning aviation interests.
Answer (A) is incorrect because En Route Flight Advisory Service (EFAS), not TIBS, is a weather service on a common frequency of 122.0 mHz. Answer (B) is incorrect because Pilot's Automatic Telephone Weather Answering System (PATWAS), not TIBS, is a recorded telephone briefing service for the local area, usually within a 50-NM radius of the station. A few selected stations also provide route forecasts.

3. *OK*

5400. The Hazardous Inflight Weather Advisory Service (HIWAS) is a broadcast service over selected VORs that provides

A— SIGMETs and AIRMETs at 15 minutes and 45 minutes past the hour for the first hour after issuance.
B— continuous broadcast of inflight weather advisories.
C— SIGMETs, CONVECTIVE SIGMETs and AIRMETs at 15 minutes and 45 minutes past the hour.

Answer (B) is correct (5400). *(AWS Sect 1)*
The Hazardous Inflight Weather Advisory Service (HIWAS) is a continuous broadcast service over selected VORs of in-flight weather advisories; i.e., SIGMETs, convective SIGMETs, AIRMETs, severe weather forecast alerts (AWW), and center weather advisories (CWA).
Answer (A) is incorrect because a FSS, not HIWAS, may broadcast SIGMETs and AIRMETs in their entirety upon receipt and at 15 min. and 45 min. past the hour for the first hour after issuance if there is no local HIWAS outlet. Answer (C) is incorrect because a FSS, not HIWAS, may broadcast a summarized alert notice at 15 min. and 45 min. past the hour of any in-flight weather advisory, including SIGMETs, convective SIGMETs, and AIRMETs, if there is no HIWAS outlet.

4.

5559. En route Flight Advisory Service (EFAS) is a service that provides en route aircraft with timely and meaningful weather advisories pertinent to the type of flight intended, route, and altitude. This information is received by

A— listening to en route VORs at 15 and 45 minutes past the hour.
B— contacting flight watch, using the name of the ARTCC facility identification in your area, your aircraft identification, and name of nearest VOR, on 122.0 MHz below 17,500 feet MSL.
C— contacting the AFSS facility in your area, using your airplane identification, and the name of the nearest VOR.

Answer (B) is correct (5559). *(AIM Para 7-1-4)*
En route Flight Advisory Service (EFAS) is a service specifically designed to provide en route aircraft with timely and meaningful weather advisories pertinent to the type of flight intended, route of flight, and altitude. This information is received by contacting flight watch, using the name of the ARTCC facility identification in your area, followed by your aircraft identification, and the name of the nearest VOR to your position on 122.0 MHz, when below 17,500 ft. MSL.
Answer (A) is incorrect because, in some areas, in-flight weather advisories, not EFAS, are broadcasted on VORs at 15 and 45 min. past the hour. Answer (C) is incorrect because only selected, not all, AFSSs have specially trained Flight Watch (EFAS) specialists.

5.

5398. During preflight preparation, weather report forecasts which are not routinely available at the local service outlet (AFSS) can best be obtained by means of contacting

A— weather forecast office (WFO).
B— air route traffic control center.
C— pilot's automatic telephone answering service.

Answer (A) is correct (5398). *(AWS Sect 1)*
Weather report forecasts which are not routinely available at an AFSS can be obtained by contacting a weather forecast office (WFO).
Answer (B) is incorrect because ARTCC is concerned with air traffic control, not weather briefings. Answer (C) is incorrect because PATWAS contains the weather products available at an AFSS.

6.

5421. To obtain a continuous transcribed weather briefing including winds aloft and route forecasts for a cross-country flight, a pilot could monitor

A— a TWEB on a low-frequency and/or VOR receiver.

B— the regularly scheduled weather broadcast on a VOR frequency.

C— a high-frequency radio receiver tuned to En Route Flight Advisory Service.

Answer (A) is correct (5421). *(AIM Para 7-1-8)*

Transcribed Weather Broadcasts (TWEBs) are route-oriented weather data recorded on tape and broadcast continuously over selected low-frequency navigational aids (i.e., NDBs) and/or VORs.

Answer (B) is incorrect because weather broadcasts include observed weather only at specific stations, not en route or forecast weather. Answer (C) is incorrect because one can only communicate and discuss weather with Flight Watch; i.e., it has no continuous transcribed weather data.

7.

5560. Weather Advisory Broadcasts, including Severe Weather Forecast Alerts (AWW), Convective SIGMETs, and SIGMETs, are provided by

A—ARTCCs on all frequencies, except emergency, when any part of the area described is within 150 miles of the airspace under their jurisdiction.

B—AFSSs on 122.2 MHz and adjacent VORs, when any part of the area described is within 200 miles of the airspace under their jurisdiction.

C—selected low-frequency and/or VOR navigational aids.

Answer (A) is correct (5560). *(AIM Para 7-1-9)*

ARTCCs broadcast a Severe Weather Forecast Alert (AWW), convective SIGMET, SIGMET, or center weather advisory (CWA) alert once on all frequencies, except emergency, when any part of the area described is within 150 mi. of the airspace under their jurisdiction.

Answer (B) is incorrect because weather advisory broadcasts are provided by ARTCCs on all frequencies (except emergency), not by AFSSs on 122.2 MHz and adjacent VORs, when any part of the area described is within 150 mi., not 200 mi., of the airspace under their jurisdiction. Answer (C) is incorrect because Transcribed Weather Broadcasts (TWEB), not weather advisory broadcasts, are provided by selected low-frequency and/or VOR navigational aids.

8.2 Aviation Routine Weather Report (METAR)

8.

5331. Refer to the excerpt from the following METAR report:

KTUS.....08004KT 4SM HZ .....26/04 A2995 RMK RAE36

At approximately what altitude AGL should bases of convective-type cumuliform clouds be expected?

A—4,400 feet.

B—8,800 feet.

C—17,600 feet.

Answer (B) is correct (5331). *(AvW Chap 6)*

To determine the approximate height of the cloud bases, you need the temperature and dew point. In the METAR report, the temperature is 26°C and the dew point is 4°C (26/04).

In a convective current, temperature and dew point converge at a rate of 2.5°C per 1,000 ft.

We can estimate the cumuliform cloud base in thousands of feet by dividing the temperature/dew point spread by 2.5. Given a temperature/dew point spread of 22°C (26-4), the base of the convective-type cumuliform clouds is approximately 8,800 ft. AGL (22 ÷ 2.5).

Answer (A) is incorrect because 4,400 ft. AGL is the approximate height of the base of cumuliform clouds if the temperature/dew point spread is 11°C, not 22°C. Answer (C) is incorrect because 17,600 ft. AGL is the approximate height of the base of cumuliform clouds if the temperature/dew point spread is 44°C, not 22°C.

9.

5406. What significant cloud coverage is reported by this pilot report?

KMOB
UA/OV 15NW MOB 1340Z/SK OVC 025/045 OVC 090

A— Three (3) separate overcast layers exist with bases at 250, 7,500, and 9,000 feet.

B— The top of the lower overcast is 2,500 feet; base and top of second overcast layer is 4,500 and 9,000 feet, respectively.

C— The base of the second overcast layer is 2,500 feet; top of second overcast layer is 7,500 feet; base of third layer is 9,000 feet.

Answer (B) is correct (5406). *(AWS Sect 3)*

In a PIREP, the significant cloud coverage is located in the sky cover (/SK) element. This PIREP states the top of the lower overcast cloud layer is 2,500 ft. (OVC 025/) and the base and top of the second overcast cloud layer is 4,500 ft. and 9,000 ft., respectively (045 OVC 090).

Answer (A) is incorrect because there are two, not three, overcast cloud layers. Answer (C) is incorrect because there are two, not three, overcast cloud layers.

10.
5402. The remarks section of the Aviation Routine Weather Report (METAR) contains the following coded information. What does it mean?

RMK FZDZB42 WSHFT 30 FROPA

A— Freezing drizzle with cloud bases below 4,200 feet.
B— Freezing drizzle below 4,200 feet and wind shear.
C— Wind shift at three zero due to frontal passage.

11.
5404. The station originating the following METAR observation has a field elevation of 3,500 feet MSL. If the sky cover is one continuous layer, what is the thickness of the cloud layer? (Top of overcast reported at 7,500 feet MSL.)

METAR KHOB 151250Z 17006KT 4SM OVC005 13/11 A2998

A— 2,500 feet.
B— 3,500 feet.
C— 4,000 feet.

12.
5403. What is meant by the Special METAR weather observation for KBOI?

SPECI KBOI 091854Z 32005KT 1 1/2SM RA BR OVC007 17/16 A2990 RMK RAB12

A— Rain and fog obscuring two-tenths of the sky; rain began at 1912Z.
B— Rain and mist obstructing visibility; rain began at 1812Z.
C— Rain and overcast at 1,200 feet AGL.

8.3 Radar Weather Report (SD)

13.
5408. Which is true concerning the radar weather report (SD) for KOKC?

KOKC 1934 LN 8TRW++/+ 86/40 164/60 199/115 15W L2425 MT 570 AT 159/65 2 INCH HAIL RPRTD THIS CELL

A— There are three cells with tops at 11,500, 40,000, and 60,000 feet.
B— The line of cells is moving 060° with winds reported up to 40 knots.
C— The maximum tops of the cells is 57,000 feet located 65 NM southeast of the station.

Answer (C) is correct (5402). *(AIM Para 7-1-28)*
The remark is decoded as freezing drizzle that began at 42 min. past the hour (FZDZB42) and a wind shift at 30 min. past the hour due to frontal passage (WSHFT 30 FROPA).
Answer (A) is incorrect because FZDZB42 means that freezing drizzle began at 42 min. past the hour, not that the cloud bases are below 4,200 ft. Answer (B) is incorrect because freezing drizzle began at 42 min. past the hour, not below 4,200 ft., and there was a wind shift, not wind shear, reported at 30 min. past the hour due to frontal passage.

Answer (B) is correct (5404). *(AIM Para 7-1-28)*
In the METAR report, the base of the overcast cloud layer is reported as 500 ft. AGL (OVC005) or 4,000 ft. MSL (3,500 ft. field elevation plus 500 ft. AGL). If the overcast cloud layer top is reported at 7,500 ft. MSL, the cloud layer is 3,500 ft. thick (7,500 – 4,000).
Answer (A) is incorrect because the cloud layer would be 2,500 ft. thick if the base of the overcast cloud layer was reported at 1,500 ft. (OVC015), not 500 ft. (OVC005). Answer (C) is incorrect because the top of the overcast cloud layer, not the thickness of the cloud layer, is 4,000 ft. AGL.

Answer (B) is correct (5403). *(AIM Para 7-1-28)*
The SPECI report for KBOI is reporting a visibility of 1½ SM in rain and mist (1 1/2SM RA BR), and the remarks indicate that the rain began at 12 min. past the hour, or 1812Z (RMK RAB12). Note the time of the SPECI is 1854Z.
Answer (A) is incorrect because the obscuration is reported as mist (BR), not fog (FG), since the visibility is between 5/8 to 6 SM. Additionally, the rain began at 12 min. past the hour or 1812Z, not 1912Z. Answer (C) is incorrect because the base of the overcast layer is reported at 700 ft. AGL (OVC007), not 1,200 ft. AGL.

Answer (C) is correct (5408). *(AWS Sect 3)*
In the SD for KOKC, the coded information **MT 570 AT 159/65** means the maximum tops of the cells are 57,000 ft. MSL, located on 159° from KOKC (i.e., southeast) at 65 NM.
Answer (A) is incorrect because the coded information **86/40 164/60 199/115** is the azimuth, referenced to true north, and range (NM) of points defining the echo pattern, not the tops of three cells. Answer (B) is incorrect because the coded information **L2425** means the line (L) echo pattern movement is from 240° at 25 kt., not winds reported up to 40 kt.

8.4 Surface Analysis Chart

14.
5425. On a Surface Analysis Chart, the solid lines that depict sea level pressure patterns are called

A— isobars.
B— isogons.
C— millibars.

Answer (A) is correct (5425). *(AWS Sect 5)*
    Isobars are solid lines on the Surface Analysis Chart depicting the sea level pressure pattern. They are usually spaced at 4-mb intervals and connect points of equal or constant pressure.
    Answer (B) is incorrect because isogons are lines of magnetic variation found on navigational charts. Answer (C) is incorrect because millibars are units of pressure, not lines that depict pressure patterns.

15.
5429. The Surface Analysis Chart depicts

A— frontal locations and expected movement, pressure centers, cloud coverage, and obstructions to vision at the time of chart transmission.
B— actual frontal positions, pressure patterns, temperature, dew point, wind, weather, and obstructions to vision at the valid time of the chart.
C— actual pressure distribution, frontal systems, cloud heights and coverage, temperature, dew point, and wind at the time shown on the chart.

Answer (B) is correct (5429). *(AWS Sect 5)*
    The Surface Analysis Chart depicts actual frontal positions, pressure patterns, temperature, dew point, wind, weather, and obstructions to vision at the valid time of the chart.
    Answer (A) is incorrect because the Surface Analysis Chart reports actual surface weather as it exists at the time of observation, i.e., no forecasts. Answer (C) is incorrect because Surface Analysis Charts do not indicate cloud heights.

16.
5426. Dashed lines on a Surface Analysis Chart, if depicted, indicate that the pressure gradient is

A— weak.
B— strong.
C— unstable.

Answer (A) is correct (5426). *(AWS Sect 5)*
    When the pressure gradient is weak, dashed isobars are sometimes inserted at 2-mb intervals on the Surface Analysis Chart to more clearly define the pressure pattern.
    Answer (B) is incorrect because strong pressure gradients are depicted by closely spaced solid isobars at 4-mb intervals, not by dashed isobars at 2-mb intervals. Answer (C) is incorrect because stability has to do with temperature lapse rates, not pressure levels.

17.
5428. On a Surface Analysis Chart, close spacing of the isobars indicates

A— weak pressure gradient.
B— strong pressure gradient.
C— strong temperature gradient.

Answer (B) is correct (5428). *(AWS Sect 5)*
    On a Surface Analysis Chart, close spacing of the isobars indicates a strong pressure gradient. Each line represents a 4-mb change. If the lines are close together, the pressure is changing more rapidly over a given area.
    Answer (A) is incorrect because the isobars will be widely, not closely, spaced when there is a weak pressure gradient. Answer (C) is incorrect because isotherms, not isobars, indicate changing temperatures.

18.
5427. Which chart provides a ready means of locating observed frontal positions and pressure centers?

A— Surface Analysis Chart.
B— Constant Pressure Analysis Chart.
C— Weather Depiction Chart.

Answer (A) is correct (5427). *(AWS Sect 5)*
    The Surface Analysis Chart provides a ready means of locating pressure systems and fronts. It also gives an overview of winds, temperatures, and dew point temperatures at chart time.
    Answer (B) is incorrect because Constant Pressure Analysis Charts have to do with observed moisture content, temperatures, and winds aloft. Answer (C) is incorrect because the Weather Depiction Chart shows frontal location, cloud coverage and height, VFR-MVFR-IFR, etc., but not pressure centers.

8.5 Constant Pressure Charts

19.
5441. What flight planning information can a pilot derive from Constant Pressure Analysis Charts?

A— Winds and temperatures aloft.
B— Clear air turbulence and icing conditions.
C— Frontal systems and obstructions to vision aloft.

Answer (A) is correct (5441). *(AWS Sect 12)*
Constant Pressure Analysis Charts provide information about the observed upper-air temperature, wind, and temperature/dew point spread along your proposed route.
Answer (B) is incorrect because clear air turbulence is shown on prognostic charts and is included in area forecasts. Answer (C) is incorrect because frontal systems and obstructions to vision aloft are shown on Surface Analysis and Weather Depiction Charts.

20.
5442. From which of the following can the observed temperature, wind, and temperature/dewpoint spread be determined at a specified altitude?

A— Stability Charts.
B— Winds Aloft Forecasts.
C— Constant Pressure Analysis Charts.

Answer (C) is correct (5442). *(AWS Sect 12)*
Constant Pressure Analysis Charts provide pilots with information about observed temperature, wind, and temperature/dew point spread at specified pressure altitudes. The altitudes are 850 mb (5,000 ft.), 700 mb (10,000 ft.), 500 mb (18,000 ft.), 300 mb (30,000 ft.), and 200 mb (approximately 39,000 ft.).
Answer (A) is incorrect because Stability Charts provide information about stability, freezing level, precipitable water, and average relative humidity, but they do not contain the temperature/dew point spread. Answer (B) is incorrect because Winds Aloft Forecasts do not give the temperature/dew point spread aloft.

21.
5440. Hatching on a Constant Pressure Analysis Chart indicates

A— hurricane eye.
B— windspeed 70 knots to 110 knots.
C— windspeed 110 knots to 150 knots.

Answer (B) is correct (5440). *(AWS Sect 12)*
On Constant Pressure Analysis Charts, areas of strong winds are indicated by hatching, or shading, which indicates winds of 70 to 110 kt.
Answer (A) is incorrect because hurricane eyes have very low winds. Answer (C) is incorrect because wind speeds between 110 and 150 kt. are shown by a clear area within a hatched area.

8.6 Terminal Aerodrome Forecast (TAF)

22.
5409. What is the meaning of the terms PROB40 2102 +TSRA as used in a Terminal Aerodrome Forecast (TAF)?

A— Probability of heavy thunderstorms with rain showers below 4,000 feet at time 2102.
B— Between 2100Z and 0200Z there is a forty percent (40%) probability of thunderstorms with heavy rain.
C— Beginning at 2102Z forty percent (40%) probability of heavy thunderstorms and rain showers.

Answer (B) is correct (5409). *(AIM Para 7-1-28)*
A PROB40 group in a TAF indicates the probability of occurrence of thunderstorms or other precipitation events in the 40% to 49% range; thus the value 40% is appended to the PROB contraction. The forecast **PROB40 2102 +TSRA** means that between 2100Z and 0200Z there is a 40% probability of thunderstorms with heavy rain.
Answer (A) is incorrect because there is a 40% probability of thunderstorms with heavy rain (+RA), not rain showers (SHRA), between 2100Z and 0200Z, not at 2102Z. The intensity symbol (+) refers to the precipitation, not the descriptor. Answer (C) is incorrect because there is a 40% probability of thunderstorms with heavy rain (+RA), not rain showers (SHRA), between 2100Z and 0200Z, not beginning at 2102Z. The intensity symbol (+) refers to the precipitation (RA), not the descriptor (TS).

23.
5410. What does the contraction VRB in the Terminal Aerodrome Forecast (TAF) mean?

A— Wind speed is variable throughout the period.
B— Cloud base is variable.
C— Wind direction is variable.

Answer (C) is correct (5410). *(AWS Sect 4)*
A variable wind direction forecast is noted by the contraction VRB where the three-digit wind direction usually appears.
Answer (A) is incorrect because the contraction VRB indicates that the wind direction, not wind speed, is variable. Answer (B) is incorrect because the contraction VRB indicates that the wind direction, not cloud base, is variable.

24.

5411. Which statement pertaining to the following Terminal Aerodrome Forecast (TAF) is true?

TAF
KMEM 091135Z 0915 15005KT 5SM HZ BKN060
FM1600 VRB04KT P6SM SKC

A— Wind in the valid period implies surface winds are forecast to be greater than 5 KTS.

B— Wind direction is from 160° at 4 KTS and reported visibility is 6 statute miles.

C— SKC in the valid period indicates no significant weather and sky clear.

25.

5412. The visibility entry in a Terminal Aerodrome Forecast (TAF) of P6SM implies that the prevailing visibility is expected to be greater than

A— 6 nautical miles.

B— 6 statute miles.

C— 6 kilometers.

26.

5413. Terminal Aerodrome Forecasts (TAF) are issued how many times a day and cover what period of time?

A— Four times daily and are usually valid for a 24 hour period.

B— Six times daily and are usually valid for a 24 hour period including a 4-hour categorical outlook.

C— Six times daily and are valid for 12 hours including a 6-hour categorical outlook.

8.7 Aviation Area Forecast (FA)

27.

5419. The Aviation Weather Center (AWC) prepares FA's for the contiguous U.S.

A— twice each day.

B— three times each day.

C— every 6 hours unless significant changes in weather require it more often.

28.

5414. Which information section is contained in the Aviation Area Forecast (FA)?

A—Winds aloft, speed and direction.

B—VFR Clouds and Weather (VFR CLDS/WX).

C—In-Flight Aviation Weather Advisories.

Answer (C) is correct (5411). *(AIM Para 7-1-28)*
    The TAF indicates that from 1600Z the wind is forecast variable at 4 kt., visibility greater than 6 SM, no significant weather (implied since the weather element is omitted) and sky clear.
    Answer (A) is incorrect because prior to 1600 UTC the forecast wind is 150° at 5 kt., not greater than 5 kt. Answer (B) is incorrect because the wind direction is forecast to be variable, not 160°, and visibility is forecast to be greater than 6 SM (P6SM), not 6 SM (6SM).

Answer (B) is correct (5412). *(AWS Sect 4)*
    The visibility entry in a TAF of P6SM implies that the prevailing visibility is expected to be more than 6 statute miles (SM).
    Answer (A) is incorrect because the units of measure is statute miles (SM), not nautical miles (NM). Answer (C) is incorrect because the unit of measure is statute miles (SM), not kilometers.

Answer (A) is correct (5413). *(AIM Para 7-1-28)*
    TAFs are issued four times daily and are usually valid for a 24-hr. period.
    Answer (B) is incorrect because TAFs are issued four, not six, times daily, and TAFs do not have a categorical outlook. Answer (C) is incorrect because TAFs are valid for a 24-hr., not 12-hr., period, and TAFs do not have a categorical outlook.

Answer (B) is correct (5419). *(AWS Sect 4)*
    The Aviation Weather Center (AWC) prepares Area Forecasts (FAs) for the contiguous United States three times each day. They cover an 18-hr. period, including a 6-hr. outlook.
    Answer (A) is incorrect because FAs are issued three, not two, times each day. Answer (C) is incorrect because FAs are issued three, not two, times each day, not every 6 hr.

Answer (B) is correct (5414). *(AWS Sect 4)*
    The FA is comprised of four sections: a communications and product header section; a precautionary statement section; and two weather sections, a SYNOPSIS section and a VFR CLDS/WX section.
    Answer (A) is incorrect because winds aloft, speed, and direction are contained in the winds and temperatures aloft forecast (FD), not the FA. Answer (C) is incorrect because in-flight aviation weather advisories include convective SIGMETs, SIGMETs, AIRMETs, severe weather forecast alerts (AWW), and center weather advisories (CWA), none of which are included in the FA.

29.
5415. The section of the Aviation Area Forecast (FA) entitled VFR Clouds and Weather contains a summary of

A—forecast sky cover, cloud tops, visibility, and obstructions to vision along specific routes.
B—only those weather systems producing liquid or frozen precipitation, fog, thunderstorms, or IFR ceilings.
C—sky condition, cloud heights, visibility, obstructions to vision, precipitation, and sustained surface winds of 20 knots or greater.

Answer (C) is correct (5415). *(AWS Sect 4)*
The VFR Clouds and Weather (VFR CLDS/WX) section is usually several paragraphs long. The specific forecast section gives a general description of clouds and weather, which cover an area greater than 3,000 sq. mi., and is significant to VFR operations. Surface visibility and obstructions to vision are included when the forecast visibility is 6 SM or less. Precipitation, thunderstorms, and sustained winds of 20 kt. or greater are always included when forecast.
Answer (A) is incorrect because a TWEB Route Forecast, not an FA, contains a forecast of sky cover, cloud tops, visibility, and obstructions to vision along specific routes. Answer (B) is incorrect because hazardous weather, e.g., IMC and icing, is found in the in-flight aviation weather advisories, not an FA.

8.8 In-Flight Weather Advisories

30.
5418. What single reference contains information regarding a volcanic eruption, that is occurring or expected to occur?

A—In-Flight Weather Advisories.
B—Terminal Area Forecasts (TAF).
C—Weather Depiction Chart.

Answer (A) is correct (5418). *(AIM Para 7-1-5)*
A SIGMET, which is a type of in-flight weather advisory, will contain information regarding a volcanic eruption that is occurring or expected to occur.
Answer (B) is incorrect because a SIGMET, not a TAF, is the single reference containing information regarding a volcanic eruption that is occurring or expected to occur. Answer (C) is incorrect because a weather depiction chart is prepared from METAR reports and does not provide information regarding a volcanic eruption.

31.
5416. In-Flight Aviation Weather Advisories include what type of information?

A—Forecasts for potentially hazardous flying conditions for en route aircraft.
B—State and geographic areas with reported ceilings and visibilities below VFR minimums.
C—IFR conditions, turbulence, and icing within a valid period for the listed states.

Answer (A) is correct (5416). *(AIM Para 7-1-5)*
In-flight aviation weather advisories serve to notify en route pilots of the possibility of encountering hazardous flying conditions which may not have been forecast at the time of the preflight briefing. Whether or not the condition described is potentially hazardous to a particular flight is for the pilot to evaluate on the basis of experience and the operational limits of the aircraft.
Answer (B) is incorrect because in-flight aviation weather advisories are forecasts, not reported or observed conditions. Answer (C) is incorrect because in-flight aviation weather advisories have a defined maximum forecast period and do not necessarily cover the entire time that IFR weather conditions, turbulence, and icing may be experienced.

32.
5417. What type of In-Flight Weather Advisories provides an en route pilot with information regarding the possibility of moderate icing, moderate turbulence, winds of 30 knots or more at the surface and extensive mountain obscurement?

A—Convective SIGMETs and SIGMETs.
B—Severe Weather Forecast Alerts (AWW) and SIGMETs.
C—AIRMETs and Center Weather Advisories (CWA).

Answer (C) is correct (5417). *(AIM Para 7-1-5)*
AIRMETs are issued for the possibility of moderate icing, moderate turbulence, sustained winds of 30 kt. or more at the surface, widespread area of ceilings less than 1,000 ft. and/or visibility less than 3 SM, and extensive mountain obscurement. A center weather advisory (CWA) may be issued to supplement an AIRMET or to inform pilots when existing conditions meet AIRMET criteria but an AIRMET has not been issued.
Answer (A) is incorrect because convective SIGMETs concern only thunderstorms and related phenomena and imply the associated occurrence of turbulence and icing. A SIGMET is issued for severe, not moderate, icing and severe to extreme, not moderate, turbulence. Answer (B) is incorrect because a severe weather forecast alert (AWW) defines an area of possible severe thunderstorms or tornado activity. A SIGMET is issued for severe, not moderate, icing and severe to extreme, not moderate, turbulence.

33.
5422. SIGMET's are issued as a warning of weather conditions which are hazardous

A— to all aircraft.
B— particularly to heavy aircraft.
C— particularly to light airplanes.

Answer (A) is correct (5422). *(AWS Sect 4)*
SIGMETs (significant meteorological information) advise of weather potentially hazardous to all aircraft other than convective activity (which is reported in a convective SIGMET). SIGMETs cover severe icing; severe or extreme turbulence; or duststorms, sandstorms, or volcanic ash lowering visibility to less than 3 SM.
Answer (B) is incorrect because SIGMETs pertain to all, not just heavy, aircraft. Answer (C) is incorrect because SIGMETs pertain to all, not just light, aircraft.

34.
5423. Which correctly describes the purpose of convective SIGMET's (WST)?

A— They consist of an hourly observation of tornadoes, significant thunderstorm activity, and large hailstone activity.
B— They contain both an observation and a forecast of all thunderstorm and hailstone activity. The forecast is valid for 1 hour only.
C— They consist of either an observation and a forecast or just a forecast for tornadoes, significant thunderstorm activity, or hail greater than or equal to 3/4 inch in diameter.

Answer (C) is correct (5423). *(AWS Sect 4)*
Convective SIGMETs are issued for severe thunderstorms resulting in surface winds greater than 50 kt., hail at the surface, hail of 3/4 in. diameter, tornadoes, embedded thunderstorms, lines of thunderstorms, and very severe thunderstorms.
Answer (A) is incorrect because a WST is an unscheduled, not scheduled, forecast. Answer (B) is incorrect because WSTs are issued only for severe thunderstorms and hail 3/4 in. or larger. Also, WSTs can be for periods up to 2 hr., not 1 hr.

35.
5405. What wind conditions would you anticipate when squalls are reported at your destination?

A— Rapid variations in windspeed of 15 knots or more between peaks and lulls.
B— Peak gusts of at least 35 knots combined with a change in wind direction of 30° or more.
C— Sudden increases in windspeed of at least 16 knots to a sustained speed of 22 knots or more for at least 1 minute.

Answer (C) is correct (5405). *(AvW Glossary)*
A squall is a sudden increase in wind speed of at least 16 kt. to a sustained speed of 22 kt. or more and lasting for at least 1 min.
Answer (A) is incorrect because rapid variations in wind speed describes gusts (not squalls). Answer (B) is incorrect because abrupt changes in both direction and speed describe wind shear (not squalls).

8.9 Low-Level and High-Level Prognostic Charts

36.
5433. Which weather chart depicts conditions forecast to exist at a specific time in the future?

A— Freezing Level Chart.
B— Weather Depiction Chart.
C— 12-hour Significant Weather Prognostic Chart.

Answer (C) is correct (5433). *(AWS Sect 8)*
U.S. Low-Level Significant Weather Prog Charts are issued four times daily. They contain 12- and 24-hr. forecasts indicating forecast weather at 00Z, 06Z, 12Z, and 18Z.
Answer (A) is incorrect because there is no Freezing Level Weather Chart, per se. Answer (B) is incorrect because Weather Depiction Charts report current observed, not forecast, weather.

37.
5436. What is the upper limit of the Low Level Significant Weather Prognostic Chart?

A— 30,000 feet.
B— 24,000 feet.
C— 18,000 feet.

Answer (B) is correct (5436). *(AWS Sect 8)*
The upper limit of the Low-Level Significant Weather Prognostic Chart is 24,000 ft. MSL. The lower limit is the surface.
Answer (A) is incorrect because the upper limit of the Low-Level Significant Weather Prognostic Chart is 24,000 ft. MSL, not 30,000 ft. MSL. Answer (C) is incorrect because the upper limit of the Low-Level Significant Weather Prognostic Chart is 24,000 ft. MSL (not 18,000 ft. MSL).

38.
5434. What weather phenomenon is implied within an area enclosed by small scalloped lines on a U.S. High-Level Significant Weather Prognostic Chart?

A— Cirriform clouds, light to moderate turbulence, and icing.
B— Cumulonimbus clouds, icing, and moderate or greater turbulence.
C— Cumuliform or standing lenticular clouds, moderate to severe turbulence, and icing.

39.
5435. The U.S. High-Level Significant Weather Prognostic Chart forecasts significant weather for what airspace?

A— 18,000 feet to 45,000 feet.
B— 24,000 feet to 45,000 feet.
C— 24,000 feet to 63,000 feet.

8.10 Other Charts and Forecasts

40.
5407. To best determine observed weather conditions between weather reporting stations, the pilot should refer to

A— pilot reports.
B— Area Forecasts.
C— prognostic charts.

41.
5431. When total sky cover is few or scattered, the height on the Weather Depiction Chart is the

A— top of the lowest layer.
B— base of the lowest layer.
C— base of the highest layer.

42.
5430. Which provides a graphic display of both VFR and IFR weather?

A— Surface Weather Map.
B— Radar Summary Chart.
C— Weather Depiction Chart.

Answer (B) is correct (5434). *(AWS Sect 8)*
Small scalloped lines are used on High-Level Significant Weather Prognostic Charts to indicate expected cumulonimbus clouds. This automatically implies moderate or greater turbulence and icing (which are not depicted separately).
Answer (A) is incorrect because cumulonimbus, not cirriform, clouds are indicated by small scalloped lines. Answer (C) is incorrect because standing lenticular clouds would be indicated as clear air turbulence by heavy dashed lines encircling the forecast area.

Answer (C) is correct (5435). *(AWS Sect 8)*
High-Level Significant Weather Prognostic Charts forecast significant weather for the altitudes from 24,000 ft. MSL to 63,000 ft. MSL.
Answer (A) is incorrect because the base is 24,000 ft. MSL, not 18,000 ft. MSL, and the ceiling is 63,000 ft. MSL, not 45,000 ft. MSL. Answer (B) is incorrect because the ceiling is 63,000 ft. MSL, not 45,000 ft. MSL.

Answer (A) is correct (5407). *(AWS Sect 4)*
Pilot Weather Reports (PIREPs) are observed weather conditions usually between weather reporting stations.
Answer (B) is incorrect because area forecasts are forecasts, not observed weather. Answer (C) is incorrect because prognostic charts are forecasts, not observed weather.

Answer (B) is correct (5431). *(AWS Sect 6)*
On the Weather Depiction Chart, cloud height above ground level is entered under the station circle in hundreds of feet, similar to hourly weather reports. If the total sky cover is scattered, the height entered is the base of the lowest layer. If total sky cover is broken or greater, the cloud height entered is the ceiling.
Answer (A) is incorrect because the base, not the top, of the lowest layer is indicated. Answer (C) is incorrect because the base of the lowest, not the highest, layer is indicated.

Answer (C) is correct (5430). *(AWS Sect 6)*
The Weather Depiction Chart is computer-prepared from METAR reports to give a broad overview of observed flying category conditions as of the valid time of the chart. It provides information concerning cloud heights and ceilings, weather, and obstructions to vision on a national map. Areas that are marginal VFR are indicated by shading. Frontal systems are also depicted.
Answer (A) is incorrect because a Surface Weather Map, also known as a Surface Analysis Chart, shows pressure systems rather than VFR vs. IFR areas due to visibilities and ceilings. Answer (B) is incorrect because a Radar Summary Chart graphically depicts a collection of radar reports. It is a national map which displays the kind of precipitation echoes, their intensity, trends, configurations, and coverage, i.e., not VFR vs. IFR.

43.
5432. What information is provided by the Radar Summary Chart that is not shown on other weather charts?

A— Lines and cells of hazardous thunderstorms.
B— Ceilings and precipitation between reporting stations.
C— Areas of cloud cover and icing levels within the clouds.

Answer (A) is correct (5432). *(AWS Sect 7)*
    The Radar Summary Chart shows lines and cells of significant thunderstorms. It is a national map displaying a collection of radar reports including the type of precipitation echoes, their intensity, trend, configuration, coverage, echo tops and bases, and movement.
    Answer (B) is incorrect because ceilings and precipitation between reporting stations must be inferred from the Weather Depiction Chart, not the Radar Summary Chart. Answer (C) is incorrect because areas of cloud cover and icing levels are forecast on the prog charts, not shown on the Radar Summary Chart.

44.
5424. What values are used for Winds Aloft Forecasts?

A— True direction and MPH.
B— True direction and knots.
C— Magnetic direction and knots.

Answer (B) is correct (5424). *(AWS Sect 4)*
    In the Winds Aloft Forecast, the temperature is in Celsius, and the winds are the true direction and in knots.
    Answer (A) is incorrect because the wind measurement is in knots, not mph. Answer (C) is incorrect because the wind direction is true, not magnetic.

45.
5438. A freezing level panel of the composite moisture stability chart is an analysis of

A— forecast freezing level data from surface observations.
B— forecast freezing level data from upper air observations.
C— observed freezing level data from upper air observations.

Answer (C) is correct (5438). *(AWS Sect 10)*
    The freezing level panel found on the Composite Moisture Stability Chart is an analysis of observed freezing level data from upper air observations.
    Answer (A) is incorrect because the freezing level panel contains observed, not forecast, freezing level data from upper, not surface, air observations. Answer (B) is incorrect because the freezing level panel contains observed, not forecast, freezing level data.

46.
5420. Which forecast provides specific information concerning expected sky cover, cloud tops, visibility, weather, and obstructions to vision in a route format?

A— Area Forecast.
B— Terminal Aerodrome Forecast.
C— Transcribed Weather Broadcast.

Answer (C) is correct (5420). *(AWS Sect 4)*
    The TWEB Route Forecast is similar to the area forecast except that information is issued in a route format. It forecasts sky cover, height and amount of cloud bases, cloud tops, visibility, weather, and obstructions to vision for a corridor 25 NM either side of the route.
    Answer (A) is incorrect because an area forecast is not issued in a route format. Answer (B) is incorrect because a Terminal Aerodrome Forecast is not issued in a route format.

END OF CHAPTER

CHAPTER NINE
NAVIGATION: CHARTS, PUBLICATIONS, FLIGHT COMPUTERS

This chapter contains outlines of major concepts tested, all FAA test questions and answers regarding navigation, and an explanation of each answer. Each module, or subtopic, within this chapter is listed above with the number of questions from the FAA pilot knowledge test pertaining to that particular module. For each module, the first number following the parentheses is the page number on which the outline begins, and the next number is the page number on which the questions begin.

CAUTION: Recall that the **sole purpose** of this book is to expedite your passing the FAA pilot knowledge test for the commercial pilot certificate. Accordingly, all extraneous material (i.e., topics or regulations not directly tested on the FAA pilot knowledge test) is omitted, even though much more information and knowledge are necessary to become a proficient commercial pilot. This additional material is presented in *Commercial Pilot Flight Maneuvers and Practical Test Prep* and *Pilot Handbook*, available from Gleim Publications, Inc. See the order form on page 284.

9.1 SECTIONAL CHARTS (Questions 1-16)

1. Blue airport symbols indicate airports with at least a part-time control tower.

    a. Magenta airport symbols indicate airports without a control tower.

2. True course measurements on a sectional chart should be made along a meridian (line of longitude) near the midpoint of the course because the angles formed by lines of longitude and the course line vary from point to point.

    a. Lines of longitude are not parallel because they go from pole to pole.

3. Each rectangular area bounded by lines of latitude and longitude contains a pair of numbers in large, bold print to indicate the height of the maximum elevation of terrain or obstructions within that area of latitude and longitude. This is called the **maximum elevation figure (MEF)**.

    a. The larger number to the left indicates thousands of feet.
    b. The smaller number to the right indicates hundreds of feet.

4. Obstructions on sectional charts are marked as shown below:

a. The elevation (MSL) of the terrain at the base of the obstruction is the bold figure minus the light figure.

    1) Use this computation to compute terrain elevation.

    2) Airport elevation is also given in the airport identifier for each airport.

5. Airport identifiers include the following information:

a. The name of the airport

b. The elevation of the airport, followed by the length of the longest hard-surfaced runway. An L between the altitude and length indicates lighting.

    1) EXAMPLE: "1008 L 70" means an airport elevation of 1,008 ft. MSL, lighting sunset to sunrise, and a length of 7,000 ft. for the longest hard-surfaced runway.

    2) If the L has an asterisk beside it (*L), it means part-time or pilot-controlled lighting.

c. Private "**(Pvt)**" indicating a nonpublic-use airport having emergency or landmark value

6. Class E airspace extends upward from 700 ft. AGL in areas marked to the inside of magenta shading.

a. Where the outer edge of magenta shading ends, the floor of Class E airspace is 1,200 ft. AGL.

7. In Class G airspace at or below 1,200 ft. AGL during the day, the minimum flight visibility for VFR operations is 1 SM.

a. In Class E airspace below 10,000 ft. MSL, the minimum flight visibility for VFR operations is 3 SM.

8. An **Alert Area** is airspace within which there is a high volume of pilot training or an unusual type of aerial activity. Pilots should be particularly alert when flying in these areas.

a. Alert Areas are depicted on sectional charts by a blue box.

9. **Military training routes** are depicted on sectional charts by a thin gray line.

10. **Class D airspace** is an area of controlled airspace surrounding an airport with an operating control tower, not associated with Class B or Class C airspace areas.

   a. Class D airspace is depicted by a segmented (dashed) blue line on sectional charts.

   b. The height of the Class D airspace is shown in a broken box and is expressed in hundreds of feet MSL.

      1) EXAMPLE: $\lceil_{31}\rceil$ means the height of the Class D airspace is 3,100 ft. MSL.

   c. Two-way radio communication is not required to take off or land at the primary Class D airport if weather conditions are at or above basic VFR weather minimums and you received the appropriate clearance from the tower, i.e., light signals.

      1) A transponder is not required in Class D airspace.

11. **Class C airspace** areas are depicted by solid magenta lines on sectional charts.

   a. The vertical limits are indicated on the chart within each area and are expressed in hundreds of feet MSL. The top limit is shown above a straight line and the bottom limit beneath the line.

      1) EXAMPLE: The Metropolitan Oakland International (OAK) Class C airspace is shown on Fig. 54, point 6, on the outside back cover.

         a) $\frac{T}{SFC}$ over OAK means the Class C airspace extends from the surface to the base of the overlying Class B airspace.

            i) Note the blue line depicting Class B airspace is drawn over OAK. Thus, the top of Class C airspace is at 2,100 ft. MSL to the left of OAK and 3,000 ft. MSL to the right of OAK.

9.2 FUEL CONSUMPTION (Questions 17-22)

1. To determine the time en route, divide the number of miles by your groundspeed.

2. To determine the fuel consumed, multiply the time en route by the fuel consumed per hour.

3. EXAMPLE: If an airplane uses 10.5 GPH and has a TAS (or groundspeed) of 145 kt., you may be asked to estimate the fuel burn on a 460 NM trip. First, determine the time en route by dividing the distance of 460 NM by 145 kt. to arrive at 3.17 hr. Second, multiply the time of 3.17 hr. by 10.5 GPH to arrive at 33 gal.

9.3 TIME, DISTANCE, AND FUEL TO STATION (Questions 23-48)

1. The time/distance to station can also be found by application of the isosceles triangle principle (i.e., if two angles of a triangle are equal, two of the sides are also equal).

   a. The formula may be applied as follows:

      1) With the aircraft established on a radial, inbound, rotate the OBS 10° to the left (90° − 10° = 80°, i.e., now using 260° radial).

      2) Turn 10° to the right and note the time.

      3) Maintain constant heading until the CDI centers, and note the elapsed time.

4) Time to station is the same as the time taken to complete the 10° change of bearing.

FIGURE 21.—Isosceles Triangle.

b. This same formula can also be used for left turns, as well as varying angles (i.e., 5°, 10°, 15°, etc.).

2. When tracking inbound to a VOR or an NDB, you can determine the time and distance to the station using the following method:

a. Note the radial or bearing you are on.

b. Turn 90° to the left or right.

c. Note the time elapsed between bearings.

$$\text{Time to station (min.)} = \frac{60 \times \text{Min. flown between bearing change}}{\text{Degrees of bearing change}}$$

$$\text{Distance to station (NM)} = \frac{\text{TAS} \times \text{Min. flown between bearing change}}{\text{Degrees of bearing change}}$$

d. EXAMPLE: The ADF indicates a 5° wingtip bearing change in 2.5 min. If the TAS is 125 kt., what is the time and distance to the station?

$$\text{Time to station} = \frac{60 \times 2.5}{5} = \frac{150}{5} = 30 \text{ min.}$$

$$\text{Distance to station} = \frac{125 \times 2.5}{5} = \frac{312.5}{5} = 62.5 \text{ NM}$$

3. To determine the fuel required, convert the time to station into hours and multiply by the fuel consumption as shown.

$$\text{Fuel required} = \frac{\text{Rate of fuel consumption} \times \text{Min. to station}}{60}$$

EXAMPLE: You are 20 min. from the station and your fuel burn is 15 GPH.

$$\text{Fuel required} = \frac{15 \times 20}{60} = \frac{300}{60} = 5 \text{ gal.}$$

4. When a relative bearing doubles in a specific time, the time to the station is that time (the time to double the relative bearing); e.g., if it takes 5 min. to double your relative bearing, you are 5 min. from the station.

9.4 WIND DIRECTION AND SPEED (Questions 49-52)

1. To estimate your wind given true heading and a true course, simply use the wind side of your flight computer backwards.

   a. Place the groundspeed under the grommet (the hole in the center) with the true course under the true index.

   b. Then on the true airspeed arc, place a pencil mark reflecting the right or left wind correction angle you are holding.

   c. Rotate the inner scale so the pencil mark is on the centerline and read the wind direction under the true index.

   d. The distance up from the grommet is the wind speed.

2. To determine the total course correction needed to converge on (fly direct to) your destination, use the following steps:

   a. Since 1° off course equals 1 NM per 60 NM from the station, the following formula applies:

   $$\frac{NM\ off}{NM\ flown} \times 60 = Degrees\ off\ course\ from\ departure\ point$$

      1) Turning back this number of degrees will parallel the original course.

   b. To fly direct to your destination, calculate the number of degrees off course.

   $$\frac{NM\ off}{NM\ remaining} \times 60 = Degrees\ off\ course\ to\ destination$$

      1) Turning this number of degrees farther will take you direct to your destination.

   c. EXAMPLE: You are 140 NM from your departure point and have determined that you are 11 NM off course. If 71 NM remain to be flown, the approximate total correction to be made to converge on the destination is 14°, as computed below.

   $$\frac{11\ NM}{140\ NM} \times 60 = 4.7°$$

   $$\frac{11\ NM}{71\ NM} \times 60 = \underline{9.3°}$$
   $$\underline{14.0°}$$

9.5 TIME, COMPASS HEADING, ETC., ON CLIMBS AND EN ROUTE (Questions 53-55)

1. You may be asked to determine the minutes, compass heading, distance, and fuel consumed during a climb or en route.

2. The first step is to determine the number of minutes to climb.

   a. Divide the amount of climb required by the rate of climb.

      1) EXAMPLE: If you must climb 5,000 ft. at 500 fpm, the climb takes 10 min. (5,000 ÷ 500).

3. If there are several alternative answers with the correct number of minutes, you may be able to determine the correct answer based upon the amount of fuel burned.

   a. Convert the time required to climb into hours by dividing by 60.

   b. Then multiply by the rate of fuel consumption to determine the amount of fuel used.

4.   Finally, if you must determine the compass heading, begin by converting the true course to true heading by adjusting for wind effect using the wind side of your flight computer.

   a.   Align the wind direction on the inner scale under the true index (top of the computer) on the outer scale.

   b.   Measure up the vertical line the amount of wind speed in kt., and put a pencil mark on the plastic.

   c.   Rotate the inner scale so the true course is under the true index.

   d.   Slide the grid so that your pencil dot is superimposed over the true airspeed. The location of the grommet will indicate the groundspeed.

   e.   The pencil mark will indicate the wind correction angle (if to the left, it is a negative wind correction, and if to the right, a positive wind correction).

   f.   True heading is found by adjusting the true course for the wind correction.

   g.   Magnetic heading is found by adjusting the true heading for magnetic variation.

      1)   Subtract easterly variation ("east is least").
      2)   Add westerly variation ("west is best").

   h.   Convert magnetic heading to compass heading by adjusting for the compass deviation, which is given in these questions as + or −.

9.6 TIME, COMPASS HEADING, ETC., ON DESCENTS (Questions 56-58)

1.   These questions are calculated the same as for climbs (previous page), except you are descending.

2.   Note that the questions require you to arrive at some elevation AGL above the airport, not the airport elevation.

   a.   Add the airport elevation to the altitude AGL required; then subtract that amount from the cruising altitude.

QUESTIONS AND ANSWER EXPLANATIONS

All the FAA questions from the pilot knowledge test for the commercial pilot certificate relating to navigation and the material outlined previously are reproduced on the following pages in the same modules as the outlines. To the immediate right of each question are the correct answer and answer explanation. You should cover these answers and answer explanations while responding to the questions. (A bookmark for this purpose has been provided in the back of the book.) Refer to the general discussion in the Introduction on how to take the FAA pilot knowledge test.

Remember that the questions from the FAA pilot knowledge test bank have been reordered by topic, and the topics have been organized into a meaningful sequence. Accordingly, the first line of the answer explanation gives the FAA question number and the citation of the authoritative source for the answer.

9.1 Sectional Charts

1.
5564. Which is true concerning the blue and magenta colors used to depict airports on Sectional Aeronautical Charts?

A— Airports with control towers underlying Class A, B, and C airspace are shown in blue; Class D and E airspace are magenta.

B— Airports with control towers underlying Class C, D, and E airspace are shown in magenta.

C— Airports with control towers underlying Class B, C, D, and E airspace are shown in blue.

Answer (C) is correct (5564). *(ACL)*
On sectional charts, airports with contr... underlying Class B, C, D, E, or G airspace are ... blue. Airports with no control towers are shown in magenta.
Answer (A) is incorrect because there are no airports in Class A airspace. Airports with control towers are shown in blue, all others in magenta. Answer (B) is incorrect because airports with control towers are shown in blue, not magenta.

2.
5479. True course measurements on a Sectional Aeronautical Chart should be made at a meridian near the midpoint of the course because the

A— values of isogonic lines change from point to point.

B— angles formed by isogonic lines and lines of latitude vary from point to point.

C— angles formed by lines of longitude and the course line vary from point to point.

Answer (C) is correct (5479). *(PHAK Chap 8)*
Because meridians (lines of longitude) converge toward the poles, the angles formed by meridians and the course line may vary from point to point. Thus, course measurement should be taken at a meridian near the midpoint of the course rather than at the departure point.
Answer (A) is incorrect because isogonic lines are used to calculate magnetic (not true) course. Answer (B) is incorrect because isogonic lines are used to calculate magnetic (not true) course.

3.
5577. When a dashed blue circle surrounds an airport on a sectional aeronautical chart, it will depict the boundary of

A— Special VFR airspace.

B— Class B airspace.

C— Class D airspace.

Answer (C) is correct (5577). *(AIM Para 3-2-5)*
On a sectional aeronautical chart, the boundary of Class D airspace is depicted by a dashed (segmented) blue circle around an airport.
Answer (A) is incorrect because there is no airspace designated as special VFR. Answer (B) is incorrect because, on a sectional chart, a solid, not dashed, blue circle that surrounds an airport depicts the boundary of Class B airspace.

The next 13 questions refer to Figures 52, 53, and 54. These figures are reproduced on the covers of this book as follows:

Figure 52 -- inside front cover
Figure 53 -- inside back cover
Figure 54 -- outside back cover

4.
5583. (Refer to figure 52, point 6, on the inside front cover.) Mosier Airport is

A— an airport restricted to use by private and recreational pilots.

B— a restricted military stage field within restricted airspace.

C— a nonpublic use airport.

Answer (C) is correct (5583). *(ACL)*
Mosier Airport (west of 6) is a private, i.e., nonpublic-use, airport as indicated by the term "(Pvt)" after the airport name. Private airports that are shown on the sectional charts have an emergency or landmark value.
Answer (A) is incorrect because the airport symbol with the letter "R" in the center means it is a nonpublic-use airport, not that only private and recreational pilots may use the airport. Answer (B) is incorrect because military airfields are labeled as AFB, NAS, AAF, NAAS, NAF, MCAS, or DND.

575. (Refer to figure 52, point 9, on the inside front cover.) The alert area depicted within the blue lines is an area in which

A— there is a high volume of pilot training activities or an unusual type of aerial activity, neither of which is hazardous to aircraft.
B— the flight of aircraft is prohibited.
C— the flight of aircraft, while not prohibited, is subject to restriction.

Answer (A) is correct (5575). *(ACL)*
Alert Areas are depicted on charts to inform nonparticipating pilots of areas that may contain a high volume of pilot training or an unusual type of aerial activity, neither of which is hazardous to aircraft.
Answer (B) is incorrect because a Prohibited Area, not an Alert Area, is airspace within which the flight of aircraft is prohibited. Answer (C) is incorrect because a Restricted Area, not an Alert Area, is airspace within which the flight of aircraft, while not prohibited, is subject to restriction.

6.
5566. (Refer to figure 52, point 7, on the inside front cover.) The floor of Class E airspace over the town of Woodland is

A— 700 feet AGL over part of the town and no floor over the remainder.
B— 1,200 feet AGL over part of the town and no floor over the remainder.
C— both 700 feet and 1,200 feet AGL.

Answer (C) is correct (5566). *(ACL)*
The town of Woodland (right of point 7) has magenta shading over part of the town. To the inside of the shading, Class E airspace begins at 700 ft. AGL. Where the outer edge of the magenta area ends, Class E airspace begins at 1,200 ft. AGL.
Answer (A) is incorrect because the outer edge of the magenta shading indicates the floor of Class E airspace is at 1,200 ft. AGL. Answer (B) is incorrect because the area to the inside of the magenta shading indicates the floor of Class E airspace is at 700 ft. AGL.

7.
5568. (Refer to figure 52, point 8, on the inside front cover.) The floor of the Class E airspace over the town of Auburn is

A— 1,200 feet MSL.
B— 700 feet AGL.
C— 1,200 feet AGL.

Answer (B) is correct (5568). *(ACL)*
The town of Auburn (southeast of point 8) is located inside the magenta shaded area, which means the floor of Class E airspace is 700 ft. AGL.
Answer (A) is incorrect because the floor of Class E airspace over the town of Auburn is 700 ft. AGL, not 1,200 ft. MSL. The town of Auburn is within the magenta shading. Answer (C) is incorrect because 1,200 ft. AGL is the floor of Class E airspace outside, not inside, the magenta shaded area.

8.
5565. (Refer to figure 52, point 1, on the inside front cover.) The floor of the Class E airspace above Georgetown Airport (Q61) is at

A— the surface.
B— 3,823 feet MSL.
C— 700 feet AGL.

Answer (B) is correct (5565). *(ACL)*
Georgetown Airport is located outside the magenta shaded area, which means the floor of Class E airspace is at 1,200 ft. AGL. The airport elevation is given in the first line of the airport data as 2,623 ft. MSL. Thus, the floor of Class E airspace above Georgetown Airport is 3,823 ft. MSL (2,623 + 1,200).
Answer (A) is incorrect because Class E airspace would begin at the surface only if the airport were surrounded by a magenta segmented circle. Answer (C) is incorrect because the floor of Class E airspace would begin at 700 ft. AGL if Georgetown Airport were inside, not outside, the magenta shaded areas.

9.
5567. (Refer to figure 52, point 5, on the inside front cover.) The floor of the Class E airspace over University Airport (0O5) is

A— the surface.
B— 700 feet AGL.
C— 1,200 feet AGL.

Answer (B) is correct (5567). *(ACL)*
University Airport (east of point 5) is located within the magenta shading, which means the floor of Class E airspace is at 700 ft. AGL.
Answer (A) is incorrect because Class E airspace would begin at the surface only if the airport were surrounded by a magenta segmented circle. Answer (C) is incorrect because 1,200 ft. AGL is the floor of Class E airspace outside, not inside, the magenta shaded area.

10.
5581. (Refer to figure 52, point 4, on the inside front cover.) The highest obstruction with high intensity lighting within 10 NM of Lincoln Regional Airport (LHM) is how high above the ground?

A— 1,254 feet.
B— 662 feet.
C— 299 feet.

Answer (C) is correct (5581). *(ACL)*
Obstructions with high-intensity lights are depicted by lightning bolt symbols around the top of the obstruction symbol. The only symbol having high-intensity lights within 10 NM of Lincoln Airport is located approximately 3.5 NM south of the airport. The height above ground of this obstruction is the number in parentheses, which is 299 ft. AGL.
Answer (A) is incorrect because 1,254 ft. is the height of the obstruction above sea level, not the ground, located approximately 8.5 NM east of the airport. This obstruction does not have high-intensity lights. Answer (B) is incorrect because 662 ft. is the height above ground of the group of obstructions located approximately 8 NM southwest of the airport. While these obstructions are the highest above ground, they do not have high-intensity lighting.

11.
5585. (Refer to figure 52, point 4, on the inside front cover.) The terrain at the obstruction approximately 8 NM east southeast of the Lincoln Airport is approximately how much higher than the airport elevation?

A— 376 feet.
B— 835 feet.
C— 1,135 feet.

Answer (B) is correct (5585). *(ACL)*
The obstruction approximately 8 NM east-southeast of the Lincoln Airport (point 4) is marked as having an elevation of 1,254 ft. MSL, and a height of 300 ft. AGL. Thus, the terrain elevation at that point is 954 ft. MSL (1,254 − 300). The Lincoln Airport elevation is shown to be 119 ft. MSL, which is 835 ft. (954 − 119) lower than the terrain elevation at the obstruction.
Answer (A) is incorrect because the terrain at the obstruction is 835 ft., not 376 ft., higher than the Lincoln Airport elevation. Answer (C) is incorrect because 1,135 ft. is the height of the obstruction above the airport elevation.

12.
5569. (Refer to figure 53, point 1, on the inside back cover.) This thin black shaded line is most likely

A— an arrival route.
B— a military training route.
C— a state boundary line.

Answer (B) is correct (5569). *(ACL)*
The thin black shaded line is most likely a military training route (MTR). Generally, MTRs are established below 10,000 ft. MSL for operations at speeds in excess of 250 kt. MTRs are normally labeled on sectional charts with either IR (IFR operations) or VR (VFR operations) and followed by either three or four number characters.
Answer (A) is incorrect because arrival routes are not depicted on sectional charts. Answer (C) is incorrect because a state boundary line is depicted on sectional charts by a thin black broken line, not a thin black shaded line.

13.
5570. (Refer to figure 53, point 2, on the inside back cover.) The 16 indicates

A— an antenna top at 1,600 feet AGL.
B— the maximum elevation figure for that quadrangle.
C— the minimum safe sector altitude for that quadrangle.

Answer (B) is correct (5570). *(ACL)*
The large bold 1 and somewhat smaller 6 (point 2) refers to the maximum elevation figure (MEF) in feet MSL of the highest obstruction or terrain in the quadrangle bounded by tick lines of longitude and latitude. On sectional charts, the MEF is provided in each square bounded by lines of longitude and latitude.
Answer (A) is incorrect because an antenna is shown by an obstruction symbol (as shown to the southeast of 2) and the height above ground is the number in parentheses, not large, bold numbers. Answer (C) is incorrect because minimum safe altitudes are depicted on IAP, not sectional, charts.

14.

5588. (Refer to figure 53 on the inside back cover.)

GIVEN:

Location . . . . Madera Airport (MAE)
Altitude . . . . 1,000 ft AGL
Position . . . . 7 NM north of Madera (MAE)
Time . . . . 3 p.m. local
Flight visibility . . . . 1 SM

You are VFR approaching Madera Airport for a landing from the north. You

A— are in violation of the CFR's; you need 3 miles of visibility under VFR.

B— are required to descend to below 700 feet AGL to remain clear of Class E airspace and may continue for landing.

C— may descend to 800 feet AGL (Pattern Altitude) after entering Class E airspace and continue to the airport.

Answer (B) is correct (5588). *(ACL)*
If you are 7 NM north of Madera Airport (middle of Fig. 53), you are outside of the magenta shaded area which means the floor of Class E airspace is at 1,200 ft. AGL. Since you are flying at 1,000 ft. AGL (i.e., Class G airspace) during daylight hours, the minimum flight visibility required for VFR flight is 1 SM. At the edge of the magenta shading the floor of Class E is at 700 ft. AGL. Thus, to maintain VFR you must remain in Class G airspace and descend below 700 ft. AGL to remain clear of Class E airspace, and you may continue for landing.
Answer (A) is incorrect because you are currently in Class G airspace at 1,000 ft. AGL during daylight hours, and thus you need only 1 SM, not 3 SM, visibility. Answer (C) is incorrect because, in order to remain VFR, you must descend below 700 ft. AGL, not the pattern altitude of 800 ft. AGL, to remain clear of Class E airspace.

15.

5587. (Refer to figure 54, point 6, on the outside back cover.) The Class C airspace at Metropolitan Oakland International (OAK) which extends from the surface upward has a ceiling of

A— both 2,100 feet and 3,000 feet MSL.

B— 8,000 feet MSL.

C— 2,100 feet AGL.

Answer (A) is correct (5587). *(ACL)*
The Class C airspace at OAK (point 6) is shown in solid magenta lines. The surface area over the airport indicates the Class C airspace extends from the surface (SFC) upward to T, which means the ceiling ends at the base of the San Francisco Class B airspace. The base of the Class B airspace changes over OAK. To the left of OAK the base is 2,100 ft. MSL and to the right of OAK the base is 3,000 ft. MSL.
Answer (B) is incorrect because 8,000 ft. is the ceiling of the Class B, not the Class C, airspace over OAK. Answer (C) is incorrect because 2,100 ft. AGL is the approximate ceiling of the Class C airspace on the west side of OAK, but the ceiling on the east side is 3,000 ft. MSL.

16.

5572. (Refer to figure 54, point 1, on the outside back cover.) What minimum altitude is required to avoid the Livermore Airport (LVK) Class D airspace?

A— 2,503 feet MSL.

B— 2,901 feet MSL.

C— 3,297 feet MSL.

Answer (B) is correct (5572). *(AIM Para 3-2-5)*
The Class D airspace at Livermore Airport extends from the surface to 2,900 ft. MSL, as indicated by the ⌐29⌐ within the blue segmented circle. Thus, the minimum altitude to fly over and avoid the Livermore Airport Class D airspace is 2,901 ft. MSL.
Answer (A) is incorrect because at 2,503 ft. MSL you would be in Class D airspace. Answer (C) is incorrect because, although at 3,297 ft. MSL you would be above the Class D airspace, it is not the minimum altitude at which you could avoid the airspace.

9.2 Fuel Consumption

17.

5470. If an airplane is consuming 95 pounds of fuel per hour at a cruising altitude of 6,500 feet and the groundspeed is 173 knots, how much fuel is required to travel 450 NM?

A— 248 pounds.

B— 265 pounds.

C— 284 pounds.

Answer (A) is correct (5470). *(PHAK Chap 8)*
At a groundspeed of 173 kt., it will take 2.60 hr. to go 450 NM (450 ÷ 173). At 95 lb./hr., it will take approximately 248 lb. (2.60 x 95) of fuel.
Answer (B) is incorrect because 265 lb. is required to travel 483 NM, not 450 NM. Answer (C) is incorrect because 284 lb. is required to travel 517 NM, not 450 NM.

18.
5469. If fuel consumption is 80 pounds per hour and groundspeed is 180 knots, how much fuel is required for an airplane to travel 460 NM?

A— 205 pounds.
B— 212 pounds.
C— 460 pounds.

Answer (A) is correct (5469). *(PHAK Chap 8)*
At a groundspeed of 180 kt., it will take 2.55 hr. to go 460 NM (460 ÷ 180). At 80 lb./hr., it will take approximately 205 lb. (2.55 x 80) of fuel.
Answer (B) is incorrect because 212 lb. is required to travel 477 NM, not 460 NM. Answer (C) is incorrect because 460 lb. is required to travel 1,035 NM, not 460 NM.

19.
5471. If an airplane is consuming 12.5 gallons of fuel per hour at a cruising altitude of 8,500 feet and the groundspeed is 145 knots, how much fuel is required to travel 435 NM?

A— 27 gallons.
B— 34 gallons.
C— 38 gallons.

Answer (C) is correct (5471). *(PHAK Chap 8)*
At a groundspeed of 145 kt., it will take 3.0 hr. to go 435 NM (435 ÷ 145). At 12.5 GPH, it will take approximately 38 gal. (3 x 12.5) of fuel.
Answer (A) is incorrect because 27 gal. is required to travel 313 NM, not 435 NM. Answer (B) is incorrect because 34 gal. is required to travel 394 NM, not 435 NM.

20.
5472. If an airplane is consuming 9.5 gallons of fuel per hour at a cruising altitude of 6,000 feet and the groundspeed is 135 knots, how much fuel is required to travel 490 NM?

A— 27 gallons.
B— 30 gallons.
C— 35 gallons.

Answer (C) is correct (5472). *(PHAK Chap 8)*
At a groundspeed of 135 kt., it will take 3.63 hr. to go 490 NM (490 ÷ 135). At 9.5 GPH, it will take approximately 35 gal. (3.63 x 9.5) of fuel.
Answer (A) is incorrect because 27 gal. is required to travel 384 NM, not 490 NM. Answer (B) is incorrect because 30 gal. is required to travel 426 NM, not 490 NM.

21.
5473. If an airplane is consuming 14.8 gallons of fuel per hour at a cruising altitude of 7,500 feet and the groundspeed is 167 knots, how much fuel is required to travel 560 NM?

A— 50 gallons.
B— 53 gallons.
C— 57 gallons.

Answer (A) is correct (5473). *(PHAK Chap 8)*
At a groundspeed of 167 kt., it will take 3.35 hr. to go 560 NM (560 ÷ 167). At 14.8 GPH, it will take approximately 50 gal. (3.35 x 14.8) of fuel.
Answer (B) is incorrect because 53 gal. is required to travel 598 NM, not 560 NM. Answer (C) is incorrect because 57 gal. is required to travel 643 NM, not 560 NM.

22.
5474. If fuel consumption is 14.7 gallons per hour and groundspeed is 157 knots, how much fuel is required for an airplane to travel 612 NM?

A— 58 gallons.
B— 60 gallons.
C— 64 gallons.

Answer (A) is correct (5474). *(PHAK Chap 8)*
At a groundspeed of 157 kt., it will take 3.90 hr. to go 612 NM (612 ÷ 157). At 14.7 GPH, it will take approximately 58 gal. (3.90 x 14.7) of fuel.
Answer (B) is incorrect because 60 gal. is required to travel 641 NM, not 612 NM. Answer (C) is incorrect because 64 gal. is required to travel 684 NM, not 612 NM.

9.3 Time, Distance, and Fuel to Station

23.
5540. (Refer to figure 21 below.) If the time flown between aircraft positions 2 and 3 is 13 minutes, what is the estimated time to the station?

A— 13 minutes.
B— 17 minutes.
C— 26 minutes.

Answer (A) is correct (5540). *(IFH Chap VIII)*
The time/distance to station can be found by application of the isosceles triangle principle (i.e., if two angles of a triangle are equal, two of the sides are also equal), as follows:

1. With the aircraft established on a radial (here 270°), inbound, rotate the OBS 10° to the left, i.e., 260°.
2. Turn 10° to the right and note the time.
3. Maintain constant heading until the CDI centers, and note the elapsed time.
4. Time to station is the same as the time taken to complete the 10° change of bearing.

Thus, if the time flown between aircraft positions 2 and 3 is 13 min., the estimated time to the station is also 13 min.
Answer (B) is incorrect because the time between positions 2 and 3 and between position 3 and the station should be equal, i.e., 13 min. Answer (C) is incorrect because the time between positions 2 and 3 and between position 3 and the station should be equal, i.e., 13 min.

FIGURE 21.—Isosceles Triangle.

24.
5543. (Refer to figure 24 on page 219.) If the time flown between aircraft positions 2 and 3 is 15 minutes, what is the estimated time to the station?

A— 15 minutes.
B— 30 minutes.
C— 60 minutes.

Answer (A) is correct (5543). *(IFH Chap VIII)*
The time/distance to station can be found by application of the isosceles triangle principle (i.e., if two angles of a triangle are equal, two of the sides are also equal), as follows:

1. With the aircraft established on a radial (here 105°), inbound, rotate the OBS 15° to the left, i.e., 90°.
2. Turn 15° to the right and note the time.
3. Maintain constant heading until the CDI centers, and note the elapsed time.
4. Time to station is the same as the time taken to complete the 15° change of bearing.

Thus, if the time flown between aircraft positions 2 and 3 is 15 min., the estimated time to the station is also 15 min.
Answer (B) is incorrect because the time between positions 2 and 3 and between position 3 and the station should be equal, i.e., 15 min. Answer (C) is incorrect because the time between positions 2 and 3 and between position 3 and the station should be equal, i.e., 15 min.

FIGURE 24.—Isosceles Triangle.

25.

5542. (Refer to figure 23 below.) If the time flown between aircraft positions 2 and 3 is 13 minutes, what is the estimated time to the station?

A— 7.8 minutes.
B— 13 minutes.
C— 26 minutes.

Answer (B) is correct (5542). *(IFH Chap VIII)*

The time/distance to station can be found by application of the isosceles triangle principle (i.e., if two angles of a triangle are equal, two of the sides are also equal), as follows:

1. With the aircraft established on a radial (here 90°), inbound, rotate the OBS 20° to the right, i.e., 110°.
2. Turn 20° to the left and note the time.
3. Maintain constant heading until the CDI centers, and note the elapsed time.
4. Time to station is the same as the time taken to complete the 20° change of bearing.

Thus, if the time flown between aircraft positions 2 and 3 is 13 min., the estimated time to the station is also 13 min.

Answer (A) is incorrect because the time between positions 2 and 3 and between position 3 and the station should be equal, i.e., 13 min. Answer (C) is incorrect because the time between positions 2 and 3 and between position 3 and the station should be equal, i.e., 13 min.

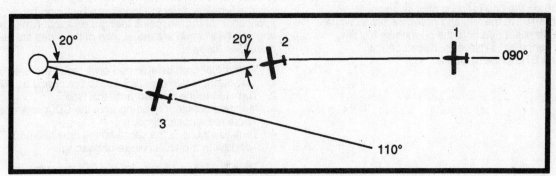

FIGURE 23.—Isosceles Triangle.

26.
5541. (Refer to figure 22 below.) If the time flown between aircraft positions 2 and 3 is 8 minutes, what is the estimated time to the station?

A— 8 minutes.
B— 16 minutes.
C— 48 minutes.

Answer (A) is correct (5541). *(IFH Chap VIII)*
The time/distance to station can be found by application of the isosceles triangle principle (i.e., if two angles of a triangle are equal, two of the sides are also equal), as follows:

1. With the aircraft established on a radial (here 270°), inbound, rotate the OBS 5° to the left, i.e., 265°.
2. Turn 5° to the right and note the time.
3. Maintain constant heading until the CDI centers, and note the elapsed time.
4. Time to station is the same as the time taken to complete the 5° change of bearing.

Thus, if the time flown between aircraft positions 2 and 3 is 8 min., the estimated time to the station is also 8 min.
Answer (B) is incorrect because the time between positions 2 and 3 and between position 3 and the station should be equal, i.e., 8 min. Answer (C) is incorrect because the time between positions 2 and 3 and between position 3 and the station should be equal, i.e., 8 min.

FIGURE 22.—Isosceles Triangle.

27.
5544. Inbound on the 040 radial, a pilot selects the 055 radial, turns 15° to the left, and notes the time. While maintaining a constant heading, the pilot notes the time for the CDI to center is 15 minutes. Based on this information, the ETE to the station is

A— 8 minutes.
B— 15 minutes.
C— 30 minutes.

Answer (B) is correct (5544). *(IFH Chap VIII)*
The time/distance to station can be found by application of the isosceles triangle principle (i.e., if two angles of a triangle are equal, two of the sides are also equal), as follows:

1. With the aircraft established on a radial (here 40°), inbound, rotate the OBS 15° to the right, i.e., 55°.
2. Turn 15° to the left and note the time.
3. Maintain constant heading until the CDI centers, and note the elapsed time.
4. Time to station is the same as the time taken to complete the 15° change of bearing.

Thus, if it takes 15 min. for the CDI to center, the estimated time to the station is also 15 min.
Answer (A) is incorrect because the time to the station is the same as the time between bearings, i.e., 15 min. Answer (C) is incorrect because the time to the station is the same as the time between bearings, i.e., 15 min.

28.
5545. Inbound on the 090 radial, a pilot rotates the OBS 010° to the left, turns 010° to the right, and notes the time. While maintaining a constant heading, the pilot determines that the elapsed time for the CDI to center is 8 minutes. Based on this information, the ETE to the station is

A— 8 minutes.
B— 16 minutes.
C— 24 minutes.

29.
5546. Inbound on the 315 radial, a pilot selects the 320 radial, turns 5° to the left, and notes the time. While maintaining a constant heading, the pilot notes the time for the CDI to center is 12 minutes. The ETE to the station is

A— 10 minutes.
B— 12 minutes.
C— 24 minutes.

30.
5547. Inbound on the 190 radial, a pilot selects the 195 radial, turns 5° to the left, and notes the time. While maintaining a constant heading, the pilot notes the time for the CDI to center is 10 minutes. The ETE to the station is

A— 10 minutes.
B— 15 minutes.
C— 20 minutes.

Answer (A) is correct (5545). *(IFH Chap VIII)*
The time/distance to station can be found by application of the isosceles triangle principle (i.e., if two angles of a triangle are equal, two of the sides are also equal), as follows:

1. With the aircraft established on a radial (here 90°), inbound, rotate the OBS 10° to the left, i.e., 80°.
2. Turn 10° to the right and note the time.
3. Maintain constant heading until the CDI centers, and note the elapsed time.
4. Time to station is the same as the time taken to complete the 10° change of bearing.

Thus, if it takes 8 min. for the CDI to center, the estimated time to the station is also 8 min.
Answer (B) is incorrect because the time to the station is the same as the time between bearings, i.e., 8 min. Answer (C) is incorrect because the time to the station is the same as the time between bearings, i.e., 8 min.

Answer (B) is correct (5546). *(IFH Chap VIII)*
The time/distance to station can be found by application of the isosceles triangle principle (i.e., if two angles of a triangle are equal, two of the sides are also equal), as follows:

1. With the aircraft established on a radial (here 315°), inbound, rotate the OBS 5° to the right, i.e., 320°.
2. Turn 5° to the left and note the time.
3. Maintain constant heading until the CDI centers, and note the elapsed time.
4. Time to station is the same as the time taken to complete the 5° change of bearing.

Thus, if it takes 12 min. for the CDI to center, the estimated time to the station is also 12 min.
Answer (A) is incorrect because the time to the station is the same as the time between bearings, i.e., 12 min. Answer (C) is incorrect because the time to the station is the same as the time between bearings, i.e., 12 min.

Answer (A) is correct (5547). *(IFH Chap VIII)*
The time/distance to station can be found by application of the isosceles triangle principle (i.e., if two angles of a triangle are equal, two of the sides are also equal), as follows:

1. With the aircraft established on a radial (here 190°), inbound, rotate the OBS 5° to the right, i.e., 195°.
2. Turn 5° to the left and note the time.
3. Maintain constant heading until the CDI centers, and note the elapsed time.
4. Time to station is the same as the time taken to complete the 5° change of bearing.

Thus, if it takes 10 min. for the CDI to center, the estimated time to the station is also 10 min.
Answer (B) is incorrect because the time to the station is the same as the time between bearings, i.e., 10 min. Answer (C) is incorrect because the time to the station is the same as the time between bearings, i.e., 10 min.

31.
5539. While maintaining a magnetic heading of 270° and a true airspeed of 120 knots, the 360 radial of a VOR is crossed at 1237 and the 350 radial is crossed at 1244. The approximate time and distance to this station are

A— 42 minutes and 84 NM.
B— 42 minutes and 91 NM.
C— 44 minutes and 96 NM.

Answer (A) is correct (5539). *(IFH Chap VIII)*
To determine the time and distance to the station, use the following formulas:

$$\text{Time to station} = \frac{60 \times \text{Min. flown between bearing change}}{\text{Degrees of bearing change}}$$

$$= \frac{60 \times 7}{10} = \frac{420}{10} = 42\,min.$$

$$\text{Distance to station} = \frac{TAS \times \text{Min. flown between bearing change}}{\text{Degrees of bearing change}}$$

$$= \frac{120 \times 7}{10} = \frac{840}{10} = 84\,NM$$

Answer (B) is incorrect because the distance would be 91 NM if the TAS were 132 kt., not 120 kt. Answer (C) is incorrect because the time to the station is 42 min., not 44 min., and the distance is 84 NM, not 96 NM.

32.
5515. The relative bearing on an ADF changes from 265° to 260° in 2 minutes of elapsed time. If the groundspeed is 145 knots, the distance to that station would be

A— 26 NM.
B— 37 NM.
C— 58 NM.

Answer (C) is correct (5515). *(IFH Chap VIII)*
To determine the distance to the station use the following formula:

$$\text{Distance to station} = \frac{TAS \times \text{Min. flown between bearing change}}{\text{Degrees of bearing change}}$$

$$= \frac{145 \times 2}{5} = \frac{290}{5} = 58\,NM$$

Note the FAA incorrectly uses groundspeed instead of TAS to calculate the distance to the station.
Answer (A) is incorrect because a distance of 26 NM to the station would require a TAS of 65 kt., not 145 kt. Answer (B) is incorrect because a distance of 37 NM to the station would require a TAS of 93 kt., not 145 kt.

33.
5516. The ADF indicates a wingtip bearing change of 10° in 2 minutes of elapsed time, and the TAS is 160 knots. What is the distance to the station?

A— 15 NM.
B— 32 NM.
C— 36 NM.

Answer (B) is correct (5516). *(IFH Chap VIII)*
To determine the distance to the station use the following formula:

$$\text{Distance to station} = \frac{TAS \times \text{Min. flown between bearing change}}{\text{Degrees of bearing change}}$$

$$= \frac{160 \times 2}{10} = \frac{320}{10} = 32\,NM$$

Answer (A) is incorrect because a distance of 15 NM to the station would require a TAS of 75 kt., not 160 kt. Answer (C) is incorrect because a distance of 36 NM to the station would require a TAS of 180 kt., not 160 kt.

34.
5517. With a TAS of 115 knots, the relative bearing on an ADF changes from 090° to 095° in 1.5 minutes of elapsed time. The distance to the station would be

A— 12.5 NM.
B— 24.5 NM.
C— 34.5 NM.

Answer (C) is correct (5517). *(IFH Chap VIII)*
To determine the distance to the station use the following formula:

$$\text{Distance to station} = \frac{TAS \times \text{Min. flown between bearing change}}{\text{Degrees of bearing change}}$$

$$= \frac{115 \times 1.5}{5} = \frac{172.5}{5} = 34.5\,NM$$

Answer (A) is incorrect because a distance of 12.5 NM to the station would require a TAS of 42 kt., not 115 kt. Answer (B) is incorrect because a distance of 24.5 NM to the station would require a TAS of 82 kt., not 115 kt.

35.
5518. GIVEN:

Wingtip bearing change . . . . 5°
Time elapsed between bearing change . . . . 5 min
True airspeed . . . . 115 kts

The distance to the station is

A— 36 NM.
B— 57.5 NM.
C— 115 NM.

36.
5519. The ADF is tuned to a nondirectional radiobeacon and the relative bearing changes from 095° to 100° in 1.5 minutes of elapsed time. The time en route to that station would be

A— 18 minutes.
B— 24 minutes.
C— 30 minutes.

37.
5531. While maintaining a constant heading, a relative bearing of 10° doubles in 5 minutes. If the true airspeed is 105 knots, the time and distance to the station being used is approximately

A— 5 minutes and 8.7 miles.
B— 10 minutes and 17 miles.
C— 15 minutes and 31.2 miles.

38.
5526. GIVEN:

Wingtip bearing change . . . . 15°
Elapsed time between bearing change . . . . 6 min
Rate of fuel consumption . . . . 8.6 gal/hr

Calculate the approximate fuel required to fly to the station.

A— 3.44 gallons.
B— 6.88 gallons.
C— 17.84 gallons.

Answer (C) is correct (5518). *(IFH Chap VIII)*
To determine the distance to the station use the following formula:

$$\text{Distance to station} = \frac{\text{TAS} \times \text{Min. flown between bearing change}}{\text{Degrees of bearing change}}$$

$$= \frac{115 \times 5}{5} = \frac{575}{5} = 115\,NM$$

Answer (A) is incorrect because a distance of 36 NM to the station would require a TAS of 36 kt., not 115 kt. Answer (B) is incorrect because a distance of 57.5 NM to the station would require a TAS of 57.5 kt., not 115 kt.

Answer (A) is correct (5519). *(IFH Chap VIII)*
The time to the station is determined by the following formula:

$$\text{Time to station} = \frac{60 \times \text{Min. flown between bearing change}}{\text{Degrees of bearing change}}$$

$$= \frac{60 \times 1.5}{5} = \frac{90}{5} = 18\,min.$$

Answer (B) is incorrect because 2 min., not 1.5 min., of elapsed time between 5° of bearing change would indicate 24 min. to the station. Answer (C) is incorrect because 2.5 min., not 1.5 min., of elapsed time between 5° of bearing change would indicate 30 min. to the station.

Answer (A) is correct (5531). *(IFH Chap VIII)*
When a relative bearing doubles in a specific time, the time to the station is that time (the time to double the relative bearing). Thus, the time to the station is 5 min. Since the TAS is 105 kt., the distance would be 8.7 NM (5 ÷ 60 x 105).
Answer (B) is incorrect because the time to the station is the same as the time to double the relative bearing, i.e., 5 min. Answer (C) is incorrect because the time to the station is the same as the time to double the relative bearing, i.e., 5 min.

Answer (A) is correct (5526). *(IFH Chap VIII)*
To determine the time and fuel required to fly to the station use the following steps:

1. $$\text{Time to station} = \frac{60 \times \text{Min. flown between bearing change}}{\text{Degrees of bearing change}}$$

$$= \frac{60 \times 6}{15} = \frac{360}{15} = 24\,min.$$

2. Use your flight computer or your calculator to determine the fuel required.

$$\text{Fuel required} = \frac{\text{Rate of fuel consumption} \times \text{Min. to station}}{60}$$

$$= \frac{8.6 \times 24}{60} = \frac{206.4}{60} = 3.44\,gal.$$

Answer (B) is incorrect because 6.88 gal. would be required if the fuel consumption were 17.2 gal./hr., not 8.6 gal./hr. Answer (C) is incorrect because 17.84 gal. would be required if the fuel consumption were 44.6 gal./hr., not 8.6 gal./hr.

39.
5527. GIVEN:

Wingtip bearing change . . . . 15°
Elapsed time between bearing change . . . . 7.5 min
True airspeed . . . . 85 kts
Rate of fuel consumption . . . . 9.6 gal/hr

The time, distance, and fuel required to fly to the station is

A— 30 minutes; 42.5 miles; 4.80 gallons.
B— 32 minutes; 48 miles; 5.58 gallons.
C— 48 minutes; 48 miles; 4.58 gallons.

40.
5528. While maintaining a constant heading, a relative bearing of 15° doubles in 6 minutes. The time to the station being used is

A— 3 minutes.
B— 6 minutes.
C— 12 minutes.

41.
5529. While maintaining a constant heading, the ADF needle increases from a relative bearing of 045° to 090° in 5 minutes. The time to the station being used is

A— 5 minutes.
B— 10 minutes.
C— 15 minutes.

42.
5530. While cruising at 135 knots and on a constant heading, the ADF needle decreases from a relative bearing of 315° to 270° in 7 minutes. The approximate time and distance to the station being used is

A— 7 minutes and 16 miles.
B— 14 minutes and 28 miles.
C— 19 minutes and 38 miles.

Answer (A) is correct (5527). *(IFH Chap VIII)*
To determine the time, distance, and fuel required to fly to the station use the following steps:

1. $\text{Time to station} = \dfrac{60 \times \text{Min. flown between bearing change}}{\text{Degrees of bearing change}}$

$$= \frac{60 \times 7.5}{15} = \frac{450}{15} = 30\,min.,$$

2. $\text{Distance to station} = \dfrac{\text{TAS} \times \text{Min. flown between bearing change}}{\text{Degrees of bearing change}}$

$$= \frac{85 \times 7.5}{15} = \frac{637.5}{15} = 42.5\,NM,\ and$$

3. $\text{Fuel required} = \dfrac{\text{Rate of fuel consumption} \times \text{Min. to station}}{60}$

$$= \frac{9.6 \times 30}{60} = \frac{288}{60} = 4.80\,gal.$$

Answer (B) is incorrect because 8 min., not 7.5 min., of elapsed time between 15° of bearing change would indicate 32 min. to the station. Answer (C) is incorrect because 12 min., not 7.5 min., of elapsed time between 15° of bearing change would indicate 48 min. to the station.

Answer (B) is correct (5528). *(IFH Chap VIII)*
When a relative bearing doubles in a specific time, the time to the station is that time (the time to double the relative bearing). Thus, the time to the station is 6 min.
Answer (A) is incorrect because the time to the station is the same as the time to double the relative bearing, i.e., 6 min. Answer (C) is incorrect because the time to the station is the same as the time to double the relative bearing, i.e., 6 min.

Answer (A) is correct (5529). *(IFH Chap VIII)*
When a relative bearing doubles in a specific time, the time to the station is that time (the time to double the relative bearing). Thus, the time to the station is 5 min.
Answer (B) is incorrect because the time to the station is the same as the time to double the relative bearing, i.e., 5 min. Answer (C) is incorrect because the time to the station is the same as the time to double the relative bearing, i.e., 5 min.

Answer (A) is correct (5530). *(IFH Chap VIII)*
When a relative bearing doubles in a specific time, the time to the station is that time (the time to double the relative bearing). Thus, the time to the station is 7 min. Since the TAS is 135 kt., the distance to the station is 15.7 NM (7 ÷ 60 x 135).
Answer (B) is incorrect because the time to the station is the same as the time to double the relative bearing, i.e., 7 min. Answer (C) is incorrect because the time to the station is the same as the time to double the relative bearing, i.e., 7 min.

43.

5520. The ADF is tuned to a nondirectional radiobeacon and the relative bearing changes from 270° to 265° in 2.5 minutes of elapsed time. The time en route to that beacon would be

A— 9 minutes.
B— 18 minutes.
C— 30 minutes.

44.

5521. The ADF is tuned to a nondirectional radiobeacon and the relative bearing changes from 085° to 090° in 2 minutes of elapsed time. The time en route to the station would be

A— 15 minutes.
B— 18 minutes.
C— 24 minutes.

45.

5522. If the relative bearing changes from 090° to 100° in 2.5 minutes of elapsed time, the time en route to the station would be

A— 12 minutes.
B— 15 minutes.
C— 18 minutes.

46.

5523. The ADF is tuned to a nondirectional radiobeacon and the relative bearing changes from 090° to 100° in 2.5 minutes of elapsed time. If the true airspeed is 90 knots, the distance and time en route to that radiobeacon would be

A— 15 miles and 22.5 minutes.
B— 22.5 miles and 15 minutes.
C— 32 miles and 18 minutes.

Answer (C) is correct (5520). *(IFH Chap VIII)*

To determine the time to the station use the following formula:

$$\text{Time to station} = \frac{60 \times \text{Min. flown between bearing change}}{\text{Degrees of bearing change}}$$

$$= \frac{60 \times 2.5}{5} = \frac{150}{5} = 30 \, min.$$

Answer (A) is incorrect because 45 sec., not 2.5 min., of elapsed time between 5° of bearing change would indicate 9 min. to the station. Answer (B) is incorrect because 1.5 min., not 2.5 min., of elapsed time between 5° of bearing change would indicate 18 min. to the station.

Answer (C) is correct (5521). *(IFH Chap VIII)*

To determine the time to the station use the following formula:

$$\text{Time to station} = \frac{60 \times \text{Min. flown between bearing change}}{\text{Degrees of bearing change}}$$

$$= \frac{60 \times 2}{5} = \frac{120}{5} = 24 \, min.$$

Answer (A) is incorrect because 1.25 min., not 2 min., of elapsed time between 5° of bearing change would indicate 15 min. to the station. Answer (B) is incorrect because 1.5 min., not 2 min., of elapsed time between 5° of bearing change would indicate 18 min. to the station.

Answer (B) is correct (5522). *(IFH Chap VIII)*

To determine the time to the station use the following formula:

$$\text{Time to station} = \frac{60 \times \text{Min. flown between bearing change}}{\text{Degrees of bearing change}}$$

$$= \frac{60 \times 2.5}{10} = \frac{150}{10} = 15 \, min.$$

Answer (A) is incorrect because 2 min., not 2.5 min., of elapsed time between 10° of bearing change would indicate 12 min. to the station. Answer (C) is incorrect because 3 min., not 2.5 min., of elapsed time between 10° of bearing change would indicate 18 min. to the station.

Answer (B) is correct (5523). *(IFH Chap VIII)*

To determine the time and distance to the station, use the following formulas:

$$\text{Time to station} = \frac{60 \times \text{Min. flown between bearing change}}{\text{Degrees of bearing change}}$$

$$= \frac{60 \times 2.5}{10} = \frac{150}{10} = 15 \, min.$$

$$\text{Distance to station} = \frac{\text{TAS} \times \text{Min. flown between bearing change}}{\text{Degrees of bearing change}}$$

$$= \frac{90 \times 2.5}{10} = \frac{225}{10} = 22.5 \, NM$$

Answer (A) is incorrect because the time, not distance, is 15 min., and the distance, not time, is 22.5 NM. Answer (C) is incorrect because 3 min., not 2.5 min., of elapsed time between 10° of bearing change would indicate 18 min. to the station.

47.
5524. GIVEN:

Wingtip bearing change . . . . 10°
Elapsed time between bearing change . . . . 4 min
Rate of fuel consumption . . . . 11 gal/hr

Calculate the fuel required to fly to the station.

A— 4.4 gallons.
B— 8.4 gallons.
C— 12 gallons.

Answer (A) is correct (5524). *(IFH Chap VIII)*
To calculate the fuel required to fly to the station use the following steps:

1. $\text{Time to station} = \dfrac{60 \times \text{Min. flown between bearing change}}{\text{Degrees of bearing change}}$

$$= \frac{60 \times 4}{10} = \frac{240}{10} = 24 \, min.$$

2. $\text{Fuel required} = \dfrac{\text{Rate of fuel consumption} \times \text{Min. to station}}{60}$

$$= \frac{11 \times 24}{60} = \frac{264}{60} = 4.4 \, gal.$$

Answer (B) is incorrect because 8.4 gal. would be required if the fuel consumption were 21 gal./hr., not 11 gal./hr. Answer (C) is incorrect because 12 gal. would be required if the fuel consumption were 30 gal./hr., not 11 gal./hr.

48.
5525. GIVEN:

Wingtip bearing change . . . . 5°
Elapsed time between bearing change . . . . 6 min
Rate of fuel consumption . . . . 12 gal/hr

The fuel required to fly to the station is

A— 8.2 gallons.
B— 14.4 gallons.
C— 18.7 gallons.

Answer (B) is correct (5525). *(IFH Chap VIII)*
To calculate the fuel required to fly to the station use the following steps:

1. $\text{Time to station} = \dfrac{60 \times \text{Min. flown between bearing change}}{\text{Degrees of bearing change}}$

$$= \frac{60 \times 6}{5} = \frac{360}{5} = 72 \, min.$$

2. $\text{Fuel required} = \dfrac{\text{Rate of fuel consumption} \times \text{Min. to station}}{60}$

$$= \frac{12 \times 72}{60} = \frac{864}{60} = 14.4 \, gal.$$

Answer (A) is incorrect because 8.2 gal. would be required if the fuel consumption were 6.8 gal./hr., not 12 gal./hr. Answer (C) is incorrect because 18.7 gal. would be required if the fuel consumption were 15.6 gal./hr., not 12 gal./hr.

9.4 Wind Direction and Speed

49.
5475. GIVEN:

True course . . . . 105°
True heading . . . . 085°
True airspeed . . . . 95 kts
Groundspeed . . . . 87 kts

Determine the wind direction and speed.

A— 020° and 32 knots.
B— 030° and 38 knots.
C— 200° and 32 knots.

Answer (A) is correct (5475). *(FI Comp)*
To estimate your wind given a true heading and a true course, simply use the wind side of your flight computer backwards. First, place your groundspeed of 87 kt. under the grommet with your true course of 105° under the true index. Since your true heading is 085°, you are holding a 20° left wind correction angle. Next, place a pencil mark on the 95-kt. true airspeed arc, 20° left of the centerline. Finally, rotate the wheel until the pencil mark is on the centerline, and read a wind of 020° (under the true index) at 32 kt. (up from the grommet).
Answer (B) is incorrect because a wind from 030° at 38 kt. would result in less wind correction and a slower groundspeed. Answer (C) is incorrect because a wind from 200° at 32 kt. would result in a higher, not lower, groundspeed than airspeed.

50.

5476. GIVEN:

True course	345°
True heading	355°
True airspeed	85 kts
Groundspeed	95 kts

Determine the wind direction and speed.

A— 095° and 19 knots.
B— 113° and 19 knots.
C— 238° and 18 knots.

51.

5477. You have flown 52 miles, are 6 miles off course, and have 118 miles yet to fly. To converge on your destination, the total correction angle would be

A— 3°.
B— 6°.
C— 10°.

Answer (B) is correct (5476). *(FI Comp)*

To estimate your wind given a true heading and a true course, simply use the wind side of your flight computer backwards. First, place your groundspeed of 95 kt. under the grommet with your true course of 345° under the true index. Since your true heading is 355°, you are holding a 10° right wind correction angle. Next, place a pencil mark on the 85-kt. true airspeed arc, 10° right of centerline. Finally, rotate the wheel until the pencil mark is on the centerline, and read a wind of 113° (under the true index) at 19 kt. (up from the grommet).

Answer (A) is incorrect because a wind from 095° at 19 kt. would result in more wind correction angle and a slower groundspeed. Answer (C) is incorrect because a wind from 238° at 18 kt. would require a left, not right, wind correction angle.

Answer (C) is correct (5477). *(IFH Chap VIII)*

To determine the total correction angle to converge on your destination use the following steps:

1. Since 1° off course equals 1 NM per 60 NM from the station, the following formula applies:

$$\frac{NM\ off}{NM\ flown} \times 60 = Degrees\ off\ course\ from\ departure\ point$$

$$\frac{6\ NM}{52\ NM} \times 60 = 6.92°$$

Turning back this number of degrees will parallel the original course.

2. To converge on your destination, calculate the number of degrees off it:

$$\frac{NM\ off}{NM\ remaining} \times 60 = Degrees\ off\ course\ to\ destination$$

$$\frac{6\ NM}{118\ NM} \times 60 = 3.05°$$

3. Turning this number of degrees farther will take you to your destination. Thus, the total correction angle is approximately 10° (6.92 + 3.05).

Answer (A) is incorrect because turning 3° would converge you on your destination if you were already paralleling the original course. Answer (B) is incorrect because 6° is the amount of correction required to parallel the original course.

52.
5478. GIVEN:

Distance off course . . . . 9 mi
Distance flown . . . . 95 mi
Distance to fly . . . . 125 mi

To converge at the destination, the total correction angle
would be

A— 4°.
B— 6°.
C— 10°.

Answer (C) is correct (5478). *(IFH Chap VIII)*
   To determine the total correction angle to converge
on your destination use the following steps:

1. Since 1° off course equals 1 NM per 60 NM from the
   station, the following formula applies:

   $$\frac{NM\ off}{NM\ flown} \times 60 = Degrees\ off\ course\ from\ departure\ point$$

   $$\frac{9\ NM}{95\ NM} \times 60 = 5.68°$$

   Turning back this number of degrees will parallel the
   original course.

2. To converge on your destination, calculate the
   number of degrees off it:

   $$\frac{NM\ off}{NM\ remaining} \times 60 = Degrees\ off\ course\ to\ destination$$

   $$\frac{9\ NM}{125\ NM} \times 60 = 4.32°$$

3. Turning this number of degrees farther will take you to
   your destination. Thus, the total correction angle is
   10° (5.68 + 4.32).

   Answer (A) is incorrect because turning 4° would
converge you on your destination if you were already
paralleling the original course. Answer (B) is incorrect
because 6° is the amount of correction required to
parallel the original course.

9.5 Time, Compass Heading, etc., on Climbs and En Route

53.
5488. An airplane departs an airport under the following
conditions:

Airport elevation . . . . 1,000 ft
Cruise altitude . . . . 9,500 ft
Rate of climb . . . . 500 ft/min
Average true airspeed . . . . 135 kts
True course . . . . 215°
Average wind velocity . . . . 290° at 20 kts
Variation . . . . 3° W
Deviation . . . . −2°
Average fuel consumption . . . . 13 gal/hr

Determine the approximate time, compass heading,
distance, and fuel consumed during the climb.

A— 14 minutes, 234°, 26 NM, 3.9 gallons.
B— 17 minutes, 224°, 36 NM, 3.7 gallons.
C— 17 minutes, 242°, 31 NM, 3.5 gallons.

Answer (B) is correct (5488). *(FI Comp)*
   The requirement is the time, compass heading,
distance, and fuel consumed during the climb. The
airport elevation is 1,000 ft. and the climb is to 9,500 ft.,
which is a climb of 8,500 ft. At 500 fpm, this requires
17 min., which narrows the answer down to (B) or (C). In
17 min., the fuel burned would be 3.7 gal. (17 ÷ 60 x 13).
Thus, the answer is (B).
   To determine the compass heading, first determine
the true heading using the wind side of your flight
computer. Then adjust the true heading to magnetic
heading, and then to compass heading.
   To determine the distance, multiply the time by the
groundspeed also found on the wind side of the
computer.
   Answer (A) is incorrect because the time required to
climb is 17 min., not 14 min. Answer (C) is incorrect
because the fuel used during 17 min. of climb is 3.7 gal.,
not 3.5 gal.

54.

5489. An airplane departs an airport under the following conditions:

Airport elevation	1,500 ft
Cruise altitude	9,500 ft
Rate of climb	500 ft/min
Average true airspeed	160 kts
True course	145°
Average wind velocity	080° at 15 kts
Variation	5° E
Deviation	−3°
Average fuel consumption	14 gal/hr

Determine the approximate time, compass heading, distance, and fuel consumed during the climb.

A— 14 minutes, 128°, 35 NM, 3.2 gallons.
B— 16 minutes, 132°, 41 NM, 3.7 gallons.
C— 16 minutes, 128°, 32 NM, 3.8 gallons.

55.

5481. GIVEN

Wind	175° at 20 kts
Distance	135 NM
True course	075°
True airspeed	80 kts
Fuel consumption	105 lb/hr

Determine the time en route and fuel consumption.

A— 1 hour 28 minutes and 73.2 pounds.
B— 1 hour 38 minutes and 158 pounds.
C— 1 hour 40 minutes and 175 pounds.

9.6 Time, Compass Heading, etc., on Descents

56.

5466. An airplane descends to an airport under the following conditions:

Cruising altitude	6,500 ft
Airport elevation	700 ft
Descends to	800 ft AGL
Rate of descent	500 ft/min
Average true airspeed	110 kts
True course	335°
Average wind velocity	060° at 15 kts
Variation	3° W
Deviation	+2°
Average fuel consumption	8.5 gal/hr

Determine the approximate time, compass heading, distance, and fuel consumed during the descent.

A— 10 minutes, 348°, 18 NM, 1.4 gallons.
B— 10 minutes, 355°, 17 NM, 2.4 gallons.
C— 12 minutes, 346°, 18 NM, 1.6 gallons.

Answer (B) is correct (5489). *(Fl Comp)*

The requirement is the time, compass heading, distance, and fuel consumed during the climb. The airport elevation is 1,500 ft. and the climb is to 9,500 ft., which is a climb of 8,000 ft. At 500 fpm, this requires 16 min., which narrows the answer down to (B) or (C). In 16 min. at 14 gal./hr., just over one-fourth of 14 gal. would be burned, which is approximately 3.7 gal., or answer (B). To determine the compass heading, first determine the true heading using the wind side of your flight computer. Then adjust the true heading to magnetic heading, and then to compass heading. To determine the distance, multiply the time by the groundspeed also found on the wind side of the computer.

Answer (A) is incorrect because the time required to climb is 16 min., not 14 min. Answer (C) is incorrect because the fuel used during 16 min. of climb is 3.7 gal., not 3.8 gal.

Answer (C) is correct (5481). *(Fl Comp)*

Using the wind side of your flight computer, follow these steps:

1. Place the wind direction under the true index (175°).
2. Mark the wind velocity up from the grommet (+20 kt.).
3. Place the true course under the true index (75°).
4. Slide the wind velocity mark to the (80-kt.) TAS line, and the groundspeed is under the grommet which is 81 kt.

Using the computer side, determine the time it takes to travel 135 NM by placing the index under 81 kt., then locate 135 NM on the outer scale, and under it is the time of 1 hr. 40 min. Next, place the index under 105 lb./hr. and locate 1 hr. 40 min. on the inner scale, and determine the fuel consumption on the outer scale to be 175 lb.

Answer (A) is incorrect because to travel 135 NM in 1 hr. and 28 min. would require a groundspeed of 92 kt., not 81 kt. Answer (B) is incorrect because in 1 hr. and 38 min. at 105 lb./hr., the fuel consumption would be 171 lb., not 158 lb.

Answer (A) is correct (5466). *(Fl Comp)*

A descent is to be made from 6,500 ft. to 1,500 ft. MSL (airport elevation of 700 ft. + 800 ft. AGL), which is a 5,000-ft. descent. At 500 fpm, it would take 10 min. Thus, the correct answer must either be (A) or (B). At 8.5 gal./hr., 1.4 gal. would be burned in 10 min. (10/60 x 8.5). Thus, (A) is correct.

Compute the compass heading by using the wind side of your flight computer. Convert true course to true heading based upon the wind effect. Then convert the true heading to magnetic heading by adjusting for the magnetic variation. The compass heading is determined by adjusting the magnetic heading for the compass deviation.

Answer (B) is incorrect because at 8.5 gal./hr., 1.4 gal., not 2.4 gal., would be used in 10 min. Answer (C) is incorrect because it would take approximately 12 min. to descend from 6,500 ft. MSL to the surface of the airport, not the level altitude of 1,500 ft. MSL (800 ft. AGL).

57.

5467. An airplane descends to an airport under the following conditions:

Cruising altitude	7,500 ft
Airport elevation	1,300 ft
Descends to	800 ft AGL
Rate of descent	300 ft/min
Average true airspeed	120 kts
True course	165°
Average wind velocity	240° at 20 kts
Variation	4° E
Deviation	−2°
Average fuel consumption	9.6 gal/hr

Determine the approximate time, compass heading, distance, and fuel consumed during the descent.

A— 16 minutes, 168°, 30 NM, 2.9 gallons.
B— 18 minutes, 164°, 34 NM, 3.2 gallons.
C— 18 minutes, 168°, 34 NM, 2.9 gallons.

Answer (C) is correct (5467). (FI Comp)
    A descent is to be made from 7,500 ft. to 2,100 ft. MSL (airport elevation of 1,300 ft. + 800 ft. AGL), which is a 5,400-ft. descent. At 300 fpm, it would take 18 min. Thus, the correct answer must either be (B) or (C). Based on fuel consumption of 9.6 gal./hr., the fuel consumption would be 2.9 gal. (18/60 x 9.6), which makes answer (C) correct.
    Compute the compass heading by using the wind side of your flight computer. Convert true course to true heading based upon the wind effect. Then convert the true heading to magnetic heading by adjusting for the magnetic variation. The compass heading is determined by adjusting the magnetic heading for the compass deviation.
    Answer (A) is incorrect because the time to descend is 18 min., not 16 min. Answer (B) is incorrect because at 9.6 gal./hr., 2.9 gal., not 3.2 gal., would be used in 18 min.

58.

5468. An airplane descends to an airport under the following conditions:

Cruising altitude	10,500 ft
Airport elevation	1,700 ft
Descends to	1,000 ft AGL
Rate of descent	600 ft/min
Average true airspeed	135 kts
True course	263°
Average wind velocity	330° at 30 kts
Variation	7° E
Deviation	+3°
Average fuel consumption	11.5 gal/hr

Determine the approximate time, compass heading, distance, and fuel consumed during the descent.

A— 9 minutes, 274°, 26 NM, 2.8 gallons.
B— 13 minutes, 274°, 28 NM, 2.5 gallons.
C— 13 minutes, 271°, 26 NM, 2.5 gallons.

Answer (C) is correct (5468). (FI Comp)
    A descent is to be made from 10,500 ft. to 2,700 ft. MSL (airport elevation of 1,700 ft. + 1,000 ft. AGL), which is a 7,800-ft. descent. At 600 fpm, it would take 13 min. Thus, the correct answer must either be (B) or (C) and you must compute the compass heading.
    Place the wind direction of 330° under the true index. With a pencil, mark the wind velocity of 30 kt. above the grommet. Then turn the inner scale so that the true course of 263° is under the true index. Next, slide the wind scale such that the pencil mark is on the true airspeed of 135 kt., and note that the groundspeed is 121 kt. Also note that a 12° right correction is required. Thus, the true heading will be 275° (263° + 12°). To convert to magnetic, subtract the 7° easterly variation to get 268° (275° − 7°). Then add the compass deviation of 3° to determine the compass heading of 271° (268° + 3°). Thus, answer (C) is correct.
    Answer (A) is incorrect because the time to descend is 13 min., not 9 min. Answer (B) is incorrect because the compass heading is 271°, not 274°.

END OF CHAPTER

CHAPTER TEN
NAVIGATION SYSTEMS

This chapter contains outlines of major concepts tested, all FAA test questions and answers regarding navigation systems, and an explanation of each answer. Each module, or subtopic, within this chapter is listed above with the number of questions from the FAA pilot knowledge test pertaining to that particular module. For each module, the first number following the parentheses is the page number on which the outline begins, and the next number is the page number on which the questions begin.

CAUTION: Recall that the **sole purpose** of this book is to expedite your passing the FAA pilot knowledge test for the commercial pilot certificate. Accordingly, all extraneous material (i.e., topics or regulations not directly tested on the FAA pilot knowledge test) is omitted, even though much more information and knowledge are necessary to become a proficient commercial pilot. This additional material is presented in *Commercial Pilot Flight Maneuvers and Practical Test Prep* and *Pilot Handbook*, available from Gleim Publications, Inc. See the order form on page 284.

10.1 AUTOMATIC DIRECTION FINDER (ADF) (Questions 1-14)

1. The ADF indicator always has its needle pointing toward the NDB station (nondirectional beacon, also known as a radio beacon).
   a. If the NDB is directly in front of the airplane, the needle will point straight up.
   b. If the NDB is directly off the right wing; i.e., at 3 o'clock, the needle will point directly to the right.
   c. If the NDB is directly behind the airplane, the needle will point straight down, etc.
2. Homing to a station is accomplished by keeping the needle centered on the top index of your ADF.
   a. A wind will cause you to drift on your inbound course and fly a curved path to the station.
3. When properly correcting for crosswind while heading to the NDB, the needle will point (not straight up) to the side the crosswind is blowing to. The amount of deflection depends on the amount of crosswind correction.
   a. When tracking away from the station, the head of the needle will point to the side from which the crosswind is blowing.
4. To compute magnetic heading, relative bearing, or magnetic bearing, use the formula:

$$MH + RB = MB$$

   a. Magnetic heading (MH) is the magnetic heading of the airplane.

    b.   Relative bearing (RB) is the direction of the magnetic bearing relative to the airplane.

    c.   Magnetic bearing (MB) is the relative direction from north.

    d.   In order to obtain answers ranging between 0° and 360°, you may need to add or subtract 360° to or from your answer.

    e.   The preceding formula is for magnetic bearing TO the station. If magnetic bearing FROM the station is desired, add or subtract 180°.

5.   EXAMPLE: Given a 300° magnetic heading and a relative bearing of 30°, the magnetic bearing is 300° + 30° = 330° (MH + RB = MB).

    a.   Or if you know your MH is 300° and the MB is 330°, the ADF would indicate 30°, which is the RB.

6.   There is a series of questions referring to the interception of a magnetic bearing from an ADF at a specified angle.

    a.   Remember a bearing from an ADF is the same as a VOR radial; e.g., spokes FROM the axle of a wheel.

        1)   Bearings TO are the opposite direction. A 90° bearing FROM is to the east. A 90° bearing TO is west of the station.

    b.   Begin by constructing a diagram.

        1)   Start with a point indicating the ADF station.

        2)   Extend the "desired" bearing FROM or TO the station.

        3)   Draw your airplane based on your relative bearing (indicated by an ADF indicator or stated in the question) and your magnetic heading (also given).

        4)   Trace your current ground track on the diagram and compute your angle of interception with the "desired" bearing.

        5)   If a revised MH is required, first compute your present angle of interception and then determine the amount of MH change needed to obtain the desired angle of interception.

10.2 VOR USE AND RECEIVER CHECKS (Questions 15-22a)

1.   When checking the course sensitivity of a VOR receiver, the OBS should be rotated 10° to 12° to move the CDI from the center to the last dot.

    a.   One-fifth deflection represents 2° off course, or 2 NM at 60 NM from the VOR station.

2.   When using a VOT to make a VOR receiver check, the CDI should be centered and the OBS should indicate that the aircraft is on the 360° radial.

    a.   To use a designated checkpoint on an airport surface, set the OBS on the designated radial.

        1)   The CDI must center within ±4° of that radial with a FROM indication.

    b.   When the CDI is centered during an airborne check, the OBS and the TO/FROM indicator should read within ±6° of the selected radial.

3.   To track outbound on a VOR radial, set the OBS to the desired radial, and make heading corrections toward the CDI.

    a.   To track inbound on a VOR radial, set the OBS to the reciprocal of the desired radial, and make heading corrections toward the CDI.

    b.   Flying a heading that is reciprocal to the bearing selected on the OBS would result in reverse sensing of the VOR receiver.

4.   For IFR operations off established airways, VORs which are no more than 80 NM apart should be listed in the "route of flight" portion of an IFR flight plan.

10.3 RADIO MAGNETIC INDICATOR (RMI) (Questions 23-27)

1.   The radio magnetic indicator (RMI) consists of a rotating compass card (heading indicator) and one or more navigation indicators which point to stations.

2.   The magnetic heading of the airplane is always directly under the index at the top of the instrument.

3.   The bearing pointer displays magnetic bearings to selected navigation stations.

   a.   The tail of the indicator tells you which radial you are on.

   b.   For example, the RMI above indicates a 015° magnetic heading, crossing the R-270 of VOR 1 (thin needle) and crossing the R-130 of VOR 2 (wide needle).

10.4 HORIZONTAL SITUATION INDICATOR (HSI) (Questions 28-32)

1.   The horizontal situation indicator (HSI) is a combination of a heading indicator and a VOR/ILS indicator, as illustrated and described below.

   a.   The azimuth card, which rotates so that the heading is shown under the index at the top of the instrument.

      1)   The azimuth card may be part of a remote indicating compass (RIC).

      2)   Or the azimuth card must be checked against the magnetic compass and reset with a heading set knob.

b.   The course indicating arrow, which is the VOR (OBS) indicator.

c.   The TO/FROM indicator for the VOR.

d.   Glide slope deviation pointer. It indicates above or below the glide slope, which is the longer center line.

e.   Glide slope warning flag, which comes out when reliable signals are not received by the glide slope deviation pointer.

f.   Heading set knob, which is used to coordinate the heading indicator (directional gyro, etc.) with the actual compass.

1)   If the azimuth card is part of an RIC, normally a heading bug (pointer) set knob moves a bug around the periphery of the azimuth card.

g.   Lubber line, which shows the current heading.

h.   Course deviation bar, which indicates the direction one would have to turn to intercept the desired radial if one were on the approximate heading of the OBS selection.

i.   The airplane symbol, which is fixed, showing the airplane relative to the selected course if seen from above the airplane looking down.

j.   The tail of the course-indicating arrow, which shows the reciprocal of the OBS heading.

k.   The course setting knob, which is used to adjust the OBS.

QUESTIONS AND ANSWER EXPLANATIONS

All the FAA questions from the pilot knowledge test for the commercial pilot certificate relating to navigation systems and the material outlined previously are reproduced on the following pages in the same modules as the outlines. To the immediate right of each question are the correct answer and answer explanation. You should cover these answers and answer explanations while responding to the questions. (A bookmark for this purpose has been provided in the back of the book.) Refer to the general discussion in the Introduction on how to take the FAA pilot knowledge test.

Remember that the questions from the FAA pilot knowledge test bank have been reordered by topic, and the topics have been organized into a meaningful sequence. Accordingly, the first line of the answer explanation gives the FAA question number and the citation of the authoritative source for the answer.

10.1 Automatic Direction Finder (ADF)

1.
5490b. Which is true about homing when using ADF during crosswind conditions? Homing

A— to a radio station results in a curved path that leads to the station.
B— is a practical navigation method for flying both to and from a radio station.
C— to a radio station requires that the ADF have an automatically or manually rotatable azimuth.

Answer (A) is correct (5490b). *(IFH Chap VII)*
Homing to a station is accomplished by keeping the needle centered on the top index of your ADF. As a result, any wind will cause you to drift on your inbound course and fly a curved path to the station.
Answer (B) is incorrect because homing is an impractical means of navigating to the station and an absolutely faulty means of "navigating from the station." Answer (C) is incorrect because homing can be accomplished with any ADF by keeping the needle pointed to the top of your ADF dial, regardless if the ADF has an automatically or manually rotatable azimuth.

2.
5491c. Which is true regarding tracking on a desired bearing when using ADF during crosswind conditions?

A— To track outbound, heading corrections should be made away from the ADF pointer.
B— When on the desired track outbound with the proper drift correction established, the ADF pointer will be deflected to the windward side of the tail position.
C— When on the desired track inbound with the proper drift correction established, the ADF pointer will be deflected to the windward side of the nose position.

3.
5493b. The magnetic heading is 315° and the ADF shows a relative bearing of 140°. The magnetic bearing FROM the radiobeacon would be

A— 095°.
B— 175°.
C— 275°.

4.
5494b. The magnetic heading is 350° and the relative bearing to a radiobeacon is 240°. What would be the magnetic bearing TO that radiobeacon?

A— 050°.
B— 230°.
C— 295°.

5.
5495. The ADF is tuned to a radiobeacon. If the magnetic heading is 040° and the relative bearing is 290°, the magnetic bearing TO that radiobeacon would be

A— 150°.
B— 285°.
C— 330°.

6.
5496. If the relative bearing to a nondirectional radio beacon is 045° and the magnetic heading is 355°, the magnetic bearing TO that radio beacon would be

A— 040°.
B— 065°.
C— 220°.

Answer (B) is correct (5491c). *(IFH Chap VII)*
When tracking outbound from an NDB station, the nose of the aircraft will be crabbed into the wind. As a result of this crab and flying away from the station, the ADF needle will be deflected towards the windward side (the side the wind is coming from).
Answer (A) is incorrect because, when tracking outbound, corrections should be made towards, not away from, the ADF pointer. Answer (C) is incorrect because, when inbound, the pointer is deflected to the leeward (the side the wind is blowing toward), not the windward side.

Answer (C) is correct (5493b). *(IFH Chap VII)*
To compute the magnetic bearing to an NDB, you use the formula below. The MH is given as 315° and the RB is given as 140°.

$$MH + RB = MB \text{ (TO)}$$
$$315° + 140° = MB \text{ (TO) } 455° - 360° = 095°$$

You adjust by 180° to get MB (FROM)

$$095° + 180° = 275°$$

Answer (A) is incorrect because 095° is the MB TO the station, not FROM the station. Answer (B) is incorrect because 175° is not a related direction in this problem.

Answer (B) is correct (5494b). *(IFH Chap VII)*
To compute the magnetic bearing to an NDB, you use the formula below. The MH is given as 350° and the RB is given as 240°.

$$MH + RB = MB \text{ (TO)}$$
$$350° + 240° = MB \text{ (TO)}$$
$$MB \text{ (TO)} = 590° - 360° = 230°$$

Answer (A) is incorrect because 050° is the MB FROM the station, not TO the station. Answer (C) is incorrect because 295° is not a related direction in this problem.

Answer (C) is correct (5495). *(IFH Chap VII)*
To compute the magnetic bearing to an NDB, you use the formula below. The MH is given as 040° and the RB is 290°.

$$MH + RB = MB \text{ (TO)}$$
$$040° + 290° = 330°$$

Answer (A) is incorrect because 150° is the MB FROM the station, not TO the station. Answer (B) is incorrect because 285° is not a related direction in this problem.

Answer (A) is correct (5496). *(IFH Chap VII)*
To compute the magnetic bearing to an NDB, you use the formula below. The MH is given as 355° and the RB is given as 045°.

$$MH + RB = MB \text{ (TO)}$$
$$355° + 045° = MB \text{ (TO)}$$
$$MB \text{ (TO)} = 400° - 360° = 040°$$

Answer (B) is incorrect because 065° is not a related direction in this problem. Answer (C) is incorrect because 220° is the MB FROM the station, not TO the station.

7.
5492b. An aircraft is maintaining a magnetic heading of 265° and the ADF shows a relative bearing of 065°. This indicates that the aircraft is crossing the

A— 065° magnetic bearing FROM the radiobeacon.
B— 150° magnetic bearing FROM the radiobeacon.
C— 330° magnetic bearing FROM the radiobeacon.

8.
5511. (Refer to figure 18 below.) To intercept a magnetic bearing of 240° FROM at a 030° angle (while outbound), the airplane should be turned

A— left 065°.
B— left 125°.
C— right 270°.

FIGURE 18.—Magnetic Heading/Radio Compass.

9.
5512. (Refer to figure 18 above.) If the airplane continues to fly on the heading as shown, what magnetic bearing FROM the station would be intercepted at a 35° angle outbound?

A— 035°.
B— 070°.
C— 215°.

Answer (B) is correct (5492b). *(IFH Chap VII)*
To compute the magnetic bearing to an NDB, you use the formula below. The MH is given as 265° and the RB is given as 065°.

MH + RB = MB (TO)
265° + 065° = 330°

You adjust by 180° to get MB (FROM)

330° − 180° = 150°

Answer (A) is incorrect because 065° is the RB TO the station, not MB FROM the station. Answer (C) is incorrect because 330° is the MB TO the station, not MB FROM the station.

Answer (B) is correct (5511). *(IFH Chap VIII)*
Draw a diagram as illustrated below. Read the illustration from right to left. You are on a 35° MH. Your RB is 310°. That identifies where the NDB is. Finally you want to draw the 240° MB outbound. To intercept the 240° MB at a 30° angle, you need a left turn from 35° to 270° which is 125°.

MH + RB = MB
035° + 310° = MB (TO) = 345°

Answer (A) is incorrect because a left 65° turn brings the airplane to a 330° MH, which will intercept the 240° MB FROM the station at a 90° angle, not 30°angle. Answer (C) is incorrect because a right 270° turn brings the airplane to a 305° MH, which will intercept the 240° MB FROM the station at a 65° angle, not a 30° angle.

Answer (B) is correct (5512). *(IFH Chap VIII)*
You are currently on the 165° MB (FROM). With a 35° MH, you will cross the 70° MB (FROM) at a 35° intersection angle (70° − 35° = 35°). Note that the 70° MB (FROM) is in front of us when you are northeast bound currently crossing the 165° MB (FROM).
Answer (A) is incorrect because with a 35° MH you will parallel the 35° MB (FROM). Answer (C) is incorrect because you will not cross the 215° MB (FROM) the station.

10.

5513. (Refer to figure 19 below.) If the airplane continues to fly on the magnetic heading as illustrated, what magnetic bearing FROM the station would be intercepted at a 35° angle?

A— 090°.
B— 270°.
C— 305°.

FIGURE 19.—Magnetic Heading/Radio Compass.

11.

5514. (Refer to figure 19 above.) If the airplane continues to fly on the magnetic heading as illustrated, what magnetic bearing FROM the station would be intercepted at a 30° angle?

A— 090°.
B— 270°.
C— 310°.

Answer (C) is correct (5513). *(IFH Chap VIII)*
    Draw a diagram as illustrated below. Begin by determining your present MB.

$$MH + RB = MB (TO)$$
ADD 180° for MB (FROM)

$340° + 110° + 180° = MB (FROM) = 630° - 360° = 270°$

You are now on the 270° MB (FROM). When you cross the 305° MB (FROM) of the NDB, you will have a 35° interception angle (340° – 305° = 35°).
    Answer (A) is incorrect because on this heading, you will never cross the 090° MB (FROM). Answer (B) is incorrect because you are already on the 270° MB (FROM).

Answer (C) is correct (5514). *(IFH Chap VIII)*
    Refer to the diagram above. Begin by determining your present MB.

$$MH + RB = MB (TO)$$

Add 180° for MB (FROM)

$340° + 110° + 180° = MB (FROM) = 630° - 360° = 270°$

When you cross the 310° MB (FROM) of the NDB, you will have a 30° interception angle (340° – 310° = 30°).
    Answer (A) is incorrect because on this heading, you will never cross the 090° MB (FROM). Answer (B) is incorrect because you are already on the 270° MB (FROM).

FIGURE 16.—Magnetic Compass/ADF.

12.

5499. (Refer to figure 16 on page 238.) At the position indicated by instrument group 1, to intercept the 330° magnetic bearing to the NDB at a 30° angle, the aircraft should be turned

A— left to a heading of 270°.
B— right to a heading of 330°.
C— right to a heading of 360°.

13.

5497. (Refer to figure 16 on page 238.) If the aircraft continues its present heading as shown in instrument group 3, what will be the relative bearing when the aircraft reaches the magnetic bearing of 030° FROM the NDB?

A— 030°.
B— 060°.
C— 240°.

14.

5498. (Refer to figure 16 on page 238.) At the position indicated by instrument group 1, what would be the relative bearing if the aircraft were turned to a magnetic heading of 090°?

A— 150°.
B— 190°.
C— 250°.

Answer (C) is correct (5499). *(IFH Chap VIII)*
Draw a diagram as illustrated below.

Note you are west of the 330° MB because your RB is greater than 30° (on the 330° MB, you will have a 30° RB). Thus, you need to turn right. Since you wish a 30° intersection angle with the 330° MB, your heading should be 360°.
   Answer (A) is incorrect because a MH of 270° will take you further from the 330° MB TO the station. Answer (B) is incorrect because a MH of 330° will parallel, not intercept, the 330° MB TO the station.

Answer (C) is correct (5497). *(IFH Chap VIII)*
Draw a diagram as illustrated below.

Recall the formula

$$MH + RB = MB\ (TO)$$
$$MH + RB = MB\ (FROM) + 180°$$
$$330° + RB = 30° + 180° + 360°$$
$$RB = 240°$$

   Answer (A) is incorrect because a 030° RB would mean that the NDB is north of the airplane. Answer (B) is incorrect because a 060° RB would mean that the NDB is northeast of the airplane.

Answer (C) is correct (5498). *(IFH Chap VIII)*
   The requirement is your new RB if you change your MH from 300° to 90°. Begin by solving for your MB.

$$MH + RB = MB$$
$$300° + 40° = MB = 340°$$

Note your MB will remain the same but your MH changes. Resolve the above equation.

$$MH + RB = MB$$
$$90° + RB = 340°$$
$$RB = 250°$$

   Answer (A) is incorrect because to have a RB of 150° after a turn to a MH of 090° would mean the airplane is on the 240°, not 340°, MB TO the station. Answer (B) is incorrect because to have a RB of 190° after a turn to a MH of 090° would mean the airplane is on the 280°, not 340°, MB TO the station.

10.2 VOR Use and Receiver Checks

15.
5532. When checking the course sensitivity of a VOR receiver, how many degrees should the OBS be rotated to move the CDI from the center to the last dot on either side?

A— 5° to 10°.
B— 10° to 12°.
C— 18° to 20°.

16.
5552. When using VOT to make a VOR receiver check, the CDI should be centered and the OBS should indicate that the aircraft is on the

A— 090 radial.
B— 180 radial.
C— 360 radial.

17.
5551. How should the pilot make a VOR receiver check when the aircraft is located on the designated checkpoint on the airport surface?

A— Set the OBS on 180° plus or minus 4°; the CDI should center with a FROM indication.
B— Set the OBS on the designated radial. The CDI must center within plus or minus 4° of that radial with a FROM indication.
C— With the aircraft headed directly toward the VOR and the OBS set to 000°, the CDI should center within plus or minus 4° of that radial with a TO indication.

18.
5533. An aircraft 60 miles from a VOR station has a CDI indication of one-fifth deflection, this represents a course centerline deviation of approximately

A— 6 miles.
B— 2 miles.
C— 1 mile.

Answer (B) is correct (5532). *(IFH Chap VIII)*
Course sensitivity may be checked on a VOR by noting the number of degrees of change in the course selected as you rotate the OBS to move the CDI from center to the last dot on either side. This should be between 10° and 12°.
Answer (A) is incorrect because normal VOR sensitivity is 10° to 12°, not 5° to 10°. Answer (C) is incorrect because normal VOR sensitivity is 10° to 12°, not 18° to 20°.

Answer (C) is correct (5552). *(AIM Para 1-1-4)*
To use a VOT, tune in the published VOT frequency on your VOR receiver. With the course deviation indicator (CDI) centered, the omnibearing selector (OBS) should read 0° with the TO-FROM indicator showing FROM or the OBS should read 180° with the TO-FROM indicator showing TO. This indicates you are on the 360° radial.
Answer (A) is incorrect because a VOT sends out a 360°, not 090°, radial in all directions. Answer (B) is incorrect because a VOT sends out a 360°, not 180°, radial in all directions.

Answer (B) is correct (5551). *(AIM Para 1-1-4)*
On ground checkpoints, you must have the aircraft on the location of the checkpoint and have the designated radial set on the OBS. The CDI must center within ±4° of the designated radial.
Answer (A) is incorrect because it relates to VOT receiver checks, but on a VOT, with the OBS on 180°, there should be a TO, not a FROM, indication. Answer (C) is incorrect because it relates to VOT receiver checks, but VOTs, or any other VOR receiver check, do not require the airplane to be pointed in a particular direction.

Answer (B) is correct (5533). *(IFH Chap VIII)*
Assuming a receiver with normal course sensitivity and full-scale deflection at 5 dots, aircraft displacement from course is approximately 200 ft. per dot per NM. Since one-fifth deflection equals 1 dot, the aircraft is 12,000 ft. or 2 NM off course (200 ft./NM x 60 NM = 12,000 ft.).
Answer (A) is incorrect because 6 NM off course would be indicated by a three-fifth, not one-fifth, CDI deflection. Answer (C) is incorrect because 1 NM off course would be indicated by a one-fifth CDI deflection if the aircraft were 30 NM, not 60 NM, from the station.

19.
5553. When the CDI needle is centered during an airborne VOR check, the omnibearing selector and the TO/FROM indicator should read

A— within 4° of the selected radial.
B— within 6° of the selected radial.
C— 0° TO, only if you are due south of the VOR.

20.
5500. Which situation would result in reverse sensing of a VOR receiver?

A— Flying a heading that is reciprocal to the bearing selected on the OBS.
B— Setting the OBS to a bearing that is 90° from the bearing on which the aircraft is located.
C— Failing to change the OBS from the selected inbound course to the outbound course after passing the station.

21.
5501. To track outbound on the 180 radial of a VOR station, the recommended procedure is to set the OBS to

A— 360° and make heading corrections toward the CDI needle.
B— 180° and make heading corrections away from the CDI needle.
C— 180° and make heading corrections toward the CDI needle.

22.
5502. To track inbound on the 215 radial of a VOR station, the recommended procedure is to set the OBS to

A— 215° and make heading corrections toward the CDI needle.
B— 215° and make heading corrections away from the CDI needle.
C— 035° and make heading corrections toward the CDI needle.

22a.
0601-577. For IFR operations off established airways, ROUTE OF FLIGHT portion of an IFR flight plan should list VOR navigational aids which are no more than

A— 80 miles apart.
B— 70 miles apart.
C— 40 miles apart.

Answer (B) is correct (5553). *(AIM Para 1-1-4)*
For an airborne VOR receiver check, the maximum permissible bearing error of a VOR is ±6°.
Answer (A) is incorrect because the airborne check tolerance is 6°, not 4°. Answer (C) is incorrect because the airborne check is performed over points designated by the FAA or over specific landmarks, not just due south of the VOR.

Answer (A) is correct (5500). *(IFH Chap VIII)*
By flying a heading which is a reciprocal of the course set in the OBS you will have two situations. You will be flying to the station with a FROM indication or you will fly from the station with a TO indication. Either will result in reverse sensing.
Answer (B) is incorrect because it will result in the TO/FROM flag indicating the "cone of confusion." Answer (C) is incorrect because although it may put you off course, it would not cause reverse sensing.

Answer (C) is correct (5501). *(IFH Chap VIII)*
The recommended procedure is to set 180° on the OBS (your outbound course). This will give you a FROM indication while flying away from the station. This is normal sensing and you correct towards the needle.
Answer (A) is incorrect because it would give you reverse sensing. Thus, corrections are made away from, not toward, the needle. Answer (B) is incorrect because it would take you away from your course (it is the way you navigate when using reverse sensing, e.g., on the back course of a localizer approach).

Answer (C) is correct (5502). *(IFH Chap VIII)*
Since radials emanate outward from the VOR, tracking inbound on R-215 means you are flying the reciprocal course of 035°. Thus, you should set 035° on the OBS, and make heading corrections toward the needle.
Answer (A) is incorrect because it would result in reverse sensing by the CDI. Answer (B) is incorrect because it would result in reverse sensing by the CDI.

Answer (A) is correct (0601-577). *(AIM Para 5-1-73.c)*
The *Aeronautical Information Manual* indicates that, in order to facilitate the use of VOR signals, the distance between VORs defining a direct route of flight in controlled airspace off established airways below 18,000 ft. MSL should not exceed 80 NM.
Answer (B) is incorrect because the recommended maximum distance between VOR navigational aids is 80 NM, not 70 NM. Answer (C) is incorrect because the recommended maximum distance between VOR navigational aids is 80 NM, not 40 NM.

FIGURE 20.—Radio Magnetic Indicator (RMI).

10.3 Radio Magnetic Indicator (RMI)

23.
5534. (Refer to figure 20 on page 242.) Using instrument group 3, if the aircraft makes a 180° turn to the left and continues straight ahead, it will intercept which radial?

A— 135 radial.
B— 270 radial.
C— 360 radial.

Answer (A) is correct (5534). *(IFH Chap VIII)*
RMI 3 is on R-135 of the VOR, based on the tail of the wide needle. It has a heading of 300° (under the arrow at the top). A 180° turn to the left will result in a 120° course. The left turn takes the airplane southwest of the R-135 and the 120° heading takes the airplane back through R-135.
Answers (B) is incorrect because R-270 is west of the VOR, so an airplane southeast of the VOR that turns to a southeast heading would not cross this radial. Answer (C) is incorrect because R-360 is north of the VOR, so an airplane southeast of the VOR that turns to a southeast heading would not cross this radial.

24.
5536. (Refer to figure 20 on page 242.) Which instrument shows the aircraft in a position where a straight course after a 90° left turn would result in intercepting the 180 radial?

A— 2.
B— 3.
C— 4.

Answer (B) is correct (5536). *(IFH Chap VIII)*
RMI 3 shows the airplane on R-135 of the VOR, i.e., southeast, and on a heading of 300°. A 90° left turn to 210° would cause the airplane to fly southwest, and thus intercept R-180.
Answer (A) is incorrect because RMI 2 shows the airplane on R-310 (northwest), and heading 125°. A 90° left turn to 035° would not intercept R-180. Answer (C) is incorrect because RMI 4 shows the airplane on R-015 (northeast), and heading 360°. A 90° left turn to 270° would intercept R-360, not R-180.

25.
5535. (Refer to figure 20 on page 242.) Which instrument shows the aircraft in a position where a 180° turn would result in the aircraft intercepting the 150 radial at a 30° angle?

A— 2.
B— 3.
C— 4.

Answer (C) is correct (5535). *(IFH Chap VIII)*
RMI 4 is on R-015 of the VOR, i.e., north-northeast, and on a heading of 360°. A 180° turn to 180° would cause the airplane to intercept R-150 at a 30° angle (180° − 150° = 30°).
Answer (A) is incorrect because RMI 2 shows the airplane on R-310 (northwest) and heading 125°. A 180° turn to 305° would not intercept R-150. Answer (B) is incorrect because, on the present heading of 300°, not after a 180° turn to 120°, you would intercept the R-150 at a 30° angle.

26.
5537. (Refer to figure 20 on page 242.) Which instrument shows the aircraft to be northwest of the VORTAC?

A— 1.
B— 2.
C— 3.

Answer (B) is correct (5537). *(IFH Chap VIII)*
RMI 2 shows the aircraft to be on R-310 of the VORTAC, i.e., northwest.
Answer (A) is incorrect because RMI 1 shows R-160 which is southeast. Answer (C) is incorrect because RMI 3 shows R-135 which is southeast.

27.
5538. (Refer to figure 20 on page 242.) Which instrument(s) show(s) that the aircraft is getting further from the selected VORTAC?

A— 4.
B— 1 and 4.
C— 2 and 3.

Answer (A) is correct (5538). *(IFH Chap VIII)*
On an RMI, the head of the needle points to the selected station. Thus, RMI 4 shows the aircraft flying away from the VORTAC.
Answer (B) is incorrect because RMI 1 shows the aircraft flying toward, not away from, the VORTAC. Answer (C) is incorrect because RMIs 2 and 3 show the aircraft flying toward, not away from, the VORTAC.

FIGURE 17.—Horizontal Situation Indicator (HSI).

10.4 Horizontal Situation Indicator (HSI)

28.
5508. (Refer to figure 17 above.) Which illustration indicates that the airplane will intercept the 060 radial at a 75° angle outbound, if the present heading is maintained?

A— 4.
B— 5.
C— 6.

Answer (B) is correct (5508). *(IFH Chap VIII)*
    The present magnetic heading of the airplane in illustration 5 is 345° so you will cross R-060 at a 75° angle. The TO indication indicates you are east of the 330° – 150° radials. The right deflection on the 240° OBS selection means you are south of the 060° radial.
    Answer (A) is incorrect because illustration 4 shows the airplane intercepting R-060 at a 15° angle (255° – 240°). Answer (C) is incorrect because illustration 6 shows the airplane intercepting R-060 at a 60° angle (300° – 240°).

29.
5507. (Refer to figure 17 on page 244.) Which statement is true regarding illustration 2, if the present heading is maintained? The airplane will

A— cross the 180 radial at a 45° angle outbound.
B— intercept the 225 radial at a 45° angle.
C— intercept the 360 radial at a 45° angle inbound.

30.
5506. (Refer to figure 17 on page 244.) Which illustration indicates that the airplane will intercept the 060 radial at a 60° angle inbound, if the present heading is maintained?

A— 6.
B— 4.
C— 5.

31.
5509. (Refer to figure 17 on page 244.) Which illustration indicates that the airplane should be turned 150° left to intercept the 360 radial at a 60° angle inbound?

A— 1.
B— 2.
C— 3.

32.
5510. (Refer to figure 17 on page 244.) Which is true regarding illustration 4, if the present heading is maintained? The airplane will

A— cross the 060 radial at a 15° angle.
B— intercept the 240 radial at a 30° angle.
C— cross the 180 radial at a 75° angle.

Answer (A) is correct (5507). *(IFH Chap VIII)*
Illustration 2 indicates that the airplane is heading approximately 227°. The bearing pointer indicates that a heading of 235° will take you to the station; thus, you are on the 055 radial (i.e., east-northeast of the station heading southwest). If you maintain the present heading, the station will remain to the right of the aircraft and you will cross the 180 radial at approximately a 45° angle outbound (227 – 180 = 47).
Answer (B) is incorrect because you would intercept the 180 radial, not the 225 radial, at a 45° angle outbound. Answer (C) is incorrect because the bearing point is presently to the right of the airplane's heading; thus, the station would remain to the right. The airplane would fly south, not north, of the station and would cross the 180, not the 360, radial at a 45° angle outbound, not inbound.

Answer (A) is correct (5506). *(IFH Chap VIII)*
Illustration 6 indicates that the airplane is east of the station on a heading of 300°. The course selector is set to 240 and a TO indication. On a heading of 300°, the airplane will intercept the 060 radial inbound, which is 240° TO the station, at a 60° angle (300-240).
Answer (B) is incorrect because in illustration 4 the airplane is east of the station heading 255°. The airplane will intercept the 240 radial, not the 060 radial, at a 15° angle outbound. Answer (C) is incorrect because in illustration 5 the airplane is east of the station heading 345°. The airplane will intercept the 060 radial at a 105° angle inbound (345-240), not a 60° angle inbound.

Answer (A) is correct (5509). *(IFH Chap VIII)*
By turning the airplane as indicated in illustration 1, 150° left you would be heading 240°. This would be a 60° interception to the 360° radial.
Note the TO indication on a 180° OBS means you are north. The right deflection on the 180° OBS means you are east of the 360° radial. A 240° MH will intercept the 360° radial at a 60° angle.
Answer (B) is incorrect because airplane 2 is inbound from the northeast. If you turn 150° left from 227°, your new heading will be 077°. You will fly away from the 360° radial. Answer (C) is incorrect because airplane 3 is inbound from the northeast. If you make a 150° left turn from 244°, your new heading will be 094°. You will fly east, away from the 360° radial.

Answer (C) is correct (5510). *(IFH Chap VIII)*
Illustration 4 indicates that the airplane is heading 255°. The bearing pointer indicates that a heading of 275° will take you to the station; thus, you are on the 095 radial (i.e., east of the station heading southwest). If you maintain the present heading, you will cross the R-180 at a 75° angle (255 – 180 = 75).
Answer (A) is incorrect because you will cross the 240 radial, not the 060 radial, at a 15° angle. Answer (B) is incorrect because you will cross the 240 radial at a 15°, not 30°, angle.

END OF CHAPTER

CHAPTER ELEVEN
FLIGHT OPERATIONS

This chapter contains outlines of major concepts tested, all FAA test questions and answers regarding flight operations, and an explanation of each answer. Each module, or subtopic, within this chapter is listed above with the number of questions from the FAA pilot knowledge test pertaining to that particular module. For each module, the first number following the parentheses is the page number on which the outline begins, and the next number is the page number on which the questions begin.

CAUTION: Recall that the **sole purpose** of this book is to expedite your passing the FAA pilot knowledge test for the commercial pilot certificate. Accordingly, all extraneous material (i.e., topics or regulations not directly tested on the FAA pilot knowledge test) is omitted, even though much more information and knowledge are necessary to become a proficient commercial pilot. This additional material is presented in *Commercial Pilot Flight Maneuvers and Practical Test Prep* and *Pilot Handbook*, available from Gleim Publications, Inc. See the order form on page 284.

11.1 FLIGHT FUNDAMENTALS (Question 1)

1. The four flight fundamentals involved in maneuvering an airplane are
    a. Straight-and-level flight
    b. Turns
    c. Climbs
    d. Descents

11.2 TAXIING (Questions 2-4)

1. When taxiing in a strong quartering tailwind, the aileron control should be opposite the direction from which the wind is blowing.
    a. This keeps the aileron down on the side from which the wind is blowing.

2. On crosswind takeoffs,
    a. The rudder is used to maintain directional control,
    b. The aileron pressure should be into the wind to keep the upwind wing down, and
    c. There should be a higher-than-normal liftoff speed so the airplane does not skip sideways during liftoff.

11.3 LANDINGS (Questions 5-7)

1. During gusty wind conditions, a power-on approach and power-on landing should be conducted.

2. On crosswind landings, at the moment of touchdown, the direction of motion of the airplane and its longitudinal axis should be parallel to the runway; i.e., not skipping sideways, which would impose side loads on the landing gear.

3. When turbulence is encountered during the approach to a landing, you should increase the airspeed slightly above normal approach speed to attain more positive control.

11.4 EMERGENCIES (Questions 8-9)

1. The vital and most immediate concern in the event of complete power failure after becoming airborne on takeoff is maintaining a safe, i.e., best glide, airspeed so as to avoid stalls/spins.

2. When diverting to an alternate airport in an emergency, time is usually of the essence. Accordingly, you should divert to the new course as soon as possible. Rule of thumb computations, estimates, and any other shortcuts are appropriate.

11.5 ANTI-COLLISION LIGHT SYSTEM (Question 10)

1. Pilots are required to have the aircraft's anti-collision lighting system operating during all operations, night and day, unless the pilot in command determines that it should be turned off for safety reasons.

11.6 COLD WEATHER OPERATION (Questions 11-13)

1. The cabin area as well as the engine should be preheated for cold weather operation.

2. In cold weather, crankcase breather lines should be inspected to determine whether they are clogged with ice from crankcase vapors that have condensed and frozen.

3. When taking off from a slushy runway, you can minimize the freezing of landing gear mechanisms by recycling the gear several times after takeoff.

11.7 TURBULENCE (Questions 14-16)

1. In severe turbulence, set power for the design maneuvering airspeed (V_A) and maintain a level flight attitude.

    a. Accept changes in airspeed and altitude.

2. Flight at or below V_A means the airplane will stall before excessive loads can be imposed on the wings.

3. When entering an area where significant clear air turbulence (CAT) has been reported, reduce the airspeed to that recommended for rough air at the first indication of turbulence.

11.8 NIGHT FLYING OPERATIONS (Questions 17-22)

1. For night flying operations, the best night vision is achieved when the rods in the eyes become adjusted to the darkness in approximately 30 min.

2. When planning a night cross-country flight, you should check the availability and status of en route and destination airport lighting systems.

3. Light beacons producing red flashes indicate obstructions or areas considered hazardous to aerial navigation.

4. When flying VFR at night, the first indication of flying into restricted visibility conditions is the gradual disappearance of lights on the ground.

5. When planning for an emergency landing at night, two of the primary considerations should include

    a. Planning the emergency approach and landing to an unlighted portion of an area.
    b. Selecting a landing close to public access, if possible.

QUESTIONS AND ANSWER EXPLANATIONS

All the FAA questions from the pilot knowledge test for the commercial pilot certificate relating to flight operations and the material outlined previously are reproduced on the following pages in the same modules as the outlines. To the immediate right of each question are the correct answer and answer explanation. You should cover these answers and answer explanations while responding to the questions. (A bookmark for this purpose has been provided in the back of the book.) Refer to the general discussion in the Introduction on how to take the FAA pilot knowledge test.

Remember that the questions from the FAA pilot knowledge test bank have been reordered by topic, and the topics have been organized into a meaningful sequence. Accordingly, the first line of the answer explanation gives the FAA question number and the citation of the authoritative source for the answer.

11.1 Flight Fundamentals

1.
5191. Name the four fundamentals involved in maneuvering an aircraft.

A— Power, pitch, bank, and trim.
B— Thrust, lift, turns, and glides.
C— Straight-and-level flight, turns, climbs, and descents.

Answer (C) is correct (5191). *(FTH Chap 6)*
Maneuvering the airplane is generally divided into four flight fundamentals: straight-and-level flight, turns, climbs, and descents. All controlled flight consists of either one or a combination of more than one of these basic maneuvers.
Answer (A) is incorrect because power, pitch, bank, and trim are the components of aircraft control by which the four fundamental maneuvers are performed.
Answer (B) is incorrect because thrust and lift are two of the forces which act on an airplane, and glides are a type of descent.

11.2 Taxiing

2.
5656c. While taxiing a light, high-wing airplane during strong quartering tailwinds, the aileron control should be positioned

A— neutral at all times.
B— toward the direction from which the wind is blowing.
C— opposite the direction from which the wind is blowing.

Answer (C) is correct (5656c). *(FTH Chap 5)*
When taxiing with a quartering tailwind, the aileron control should be positioned opposite the direction from which the wind is blowing so that the aileron is down on the side from which the wind is blowing. This will prevent the wind from lifting the wing or getting under it and blowing the airplane over.
Answer (A) is incorrect because the ailerons can assist in keeping the wind from blowing the airplane over in strong crosswinds. Answer (B) is incorrect because you position the aileron control toward the direction from which the wind is blowing when taxiing with a quartering headwind, not tailwind.

3.
5655b. When taxiing during strong quartering tailwinds, which aileron positions should be used?

A— Neutral.
B— Aileron up on the side from which the wind is blowing.
C— Aileron down on the side from which the wind is blowing.

Answer (C) is correct (5655b). *(FTH Chap 5)*
When taxiing with a quartering tailwind, the aileron control should be positioned opposite the direction from which the wind is blowing so that the aileron is down on the side from which the wind is blowing. This will prevent the wind from lifting the wing or getting under it and blowing the airplane over.
Answer (A) is incorrect because the ailerons can assist in keeping the wind from blowing the airplane over in strong crosswinds. Answer (B) is incorrect because you should position the aileron up on the side from which the wind is blowing in a quartering headwind, not tailwind.

4.

5661. With regard to the technique required for a crosswind correction on takeoff, a pilot should use

A— aileron pressure into the wind and initiate the lift-off at a normal airspeed in both tailwheel- and nosewheel-type airplanes.

B— right rudder pressure, aileron pressure into the wind, and higher than normal lift-off airspeed in both tricycle- and conventional-gear airplanes.

C— rudder as required to maintain directional control, aileron pressure into the wind, and higher than normal lift-off airspeed in both conventional- and nosewheel-type airplanes.

Answer (C) is correct (5661). *(FTH Chap 8)*

For crosswind takeoffs, the aileron control must be held into the crosswind, which raises the aileron on the upwind wing to impose a downward force on the wing to counteract the lifting force of the crosswind and prevents that wing from rising. The rudder is used to maintain directional control. Finally, a higher than normal lift-off airspeed is appropriate in both conventional and nosewheel-type airplanes to keep the airplane from skipping sideways during a possible slow transition from the directional control down the runway to crabbing into the wind once you are airborne.

Answer (A) is incorrect because the lift-off speed should be increased slightly and rudder pressure should be applied as necessary to maintain directional control. Answer (B) is incorrect because the amount of rudder pressure required to maintain directional control of the airplane should be applied, not necessarily only right rudder pressure.

11.3 Landings

5.

5665. A proper crosswind landing on a runway requires that, at the moment of touchdown, the

A— direction of motion of the airplane and its lateral axis be perpendicular to the runway.

B— direction of motion of the airplane and its longitudinal axis be parallel to the runway.

C— downwind wing be lowered sufficiently to eliminate the tendency for the airplane to drift.

Answer (B) is correct (5665). *(FTH Chap 9)*

At the moment of touchdown, the upwind wing must be held down and opposite rudder applied so that the direction of motion of the airplane and its longitudinal axis are both parallel to the runway. Failure to accomplish this results in severe sideloads being imposed on the landing gear and imparts ground looping tendencies.

Answer (A) is incorrect because the direction of motion of the airplane must be parallel, not perpendicular, to the runway. Answer (C) is incorrect because you lower the upwind wing, not the downwind wing, to eliminate drift.

6.

5664. Which type of approach and landing is recommended during gusty wind conditions?

A— A power-on approach and power-on landing.

B— A power-off approach and power-on landing.

C— A power-on approach and power-off landing.

Answer (A) is correct (5664). *(FTH Chap 9)*

Power-on approaches at airspeeds slightly above normal should be used for landing in gusty or turbulent wind conditions. To maintain good control in a gusty crosswind, the use of partial wing flaps may be necessary. The touchdown will be at a higher airspeed to ensure more positive control. An adequate amount of power should be used to maintain the proper airspeed throughout the approach, and the throttle should be retarded to idling position only after the main wheels contact the landing surface.

Answer (B) is incorrect because a power-on, not power-off, approach should be used during gusty conditions. Answer (C) is incorrect because a power-on, not power-off, landing should be used during gusty conditions.

7.
5662. When turbulence is encountered during the approach to a landing, what action is recommended and for what primary reason?

A— Increase the airspeed slightly above normal approach speed to attain more positive control.
B— Decrease the airspeed slightly below normal approach speed to avoid overstressing the airplane.
C— Increase the airspeed slightly above normal approach speed to penetrate the turbulence as quickly as possible.

Answer (A) is correct (5662). *(FTH Chap 9)*
Power-on approaches at airspeeds slightly above normal should be used for landing in gusty or turbulent wind conditions. To maintain good control in a gusty crosswind, the use of partial wing flaps may be necessary. The touchdown will be at a higher airspeed to ensure more positive control. An adequate amount of power should be used to maintain the proper airspeed throughout the approach, and the throttle should be retarded to idling position only after the main wheels contact the landing surface.
Answer (B) is incorrect because, since normal approach speed is generally well below V_A, a slightly higher approach speed will improve control effectiveness without overstressing the airplane. Answer (C) is incorrect because the increased approach speed is for improved control effectiveness. In general, turbulence should be penetrated slowly, not as quickly as possible.

11.4 Emergencies

8.
5663. A pilot's most immediate and vital concern in the event of complete engine failure after becoming airborne on takeoff is

A— maintaining a safe airspeed.
B— landing directly into the wind.
C— turning back to the takeoff field.

Answer (A) is correct (5663). *(FTH Chap 9)*
The most immediate concern in the event of complete engine failure while airborne in all phases of flight is establishing and maintaining a safe (i.e., best glide) airspeed. This is especially true when an engine failure occurs after becoming airborne on takeoff since the airplane is in a nose-up attitude and a relatively slow airspeed, which may be near the stall speed.
Answer (B) is incorrect because landing into the wind may not always be the best choice, given available landing areas and obstructions. Answer (C) is incorrect because turning back to the takeoff field will not be possible until sufficient altitude has been gained.

9.
5503. When diverting to an alternate airport because of an emergency, pilots should

A— rely upon radio as the primary method of navigation.
B— climb to a higher altitude because it will be easier to identify checkpoints.
C— apply rule-of-thumb computations, estimates, and other appropriate shortcuts to divert to the new course as soon as possible.

Answer (C) is correct (5503). *(FTH Chap 12)*
When diverting to an alternate airport because of an emergency, time is usually of the essence. Accordingly, you should divert to the new course as soon as possible. Rule of thumb computations, estimates, and any other shortcuts are appropriate.
Answer (A) is incorrect because any appropriate means of navigation is satisfactory. Answer (B) is incorrect because climbs may consume valuable time and/or fuel.

11.5 Anti-Collision Light System

10.
5748. Pilots are required to have the anti-collision light system operating

A— during all types of operations, both day and night.
B— anytime the pilot is in the cockpit.
C— anytime an engine is in operation.

Answer (A) is correct (5748). *(AIM Para 4-3-23)*
Aircraft equipped with an anti-collision lighting system are required to have that system operating during all types of operations, both day and night, except when the pilot-in-command determines that it should be turned off for safety reasons.
Answer (B) is incorrect because the anti-collision light system need not be operated if the pilot is in the cockpit of an aircraft that is not performing an operation (e.g., the system does not have to be on while the pilot preflights the cockpit). Answer (C) is incorrect because the anti-collision light system is required to be operational during all types of operations, day and night, not just when an engine is in operation (e.g., a motor-glider equipped with anti-collision lights must use them during power-off soaring as well as during powered flight).

11.6 Cold Weather Operation

11.
5767. Which is true regarding preheating an aircraft during cold weather operations?

A— The cabin area as well as the engine should be preheated.
B— The cabin area should not be preheated with portable heaters.
C— Hot air should be blown directly at the engine through the air intakes.

Answer (A) is correct (5767). *(AC 91-13C)*
Low temperatures may cause a change in the viscosity of engine oils, batteries to lose a high percentage of their effectiveness, and instruments to stick. Thus, preheating of the engine as well as the cabin area is desirable during cold weather operations.
Answer (B) is incorrect because the cockpit area can be preheated with portable heaters if they are available and appropriate. Answer (C) is incorrect because the engine should be heated by blowing warm air on the entire engine surface, not through the air intake areas.

12.
5766. During preflight in cold weather, crankcase breather lines should receive special attention because they are susceptible to being clogged by

A— congealed oil from the crankcase.
B— moisture from the outside air which has frozen.
C— ice from crankcase vapors that have condensed and subsequently frozen.

Answer (C) is correct (5766). *(AC 91-13C)*
Frozen crankcase breather lines prevent oil from circulating adequately in the engine and may even result in broken oil lines or oil being pumped out of the crankcase. Accordingly, you must always visually inspect to make sure that the crankcase breather lines are free of ice. The ice may have formed as a result of the crankcase vapors freezing in the lines after the engine has been turned off.
Answer (A) is incorrect because oil in the crankcase virtually never gets into the breather lines, but rather remains in the bottom of the crankcase. Answer (B) is incorrect because very cold outside air usually has a low moisture content.

13.
5768. If necessary to take off from a slushy runway, the freezing of landing gear mechanisms can be minimized by

A— recycling the gear.
B— delaying gear retraction.
C— increasing the airspeed to V_{LE} before retraction.

Answer (A) is correct (5768). *(AC 91-13C)*
When taking off from a slushy runway, recycling the landing gear several times after takeoff will ensure that any ice in the process of forming will be broken off and blown away before it completely freezes within the landing gear mechanisms.
Answer (B) is incorrect because delaying the landing gear retraction will impede the climbout and also may result in freezing the landing gear in the extended position. Answer (C) is incorrect because the landing gear should always be retracted well below V_{LE}.

11.7 Turbulence

14.
5670. If severe turbulence is encountered during flight, the pilot should reduce the airspeed to

A— minimum control speed.
B— design-maneuvering speed.
C— maximum structural cruising speed.

Answer (B) is correct (5670). *(PHAK Chap 3)*
Flight at or below design maneuvering speed (V_A) means the airplane will stall before excess loads can be imposed on the wings and cause structural damage.
Answer (A) is incorrect because minimum control speed is just above stall speed. In turbulence, the changing airspeeds would result in the airplane's stalling and/or significant control problems. Answer (C) is incorrect because the maximum structural cruising speed (V_{NO}) is considerably above V_A.

15.
5741. Which is the best technique for minimizing the wing-load factor when flying in severe turbulence?

A— Change power settings, as necessary, to maintain constant airspeed.
B— Control airspeed with power, maintain wings level, and accept variations of altitude.
C— Set power and trim to obtain an airspeed at or below maneuvering speed, maintain wings level, and accept variations of airspeed and altitude.

Answer (C) is correct (5741). *(AvW Chap 11)*
In severe turbulence, you should set power and trim to obtain an airspeed at or below maneuvering speed (V_A), maintain a level pitch and bank attitude, and accept variations of airspeed and altitude.
Answer (A) is incorrect because maintaining a constant airspeed in severe turbulence is impossible. Answer (B) is incorrect because maintaining a constant airspeed in severe turbulence is impossible.

16.
5669. A pilot is entering an area where significant clear air turbulence has been reported. Which action is appropriate upon encountering the first ripple?

A— Maintain altitude and airspeed.
B— Adjust airspeed to that recommended for rough air.
C— Enter a shallow climb or descent at maneuvering speed.

11.8 Night Flying Operations

17.
5490a. For night flying operations, the best night vision is achieved when the

A— pupils of the eyes have become dilated in approximately 10 minutes.
B— rods in the eyes have become adjusted to the darkness in approximately 30 minutes.
C— cones in the eyes have become adjusted to the darkness in approximately 5 minutes.

18.
5133. When planning a night cross-country flight, a pilot should check for

A— availability and status of en route and destination airport lighting systems.
B— red en route course lights.
C— location of rotating light beacons.

18a.
5491b. When planning a night cross-country flight, a pilot should check for the availability and status of

A— all VORs to be used en route.
B— airport rotating light beacon.
C— destination airport lighting systems.

Answer (B) is correct (5669). *(PHAK Chap 3)*
When entering an area where significant air turbulence has been reported, you should adjust the airspeed to that recommended for rough air (V_A) at the first indication of turbulence.
Answer (A) is incorrect because you should reduce your airspeed to V_A. Answer (C) is incorrect because you do not need to adjust altitude, just slow to V_A.

Answer (B) is correct (5490a). *(AFH Chap 10)*
In the eye's adaptation to darkness process, the pupils of the eyes first enlarge (dilate) to receive as much of the available light as possible. After about 5 to 10 min., the cones become adjusted and the eyes become 100 times more sensitive to the light than they were before the process began. The best night vision is achieved when the rods in the eyes have become adjusted to the darkness, which takes about 30 min. At this time, the eyes are about 100,000 times more sensitive to light than they were in a lighted area.
Answer (A) is incorrect because the eyes dilate (enlarge) at the beginning of the eye's adaptation to darkness. Additionally, after 10 min. the cones become adjusted, but the best night vision is achieved when the rods become adjusted in approximately 30 min. Answer (C) is incorrect because the best night vision is achieved when the rods, not cones, in the eyes become adjusted to the darkness in approximately 30 min., not 5 min.

Answer (A) is correct (5133). *(AFH Chap 10)*
When planning a night cross-country flight, you should check the availability and status of lighting systems at en route and destination airports. Information about their availability can be found on aeronautical charts and in the *Airport/Facility Directory*. The status of each facility can be determined by reviewing pertinent NOTAMs.
Answer (B) is incorrect because red lights indicate obstructions or areas considered hazardous to aircraft. There are no red en route course lights. Answer (C) is incorrect because, while knowing the location of rotating light beacons will assist you during night navigation, it is more important that you know the availability and status of en route and destination airport lighting systems. These lighting systems include runway lights, taxiway lights, and rotating beacons.

Answer (C) is correct (5491b). *(AFH Chap 10)*
When planning a night cross-country flight, you should check the availability and status of lighting systems at the destination airport. These lighting systems include runway lights, taxiway lights, and rotating beacons. Information about their availability can be found on aeronautical charts and in the *Airport/Facility Directory*. The status of each facility can be determined by reviewing pertinent Notices to Airmen (NOTAMs).
Answer (A) is incorrect because, while knowing the availability and status of VORs to be used en route will assist you in night navigation, it is more important that you know the availability and status of lighting systems at the destination airport. Answer (B) is incorrect because, while knowing the availability and status of rotating light beacons at airports along your route will assist you in night navigation, it is more important that you know the availability and status of the entire lighting system, not just the rotating beacon, at your destination airport.

19.

5491a. Light beacons producing red flashes indicate

A— end of runway warning at departure end.
B— a pilot should remain clear of an airport traffic pattern and continue circling.
C— obstructions or areas considered hazardous to aerial navigation.

Answer (C) is correct (5491a). *(AFH Chap 10)*
Light beacons producing red flashes indicate obstructions or areas considered hazardous to aerial navigation.
Answer (A) is incorrect because end of runway lights are steady, not flashing, red lights. Answer (B) is incorrect because, in the case of ATC light signals to an airplane in flight, a steady red, not a flashing red, light signal means to give way to other aircraft and continue circling.

20.

5492. When operating VFR at night, what is the first indication of flying into restricted visibility conditions?

A— Ground lights begin to take on an appearance of being surrounded by a halo or glow.
B— A gradual disappearance of lights on the ground.
C— Cockpit lights begin to take on an appearance of a halo or glow around them.

Answer (B) is correct (5492). *(AFH Chap 10)*
When operating VFR at night, the first indication of flying into restricted visibility conditions is the gradual disappearance of lights on the ground.
Answer (A) is incorrect because ground fog, not flying into restricted visibility, is indicated when ground lights begin to take on an appearance of being surrounded by a halo or glow. Caution should be used in attempting further flight in that same direction. Answer (C) is incorrect because ground fog, not flying into restricted visibility, is indicated when ground lights, not cockpit lights, begin to take on an appearance of a halo or glow around them.

21.

5493. After experiencing a powerplant failure at night, one of the primary considerations should include

A— turning off all electrical switches to save battery power for landing.
B— planning the emergency approach and landing to an unlighted portion of an area.
C— maneuvering to, and landing on a lighted highway or road.

Answer (B) is correct (5493). *(AFH Chap 10)*
After experiencing an engine failure at night, one of the primary considerations should include that you plan the emergency approach and landing to an unlighted portion of an area. This is to avoid the possibility of landing in an area where you could hurt people on the ground and/or avoiding buildings on the ground during landing.
Answer (A) is incorrect because turning off all electrical switches to save battery power for the landing is a procedure to use for an alternator failure, not an engine failure, at night. Answer (C) is incorrect because after experiencing an engine failure at night, one of the primary considerations should include turning away from, not maneuvering toward, a lighted highway or road. Highways or roads are hazardous to you and people on the ground.

22.

5494. When planning for an emergency landing at night, one of the primary considerations should include

A— selecting a landing area close to public access, if possible.
B— landing without flaps to ensure a nose-high landing attitude at touchdown.
C— turning off all electrical switches to save battery power for the landing.

Answer (A) is correct (5494). *(AFH Chap 10)*
When planning for an emergency landing at night, one of the primary considerations should include selecting an emergency landing area close to public access, if possible. This may facilitate rescue or help, if needed.
Answer (B) is incorrect because, when planning for an emergency landing at night, you should plan to land in the normal landing configuration. The flaps should be extended to ensure to land at the slowest possible speed in a nose-high attitude at touchdown. Answer (C) is incorrect because turning off all electrical switches to save battery power for landing is a procedure to use for an alternator failure, not an engine failure, at night.

END OF CHAPTER

APPENDIX A
COMMERCIAL PILOT PRACTICE TEST

The following 100 questions have been randomly selected from the 593 airplane-related questions in the FAA's commercial pilot test bank. You will be referred to figures (charts, tables, etc.) throughout this book. Be careful not to consult the answers or answer explanations when you look for and at the figures. Topical coverage in this practice test is similar to that of the FAA pilot knowledge test. Use the correct answer listing on page 266 to grade your practice test.

1.
5002. NTSB Part 830 requires an immediate notification as a result of which incident?

A— Engine failure for any reason during flight.
B— Damage to the landing gear as a result of a hard landing.
C— Any required flight crewmember being unable to perform flight duties because of illness.

2.
5013. Which is the correct symbol for the stalling speed or the minimum steady flight speed in a specified configuration?

A— V_S.
B— V_{S1}.
C— V_{SO}.

3.
5019. Which of the following are considered aircraft class ratings?

A— Transport, normal, utility, and acrobatic.
B— Airplane, rotorcraft, glider, and lighter-than-air.
C— Single-engine land, multiengine land, single-engine sea, and multiengine sea.

4.
5024. To act as pilot in command of an airplane that is equipped with retractable landing gear, flaps, and controllable pitch propeller, a person is required to

A— hold a multiengine airplane class rating.
B— make at least six takeoffs and landings in such an airplane within the preceding 6 months.
C— receive and log ground and flight training in such an airplane, and obtain a logbook endorsement certifying proficiency.

5.
5032. Pilots who change their permanent mailing address and fail to notify the FAA Airmen Certification Branch of this change, are entitled to exercise the privileges of their pilot certificate for a period of

A— 30 days.
B— 60 days.
C— 90 days.

6.
5059. If weather conditions are such that it is required to designate an alternate airport on your IFR flight plan, you should plan to carry enough fuel to arrive at the first airport of intended landing, fly from that airport to the alternate airport, and fly thereafter for

A— 30 minutes at slow cruising speed.
B— 45 minutes at normal cruising speed.
C— 1 hour at normal cruising speed.

7.
5061. In the contiguous U.S., excluding the airspace at and below 2,500 feet AGL, an operable coded transponder equipped with Mode C capability is required in all airspace above

A— 10,000 feet MSL.
B— 12,500 feet MSL.
C— 14,500 feet MSL.

8.
5067b. Approved flotation gear, readily available to each occupant, is required on each aircraft if it is being flown for hire over water,

A— in amphibious aircraft beyond 50 NM from shore.
B— beyond power-off gliding distance from shore.
C— regardless of the distance flown from shore.

9.
5071. No person may operate a large civil aircraft of U.S. registry which is subject to a lease, unless the lessee has mailed a copy of the lease to the FAA Aircraft Registration Branch, Technical Section, Oklahoma City, OK, within how many hours of its execution?

A— 24
B— 48
C— 72

10.
5076c. Airplane A is overtaking airplane B. Which airplane has the right-of-way?

A— Airplane A; the pilot should alter course to the right to pass.
B— Airplane B; the pilot should expect to be passed on the right.
C— Airplane B; the pilot should expect to be passed on the left.

11.
5085. What is the minimum flight visibility and proximity to cloud requirements for VFR flight, at 6,500 feet MSL, in Class C, D, and E airspace?

A— 1 mile visibility; clear of clouds.
B— 3 miles visibility; 1,000 feet above and 500 feet below.
C— 5 miles visibility; 1,000 feet above and 1,000 feet below.

12.
5093. Who is primarily responsible for maintaining an aircraft in an airworthy condition?

A— The lead mechanic responsible for that aircraft.
B— Pilot in command or operator.
C— Operator or owner of the aircraft.

13.
5104. A new maintenance record being used for an aircraft engine rebuilt by the manufacturer must include previous

A— operating hours of the engine.
B— annual inspections performed on the engine.
C— changes as required by Airworthiness Directives.

14.
5105. If an ATC transponder installed in an aircraft has not been tested, inspected, and found to comply with regulations within a specified period, what is the limitation on its use?

A— Its use is not permitted.
B— It may be used when in Class G airspace.
C— It may be used for VFR flight only.

15.
5111. No person may operate an aircraft in simulated instrument flight conditions unless the

A— other control seat is occupied by at least an appropriately rated commercial pilot.
B— pilot has filed an IFR flight plan and received an IFR clearance.
C— other control seat is occupied by a safety pilot, who holds at least a private pilot certificate and is appropriately rated.

16.
5121. When weather information indicates that abnormally high barometric pressure exists, or will be above ___ inches of mercury, flight operations will not be authorized contrary to the requirements published in NOTAMs.

A— 31.00
B— 32.00
C— 30.50

17.
5122b. Which data must be recorded in the aircraft logbook or other record by a pilot making a VOR operational check for IFR operations?

A— VOR name or identification, place of operational check, amount of bearing error, and date of check.
B— Date of check, place of operational check, bearing error, and signature.
C— VOR name or identification, amount of bearing error, date of check, and signature.

18.
5123b. For an airport without an approved instrument approach procedure to be listed as an alternate airport on an IFR flight plan, the forecasted weather conditions at the time of arrival must have at least a

A— ceiling of 2,000 feet and visibility 3 SM.
B— ceiling and visibility that allows for a descent, approach, and landing under basic VFR.
C— ceiling of 1,000 feet and visibility 3 NM.

19.
5126a. A person with a commercial pilot certificate may act as pilot in command of an aircraft for compensation or hire. If that person

A— is qualified in accordance with 14 CFR Part 61 and with the applicable parts that apply to the operation.
B— is qualified in accordance with 14 CFR Part 61 and has passed a pilot competency check given by an authorized check pilot.
C— holds appropriate category, class ratings, and meets the recent flight experience requirements of 14 CFR Part 61.

20.
5128. To act as pilot in command of a tailwheel airplane, without prior experience, a pilot must

A— log ground and flight training from an authorized instructor.
B— pass a competency check and receive an endorsement from an authorized instructor.
C— receive and log flight training from an authorized instructor.

21.
5157. While maintaining a constant angle of bank and altitude in a coordinated turn, an increase in airspeed will

A— decrease the rate of turn resulting in a decreased load factor.
B— decrease the rate of turn resulting in no change in load factor.
C— increase the rate of turn resulting in no change in load factor.

22.
5158. Lift on a wing is most properly defined as the

A— force acting perpendicular to the relative wind.
B— differential pressure acting perpendicular to the chord of the wing.
C— reduced pressure resulting from a laminar flow over the upper camber of an airfoil, which acts perpendicular to the mean camber.

23.
5164. Baggage weighing 90 pounds is placed in a normal category airplane's baggage compartment which is placarded at 100 pounds. If this airplane is subjected to a positive load factor of 3.5 G's, the total load of the baggage would be

A— 315 pounds and would be excessive.
B— 315 pounds and would not be excessive.
C— 350 pounds and would not be excessive.

24.
5175. For internal cooling, reciprocating aircraft engines are especially dependent on

A— a properly functioning cowl flap augmenter.
B— the circulation of lubricating oil.
C— the proper Freon/compressor output ratio.

25.
5178. Which statement is true about magnetic deviation of a compass? Deviation

A— varies over time as the agonic line shifts.
B— varies for different headings of the same aircraft.
C— is the same for all aircraft in the same locality.

26.
5185a. Detonation may occur at high-power settings when

A— the fuel mixture ignites instantaneously instead of burning progressively and evenly.
B— an excessively rich fuel mixture causes an explosive gain in power.
C— the fuel mixture is ignited too early by hot carbon deposits in the cylinder.

27.
5187. Fuel/air ratio is the ratio between the

A— volume of fuel and volume of air entering the cylinder.
B— weight of fuel and weight of air entering the cylinder.
C— weight of fuel and weight of air entering the carburetor.

28.
5205. In small airplanes, normal recovery from spins may become difficult if the

A— CG is too far rearward, and rotation is around the longitudinal axis.
B— CG is too far rearward, and rotation is around the CG.
C— spin is entered before the stall is fully developed.

29.
5207. If an airplane is loaded to the rear of its CG range, it will tend to be unstable about its

A— vertical axis.
B— lateral axis.
C— longitudinal axis.

30.
5211. The stalling speed of an airplane is most affected by

A— changes in air density.
B— variations in flight altitude.
C— variations in airplane loading.

31.
5213. (Refer to figure 3 on page 30.) If an airplane glides at an angle of attack of 10°, how much altitude will it lose in 1 mile?

A— 240 feet.
B— 480 feet.
C— 960 feet.

32.
5216. If the same angle of attack is maintained in ground effect as when out of ground effect, lift will

A— increase, and induced drag will decrease.
B— decrease, and parasite drag will increase.
C— increase, and induced drag will increase.

33.
5161. In theory, if the airspeed of an airplane is doubled while in level flight, parasite drag will become

A— twice as great.
B— half as great.
C— four times greater.

34.
5182. One of the main functions of flaps during the approach and landing is to

A— decrease the angle of descent without increasing the airspeed.
B— provide the same amount of lift at a slower airspeed.
C— decrease lift, thus enabling a steeper-than-normal approach to be made.

35.
5199. The angle of attack of a wing directly controls the

A— angle of incidence of the wing.
B— amount of airflow above and below the wing.
C— distribution of pressures acting on the wing.

36.
5218. Which is true regarding the forces acting on an aircraft in a steady-state descent? The sum of all

A— upward forces is less than the sum of all downward forces.
B— rearward forces is greater than the sum of all forward forces.
C— forward forces is equal to the sum of all rearward forces.

37.
5233. (Refer to figure 5 on page 41.) The vertical line from point D to point G is represented on the airspeed indicator by the maximum speed limit of the

A— green arc.
B— yellow arc.
C— white arc.

38.
5236. A fixed-pitch propeller is designed for best efficiency only at a given combination of

A— altitude and RPM.
B— airspeed and RPM.
C— airspeed and altitude.

39.
5304. Which conditions are favorable for the formation of a surface based temperature inversion?

A— Clear, cool nights with calm or light wind.
B— Area of unstable air rapidly transferring heat from the surface.
C— Broad areas of cumulus clouds with smooth, level bases at the same altitude.

40.
5307. GIVEN:

Pressure altitude . . . . 5,000 ft
True air temperature . . . . +30 °C

From the conditions given, the approximate density altitude is

A— 7,800 feet.
B— 7,200 feet.
C— 9,000 feet.

41.
5321. The general circulation of air associated with a high-pressure area in the Northern Hemisphere is

A— outward, downward, and clockwise.
B— outward, upward, and clockwise.
C— inward, downward, and clockwise.

42.
5338. Which cloud types would indicate convective turbulence?

A— Cirrus clouds.
B— Nimbostratus clouds.
C— Towering cumulus clouds.

43.
5346. Which is a characteristic typical of a stable air mass?

A— Cumuliform clouds.
B— Showery precipitation.
C— Continuous precipitation.

44.
5347. Which is true regarding a cold front occlusion? The air ahead of the warm front

A— is colder than the air behind the overtaking cold front.
B— is warmer than the air behind the overtaking cold front.
C— has the same temperature as the air behind the overtaking cold front.

45.
5350. Fog produced by frontal activity is a result of saturation due to

A— nocturnal cooling.
B— adiabatic cooling.
C— evaporation of precipitation.

46.
5358. During an approach, the most important and most easily recognized means of being alerted to possible wind shear is monitoring the

A— amount of trim required to relieve control pressures.
B— heading changes necessary to remain on the runway centerline.
C— power and vertical velocity required to remain on the proper glidepath.

47.
5361. Which statement is true concerning the hazards of hail?

A— Hail damage in horizontal flight is minimal due to the vertical movement of hail in the clouds.
B— Rain at the surface is a reliable indication of no hail aloft.
C— Hailstones may be encountered in clear air several miles from a thunderstorm.

48.
5368. Select the true statement pertaining to the life cycle of a thunderstorm.

A— Updrafts continue to develop throughout the dissipating stage of a thunderstorm.
B— The beginning of rain at the Earth's surface indicates the mature stage of the thunderstorm.
C— The beginning of rain at the Earth's surface indicates the dissipating stage of the thunderstorm.

49.
5371. What feature is normally associated with the cumulus stage of a thunderstorm?

A— Roll cloud.
B— Continuous updraft.
C— Beginning of rain at the surface.

50.
5388. Which is true regarding the development of convective circulation?

A— Cool air must sink to force the warm air upward.
B— Warm air is less dense and rises on its own accord.
C— Warmer air covers a larger surface area than the cool air; therefore, the warmer air is less dense and rises.

51.
5408. Which is true concerning the radar weather report (SD) for KOKC?

KOKC 1934 LN 8TRW++/+ 86/40 164/60 199/115 15W
L2425 MT 570 AT 159/65 2 INCH HAIL RPRTD THIS CELL

A— There are three cells with tops at 11,500, 40,000, and 60,000 feet.
B— The line of cells is moving 060° with winds reported up to 40 knots.
C— The maximum tops of the cells is 57,000 feet located 65 NM southeast of the station.

52.
5419. The Aviation Weather Center (AWC) prepares FA's for the contiguous U.S.

A— twice each day.
B— three times each day.
C— every 6 hours unless significant changes in weather require it more often.

53.
5424. What values are used for Winds Aloft Forecasts?

A— True direction and MPH.
B— True direction and knots.
C— Magnetic direction and knots.

54.
5433. Which weather chart depicts conditions forecast to exist at a specific time in the future?

A— Freezing Level Chart.
B— Weather Depiction Chart.
C— 12-hour Significant Weather Prognostic Chart.

55.
5442. From which of the following can the observed temperature, wind, and temperature/dewpoint spread be determined at a specified altitude?

A— Stability Charts.
B— Winds Aloft Forecasts.
C— Constant Pressure Analysis Charts.

56.
5446. Turbulence that is encountered above 15,000 feet AGL not associated with cumuliform cloudiness, including thunderstorms, should be reported as

A— severe turbulence.
B— clear air turbulence.
C— convective turbulence.

57.
5447. Which type of jetstream can be expected to cause the greater turbulence?

A— A straight jetstream associated with a low-pressure trough.
B— A curving jetstream associated with a deep low-pressure trough.
C— A jetstream occurring during the summer at the lower latitudes.

58.
5449. The Low Level Wind Shear Alert System (LLWAS) provides wind data and software process to detect the presence of a

A— rotating column of air extending from a cumulonimbus cloud.
B— change in wind direction and/or speed within a very short distance above the airport.
C— downward motion of the air associated with continuous winds blowing with an easterly component due to the rotation of the Earth.

59.
5451. (Refer to figure 8 on page 142.)

GIVEN:

Fuel quantity . . . . 47 gal
Power-cruise (lean) . . . . 55 percent

Approximately how much flight time would be available with a night VFR fuel reserve remaining?

A— 3 hours 8 minutes.
B— 3 hours 22 minutes.
C— 3 hours 43 minutes.

60.
5457. (Refer to figure 9 on page 130.) Using a normal climb, how much fuel would be used from engine start to 10,000 feet pressure altitude?

Aircraft weight . . . . 3,500 lb
Airport pressure altitude . . . . 4,000 ft
Temperature . . . . 21 °C

A— 23 pounds.
B— 31 pounds.
C— 35 pounds.

61.
5460. (Refer to figure 11 on page 136.) If the cruise altitude is 7,500 feet, using 64 percent power at 2,500 RPM, what would be the range with 48 gallons of usable fuel?

A— 635 miles.
B— 645 miles.
C— 810 miles.

62.
5465. (Refer to figure 12 on page 138.)

GIVEN:

Pressure altitude . . . . 18,000 ft
Temperature . . . . –1 °C
Power . . . . 2,200 RPM – 20" MP
Best fuel economy
  usable fuel . . . . 344 lb

What is the approximate flight time available under the given conditions? (Allow for VFR day fuel reserve.)

A— 4 hours 50 minutes.
B— 5 hours 20 minutes.
C— 5 hours 59 minutes.

63.
5466. An airplane descends to an airport under the following conditions:

Cruising altitude . . . . 6,500 ft
Airport elevation . . . . 700 ft
Descends to . . . . 800 ft AGL
Rate of descent . . . . 500 ft/min
Average true airspeed . . . . 110 kts
True course . . . . 335°
Average wind velocity . . . . 060° at 15 kts
Variation . . . . 3° W
Deviation . . . . +2°
Average fuel consumption . . . . 8.5 gal/hr

Determine the approximate time, compass heading, distance, and fuel consumed during the descent.

A— 10 minutes, 348°, 18 NM, 1.4 gallons.
B— 10 minutes, 355°, 17 NM, 2.4 gallons.
C— 12 minutes, 346°, 18 NM, 1.6 gallons.

64.
5473. If an airplane is consuming 14.8 gallons of fuel per hour at a cruising altitude of 7,500 feet and the groundspeed is 167 knots, how much fuel is required to travel 560 NM?

A— 50 gallons.
B— 53 gallons.
C— 57 gallons.

65.
5477. You have flown 52 miles, are 6 miles off course, and have 118 miles yet to fly. To converge on your destination, the total correction angle would be

A— 3°.
B— 6°.
C— 10°.

66.
5479. True course measurements on a Sectional Aeronautical Chart should be made at a meridian near the midpoint of the course because the

A— values of isogonic lines change from point to point.
B— angles formed by isogonic lines and lines of latitude vary from point to point.
C— angles formed by lines of longitude and the course line vary from point to point.

67.
5484. (Refer to figure 14 on page 126.)

GIVEN:

Aircraft weight .... 3,700 lb
Airport pressure altitude .... 4,000 ft
Temperature at 4,000 ft .... 21 °C

Using a normal climb under the given conditions, how much fuel would be used from engine start to a pressure altitude of 12,000 feet?

A— 30 pounds.
B— 37 pounds.
C— 46 pounds.

68.
5493b. The magnetic heading is 315° and the ADF shows a relative bearing of 140°. The magnetic bearing FROM the radiobeacon would be

A— 095°.
B— 175°.
C— 275°.

69.
5497. (Refer to figure 16 on page 238.) If the aircraft continues its present heading as shown in instrument group 3, what will be the relative bearing when the aircraft reaches the magnetic bearing of 030° FROM the NDB?

A— 030°.
B— 060°.
C— 240°.

70.
5506. (Refer to figure 17 on page 244.) Which illustration indicates that the airplane will intercept the 060 radial at a 60° angle inbound, if the present heading is maintained?

A— 6.
B— 4.
C— 5.

71.
5511. (Refer to figure 18 on page 236.) To intercept a magnetic bearing of 240° FROM at a 030° angle (while outbound), the airplane should be turned

A— left 065°.
B— left 125°.
C— right 270°.

72.
5519. The ADF is tuned to a nondirectional radiobeacon and the relative bearing changes from 095° to 100° in 1.5 minutes of elapsed time. The time en route to that station would be

A— 18 minutes.
B— 24 minutes.
C— 30 minutes.

73.
5523. The ADF is tuned to a nondirectional radiobeacon and the relative bearing changes from 090° to 100° in 2.5 minutes of elapsed time. If the true airspeed is 90 knots, the distance and time en route to that radiobeacon would be

A— 15 miles and 22.5 minutes.
B— 22.5 miles and 15 minutes.
C— 32 miles and 18 minutes.

74.
5529. While maintaining a constant heading, the ADF needle increases from a relative bearing of 045° to 090° in 5 minutes. The time to the station being used is

A— 5 minutes.
B— 10 minutes.
C— 15 minutes.

75.
5533. An aircraft 60 miles from a VOR station has a CDI indication of one-fifth deflection, this represents a course centerline deviation of approximately

A— 6 miles.
B— 2 miles.
C— 1 mile.

76.
5534. (Refer to figure 20 on page 242.) Using instrument group 3, if the aircraft makes a 180° turn to the left and continues straight ahead, it will intercept which radial?

A— 135 radial.
B— 270 radial.
C— 360 radial.

77.
5539. While maintaining a magnetic heading of 270° and a true airspeed of 120 knots, the 360 radial of a VOR is crossed at 1237 and the 350 radial is crossed at 1244. The approximate time and distance to this station are

A— 42 minutes and 84 NM.
B— 42 minutes and 91 NM.
C— 44 minutes and 96 NM.

78.
5541. (Refer to figure 22 on page 220.) If the time flown between aircraft positions 2 and 3 is 8 minutes, what is the estimated time to the station?

A— 8 minutes.
B— 16 minutes.
C— 48 minutes.

79.
5560. Weather Advisory Broadcasts, including Severe Weather Forecast Alerts (AWW), Convective SIGMETs, and SIGMETs, are provided by

A—ARTCCs on all frequencies, except emergency, when any part of the area described is within 150 miles of the airspace under their jurisdiction.
B—AFSSs on 122.2 MHz and adjacent VORs, when any part of the area described is within 200 miles of the airspace under their jurisdiction.
C—selected low-frequency and/or VOR navigational aids.

80.
5568. (Refer to figure 52, point 8, on the inside front cover.) The floor of the Class E airspace over the town of Auburn is

A— 1,200 feet MSL.
B— 700 feet AGL.
C— 1,200 feet AGL.

81.
5569. (Refer to figure 53, point 1, on the inside back cover.) This thin black shaded line is most likely

A— an arrival route.
B— a military training route.
C— a state boundary line.

82.
5572. (Refer to figure 54, point 1, on the outside back cover.) What minimum altitude is required to avoid the Livermore Airport (LVK) Class D airspace?

A— 2,503 feet MSL.
B— 2,901 feet MSL.
C— 3,297 feet MSL.

83.
5606. Applying carburetor heat will

A— not affect the mixture.
B— lean the fuel/air mixture.
C— enrich the fuel/air mixture.

84.
5608. What will occur if no leaning is made with the mixture control as the flight altitude increases?

A— The volume of air entering the carburetor decreases and the amount of fuel decreases.
B— The density of air entering the carburetor decreases and the amount of fuel increases.
C— The density of air entering the carburetor decreases and the amount of fuel remains constant.

85.
5615. (Refer to figure 31 on page 144.) Rwy 30 is being used for landing. Which surface wind would exceed the airplane's crosswind capability of 0.2 V_{so}, if V_{so} is 60 knots?

A— 260° at 20 knots.
B— 275° at 25 knots.
C— 315° at 35 knots.

86.
5621. (Refer to figure 32 on page 123.)

GIVEN:

Temperature . . . . 100 °F
Pressure altitude . . . . 4,000 ft
Weight . . . . 3,200 lb
Wind . . . . Calm

What is the ground roll required for takeoff over a 50-foot obstacle?

A— 1,180 feet.
B— 1,350 feet.
C— 1,850 feet.

87.
5631. (Refer to figure 35 on page 146.)

GIVEN:

Temperature . . . . 80 °F
Pressure altitude . . . . 4,000 ft
Weight . . . . 2,800 lb
Headwind . . . . 24 kts

What is the total landing distance over a 50-foot obstacle?

A— 1,125 feet.
B— 1,250 feet.
C— 1,325 feet.

88.

5635. The CG of an aircraft may be determined by

A— dividing total arms by total moments.
B— dividing total moments by total weight.
C— multiplying total weight by total moments.

89.

5643. GIVEN:

	WEIGHT	ARM	MOMENT
Empty weight	957	29.07	?
Pilot (fwd seat)	140	−45.30	?
Passenger (aft seat)	170	+1.60	?
Ballast	15	−45.30	?
TOTALS	?	?	?

The CG is located at station

A— −6.43.
B— +16.43.
C— +27.38.

90.

5648. An airplane is loaded to a gross weight of 4,800 pounds, with three pieces of luggage in the rear baggage compartment. The CG is located 98 inches aft of datum, which is 1 inch aft of limits. If luggage which weighs 90 pounds is moved from the rear baggage compartment (145 inches aft of datum) to the front compartment (45 inches aft of datum), what is the new CG?

A— 96.13 inches aft of datum.
B— 95.50 inches aft of datum.
C— 99.87 inches aft of datum.

91.

5650. (Refer to figure 38 on page 150.)

GIVEN:

Empty weight (oil is included)	1,271 lb
Empty weight moment (in-lb/1,000)	102.04
Pilot and copilot	400 lb
Rear seat passenger	140 lb
Cargo	100 lb
Fuel	37 gal

Is the airplane loaded within limits?

A— Yes, the weight and CG is within limits.
B— No, the weight exceeds the maximum allowable.
C— No, the weight is acceptable, but the CG is aft of the aft limit.

92.

5657. (Refer to figure 51 on page 65.) The pilot generally calls ground control after landing when the aircraft is completely clear of the runway. This is when you

A— pass the red symbol shown at the top of the figure.
B— are on the dashed-line side of the middle symbol.
C— are on the solid-line side of the middle symbol.

93.

5661. With regard to the technique required for a crosswind correction on takeoff, a pilot should use

A— aileron pressure into the wind and initiate the lift-off at a normal airspeed in both tailwheel- and nosewheel-type airplanes.
B— right rudder pressure, aileron pressure into the wind, and higher than normal lift-off airspeed in both tricycle- and conventional-gear airplanes.
C— rudder as required to maintain directional control, aileron pressure into the wind, and higher than normal lift-off airspeed in both conventional- and nosewheel-type airplanes.

94.

5663. A pilot's most immediate and vital concern in the event of complete engine failure after becoming airborne on takeoff is

A— maintaining a safe airspeed.
B— landing directly into the wind.
C— turning back to the takeoff field.

95.

5670. If severe turbulence is encountered during flight, the pilot should reduce the airspeed to

A— minimum control speed.
B— design-maneuvering speed.
C— maximum structural cruising speed.

96.

5749. When in the vicinity of a VOR which is being used for navigation on VFR flight, it is important to

A— make 90° left and right turns to scan for other traffic.
B— exercise sustained vigilance to avoid aircraft that may be converging on the VOR from other directions.
C— pass the VOR on the right side of the radial to allow room for aircraft flying in the opposite direction on the same radial.

97.
5752. Which procedure should you follow to avoid wake turbulence if a large jet crosses your course from left to right approximately 1 mile ahead and at your altitude?

A— Make sure you are slightly above the path of the jet.
B— Slow your airspeed to V_A and maintain altitude and course.
C— Make sure you are slightly below the path of the jet and perpendicular to the course.

98.
5757. As hyperventilation progresses a pilot can experience

A— decreased breathing rate and depth.
B— heightened awareness and feeling of well-being.
C— symptoms of suffocation and drowsiness.

99.
5764. Hypoxia susceptibility due to inhalation of carbon monoxide increases as

A— humidity decreases.
B— altitude increases.
C— oxygen demand increases.

100.
5766. During preflight in cold weather, crankcase breather lines should receive special attention because they are susceptible to being clogged by

A— congealed oil from the crankcase.
B— moisture from the outside air which has frozen.
C— ice from crankcase vapors that have condensed and subsequently frozen.

For additional practice tests, use **FAA Test Prep** software. Call (800) 87-GLEIM to order. Our CD-ROM version costs $59.95 and includes all questions, outlines, and figures for the test. The software has the following advantages:

1. You cannot cheat (yourself) when taking practice tests.

2. You can make up as many tests as you desire, and you can have the software rearrange the question sequence and answer order.

3. The questions on each test are randomly selected from the FAA's actual test questions so that the coverage of topics (weather, FARs, etc.) is the same as on actual FAA tests.

The software also emulates AvTEST, CATS, and LaserGrade to help you understand exactly what will occur at your pilot knowledge test.

PRACTICE TEST LIST OF ANSWERS

Q. #	Answer	Page	Q. #	Answer	Page	Q. #	Answer	Page	Q. #	Answer	Page
1.	C	106	26.	A	50	51.	C	199	76.	A	243
2.	B	80	27.	B	48	52.	B	202	77.	A	222
3.	C	81	28.	B	27	53.	B	206	78.	A	220
4.	C	82	29.	B	34	54.	C	204	79.	A	198
5.	A	86	30.	C	26	55.	C	201	80.	B	214
6.	B	96	31.	B	31	56.	B	188	81.	B	215
7.	A	101	32.	A	33	57.	B	176	82.	B	216
8.	B	99	33.	C	29	58.	B	190	83.	C	47
9.	A	90	34.	B	24	59.	B	143	84.	C	49
10.	B	93	35.	C	25	60.	C	131	85.	A	145
11.	B	95	36.	C	28	61.	C	137	86.	B	123
12.	C	102	37.	A	45	62.	C	139	87.	A	147
13.	C	105	38.	B	53	63.	A	229	88.	B	149
14.	A	104	39.	A	180	64.	A	217	89.	B	152
15.	C	92	40.	A	120	65.	C	227	90.	A	154
16.	A	95	41.	A	175	66.	C	213	91.	A	151
17.	B	97	42.	C	177	67.	C	127	92.	C	64
18.	B	96	43.	C	181	68.	C	235	93.	C	250
19.	A	87	44.	B	173	69.	C	239	94.	A	251
20.	C	83	45.	C	178	70.	A	245	95.	B	252
21.	B	35	46.	C	189	71.	B	236	96.	B	67
22.	A	32	47.	C	186	72.	A	223	97.	A	68
23.	B	37	48.	B	185	73.	B	225	98.	C	160
24.	B	52	49.	B	184	74.	A	224	99.	B	159
25.	B	44	50.	A	182	75.	B	240	100.	C	252

FAA LISTING OF SUBJECT MATTER KNOWLEDGE CODES

Pages 267 through 270 reprint the FAA's subject matter knowledge codes. These are the codes that will appear on your Airman Computer Test Report. See the illustration on page 10. Your test report will list the subject matter knowledge code of each question answered incorrectly in that subject area. To determine the knowledge area in which a particular question was incorrectly answered, compare the subject matter code(s) on your Airman Computer Test Report to the subject matter outline that follows.

When you receive your Airman Computer Test Report, you can trace the subject matter knowledge codes listed on it to the following pages to find out which topics you had difficulty with. You should discuss your test results with your CFI.

Additionally, you should cross-reference the subject matter knowledge codes on your Airman Computer Test Report to our listing of FAA commercial pilot test question numbers beginning on page 273. Determine which Gleim study modules you need to review.

The total number of test items missed may differ from the number of subject matter codes shown on the test report, since you may have missed more than one question in a certain subject matter code.

Title 14, Code of Federal Regulations (14 CFR) PART 1—Definitions and Abbreviations

A01 General Definitions
A02 Abbreviations and Symbols

14 CFR PART 23—Airworthiness Standards: Normal, Utility, Acrobatic, and Commuter Category Aircraft

A150 General
A151 Flight
A152 Structure
A153 Design and Construction
A154 Powerplant
A155 Equipment
A157 Operating Limitations and Information
A159 Appendix G: Instructions for Continued Airworthiness

14 CFR PART 61—Certification: Pilots, Flight Instructors, and Ground Instructors

A20 General
A21 Aircraft Ratings and Pilot Authorizations
A22 Student Pilots
A23 Private Pilots
A24 Commercial Pilots
A25 Airline Transport Pilots
A26 Flight Instructors
A27 Ground Instructors
A29 Recreational Pilot

14 CFR PART 71—Designation of Class A, Class B, Class C, Class D, and Class E Airspace Areas; Airways; Routes; and Reporting Points

A60 General - Class A Airspace
A61 Class B Airspace
A64 Class C Airspace
A65 Class D Airspace
A66 Class E Airspace

14 CFR PART 91—General Operating and Flight Rules

B07 General
B08 Flight Rules - General
B09 Visual Flight Rules
B10 Instrument Flight Rules
B11 Equipment, Instrument, and Certificate Requirements
B12 Special Flight Operations
B13 Maintenance, Preventive Maintenance, and Alterations
B14 Large and Turbine-powered Multiengine Airplanes
B15 Additional Equipment and Operating Requirements for Large and Transport Category Aircraft
B16 Appendix A - Category II Operations: Manual, Instruments, Equipment, and Maintenance
B17 Foreign Aircraft Operations and Operations of U.S.-Registered Civil Aircraft Outside of the U.S.

NTSB 830—Rules Pertaining to the Notification and Reporting of Aircraft Accidents or Incidents and Overdue Aircraft, and Preservation of Aircraft Wreckage, Mail, Cargo, and Records

G10 General
G11 Initial Notification of Aircraft Accidents, Incidents, and Overdue Aircraft
G12 Preservation of Aircraft Wreckage, Mail, Cargo, and Records
G13 Reporting of Aircraft Accidents, Incidents, and Overdue Aircraft

FAA-H-8083-1—Aircraft Weight and Balance Handbook

H100 Why is Weight and Balance Important?
H101 Weight Control
H102 Effects of Weight
H103 Weight Changes

H104	Stability and Balance Control	H323	Moisture and Temperature
H105	Weight and Balance Theory	H324	Air Masses and Fronts
H106	Weight and Balance Documents	H325	Aviation Weather Reports, Forecasts, and
H107	Requirements		Weather Charts
H108	Equipment for Weighing	H326	Types of Airports
H109	Preparation for Weighing	H327	Sources for Airport Data
H110	Determining the Center of Gravity	H328	Airport Markings and Signs
H111	Empty-Weight Center of Gravity Formulas	H329	Airport Lighting
H112	Determining the Loaded Weight and CG	H330	Wind Direction Indicators
H113	Multiengine Airplane Weight and Balance	H331	Radio Communications
	Computations	H332	Air Traffic Services
H114	Determining the Loaded CG	H333	Wake Turbulence
H115	Equipment List	H334	Collision Avoidance
H116	Weight and Balance Revision Record	H335	Controlled Airspace
H117	Weight Changes Caused by a Repair or	H336	Uncontrolled Airspace
	Alteration	H337	Special Use Airspace
H118	Empty-Weight CG Range	H338	Other Airspace Areas
H119	Adverse-Loaded CG Checks	H339	Aeronautical Charts
H120	Ballast	H340	Latitude and Longitude
H121	Weighing Requirements	H341	Effect of Wind
H122	Locating and Monitoring Weight and CG	H342	Basic Calculations
	Location	H343	Pilotage
H123	Determining the Correct Stabilizer Trim Setting	H344	Dead Reckoning
H124	Determining CG Changes Caused by Modifying	H345	Flight Planning
	the Cargo	H346	Charting the Course
H125	Determining Cargo Pallet Loads with Regard to	H347	Filing a VFR Flight Plan
	Floor Loading Limits	H348	Radio Navigation
H126	Determining the Maximum Amount of Payload	H349	Obtaining a Medical Certificate
	That Can Be Carried	H350	Health Factors Affecting Pilot Performance
H127	Determining the Landing Weight	H351	Environmental Factors which Affect Pilot
H128	Determining the Minutes of Fuel Dump Time		Performance
H129	Weight and Balance of Commuter Category		
	Airplanes	**FAA-H-8083-3—Airplane Flying Handbook**	
H130	Determining the Loaded CG of a Helicopter		
H131	Using an Electronic Calculator to Solve Weight	H501	Choosing a Flight School
	and Balance Problems	H502	Instructor/Student Relationship
H132	Using an E6-B Flight Computer to Solve Weight	H503	Role of the FAA
	and Balance Problems	H504	Flight Standards District Offices (FSDO's)
H133	Using a Dedicated Electronic Computer to Solve	H505	Study Habits
	Weight and Balance Problems	H506	Study Materials
H134	Typical Weight and Balance Problems	H507	Collision Avoidance
H135	Glossary	H509	Pilot Assessment
		H510	Preflight Preparation and Flight Planning
AC 61-23—Pilot's Handbook of Aeronautical		H511	Airplane Preflight Inspection
Knowledge		H512	Minimum Equipment Lists (MEL's) and
			Operations with Inoperative Equipment
H300	Forces Acting on the Airplane in Flight	H513	Cockpit Management
H301	Turning Tendency (Torque Effect)	H514	Use of Checklists
H302	Airplane Stability	H515	Ground Operations
H303	Loads and Load Factors	H516	Taxiing
H304	Airplane Structure	H517	Taxi Clearances at Airports with an Operating
H305	Flight Control Systems		Control Tower
H306	Electrical System	H518	Before Takeoff Check
H307	Engine Operation	H519	After-landing
H308	Propeller	H520	Postflight
H309	Starting the Engine	H522	Terms and Definitions
H310	Exhaust Gas Temperature Gauge	H523	Prior to Takeoff
H311	Aircraft Documents, Maintenance, and	H524	Normal Takeoff
	Inspections	H525	Crosswind Takeoff
H312	The Pitot-Static System and Associated	H526	Short-field Takeoff and Climb
	Instruments	H527	Soft-field Takeoff and Climb
H313	Gyroscopic Flight Instruments	H528	Rejected Takeoff
H314	Magnetic Compass	H529	Noise Abatement
H315	Weight Control	H531	Integrated Flight Instruction
H316	Balance, Stability, and Center of Gravity	H532	Attitude Flying
H317	Airplane Performance	H533	Straight-and-level Flight
H318	Observations	H534	Turns
H319	Service Outlets	H535	Climbs
H320	Weather Briefings	H536	Descents
H321	Nature of the Atmosphere	H538	Slow Flight
H322	The Cause of Atmospheric Circulation	H539	Stalls

H540	Spins
H541	Spin Procedures
H542	Aircraft Limitations
H543	Weight and Balance Requirements
H545	Maneuvering by Reference to Ground Objects
H546	Performance Maneuvers
H548	Airport Traffic Patterns and Operations
H549	Normal Approach and Landing
H550	Crosswind Approach and Landing
H551	Short-field Approach and Landing
H552	Soft-field Approach and Landing
H553	Power-off Accuracy Approaches
H554	Faulty Approaches and Landings
H555	Final Approaches
H556	Roundout (Flare)
H557	Touchdown
H559	Basic Instrument Training
H560	Basic Instrument Flight
H561	Use of Navigation Systems
H562	Use of Radar Services
H564	Night Vision
H565	Night Illusions
H566	Pilot Equipment
H567	Airplane Equipment and Lighting
H568	Airport and Navigation Lighting Aids
H569	Preparation and Preflight
H570	Starting, Taxiing, and Runup
H571	Takeoff and Climb
H572	Orientation and Navigation
H573	Approaches and Landing
H574	Night Emergencies
H576	VOR Navigation
H577	VOR/DME RNAV
H578	LORAN-C Navigation
H579	Global Positioning System (GPS)
H580	Radar Services
H582	Systems and Equipment Malfunctions
H583	Emergency Approaches and Landings (Actual)
H585	Airplane Systems
H586	Pressurized Airplanes
H587	Oxygen Systems
H588	Physiological Altitude Limits
H589	Regulatory Requirements
H591	Multiengine Performance Characteristics
H592	The Critical Engine
H593	Vmc for Certification
H594	Performance
H595	Factors in Takeoff Planning
H596	Accelerates/Stop Distance
H597	Propeller Feathering
H598	Use of Trim Tabs
H599	Preflight Preparation
H600	Checklist
H601	Taxiing
H602	Normal Takeoffs
H603	Crosswind Takeoffs
H604	Short-field or Obstacle Clearance Takeoff
H605	Stalls
H606	Emergency Descent
H607	Approaches and Landings
H608	Crosswind Landings
H609	Short-field Landing
H610	Go-around Procedure
H611	Engine Inoperative Emergencies
H612	Engine Inoperative Procedures
H613	Vmc Demonstrations
H614	Engine Failure Before Lift-off (Rejected Takeoff)
H615	Engine Failure After Lift-off
H616	Engine Failure En Route

H617	Engine Inoperative Approach and Landing
H618	Types of Decisions
H619	Effectiveness of ADM

AC 61-27—Instrument Flying Handbook

I01	Training Considerations
I02	Instrument Flying: Coping with Illusions in Flight
I03	Aerodynamic Factors Related to Instrument Flying
I04	Basic Flight Instruments
I05	Attitude Instrument Flying — Airplanes
I06	Attitude Instrument Flying — Helicopters
I07	Electronic Aids to Instrument Flying
I08	Using the Navigation Instruments
I09	Radio Communications Facilities and Equipment
I10	The Federal Airways System and Controlled Airspace
I11	Air Traffic Control
I12	ATC Operations and Procedures
I13	Flight Planning
I14	Appendix: Instrument Instructor Lesson Guide — Airplanes
I15	Segment of En Route Low Altitude Chart

AC 00-6—Aviation Weather

I20	The Earth's Atmosphere
I21	Temperature
I22	Atmospheric Pressure and Altimetry
I23	Wind
I24	Moisture, Cloud Formation, and Precipitation
I25	Stable and Unstable Air
I26	Clouds
I27	Air Masses and Fronts
I28	Turbulence
I29	Icing
I30	Thunderstorms
I31	Common IFR Producers
I32	High Altitude Weather
I33	Arctic Weather
I34	Tropical Weather
I35	Soaring Weather
I36	Glossary of Weather Terms

AC 00-45—Aviation Weather Services

I54	The Aviation Weather Service Program
I55	Aviation Routine Weather Report (METAR)
I56	Pilot and Radar Reports, Satellite Pictures, and Radiosonde Additional Data (RADATs)
I57	Aviation Weather Forecasts
I58	Surface Analysis Chart
I59	Weather Depiction Chart
I60	Radar Summary Chart
I61	Constant Pressure Analysis Charts
I62	Composite Moisture Stability Chart
I63	Winds and Temperatures Aloft Chart
I64	Significant Weather Prognostic Charts
I65	Convective Outlook Chart
I66	Volcanic Ash Advisory Center Products
I67	Turbulence Locations, Conversion and Density Altitude Tables, Contractions and Acronyms, Station Identifiers, WSR-88D Sites, and Internet Addresses

AIM—Aeronautical Information Manual

J01	Air Navigation Radio Aids
J02	Radar Services and Procedures
J03	Airport Lighting Aids
J04	Air Navigation and Obstruction Lighting

J05	Airport Marking Aids and Signs	K47	AC 43.9-1, Instructions for Completion of FAA Form 337
J06	Airspace — General	K48	AC 43-11, Reciprocating Engine Overhaul Terminology and Standards
J07	Class G Airspace		
J08	Controlled Airspace	K49	AC 43.13-1, Acceptable Methods, Techniques, and Practices - Aircraft Inspection and Repair
J09	Special Use Airspace		
J10	Other Airspace Areas	K50	AC 43.13-2, Acceptable Methods, Techniques, and Practices - Aircraft Alterations
J11	Service Available to Pilots		
J12	Radio Communications Phraseology and Techniques	K80	AC 60-4, Pilot's Spatial Disorientation
		L05	AC 60-22, Aeronautical Decision Making
J13	Airport Operations	L10	AC 61-67, Stall and Spin Awareness Training
J14	ATC Clearance/Separations	L15	AC 61-107, Operations of Aircraft at Altitudes Above 25,000 Feet MSL and/or MACH numbers (Mmo) Greater Than .75
J15	Preflight		
J16	Departure Procedures		
J17	En Route Procedures		
J18	Arrival Procedures	L25	FAA-G-8082-11, Inspection Authorization Knowledge Test Guide
J19	Pilot/Controller Roles and Responsibilities		
J20	National Security and Interception Procedures	L34	AC 90-48, Pilots' Role in Collision Avoidance
J21	Emergency Procedures — General	L42	AC 90-87, Helicopter Dynamic Rollover
J22	Emergency Services Available to Pilots	L44	AC 90-94, Guidelines for Using Global Positioning System Equipment for IFR En Route and Terminal Operations and for Nonprecision Instrument Approaches in the U.S. National Airspace System
J23	Distress and Urgency Procedures		
J24	Two-Way Radio Communications Failure		
J25	Meteorology		
J26	Altimeter Setting Procedures		
J27	Wake Turbulence	L50	AC 91-6, Water, Slush, and Snow on the Runway
J28	Bird Hazards, and Flight Over National Refuges, Parks, and Forests	L52	AC 91-13, Cold Weather Operation of Aircraft
		L53	AC 91-14, Altimeter Setting Sources
J29	Potential Flight Hazards	L57	AC 91-43, Unreliable Airspeed Indications
J30	Safety, Accident, and Hazard Reports	L59	AC 91-46, Gyroscopic Instruments — Good Operating Practices
J31	Fitness for Flight		
J32	Type of Charts Available	L61	AC 91-50, Importance of Transponder Operation and Altitude Reporting
J33	Pilot Controller Glossary		

Other Documents

		L62	AC 91-51, Effect of Icing on Aircraft Control and Airplane Deice and Anti-Ice Systems
J34	Airport/Facility Directory		
J35	En Route Low Altitude Chart	L70	AC 91-67, Minimum Equipment Requirements for General Aviation Operations Under FAR Part 91
J36	En Route High Altitude Chart		
J37	Sectional Chart	L80	AC 103-4, Hazard Associated with Sublimation of Solid Carbon Dioxide (Dry Ice) Aboard Aircraft
J39	Terminal Area Chart		
J40	Instrument Departure Procedure Chart	L90	AC 105-2, Sport Parachute Jumping
J41	Standard Terminal Arrival (STAR) Chart	M01	AC 120-12, Private Carriage Versus Common Carriage of Persons or Property
J42	Instrument Approach Procedures		
J43	Helicopter Route Chart	M02	AC 120-27, Aircraft Weight and Balance Control
		M08	AC 120-58, Pilot Guide — Large Aircraft Ground Deicing

ADDITIONAL ADVISORY CIRCULARS

		M13	AC 121-195-1, Operational Landing Distances for Wet Runways; Transport Category Airplanes
K01	AC 00-24, Thunderstorms		
K02	AC 00-30, Atmospheric Turbulence Avoidance	M35	AC 135-17, Pilot Guide — Small Aircraft Ground Deicing
K03	AC 00-34, Aircraft Ground Handling and Servicing		
K04	AC 00-54, Pilot Wind Shear Guide	M51	AC 20-117, Hazards Following Ground Deicing and Ground Operations in Conditions Conducive to Aircraft Icing
K05	AC 00-55, Announcement of Availability: FAA Order 8130.21A		
K06	AC 43-4, Corrosion Control for Aircraft	M52	AC 00-2, Advisory Circular Checklist
K11	AC 20-34, Preventions of Retractable Landing Gear Failure		
K12	AC 20-32, Carbon Monoxide (CO) Contamination in Aircraft — Detection and Prevention		
K13	AC 20-43, Aircraft Fuel Control		
K20	AC 20-103, Aircraft Engine Crankshaft Failure		
K23	AC 20-121, Airworthiness Approval of Airborne Loran C Systems for Use in the U.S. National Airspace System		

NOTE: AC 00-2, Advisory Circular Checklist, transmits the status of all FAA advisory circulars (AC's), as well as FAA internal publications and miscellaneous flight information such as Aeronautical Information Manual, Airport/Facility Directory, knowledge test guides, practical test standards, and other material directly related to a certificate or rating. To obtain a free copy of AC 00-2, send your request to:

K26	AC 20-138, Airworthiness Approval of Global Positioning System (GPS) Navigation Equipment for Use as a VFR and IFR Supplemental Navigation System

U.S. Department of Transportation
Subsequent Distribution Office, SVC-121.23
Ardmore East Business Center
3341 Q 75th Ave.
Landover, MD 20785

K40	AC 25-4, Inertial Navigation System (INS)
K45	AC 39-7, Airworthiness Directives
K46	AC 43-9, Maintenance Records

FOR CHOOSING GLEIM

We dedicate ourselves to providing pilots with knowledge transfer systems, enabling them to pass the FAA knowledge (written) tests and FAA practical (flight) tests. We solicit your feedback. Use the last page in this book to make notes as you use *Commercial Pilot FAA Written Exam* and other Gleim products. Tear out the page and mail it to us when convenient. Alternatively, e-mail (irvin@gleim.com) or FAX (352-375-6940) your feedback to us.

GLEIM'S E-MAIL UPDATE SERVICE

update@gleim.com

Your message to Gleim must include (in the subject or body) the acronym for your book or software, followed by the edition-printing for books and version for software. The edition-printing is indicated on the book's spine and at the bottom right corner of the cover. The software version is indicated on the CD-ROM label.

	Written Exam		Flight Maneuvers
	Book	Software	Book
Private Pilot	PPWE	FAATP PP	PPFM
Instrument Pilot	IPWE	FAATP IP	IPFM
Commercial Pilot	CPWE	FAATP CP	CPFM
Flight/Ground Instructor	FIGI	FAATP FIGI	FIFM
Fundamentals of Instructing	FOI	FAATP FOI	
Airline Transport Pilot	ATP	FAATP ATP	
Flight Engineer	FEWE	FAATP FEWE	

	Reference Book
Pilot Handbook	PH
Aviation Weather and Weather Services	AWWS
Private Pilot Syllabus and Logbook	PPSYL
Instrument Pilot Syllabus	IPSYL
Commercial Pilot Syllabus	CPSYL
FAR/AIM	FARAIM

For **Commercial Pilot FAA Written Exam**, seventh edition-sixth printing:

E X A M P L E

```
To:      update@gleim.com
From:    your e-mail address
Subject: CPWE 7-6
```

For **FAA Test Prep** software, Commercial Pilot, version 4.0:

```
To:      update@gleim.com
From:    your e-mail address
Subject: FAATP CP 4-0
```

IT ONLY TAKES A MINUTE

If you do not have e-mail, have a friend send e-mail to us and print our response for you.

272   *Blank Page*

CROSS-REFERENCES TO
THE FAA PILOT KNOWLEDGE TEST
QUESTION NUMBERS

Pages 273 through 281 contain the FAA commercial pilot question numbers from the commercial pilot knowledge test bank. The questions are numbered 5001 to 0601-577. To the right of each FAA question number*, we have added the FAA's subject matter knowledge code. To the right of the subject matter knowledge code, we have listed our answer and our chapter and question number. For example, the FAA's question 5001 is cross-referenced to the FAA's subject matter knowledge code G10, NTSB Part 830, General. The correct answer is C, and the question appears with answer explanations in our book under 4-110, which means it is reproduced in Chapter 4 as question 110. Non-airplane questions (omitted from this book) are indicated as NA.

The first line of each of our answer explanations in Chapters 1 through 11 contains

1. The correct answer
2. The FAA question number
3. A reference for the answer explanation, e.g., *FTH Chap 1*. If this reference is not practical, use the following chart to identify the subject matter knowledge code to determine which reference is appropriate for the question.

Thus, our question numbers are cross-referenced throughout this book to the FAA question numbers, and this list cross-references the FAA question numbers back to this book.

FAA Q. No.	FAA Subject Code	Gleim Answer	Gleim Chap/ Q. No.	FAA Q. No.	FAA Subject Code	Gleim Answer	Gleim Chap/ Q. No.	FAA Q. No.	FAA Subject Code	Gleim Answer	Gleim Chap/ Q. No.
5001	G10	C	4-110	5021	A20	A	4-12	5044	B07	C	4-31
5002	G11	C	4-105	5022	A20	A	4-13	5045	B07	B	4-33
5003a.	G11	A	4-106	5023	A20	B	4-14	5046	B07	B	4-34
5003b.	G11	C	4-107	5024	A20	C	4-15	5047	B07	A	4-35
5004a.	G11	A	4-108	5025	A20	C	4-18	5048	B08	NA	
5004b.	G11	C	4-109	5026	A20	C	4-19	5049a.	B08	B	4-39
5005	G11	C	4-111	5027	A20	C	4-22	5049b.	B08	B	4-40
5006	G11	A	4-104	5028	A20	C	4-23	5050a.	B08	C	4-41
5007	G13	C	4-113	5029	A20	NA		5050b.	B08	C	4-42
5008	G13	C	4-112	5030	A20	NA		5051a.	B07	B	4-43
5009	J08	B	3-15	5031	A20	A	4-21	5051b.	B08	C	4-44
5010	A01	C	4-1	5032	A20	A	4-25	5052	B08	B	4-45
5011	A01	C	4-3	5033	A21	B	4-27	5053	B12	NA	
5012	A01	C	4-2	5034	A21	B	4-26	5054	B12	NA	
5013	A02	B	4-4	5035a.	A22	NA		5055	B12	B	4-86
5014	A02	A	4-5	5035b.	A22	NA		5056a.	B07	C	4-36
5015a	A02	A	4-6	5036	A22	NA		5056b.	B07	A	4-37
5015b	A02	A	4-6a	5037	A20	NA		5057	B07	NA	
5016a.	A02	A	4-7	5038	A20	NA		5058	B09	NA	
5016b.	A02	B	4-7a.	5039	A24	C	4-28	5059	B10	B	4-63
5016c.	A02	C	4-7b.	5040	A26	NA		5060	B11	A	4-83
5017	A150	C	4-8	5041	A26	NA		5061	B11	A	4-84
5018	A20	B	4-9	5042	A26	NA		5062	B10	A	4-67
5019	A20	C	4-10	5043	A66	B	3-19	5063	B11	C	4-82
5020	A20	A	4-11								

*In June 2001, the FAA test bank was released without the familiar four-digit FAA question numbers. We identified all of the new questions and added them to the end of our cross-reference chart using our own question numbering system. The first four digits of this code refer to the month and year the question first appeared. The remaining digits identify the question number used in that particular FAA test bank release.

FAA Q. No.	FAA Subject Code	Gleim Answer	Gleim Chap/Q. No.
5064	B11	C	4-81
5065	B11	A	4-76
5066	B11	B	4-75
5067a.	B11	NA	
5067b.	B11	B	4-77
5068a.	B12	NA	
5068b.	B12	C	4-87
5068c.	B12	B	4-90
5069	B12	A	4-88
5070	B11	C	4-78
5071	B07	A	4-38
5072a.	B11	NA	
5072b.	B11	A	3-5
5073a.	B08	C	4-48
5073b.	B08	A	4-49
5073c.	B08	A	4-50
5074	B08	A	4-56
5075	B08	B	4-53
5076a.	B08	C	4-54
5076b.	B08	A	4-55
5076c.	B08	B	4-51
5076d.	B08	A	4-52
5077	B08	B	3-7
5078	B08	B	3-8
5079	B12	A	4-85
5080a.	B11	A	4-79
5080b.	B11	C	4-80
5080c.	B11	NA	
5080d.	B11	NA	
5081	B11	NA	
5082a.	B08	B	3-3
5082b.	B08	B	3-4
5082c.	B08	A	3-6
5083	B08	B	4-61
5084	B08	NA	
5085	B08	B	4-60
5086	B08	NA	
5087	B08	NA	
5088	B09	A	3-13
5089	B09	B	3-12
5090	B09	C	3-14
5091	B09	B	4-62
5092	B10	C	4-72
5093	B13	C	4-92
5094	B13	C	4-91
5095	B13	B	4-93
5096	B13	A	4-94
5097	B13	B	4-95
5098	B13	B	4-101
5099	B13	C	4-97
5100	B13	B	4-96
5101	B13	C	4-99
5102	B13	C	4-100
5103	B13	B	4-102
5104	B13	C	4-103
5105	B13	A	4-98
5106	A20	C	4-16
5107	A20	C	4-24
5108	A20	C	4-20
5109	B07	B	4-32
5110a.	B08	B	4-46
5110b.	B08	NA	
5111	B08	C	4-47
5112	B08	B	3-9
5113a.	B08	NA	
5113b.	B08	NA	
5114	B08	B	4-57
5115	B08	C	4-58
5116a.	B08	A	3-18
5116b.	B08	NA	
5117	B08	C	3-17
5118	B08	C	3-16
5119a.	B08	B	3-10
5119b.	B08	A	3-11
5120a.	B08	B	3-1
5120b.	B08	B	3-2
5121	B08	A	4-59
5122a.	B10	C	4-66
5122b.	B10	B	4-68
5123a.	B10	B	4-64
5123b.	B10	B	4-65
5124a.	B10	A	4-70
5124b.	B10	A	4-69
5124c.	B10	A	4-71
5125a.	B10	B	4-73
5125b.	B10	B	4-74
5126a.	A24	A	4-29
5126b.	A24	B	4-30
5127	A20	NA	
5128	A20	C	4-17
5129	B12	C	4-89
5130	NA		
5131	A24	NA	
5132	A24	NA	
5133	H568	A	11-18
5134	NA		
5135	NA		
5136	NA		
5137	NA		
5138	NA		
5139	NA		
5140	NA		
5141	A20	B	4-10a.
5142	A20	C	4-10b.
5143	A20	C	4-10c.
5144	A20	C	4-10d.
5145	NA		
5146	NA		
5147	NA		
5148	NA		
5149	NA		
5150	NA		
5151	H303	A	1-53
5152	H303	A	1-54
5153	H303	A	1-55
5154	H303	B	1-56
5155	H303	A	1-12
5156	H303	B	1-57
5157	H303	B	1-49
5158	H300	A	1-34
5159	H303	A	1-46
5160	H303	B	1-8
5161	H300	C	1-24
5162	H300	B	1-25
5163	H303	C	1-58
5164	H303	B	1-59
5165	H300	A	1-32
5166	H300	B	1-33
5167	H300	B	1-17

FAA Q. No.	FAA Subject Code	Gleim Answer	Gleim Chap/ Q. No.	FAA Q. No.	FAA Subject Code	Gleim Answer	Gleim Chap/ Q. No.	FAA Q. No.	FAA Subject Code	Gleim Answer	Gleim Chap/ Q. No.
5168	H307	NA		5210	H317	C	1-45	5253	H706	NA	
5169	H307	B	2-29	5211	H303	C	1-10	5254	H707	NA	
5170	H307	C	2-24	5212	H300	A	1-11	5255	H706	NA	
5171	H307	A	2-30	5213	H66	B	1-29	5256	H706	NA	
5172	H307	A	2-12	5214	H66	C	1-30	5257	H709	NA	
5173	H307	C	2-31	5215	H66	C	1-31	5258	H720	NA	
5174	H307	C	2-33	5216	H317	A	1-39	5259	H720	NA	
5175	H307	B	2-34	5217	H300	B	1-26	5260	H720	NA	
5176	H307	C	2-17	5218	H300	C	1-20	5261	H745	NA	
5177	H312	C	2-7	5219	H300	B	1-23	5262	H745	NA	
5178	H312	B	2-1	5220	H300	C	1-21	5263	H745	NA	
5179	H303	C	1-14	5221	H303	C	1-61	5264	H709	NA	
5180	H303	A	1-15	5222	H303	C	1-60	5265	H708	NA	
5181	H305	B	1-2	5223	H66	C	1-18	5266	H749	NA	
5182	H305	B	1-1	5224	H66	A	1-38	5267	H739	NA	
5183	H308	C	2-40	5225	H66	A	1-19	5268	I04	C	2-11
5184	H308	B	2-44	5226	H302	A	1-40	5269	I04	A	2-10
5185a.	H308	A	2-28	5227	H302	B	1-42	5270	I05	B	1-52
5185b.	H307	C	2-26	5228	H302	B	1-41	5271	K20	A	2-32
5186	H307	C	2-27	5229	H66	B	1-22	5272	L34	C	3-26
5187	H307	B	2-18	5230	H302	B	1-43	5273	N22	NA	
5188	H307	A	2-20	5231	H66	B	2-4	5274	N22	NA	
5189	H307	A	2-22	5232	H66	A	2-5	5275	N22	NA	
5190	H51	C	2-25	5233	H317	A	2-6	5276	N20	NA	
5191	H532	C	11-1	5234	H317	A	5-1	5277	N20	NA	
5192	H534	C	1-47	5235	H308	A	2-37	5278	N20	NA	
5193	H55	A	1-48	5236	H308	B	2-39	5279	N21	NA	
5194	H534	A	1-50	5237	H308	C	2-38	5280	N20	NA	
5195	H55	B	1-51	5238	H301	B	2-45	5281	N20	NA	
5196	H303	A	1-9	5239	H702	NA		5282	N20	NA	
5197	H303	B	1-3	5240	H703	NA		5283	N20	NA	
5198	H300	A	1-4	5241	H703	NA		5284	N20	NA	
5199	H66	C	1-5	5242	H703	NA		5285	N20	NA	
5200	H300	C	1-27	5243	H703	NA		5286	N20	NA	
5201	H300	C	1-28	5244	H703	NA		5287	N21	NA	
5202	H300	B	1-35	5245	H703	NA		5288	N21	NA	
5203	H300	A	1-36	5246	H71	NA		5289	N21	NA	
5204	H300	A	1-7	5247	H71	NA		5290	N20	NA	
5205	H316	B	1-16	5248	H728	NA		5291	N20	NA	
5206	H316	A	1-13	5249	H705	NA		5292	N20	NA	
5207	H316	B	1-44	5250	H703	NA		5293	N20	NA	
5208	H317	A	5-3	5251	H706	NA		5294	N20	NA	
5209	H317	B	1-37	5252	H705	NA		5295	N21	NA	

FAA Q. No.	FAA Subject Code	Gleim Answer	Gleim Chap/ Q. No.	FAA Q. No.	FAA Subject Code	Gleim Answer	Gleim Chap/ Q. No.	FAA Q. No.	FAA Subject Code	Gleim Answer	Gleim Chap/ Q. No.
5296	N21	NA		5339	I26	B	7-31	5382	I32	A	7-17
5297	N22	NA		5340	I27	B	7-50	5383	I32	B	7-18
5298	H51	B	2-19	5341	I27	B	7-27	5384	I32	B	7-15
5299	N/A			5342	I27	A	7-44	5385	I32	A	7-16
5300	H66	C	2-21	5343	I27	B	7-48	5386	I35	NA	
5301	I21	A	7-1	5344	I27	C	7-51	5387	I35	NA	
5302	I21	A	7-22	5345	I27	C	7-45	5388	I35	A	7-52
5303	I21	C	7-24	5346	I27	C	7-46	5389	I35	NA	
5304	I21	A	7-39	5347	I27	B	7-7	5390	I35	NA	
5305	I22	A	7-23	5348	I27	B	7-28	5391	I35	NA	
5306	I22	B	5-4	5349	I27	C	7-60	5392	I35	B	7-54
5307	I22	A	5-5	5350	I27	C	7-33	5393	I35	A	7-82
5308	I22	B	5-6	5351	I28	C	7-87	5394	I35	NA	
5309	I22	B	5-7	5352	I28	C	7-89	5395	I35	NA	
5310	I23	C	7-6	5353	I28	B	7-88	5396	I35	NA	
5311	I23	A	7-3	5354	I28	A	7-90	5397	I35	NA	
5312	I23	A	7-4	5355	I28	A	7-91	5398	I40	A	8-5
5313	I23	B	7-14	5356	I28	A	7-84	5399	I40	A	8-1
5314	I23	C	7-5	5357	I28	B	7-83	5400	J25	B	8-3
5315	I23	A	7-12	5358	I28	C	7-86	5401	J25	C	8-2
5316	I23	A	7-11	5359	I28	A	7-85	5402	J25	C	8-10
5317	I23	C	7-8	5360	I29	C	7-71	5403	J25	B	8-12
5318	I23	B	7-9	5361	I30	C	7-72	5404	J25	B	8-11
5319	I23	B	7-10	5362	I30	B	7-73	5405	I41	C	8-35
5320	I24	B	7-25	5363	I30	B	7-61	5406	J25	B	8-9
5321	I24	A	7-13	5364	I30	C	7-62	5407	I42	A	8-40
5322	I24	A	7-32	5365	I30	A	7-70	5408	I56	C	8-13
5323	I24	C	7-2	5366	I30	C	7-64	5409	J25	B	8-22
5324	I24	B	7-74	5367	I30	C	7-63	5410	J25	C	8-23
5325	I24	A	7-76	5368	I30	B	7-65	5411	J25	C	8-24
5326	I24	C	7-75	5369	I30	C	7-58	5412	J25	B	8-25
5327	I25	C	7-53	5370	I30	A	7-67	5413	J25	A	8-26
5328	I25	C	7-29	5371	I30	B	7-59	5414	I43	B	8-28
5329	I25	C	7-49	5372	I30	C	7-68	5415	I43	C	8-29
5330	I25	B	7-30	5373	I30	C	7-69	5416	I43	A	8-31
5331	I25	B	8-8	5374	I31	C	7-34	5417	J25	C	8-32
5332	I25	B	7-41	5375	I31	A	7-66	5418	J25	A	8-30
5333	I25	A	7-42	5376	I31	B	7-35	5419	I43	B	8-27
5334	I25	B	7-55	5377	I31	C	7-36	5420	I43	C	8-46
5335	I25	C	7-47	5378	I31	C	7-38	5421	J25	A	8-6
5336	I25	B	7-43	5379	I31	A	7-37	5422	I43	A	8-33
5337	I26	B	7-57	5380	I31	C	7-40	5423	I43	C	8-34
5338	I26	C	7-26	5381	I32	B	7-21	5424	I43	B	8-44

FAA Q. No.	FAA Subject Code	Gleim Answer	Gleim Chap/ Q. No.	FAA Q. No.	FAA Subject Code	Gleim Answer	Gleim Chap/ Q. No.	FAA Q. No.	FAA Subject Code	Gleim Answer	Gleim Chap/ Q. No.
5425	I43	A	8-14	5468	H317	C	9-58	5506	I08	A	10-30
5426	I44	A	8-16	5469	H342	A	9-18	5507	I08	A	10-29
5427	I44	A	8-18	5470	H342	A	9-17	5508	I08	B	10-28
5428	I44	B	8-17	5471	H342	C	9-19	5509	I08	A	10-31
5429	I44	B	8-15	5472	H342	C	9-20	5510	I08	C	10-32
5430	I45	C	8-42	5473	H342	A	9-21	5511	I08	B	10-8
5431	I45	B	8-41	5474	H342	A	9-22	5512	I08	B	10-9
5432	I46	A	8-43	5475	H341	A	9-49	5513	I08	C	10-10
5433	I47	C	8-36	5476	H341	B	9-50	5514	I08	C	10-11
5434	I64	B	8-38	5477	H341	C	9-51	5515	I08	C	9-32
5435	I64	C	8-39	5478	H341	C	9-52	5516	I08	B	9-33
5436	I64	B	8-37	5479	H344	C	9-2	5517	I08	C	9-34
5437	I62	NA		5480	H344	NA		5518	I08	C	9-35
5438	I49	C	8-45	5481	H344	C	9-55	5519	I08	A	9-36
5439	I49	A	7-56	5482	H342	A	5-13	5520	I08	C	9-43
5440	I51	B	8-21	5483	H342	B	5-14	5521	I08	C	9-44
5441	I61	A	8-19	5484	H342	C	5-15	5522	I08	B	9-45
5442	I51	C	8-20	5485	H342	C	5-16	5523	I08	B	9-46
5443	I52	B	7-80	5486	H342	B	5-17	5524	I08	A	9-47
5444	I53	B	7-77	5487	H342	A	5-18	5525	I08	B	9-48
5445	I53	C	7-78	5488	H344	B	9-53	5526	I08	A	9-38
5446	I53	B	7-79	5489	H344	B	9-54	5527	I08	A	9-39
5447	K02	B	7-20	5490a.	H564	B	11-17	5528	I08	B	9-40
5448	K02	C	7-19	5490b.	H348	A	10-1	5529	I08	A	9-41
5449	J25	B	7-92	5491a.	H568	C	11-19	5530	I08	A	9-42
5450	N33	A	7-81	5491b.	H568	C	11-18a	5531	I08	A	9-37
5451	H342	B	5-35	5491c.	H348	B	10-2	5532	I08	B	10-15
5452	H342	B	5-36	5492a.	H572	B	11-20	5533	I08	B	10-18
5453	H342	C	5-37	5492b.	H348	B	10-7	5534	I08	A	10-23
5454	H342	B	5-38	5493a.	H574	B	11-21	5535	I08	C	10-25
5455	H342	A	5-39	5493b.	H348	C	10-3	5536	I08	B	10-24
5456	H317	C	5-19	5494a.	H574	A	11-22	5537	I08	B	10-26
5457	H317	C	5-20	5494b.	H348	B	10-4	5538	I08	A	10-27
5458	H317	C	5-21	5495	H348	C	10-5	5539	I08	A	9-31
5459	H317	C	5-22	5496	H348	A	10-6	5540	I08	A	9-23
5460	H317	C	5-25	5497	H348	C	10-13	5541	I08	A	9-26
5461	H317	B	5-26	5498	H348	C	10-14	5542	I08	B	9-25
5462	H317	C	5-27	5499	H348	C	10-12	5543	I08	A	9-24
5463	H317	B	5-28	5500	H348	A	10-20	5544	I08	B	9-27
5464	H317	A	5-29	5501	H348	C	10-21	5545	I08	A	9-28
5465	H317	C	5-30	5502	H348	C	10-22	5546	I08	B	9-29
5466	H317	A	9-56	5503	H61	C	11-9	5547	I08	A	9-30
5467	H317	C	9-57	5504	J22	A	3-20	5548	I10	NA	
				5505	H66	B	5-34				

FAA Q. No.	FAA Subject Code	Gleim Answer	Gleim Chap/ Q. No.	FAA Q. No.	FAA Subject Code	Gleim Answer	Gleim Chap/ Q. No.	FAA Q. No.	FAA Subject Code	Gleim Answer	Gleim Chap/ Q. No.
5549	I10	NA		5591	J37	NA		5634	H106	C	5-49
5550	I10	NA		5592	J37	NA		5635	H105	B	5-50
5551	J01	B	10-17	5593	J37	NA		5636	H106	B	5-55
5552	J01	C	10-16	5594	J42	NA		5637	H106	B	5-56
5553	J01	B	10-19	5595	J42	NA		5638	H106	A	5-58
5554	J08	NA		5596	J42	NA		5639	H106	C	5-59
5555	J15	NA		5597	J42	NA		5640	H106	NA	
5556	J16	NA		5598	J42	NA		5641	H106	NA	
5557	J18	NA		5599	J42	NA		5642	H106	NA	
5558	J18	NA		5600	J42	NA		5643	H106	B	5-57
5559	J25	B	8-4	5601	H312	A	2-8	5644	H130	NA	
5560	J25	A	8-7	5602	H312	C	2-9	5645	H130	NA	
5561	J42	NA		5603	B08	NA		5646	H105	A	5-60
5562	J14	NA		5604	H312	B	2-3	5647	H105	A	5-63
5563	J33	NA		5605	AO2	B	2-2	5648	H105	A	5-62
5564	J37	C	9-1	5606	H307	C	2-23	5649	H105	B	5-61
5565	J37	B	9-8	5607	H307	B	2-35	5650	H105	A	5-52
5566	J37	C	9-6	5608	H307	C	2-13	5651	H105	A	5-53
5567	J37	B	9-9	5609	H307	C	2-14	5652	H105	A	5-54
5568	J37	B	9-7	5610	H307	A	2-15	5653	H351	A	2-36
5569	J37	B	9-12	5611	H307	B	2-16	5654	H308	C	2-43
5570	J37	B	9-13	5612	H314	NA		5655a.	J13	C	3-36
5571	J37	NA		5613	H314	NA		5655b.	H54	C	11-3
5572	J37	B	9-16	5614	H317	B	5-8	5656a.	J13	A	3-37
5573	J37	NA		5615	H317	A	5-40	5656b.	J13	A	3-38
5574a.	J37	NA		5616	H317	C	5-43	5656c.	H54	A	11-2
5574b.	J37	NA		5617	H317	A	5-41	5657	J05	C	3-21
5575	J37	A	9-5	5618	H317	A	5-42	5658	J05	B	3-22
5576	J37	NA		5619	H317	C	5-12	5659a.	J05	C	3-23
5577	J37	C	9-3	5620	H317	A	5-11	5659b.	J05	A	3-24
5578	J37	NA		5621	H317	B	5-10	5660	J05	A	3-25
5579	J37	NA		5622	H317	C	5-9	5661	H525	C	11-4
5580	J37	NA		5623	H317	B	5-23	5662	H550	A	11-7
5581	J37	C	9-10	5624	H317	C	5-24	5663	H583	A	11-8
5582	J37	NA		5625	H317	B	5-31	5664	H550	A	11-6
5583	J37	C	9-4	5626	H317	B	5-32	5665	H550	B	11-5
5584	J37	NA		5627	H317	C	5-33	5666	H567	A	3-27
5585	J37	B	9-11	5628	H317	A	5-46	5667	H308	B	2-41
5586	J37	NA		5629	H317	A	5-47	5668	H308	A	2-42
5587	J37	A	9-15	5630	H317	B	5-44	5669	H303	B	11-16
5588	J37	B	9-14	5631	H317	A	5-45	5670	H303	B	11-14
5589	J37	NA		5632	H105	A	5-48	5671	H745	NA	
5590	J37	NA		5633	H106	B	5-51	5672	H71	NA	
								5673	H705	NA	

FAA Q. No.	FAA Subject Code	Gleim Answer	Gleim Chap/ Q. No.	FAA Q. No.	FAA Subject Code	Gleim Answer	Gleim Chap/ Q. No.	FAA Q. No.	FAA Subject Code	Gleim Answer	Gleim Chap/ Q. No.
5674	H705	NA		5717	H742	NA		5760	J31	C	6-7
5675	H705	NA		5718	H742	NA		5761	J31	B	6-2
5676	H710	NA		5719	H742	NA		5762	J31	B	6-6
5677	H719	NA		5720	H726	NA		5763	J31	C	6-3
5678	H719	NA		5721	H726	NA		5764	J31	B	6-1
5679	H719	NA		5722	H745	NA		5765	H351	C	6-8
5680	H719	NA		5723	H745	NA		5766	L52	C	11-12
5681	H719	NA		5724	H739	NA		5767	L52	A	11-11
5682	H719	NA		5725	H732	NA		5768	L52	A	11-13
5683	H720	NA		5726	H732	NA		5769	N32	NA	
5684	H720	NA		5727	H741	NA		5770	N30	NA	
5685	H720	NA		5728	H738	NA		5771	N20	NA	
5686	H717	NA		5729	H743	NA		5772	N20	NA	
5687	H720	NA		5730	H744	NA		5773	N21	NA	
5688	H720	NA		5731	H744	NA		5774	N21	NA	
5689	H720	NA		5732	H744	NA		5775	N21	NA	
5690	H720	NA		5733	H709	NA		5776	N21	NA	
5691	H720	NA		5734	H702	NA		5777	N21	NA	
5692	H720	NA		5735	H702	NA		5778	N21	NA	
5693	H720	NA		5736	H702	NA		5779	N21	NA	
5694	H720	NA		5737	H702	NA		5780	N21	NA	
5695	H745	NA		5738	H709	NA		5781	N21	NA	
5696	H745	NA		5739	I29	B	1-6	5782	N21	NA	
5697	H745	NA		5740	I04	B	5-2	5783	N21	NA	
5698	H745	NA		5741	I30	C	11-15	5784	N21	NA	
5699	H745	NA		5742	N23	NA		5785	N21	NA	
5700	H745	NA		5743	N23	NA		5786	N21	NA	
5701	H745	NA		5744	N23	NA		5787	N21	NA	
5702	H745	NA		5745	N23	NA		5788	N21	NA	
5703	H745	NA		5746	I35	NA		5789	N21	NA	
5704	H745	NA		5747	I35	NA		5790	N21	NA	
5705	H745	NA		5748	J13	A	11-10	5791	N22	NA	
5706	H745	NA		5749	J14	B	3-28	5792	N28	NA	
5707	H726	NA		5750	J27	B	3-31	5793	N29	NA	
5708	H738	NA		5751	J27	A	3-29	5794	N29	NA	
5709	H727	NA		5752	J27	A	3-32	5795	N29	NA	
5710	H727	NA		5753	J27	A	3-30	5796	N30	NA	
5711	H727	NA		5754	J27	A	3-33	5797	N30	NA	
5712	H726	NA		5755	J27	C	3-34	5798	N30	NA	
5713	H745	NA		5756	J27	B	3-35	5799	N30	NA	
5714	H746	NA		5757	J31	C	6-5	5800	N30	NA	
5715	H746	NA		5758	J31	C	6-9	5801	N30	NA	
5716	H742	NA		5759	J31	A	6-4	5802	N30	NA	

FAA Q. No.	FAA Subject Code	Gleim Answer	Gleim Chap/ Q. No.	FAA Q. No.	FAA Subject Code	Gleim Answer	Gleim Chap/ Q. No.	FAA Q. No.	FAA Subject Code	Gleim Answer	Gleim Chap/ Q. No.
5803	N30	NA		5846	O170	NA		5889	H20	NA	
5804	N30	NA		5847	O220	NA		5890	H20	NA	
5805	N31	NA		5848	O155	NA		5891	H20	NA	
5806	N31	NA		5849	O170	NA		5892	H20	NA	
5807	N31	NA		5850	O30	NA		5893	H20	NA	
5808	N31	NA		5851	O30	NA		5894	H20	NA	
5809	N31	NA		5852	O30	NA		5895	H21	NA	
5810	N31	NA		5853	O30	NA		5896	H21	NA	
5811	N31	NA		5854	O30	NA		5897	H21	NA	
5812	N31	NA		5855	O30	NA		5898	H21	NA	
5813	N32	NA		5856	O30	NA		5899	H21	NA	
5814	N32	NA		5857	O30	NA		5900	H21	NA	
5815	N32	NA		5858	O30	NA		5901	H21	NA	
5816	N32	NA		5859	O30	NA		5902	H21	NA	
5817	N32	NA		5860	O30	NA		5903	H22	NA	
5818	N33	NA		5861	O30	NA		5904	H22	NA	
5819	N33	NA		5862	O30	NA		5905	H22	NA	
5820	N33	NA		5863	O30	NA		5906	H23	NA	
5821	N34	NA		5864	P01	NA		5907	H23	NA	
5822	N34	NA		5865	P01	NA		5908	H23	NA	
5823	N34	NA		5866	P01	NA		5909	H24	NA	
5824	N34	NA		5867	P01	NA		5910	H24	NA	
5825	O277	NA		5868	P03	NA		5911	H24	NA	
5826	O171	NA		5869	P04	NA		5912	H24	NA	
5827	O220	NA		5870	P04	NA		5913	H24	NA	
5828	O263	NA		5871	P04	NA		5914	H24	NA	
5829	O252	NA		5872	P05	NA		5915	H24	NA	
5830	O220	NA		5873	P05	NA		5916	H25	NA	
5831	O220	NA		5874	P11	NA		5917	H25	NA	
5832	O257	NA		5875	P11	NA		5918	H25	NA	
5833	O270	NA		5876	P11	NA		5919	H26	NA	
5834	O265	NA		5877	P11	NA		5920	H26	NA	
5835	O261	NA		5878	P11	NA		5921	H26	NA	
5836	O150	NA		5879	P11	NA		5922	H26	NA	
5837	O150	NA		5880	P11	NA		5923	H26	NA	
5838	O220	NA		5881	P12	NA		5924	H27	NA	
5839	O220	NA		5882	H20	NA		5925	H27	NA	
5840	O220	NA		5883	H20	NA		5926	H30	NA	
5841	O220	NA		5884	H20	NA		5927	H30	NA	
5842	O220	NA		5885	H20	NA		5928	H30	NA	
5843	O220	NA		5886	H20	NA		5929	H30	NA	
5844	O220	NA		5887	H20	NA		5930	H30	NA	
5845	O170	NA		5888	H20	NA		5931	H30	NA	

FAA Q. No.	FAA Subject Code	Gleim Answer	Gleim Chap/ Q. No.	FAA Q. No.	FAA Subject Code	Gleim Answer	Gleim Chap/ Q. No.	FAA Q. No.	FAA Subject Code	Gleim Answer	Gleim Chap/ Q. No.
5932	H30	NA		5945	L05	B	6-15	5959	L05	C	6-26
5933	H30	NA		5946	L05	C	6-16	5960	L05	A	6-22
5934	H30	NA		5947	L05	A	6-13	5961	L05	B	6-32
5935	H30	NA		5948	L05	C	6-23	5962	L05	A	6-31
5936	H30	NA		5949	L05	A	6-17	5963	L05	A	6-30
5937	H30	NA		5950	L05	C	6-27	0601-35	A20	A	4-23a
5938a.	H31	NA		5951	L05	C	6-24	0601-79	B11	C	4-77a
5938b.	H31	NA		5952	L05	C	6-25	0601-577	J15	A	10-22a
5939	H31	NA		5953	L05	B	6-29	1001-1	J05	A	3-25a
5940	H32	NA		5954	L05	C	6-28	1001-11	G10	B	4-103c
5941	L05	C	6-11	5955	L05	A	6-18	1001-22	A02	A	4-7c
5942	L05	A	6-10	5956	L05	A	6-20	1001-170	C20	B	4-103a
5943	L05	C	6-10	5957	L05	A	6-19	1001-171	C20	A	4-103b
5944	L05	C	6-14	5958	L05	B	6-21	1001-172	C20	NA	
								1001-173	C20	NA	

AUTHOR'S RECOMMENDATION

The Experimental Aircraft Association, Inc. is a very successful and effective nonprofit organization that represents and serves those of us interested in flying, in general, and in sport aviation, in particular. I personally invite you to enjoy becoming a member. Visit their website at http://www.eaa.org.

$40 for a 1-year membership
$56 for a 1-year membership (International)
$23 per year for individuals under 19 years old
Family membership available for $50 per year

> Membership includes the monthly magazine *Sport Aviation*.

Write to: EAA Aviation Center
P.O. Box 3086
Oshkosh, Wisconsin 54903-3086

Or call: (920) 426-4800
(800) 564-6322

The annual EAA Oshkosh AirVenture is an unbelievable aviation spectacular with over 12,000 airplanes at one airport! Virtually everything aviation-oriented you can imagine! Plan to spend at least 1 day (not everything can be seen in a day) in Oshkosh (100 miles northwest of Milwaukee).

Convention dates: 2002 -- July 23 through July 29
2003 -- July 29 through August 4

The annual Sun 'n Fun EAA Fly-In is also highly recommended. It is held at the Lakeland, FL (KLAL) airport (between Orlando and Tampa). Visit the Sun 'n Fun web site at http://www.sun-n-fun.org.

Convention dates: 2002 -- April 7 through April 13
2003 -- April 6 through April 12

BE-A-PILOT: INTRODUCTORY FLIGHT

Be-A-Pilot is an industry-sponsored marketing program designed to inspire people to "Stop dreaming, start flying." Be-A-Pilot has sought flight schools to participate in the program and offers a $49 introductory flight certificate that can be redeemed at a participating flight school.

The goal of this program is to encourage people to experience their dreams of flying through an introductory flight and to begin taking flying lessons.

For more information, you can visit the Be-A-Pilot home page at http://www.beapilot.com or call 1-888-BE-A-PILOT.

AIRCRAFT OWNERS AND PILOTS ASSOCIATION

AOPA is the largest, most influential aviation association in the world, with more than 370,000 members--half of all pilots in the United States. AOPA's most important contribution to the world's most accessible, safest, least expensive, friendliest, easiest-to-use general aviation environment is their lobbying on our behalf at the federal, state, and local levels. AOPA also provides legal services, advice, and other assistance to the aviation community.

We recommend that you become an AOPA member, which costs only $39 annually. To join, call 1-800-USA-AOPA or visit the AOPA Web site www.aopa.org.

PILOT KNOWLEDGE TEST (WRITTEN EXAM) BOOKS AND SOFTWARE

Before pilots take their FAA knowledge tests, they want to understand the answer to every FAA test question. Gleim's *FAA Written Exam* books and *FAA Test Prep* software have set the standard in FAA knowledge test preparation. Gleim's easy-to-use format helps pilots learn and understand exactly what they need to know to pass. Each chapter includes a study outline, actual FAA questions, and answer explanations. Gleim's *FAA Test Prep* provides standard FAA tests under simulated exam conditions. Additional information can be found in our reference books.

Books

- *Private Pilot FAA Written Exam*
- *Instrument Pilot FAA Written Exam*
- *Commercial Pilot FAA Written Exam*
- *Flight/Ground Instructor FAA Written Exam*
- *Fundamentals of Instructing FAA Written Exam*
- *Airline Transport Pilot FAA Written Exam*
- *Flight Engineer FAA Written Exam*

Software

- *Private Pilot FAA Test Prep*
- *Instrument Pilot FAA Test Prep*
- *Commercial Pilot FAA Test Prep*
- *Flight/Ground Instructor FAA Test Prep* (includes *Fundamentals of Instructing*)
- *Airline Transport Pilot FAA Test Prep*
- *Flight Engineer FAA Test Prep*

REFERENCE AND FLIGHT MANEUVERS/PRACTICAL TEST PREP BOOKS

Pilot Handbook - A complete ground school text using an outline format with diagrams. This book augments and enhances Gleim's *FAA Written Exam* books in preparing pilots for the private, commercial, and flight instructor certificates and the instrument rating. A complete, organized, and detailed text makes it useful and saves time. It also contains a special section on flight reviews.

Aviation Weather and Weather Services - A complete rewrite of the FAA's *Aviation Weather* (AC 00-6A) and *Aviation Weather Services* (AC 00-45E) into a single, easy-to-understand book complete with maps, diagrams, charts, and pictures. Pilots can learn and understand the subject matter more easily and effectively with this book.

FAR/AIM - The purpose of this book is to consolidate the common parts of Title 14 of the Code of Federal Regulations (14 CFR) [formerly known as the *Federal Aviation Regulations* (FAR)] and the *Aeronautical Information Manual* (AIM) into one easy-to-use reference book. Gleim's **FAR/AIM** resets the standard with a better presentation, easier-to-read type, improved indexes, and full-color figures. Included are Parts 1, 43, 61, 67, 71, 73, 91, 97, 103, 105, 119, Appendices I and J of 121, 135, 137, 141, and 142.

Gleim's *Flight Maneuvers* books are designed to simplify and facilitate flight training and will help pilots prepare for the FAA practical test. Each task, objective, concept, requirement, etc. in the FAA Practical Test Standards is explained, analyzed, illustrated, and interpreted so pilots will gain practical test proficiency as quickly as possible. The actual FAA Practical Tests Standards are included.

- *Private Pilot Flight Maneuvers and Practical Test Prep*
- *Instrument Pilot Flight Maneuvers and Practical Test Prep*
- *Commercial Pilot Flight Maneuvers and Practical Test Prep*
- *Flight Instructor Flight Maneuvers and Practical Test Prep*

PILOT KITS

Gleim's Pilot Kits provide everything a pilot needs to complete his/her training, except an airplane, local charts, and a flight instructor. Each kit contains the easiest, most effective, and least expensive pilot training materials available.

Private Pilot Kit   *Instrument Pilot Kit*   *Commercial Pilot Kit*   *Instrument/Commercial Pilot Kit*

ONLINE REFRESHER COURSES

Flight Instructor Refresher Course is the first FAA-approved online CFI renewal program. Gleim's FIRC contains all of the lessons and tests required to renew your CFI certificate. Visit www.gleim.com/firc to try Lesson 1 FREE and begin your renewal today.

Private Pilot Refresher Course is a recurrent ground training course designed to increase pilot knowledge and safety. Gleim's PPRC is designed to meet the ground school requirement for the flight review. It also satisfies the "safety meeting" requirement for the FAA's Pilot Proficiency Award Program (Wings Program). Visit www.gleim.com/pprc to try Lesson 1 FREE.

Gleim Publications, Inc. P.O. Box 12848 Gainesville, FL 32604	TOLL FREE: LOCAL: FAX: INTERNET: E-MAIL:	(800) 87-GLEIM/(800) 874-5346 (352) 375-0772 (888) 375-6940 (toll free) http://www.gleim.com sales@gleim.com	Customer service is available: 8:00 a.m. - 7:00 p.m., Mon. - Fri. 9:00 a.m. - 2:00 p.m., Saturday Please have your credit card ready or save time by ordering online!

Gleim's PRIVATE PILOT KIT
Includes everything you need to pass the FAA pilot knowledge (written) test and FAA practical test.
Our price is far lower than similarly equipped kits found elsewhere .... $119.95 _____

Gleim's INSTRUMENT PILOT KIT
Everything you need, just like our Private Pilot Kit. With CD-ROM .... $114.95 _____

Gleim's COMMERCIAL PILOT KIT
Everything you need to prepare for your commercial certificate. With CD-ROM .... $94.95 _____

SPECIAL COMBO: INSTRUMENT/COMMERCIAL KIT .... $189.95 _____

KNOWLEDGE TEST

	Books	Software*	Book/Software	Audios**	Book/Software*/ Audios**	
Private/Recreational Pilot	☐ @ $15.95	☐ @ $49.95	☐ @ $58.95	☐ @ $60	☐ @ $106.95	_____
Instrument Pilot	☐ @ $18.95	☐ @ $59.95	☐ @ $70.95	☐ @ $60	☐ @ $117.95	_____
Commercial Pilot	☐ @ $14.95	☐ @ $59.95	☐ @ $66.95	**Please select audio format.**		_____
Fundamentals of Instructing	☐ @ $12.95	☐ } both for		☐ CDs ☐ Cassettes		_____
Flight/Ground Instructor	☐ @ $14.95	☐ } $59.95	☐ @ $66.95			_____
Airline Transport Pilot	☐ @ $26.95	☐ @ $59.95	☐ @ $77.95			_____
Flight Engineer	☐ @ $26.95	☐ @ $59.95	☐ @ $77.95			_____

*CD-ROM (Windows) includes all questions, figures, charts, and outlines for each of the pilot knowledge tests.

REFERENCE AND FLIGHT MANEUVERS/PRACTICAL TEST PREP BOOKS
FAR/AIM .... $15.95 _____
Aviation Weather and Weather Services .... 22.95 _____
Pilot Handbook .... 13.95 _____
Private Pilot Flight Maneuvers and Practical Test Prep .... 16.95 _____
Instrument Pilot Flight Maneuvers and Practical Test Prep .... 18.95 _____
Commercial Pilot Flight Maneuvers and Practical Test Prep .... 14.95 _____
Flight Instructor Flight Maneuvers and Practical Test Prep .... 17.95 _____

OTHER BOOKS AND ACCESSORIES
Private Pilot Syllabus and Logbook .... $ 9.95 _____
Instrument Pilot Syllabus .... 14.95 _____
Commercial Pilot Syllabus .... 14.95 _____
Flight Computer .... 9.95 _____
Navigational Plotter .... 5.95 _____
Flight Bag .... 29.95 _____

Shipping (nonrefundable): **First item = $5; each additional item = $1** $_____
Add applicable sales tax for shipments within the State of Florida.
Please FAX, e-mail, or write for additional charges for outside the 48 contiguous United States.   **TOTAL** $_____

Printed 11/01. Prices subject to change without notice.

1. We process and ship orders daily, within one business day over 98.8% of the time. Call by noon for same-day service!
2. Please PHOTOCOPY this order form for others.
3. No CODs. Orders from individuals must be prepaid. Library and company orders may be purchased on account.
4. Gleim Publications, Inc. guarantees the immediate refund of all resalable texts and unopened software and audios if returned within 30 days. Applies only to items purchased direct from Gleim Publications, Inc. Our shipping charge is nonrefundable.
5. Components of specially priced package deals are nonreturnable.

NAME (please print) _____

ADDRESS _____ Apt. _____
              (street address required for UPS)

_____

CITY _____ STATE _____ ZIP _____

____ MC/VISA/DISC   ____ Check/M.O.   Daytime
Telephone (____)_____

Credit Card No. _____ - _____ - _____ - _____

Exp. ____/____   Signature _____
        Mo./Yr.

020

INSTRUCTOR CERTIFICATION FORM
COMMERCIAL PILOT KNOWLEDGE TEST

Name: _____

    I certify that I have reviewed the above individual's preparation for the FAA Commercial Pilot -- Airplane knowledge test [covering the topics specified in FAR 61.125(b)(1) through (16)] using the *Commercial Pilot FAA Written Exam* book and/or software by Irvin N. Gleim and find him/her competent to pass the pilot knowledge test.

| Signed | Date | Name | CFI Number | Expiration Date |

AN OVERVIEW OF GLEIM'S *FAA TEST PREP* SOFTWARE FOR WINDOWS

Gleim's *FAA Test Prep* for Windows™ contains many of the same features found in earlier versions. However, we have simplified the study process by incorporating the outlines and figures from our books into the new software. Everything you need to study for any of the FAA knowledge tests will be contained in one unique, easy-to-use program. Below are some of the enhancements you will find with our new study software.

Index

ABBREVIATIONS AND ACRONYMS IN
COMMERCIAL PILOT FAA WRITTEN EXAM

A/FD	*Airport/Facility Directory*
AAF	Army Airfield
AC	Advisory Circular
ADF	automatic direction finder
AFB	Air Force Base
AGL	above ground level
AIM	*Aeronautical Information Manual*
AIRMET	Airman's Meteorological Information
AME	aviation medical examiner
ATC	Air Traffic Control
ATCO	air taxi/commercial operator
BHP	brake horsepower
CAT	clear air turbulence
CDI	course deviation indicator
CFI	Certificated Flight Instructor
CG	center of gravity
DUATS	Direct User Access Terminal System
ELT	emergency locator transmitter
ETE	estimated time en route
FA	area forecast
FAA	Federal Aviation Administration
FAR	Federal Aviation Regulation
FBO	Fixed-Base Operator
FSDO	Flight Standards District Office
FSS	Flight Service Station
GPH	gallons per hour
Hg	mercury
HSI	horizontal situation indicator
IAP	instrument approach procedure
IFR	instrument flight rules
ILS	Instrument landing system
IR	instrument route
ISA	international standard atmosphere
L/D	Lift-to-Drag Ratio
L/D$_{MAX}$	Maximum Lift-to-Drag Ratio
Mb	millibar
MB	magnetic bearing
MEF	maximum elevation figure
METAR	aviation routine weather report
MH	magnetic heading
MOA	Military Operations Area
MSL	mean sea level
MTR	Military Training Routes
MVFR	marginal VFR
NAS	Naval Air Station
NDB	nondirectional radio beacon
NM	nautical mile
NOTAM	notice to airmen
NTSB	National Transportation Safety Board
OAT	outside air temperature
OBS	omnibearing selector
PIC	pilot in command
PIREP	Pilot Weather Report
PPH	pounds per hour
RB	relative bearing
RMI	radio magnetic indicator
RNAV	area navigation
SD	Radar Weather Report
SFC	surface
SIGMET	Significant Meteorological Information
SL	sea level
SM	statute mile
ST	standard temperature
SVFR	Special VFR
TACAN	Tactical Air Navigation
TAS	true airspeed
TAF	terminal aerodrome forecast
TWEB	Transcribed Weather Broadcast
UTC	Coordinated Universal Time
V$_A$	maneuvering speed
V$_F$	design flap speed
V$_{FE}$	maximum flap extended speed
VFR	visual flight rules
VHF	very high frequency
VHF/DF	VHF direction finder
V$_{LE}$	maximum landing gear extended speed
V$_{NE}$	never-exceed speed
V$_{NO}$	maximum structural cruising speed
VOR	VHF omnidirectional range
VORTAC	Collocated VOR and TACAN
VOT	VOR Test Facility
VR	visual route
V$_S$	stalling speed or the minimum steady flight speed at which the airplane is controllable
V$_{SO}$	stalling speed or the minimum steady flight speed in the landing configuration
V$_{S1}$	stalling speed or the minimum steady flight speed obtained in a specific configuration
Z	Zulu or UTC time

Please forward your suggestions, corrections, and comments concerning typographical errors, etc., to **Irvin N. Gleim • c/o Gleim Publications, Inc. • P.O. Box 12848 • University Station • Gainesville, Florida • 32604**. Please include your name and address on the back of this page so we can properly thank you for your interest. Also, please refer to both the page number and the FAA question number for each item.

1. _____

2. _____

3. _____

4. _____

5. _____

6. _____

7. _____

8. _____

9. _____

10. _____

11. _____

We need your help identifying which questions the FAA is pretesting (but not grading - see page 5). After you take your exam, please e-mail, fax, or mail us a description of these questions so we can anticipate their future use by the FAA.

12. _____

13. _____

14. _____

15. _____

| Remember for superior service: | Mail, e-mail, or fax questions about our books or software. |
| | Telephone questions about orders, prices, shipments, or payments. |

Name: _____

Address: _____

City/State/Zip: _____

Telephone: Home: _____ Work: _____ FAX: _____

E-mail: _____

GLEIM
KNOWLEDGE
TRANSFER
SYSTEMS™

9 781581 940121

ISBN 158194012-2